FOR THE
LOVE OF GOD
VOLUME ONE

OTHER CROSSWAY BOOKS BY D. A. CARSON

For the Love of God, Volume 2

The Difficult Doctrine of the Love of God

Love in Hard Places
With John D. Woodbridge

Letters Along the Way

FOR THE LOVE OF GOD

VOLUME ONE

A Daily Companion for Discovering
the Riches of God's Word

D. A. CARSON

CROSSWAY BOOKS

A PUBLISHING MINISTRY OF
GOOD NEWS PUBLISHERS
WHEATON, ILLINOIS

For the Love of God, Volume One

Copyright © 1998 by D. A. Carson

Published by Crossway Books
      a publishing ministry of Good News Publishers
      1300 Crescent Street
      Wheaton, Illinois 60187

Cover design: Cindy Kiple

First printing, 1998

First trade paperback printing, 2006

ISBN-10: 1-58134-815-0
ISBN-13: 978-1-58134-815-6

Printed in the United States of America

Library of Congress Cataloging in Publication Data
Carson, D. A.
    For the Love of God : a daily companion for discovering the riches
of God's Word / D.A. Carson.
      p.   cm.
    Includes bibliographical references.
    ISBN 1-58134-008-7 (v. 1 : hardcover : alk. paper)
    ISBN 1-58134-118-0 (v. 2 : hardcover : alk. paper)
    1. Devotional use. 2. Devotional calendars. 3. Bible—Reading.
I. Title.
BS617.8.C37 1998
220'.071—dc21   98-26484

BP		16	15	14	13	12	11	10	09	08	07	06
19	18	17	16	15	14	13	12	11	10	9	8	7

This book is gratefully dedicated

to my dear wife

Joy

who is to me as her name.

CONTENTS

PREFACE

⌒

This book, the first of two volumes, is for Christians who want to read the Bible, who want to read all the Bible.

At their best, Christians have saturated themselves in the Bible. They say with Job, "I have treasured the words of his mouth more than my daily bread" (Job 23:12). That comparison was something the children of Israel were meant to learn in the wilderness. We are told that God led them into hunger and fed them with manna to teach them "that man does not live on bread alone but on every word that comes from the mouth of the Lord" (Deut. 8:3)—words quoted by the Lord Jesus when he himself faced temptation (Matt. 4:4). Not only for the book of Revelation may it properly be said, "Blessed is the one who reads the words of this prophecy, and blessed are those who hear it and take to heart what is written in it" (Rev. 1:3). On the night he was betrayed, Jesus Christ prayed for his followers in these terms: "Sanctify them by the truth; your word is truth" (John 17:17). The means by which God sanctifies men and women, setting them apart as his own people, is the Word of truth.

The challenge has become increasingly severe in recent years, owing to several factors. All of us must confront the regular sins of laziness or lack of discipline, sins of the flesh, and of the pride of life. But there are additional pressures. The sheer pace of life affords us many excuses for sacrificing the important on the altar of the urgent. The constant sensory input from all sides is gently addictive— we become used to being entertained and diverted, and it is difficult to carve out the space and silence necessary for serious and thoughtful reading of Scripture. More seriously yet, the rising biblical illiteracy in Western culture means that the Bible is increasingly a closed book, even to many Christians. As the culture drifts away from its former rootedness in a Judeo-Christian understanding of God, history, truth, right and wrong, purpose, judgment, forgiveness, and community, so the Bible seems stranger and stranger. For precisely the same reason, it becomes all the more urgent to read it and reread it, so that at least confessing Christians preserve the heritage and outlook of a mind shaped and informed by holy Scripture.

This is a book to encourage that end. Devotional guides tend to offer short, personal readings from the Bible, sometimes only a verse or two, followed by several paragraphs of edifying exposition. Doubtless they provide personal help for believers with private needs, fears, and hopes. But they do not provide the framework of what the Bible says—the "plotline" or "story line"—the big picture that makes sense of all the little bits of the Bible. Wrongly used, such devotional guides may ultimately engender the profoundly wrong-headed view that God exists to sort out my problems; they may foster profoundly mistaken interpretations of some Scriptures, simply because the handful of passages they treat are no longer placed within the framework of the big picture, which is gradually fading from view. Only systematic and repeated reading of the whole Bible can meet these challenges.

That is what this book encourages. Here you will find a plan that will help you read through the New Testament and the Psalms twice, and the rest of the Bible once, in the course of a year—or, on a modification of the plan, in the course of two years. Comment is offered for each day, but this book fails utterly in its goal if you read the comment and not the assigned biblical passages.

The reading scheme laid out here is a slight modification of one that was first developed a century-and-a-half ago by a Scottish minister, Robert Murray M'Cheyne. How it works and why this book is only Volume One (even though it goes through the entire calendar year) are laid out in the Introduction.

"Like newborn babies, crave pure spiritual milk, so that by it you may grow up in your salvation, now that you have tasted that the Lord is good" (1 Peter 2:2-3).

Soli Deo gloria.

—D. A. Carson,
Trinity Evangelical Divinity School

INTRODUCTION

∾

Robert Murray M'Cheyne was born in Edinburgh on May 21, 1813. He died in Dundee on March 25, 1843—not yet thirty years of age. He had been serving as minister of St. Peter's, Dundee, since 1836. Though so young, he was known throughout Scotland as "the saintly M'Cheyne"; nor was his remarkable influence limited to the borders of Scotland.

His friend and colleague in ministry, Andrew Bonar, collected some of M'Cheyne's letters, messages, and miscellaneous papers, and published them, along with a brief biography, in 1844 as *Robert Murray M'Cheyne: Memoir and Remains*. That work has been widely recognized as one of the great spiritual classics. Within twenty-five years of its initial publication, it went through 116 British editions, quite apart from those in America and elsewhere. Contemporary believers interested in Christian living under the shadow of genuine revival could scarcely do better than to read and reflect on this collection of writings.

One of M'Cheyne's abiding concerns was to encourage his people, and himself, to read the Bible. To one young man, he wrote, "You read your Bible regularly, of course; but do try and understand it, and still more to feel it. Read more parts than one at a time. For example, if you are reading Genesis, read a Psalm also; or if you are reading Matthew, read a small bit of an Epistle also. Turn the Bible into prayer. Thus, if you were reading the First Psalm, spread the Bible on the chair before you, and kneel and pray, 'O Lord, give me the blessedness of the man'; 'let me not stand in the counsel of the ungodly.' This is the best way of knowing the meaning of the Bible, and of learning to pray." This was not some quaint or escapist pietism, for at the same time, M'Cheyne was himself diligent in the study of Hebrew and Greek. While a theological student, he met regularly for prayer, study, and Hebrew and Greek exercises with Andrew Bonar, Horatius Bonar, and a handful of other earnest ministers-in-training. They took the Bible so seriously in their living and preaching that when the eminent Thomas Chalmers, then Professor of Divinity, heard of the way they approached the Bible, he is reported to have said, "I like these literalities."

In line with his desire to foster serious Bible reading, M'Cheyne prepared a scheme for daily reading that would take readers through the New Testament and Psalms twice each year, and through the rest of the Bible once. It is reproduced, in slightly modified form, at the end of this Introduction.[1] Some explanation of the chart may be helpful.

The first column is self-explanatory: it lists the date for every day of the year. The following points explain the other features of this chart and the way this book is laid out.

(1) Originally, M'Cheyne listed two columns labeled "Family," and two labeled "Secret." He intended that, with some exceptions, the Scripture listings in the "Family" columns be read in family devotions, and those in the "Secret" columns be read privately, in personal devotions. The choice of the word secret was drawn from Matthew 6:6, and was in common use in M'Cheyne's day. I have labeled the two pairs of columns "Family" and "Private" respectively.

(2) For those using the chart for purely private devotions, the headings are of little significance. Over the last century and a half, many, many Christians have used this chart in just this way—as a guide and a schedule for their own Bible reading.

(3) That there are two columns for "Family" readings and two columns for "Private" readings reflects M'Cheyne's view that Christians should read from more than one part of the Bible at a time. Not only will this help you link various passages in your mind, but it will help carry you through some of the parts of the Bible that are on first inspection somewhat leaner than others (e.g., 1 Chronicles 1—12).

(4) If you read through the four passages listed for each date, in the course of a year you will, as I have indicated, read through the New Testament and the Psalms twice, and the rest of the Bible once. But if for any reason you find this too fast a pace, then read the passages listed in the first two columns (headed "Family") in the first year, and the passages listed in the last two columns (headed "Private") in the second year. Obviously this halves the rate of progress.

(5) One page of this book is devoted to each day. At the top of the page is the date, followed by the references to the four readings. The first two, corresponding to the entries in the "Family" columns, are in italics; the last two, corresponding to the entries in the "Private" columns, are in Roman type. The "Comment" that occupies the rest of the page is occasionally based on some theme that links

---

[1] The original can be found in many editions of the book already referred to, viz. Andrew A. Bonar, ed., Robert Murray M'Cheyne: Memoir and Remains. My copy is from the 1966 reprint, published by Banner of Truth, taken from the 1892 edition, pp. 623-628. Some popular editions, such as the two-volume paperback edition published by Moody Press (n.d.), omit the chart. The principal changes in substance I have introduced are four places where I have changed the break in the passage by two or three verses.

all four passages, but more commonly is based on some theme or text found in the italicized passages. In Volume Two, the second pair of passages is italicized (rather than the first), and the "Comment" is based on this second pair. In this first volume, I have not restricted comment to passages in the first column, because, in agreement with M'Cheyne, I suppose that to focus on only one part of Scripture, in this case the historical books of the Old Testament (the first column), will not be as helpful as a broader exposure to Scripture. So I have normally commented on a passage of Scripture in one of the first two columns. The first time I refer to the passage on which I am commenting I put the reference in boldface type.

(6) In no way do these pages pretend to be a commentary as that word is commonly understood. My aim is much more modest: to provide edifying comments and reflections on some part of the designated texts, and thus to encourage readers to reflect further on the biblical passages they are reading. If there is something unusual about these comments, it is that I have tried to devote at least some of them to helping the reader keep the big picture of the Bible's "story line" in mind, and to see what relevance this has for our thinking and living. In other words, although I want the comments to be edifying, this edification is not always of a private, individualized sort. My aim is to show, in however preliminary a way, that reading the whole Bible must stir up thoughtful Christians to thinking theologically and holistically, as well as reverently and humbly. Volume Two includes an exhaustive index of names, subjects, and Scriptures for both volumes.

Finally, I should venture a few practical suggestions. If you must skip something, skip this book; read the Bible instead. If you fall behind, do not use that fact as an excuse for giving up the effort until next January 1. Either catch up (by an afternoon of diligent reading, perhaps some Sunday), or skip ahead to where you should be and take up there. If your schedule allows it, set a regular time and place for your Bible reading. M'Cheyne himself wrote, "Let our secret reading prevent [i.e., precede] the dawning of the day. Let God's voice be the first we hear in the morning." Whether that is the best time of the day for you is of little consequence; regular habits are of more importance. When you read, remember that God himself has declared, "This is the one I esteem: he who is humble and contrite in spirit, and trembles at my word" (Isa. 66:2). Learn to distill what a passage is saying, and pray it back to the Lord—whether in petition, thanksgiving, praise, or frank uncertainty. In time your Bible reading will so be linked with your praying that the two will not always be differentiable.[2]

---

[2] I have tried to offer some practical pointers in this respect in *A Call to Spiritual Reformation: Priorities from Paul and His Prayers* (Grand Rapids: Baker, 1992).

M'Cheyne Chart of Daily Bible Readings

DATE	FAMILY	FAMILY	PRIVATE	PRIVATE
Jan 1	Gen 1	Matt 1	Ezra 1	Acts 1
Jan 2	Gen 2	Matt 2	Ezra 2	Acts 2
Jan 3	Gen 3	Matt 3	Ezra 3	Acts 3
Jan 4	Gen 4	Matt 4	Ezra 4	Acts 4
Jan 5	Gen 5	Matt 5	Ezra 5	Acts 5
Jan 6	Gen 6	Matt 6	Ezra 6	Acts 6
Jan 7	Gen 7	Matt 7	Ezra 7	Acts 7
Jan 8	Gen 8	Matt 8	Ezra 8	Acts 8
Jan 9	Gen 9-10	Matt 9	Ezra 9	Acts 9
Jan 10	Gen 11	Matt 10	Ezra 10	Acts 10
Jan 11	Gen 12	Matt 11	Neh 1	Acts 11
Jan 12	Gen 13	Matt 12	Neh 2	Acts 12
Jan 13	Gen 14	Matt 13	Neh 3	Acts 13
Jan 14	Gen 15	Matt 14	Neh 4	Acts 14
Jan 15	Gen 16	Matt 15	Neh 5	Acts 15
Jan 16	Gen 17	Matt 16	Neh 6	Acts 16
Jan 17	Gen 18	Matt 17	Neh 7	Acts 17
Jan 18	Gen 19	Matt 18	Neh 8	Acts 18
Jan 19	Gen 20	Matt 19	Neh 9	Acts 19
Jan 20	Gen 21	Matt 20	Neh 10	Acts 20
Jan 21	Gen 22	Matt 21	Neh 11	Acts 21
Jan 22	Gen 23	Matt 22	Neh 12	Acts 22
Jan 23	Gen 24	Matt 23	Neh 13	Acts 23
Jan 24	Gen 25	Matt 24	Est 1	Acts 24
Jan 25	Gen 26	Matt 25	Est 2	Acts 25
Jan 26	Gen 27	Matt 26	Est 3	Acts 26
Jan 27	Gen 28	Matt 27	Est 4	Acts 27
Jan 28	Gen 29	Matt 28	Est 5	Acts 28
Jan 29	Gen 30	Mark 1	Est 6	Rom 1
Jan 30	Gen 31	Mark 2	Est 7	Rom 2
Jan 31	Gen 32	Mark 3	Est 8	Rom 3

M'Cheyne Chart of Daily Bible Readings

DATE	FAMILY	FAMILY	PRIVATE	PRIVATE
Feb 1	Gen 33	Mark 4	Est 9-10	Rom 4
Feb 2	Gen 34	Mark 5	Job 1	Rom 5
Feb 3	Gen 35-36	Mark 6	Job 2	Rom 6
Feb 4	Gen 37	Mark 7	Job 3	Rom 7
Feb 5	Gen 38	Mark 8	Job 4	Rom 8
Feb 6	Gen 39	Mark 9	Job 5	Rom 9
Feb 7	Gen 40	Mark 10	Job 6	Rom 10
Feb 8	Gen 41	Mark 11	Job 7	Rom 11
Feb 9	Gen 42	Mark 12	Job 8	Rom 12
Feb 10	Gen 43	Mark 13	Job 9	Rom 13
Feb 11	Gen 44	Mark 14	Job 10	Rom 14
Feb 12	Gen 45	Mark 15	Job 11	Rom 15
Feb 13	Gen 46	Mark 16	Job 12	Rom 16
Feb 14	Gen 47	Lu 1:1-38	Job 13	1 Cor 1
Feb 15	Gen 48	Lu 1:39-80	Job 14	1 Cor 2
Feb 16	Gen 49	Lu 2	Job 15	1 Cor 3
Feb 17	Gen 50	Lu 3	Job 16-17	1 Cor 4
Feb 18	Ex 1	Lu 4	Job 18	1 Cor 5
Feb 19	Ex 2	Lu 5	Job 19	1 Cor 6
Feb 20	Ex 3	Lu 6	Job 20	1 Cor 7
Feb 21	Ex 4	Lu 7	Job 21	1 Cor 8
Feb 22	Ex 5	Lu 8	Job 22	1 Cor 9
Feb 23	Ex 6	Lu 9	Job 23	1 Cor 10
Feb 24	Ex 7	Lu 10	Job 24	1 Cor 11
Feb 25	Ex 8	Lu 11	Job 25-26	1 Cor 12
Feb 26	Ex 9	Lu 12	Job 27	1 Cor 13
Feb 27	Ex 10	Lu 13	Job 28	1 Cor 14
Feb 28	Ex 11:1-12:20	Lu 14	Job 29	1 Cor 15

M'Cheyne Chart of Daily Bible Readings

DATE	FAMILY	FAMILY	PRIVATE	PRIVATE
Mar 1	Ex 12:21-51	Lu 15	Job 30	1 Cor 16
Mar 2	Ex 13	Lu 16	Job 31	2 Cor 1
Mar 3	Ex 14	Lu 17	Job 32	2 Cor 2
Mar 4	Ex 15	Lu 18	Job 33	2 Cor 3
Mar 5	Ex 16	Lu 19	Job 34	2 Cor 4
Mar 6	Ex 17	Lu 20	Job 35	2 Cor 5
Mar 7	Ex 18	Lu 21	Job 36	2 Cor 6
Mar 8	Ex 19	Lu 22	Job 37	2 Cor 7
Mar 9	Ex 20	Lu 23	Job 38	2 Cor 8
Mar 10	Ex 21	Lu 24	Job 39	2 Cor 9
Mar 11	Ex 22	John 1	Job 40	2 Cor 10
Mar 12	Ex 23	John 2	Job 41	2 Cor 11
Mar 13	Ex 24	John 3	Job 42	2 Cor 12
Mar 14	Ex 25	John 4	Prov 1	2 Cor 13
Mar 15	Ex 26	John 5	Prov 2	Gal 1
Mar 16	Ex 27	John 6	Prov 3	Gal 2
Mar 17	Ex 28	John 7	Prov 4	Gal 3
Mar 18	Ex 29	John 8	Prov 5	Gal 4
Mar 19	Ex 30	John 9	Prov 6	Gal 5
Mar 20	Ex 31	John 10	Prov 7	Gal 6
Mar 21	Ex 32	John 11	Prov 8	Eph 1
Mar 22	Ex 33	John 12	Prov 9	Eph 2
Mar 23	Ex 34	John 13	Prov 10	Eph 3
Mar 24	Ex 35	John 14	Prov 11	Eph 4
Mar 25	Ex 36	John 15	Prov 12	Eph 5
Mar 26	Ex 37	John 16	Prov 13	Eph 6
Mar 27	Ex 38	John 17	Prov 14	Phil 1
Mar 28	Ex 39	John 18	Prov 15	Phil 2
Mar 29	Ex 40	John 19	Prov 16	Phil 3
Mar 30	Lev 1	John 20	Prov 17	Phil 4
Mar 31	Lev 2-3	John 21	Prov 18	Col 1

M'Cheyne Chart of Daily Bible Readings

DATE	FAMILY	FAMILY	PRIVATE	PRIVATE
Apr 1	Lev 4	Ps 1-2	Prov 19	Col 2
Apr 2	Lev 5	Ps 3-4	Prov 20	Col 3
Apr 3	Lev 6	Ps 5-6	Prov 21	Col 4
Apr 4	Lev 7	Ps 7-8	Prov 22	1 Thess 1
Apr 5	Lev 8	Ps 9	Prov 23	1 Thess 2
Apr 6	Lev 9	Ps 10	Prov 24	1 Thess 3
Apr 7	Lev 10	Ps 11-12	Prov 25	1 Thess 4
Apr 8	Lev 11-12	Ps 13-14	Prov 26	1 Thess 5
Apr 9	Lev 13	Ps 15-16	Prov 27	2 Thess 1
Apr 10	Lev 14	Ps 17	Prov 28	2 Thess 2
Apr 11	Lev 15	Ps 18	Prov 29	2 Thess 3
Apr 12	Lev 16	Ps 19	Prov 30	1 Tim 1
Apr 13	Lev 17	Ps 20-21	Prov 31	1 Tim 2
Apr 14	Lev 18	Ps 22	Eccles 1	1 Tim 3
Apr 15	Lev 19	Ps 23-24	Eccles 2	1 Tim 4
Apr 16	Lev 20	Ps 25	Eccles 3	1 Tim 5
Apr 17	Lev 21	Ps 26-27	Eccles 4	1 Tim 6
Apr 18	Lev 22	Ps 28-29	Eccles 5	2 Tim 1
Apr 19	Lev 23	Ps 30	Eccles 6	2 Tim 2
Apr 20	Lev 24	Ps 31	Eccles 7	2 Tim 3
Apr 21	Lev 25	Ps 32	Eccles 8	2 Tim 4
Apr 22	Lev 26	Ps 33	Eccles 9	Titus 1
Apr 23	Lev 27	Ps 34	Eccles 10	Titus 2
Apr 24	Num 1	Ps 35	Eccles 11	Titus 3
Apr 25	Num 2	Ps 36	Eccles 12	Philem
Apr 26	Num 3	Ps 37	Song 1	Heb 1
Apr 27	Num 4	Ps 38	Song 2	Heb 2
Apr 28	Num 5	Ps 39	Song 3	Heb 3
Apr 29	Num 6	Ps 40-41	Song 4	Heb 4
Apr 30	Num 7	Ps 42-43	Song 5	Heb 5

M'Cheyne Chart of Daily Bible Readings

DATE	FAMILY	FAMILY	PRIVATE	PRIVATE
May 1	Num 8	Ps 44	Song 6	Heb 6
May 2	Num 9	Ps 45	Song 7	Heb 7
May 3	Num 10	Ps 46-47	Song 8	Heb 8
May 4	Num 11	Ps 48	Isa 1	Heb 9
May 5	Num 12-13	Ps 49	Isa 2	Heb 10
May 6	Num 14	Ps 50	Isa 3-4	Heb 11
May 7	Num 15	Ps 51	Isa 5	Heb 12
May 8	Num 16	Ps 52-54	Isa 6	Heb 13
May 9	Num 17-18	Ps 55	Isa 7	James 1
May 10	Num 19	Ps 56-57	Isa 8:1-9:7	James 2
May 11	Num 20	Ps 58-59	Isa 9:8-10:4	James 3
May 12	Num 21	Ps 60-61	Isa 10:5-34	James 4
May 13	Num 22	Ps 62-63	Isa 11-12	James 5
May 14	Num 23	Ps 64-65	Isa 13	1 Peter 1
May 15	Num 24	Ps 66-67	Isa 14	1 Peter 2
May 16	Num 25	Ps 68	Isa 15	1 Peter 3
May 17	Num 26	Ps 69	Isa 16	1 Peter 4
May 18	Num 27	Ps 70-71	Isa 17-18	1 Peter 5
May 19	Num 28	Ps 72	Isa 19-20	2 Peter 1
May 20	Num 29	Ps 73	Isa 21	2 Peter 2
May 21	Num 30	Ps 74	Isa 22	2 Peter 3
May 22	Num 31	Ps 75-76	Isa 23	1 John 1
May 23	Num 32	Ps 77	Isa 24	1 John 2
May 24	Num 33	Ps 78:1-39	Isa 25	1 John 3
May 25	Num 34	Ps 78:40-72	Isa 26	1 John 4
May 26	Num 35	Ps 79	Isa 27	1 John 5
May 27	Num 36	Ps 80	Isa 28	2 John
May 28	Deut 1	Ps 81-82	Isa 29	3 John
May 29	Deut 2	Ps 83-84	Isa 30	Jude
May 30	Deut 3	Ps 85	Isa 31	Rev 1
May 31	Deut 4	Ps 86-87	Isa 32	Rev 2

M'Cheyne Chart of Daily Bible Readings

DATE	FAMILY	FAMILY	PRIVATE	PRIVATE
Jun 1	Deut 5	Ps 88	Isa 33	Rev 3
Jun 2	Deut 6	Ps 89	Isa 34	Rev 4
Jun 3	Deut 7	Ps 90	Isa 35	Rev 5
Jun 4	Deut 8	Ps 91	Isa 36	Rev 6
Jun 5	Deut 9	Ps 92-93	Isa 37	Rev 7
Jun 6	Deut 10	Ps 94	Isa 38	Rev 8
Jun 7	Deut 11	Ps 95-96	Isa 39	Rev 9
Jun 8	Deut 12	Ps 97-98	Isa 40	Rev 10
Jun 9	Deut 13-14	Ps 99-101	Isa 41	Rev 11
Jun 10	Deut 15	Ps 102	Isa 42	Rev 12
Jun 11	Deut 16	Ps 103	Isa 43	Rev 13
Jun 12	Deut 17	Ps 104	Isa 44	Rev 14
Jun 13	Deut 18	Ps 105	Isa 45	Rev 15
Jun 14	Deut 19	Ps 106	Isa 46	Rev 16
Jun 15	Deut 20	Ps 107	Isa 47	Rev 17
Jun 16	Deut 21	Ps 108-109	Isa 48	Rev 18
Jun 17	Deut 22	Ps 110-111	Isa 49	Rev 19
Jun 18	Deut 23	Ps 112-113	Isa 50	Rev 20
Jun 19	Deut 24	Ps 114-115	Isa 51	Rev 21
Jun 20	Deut 25	Ps 116	Isa 52	Rev 22
Jun 21	Deut 26	Ps 117-118	Isa 53	Matt 1
Jun 22	Deut 27:1-28:19	Ps 119:1-24	Isa 54	Matt 2
Jun 23	Deut 28:20-68	Ps 119:25-48	Isa 55	Matt 3
Jun 24	Deut 29	Ps 119:49-72	Isa 56	Matt 4
Jun 25	Deut 30	Ps 119:73-96	Isa 57	Matt 5
Jun 26	Deut 31	Ps 119:97-120	Isa 58	Matt 6
Jun 27	Deut 32	Ps 119:121-144	Isa 59	Matt 7
Jun 28	Deut 33-34	Ps 119:145-176	Isa 60	Matt 8
Jun 29	Josh 1	Ps 120-122	Isa 61	Matt 9
Jun 30	Josh 2	Ps 123-125	Isa 62	Matt 10

M'Cheyne Chart of Daily Bible Readings

DATE	FAMILY	FAMILY	PRIVATE	PRIVATE
Jul 1	Josh 3	Ps 126-128	Isa 63	Matt 11
Jul 2	Josh 4	Ps 129-131	Isa 64	Matt 12
Jul 3	Josh 5	Ps 132-134	Isa 65	Matt 13
Jul 4	Josh 6	Ps 135-136	Isa 66	Matt 14
Jul 5	Josh 7	Ps 137-138	Jer 1	Matt 15
Jul 6	Josh 8	Ps 139	Jer 2	Matt 16
Jul 7	Josh 9	Ps 140-141	Jer 3	Matt 17
Jul 8	Josh 10	Ps 142-143	Jer 4	Matt 18
Jul 9	Josh 11	Ps 144	Jer 5	Matt 19
Jul 10	Josh 12-13	Ps 145	Jer 6	Matt 20
Jul 11	Josh 14-15	Ps 146-147	Jer 7	Matt 21
Jul 12	Josh 16-17	Ps 148	Jer 8	Matt 22
Jul 13	Josh 18-19	Ps 149-150	Jer 9	Matt 23
Jul 14	Josh 20-21	Acts 1	Jer 10	Matt 24
Jul 15	Josh 22	Acts 2	Jer 11	Matt 25
Jul 16	Josh 23	Acts 3	Jer 12	Matt 26
Jul 17	Josh 24	Acts 4	Jer 13	Matt 27
Jul 18	Judg 1	Acts 5	Jer 14	Matt 28
Jul 19	Judg 2	Acts 6	Jer 15	Mark 1
Jul 20	Judg 3	Acts 7	Jer 16	Mark 2
Jul 21	Judg 4	Acts 8	Jer 17	Mark 3
Jul 22	Judg 5	Acts 9	Jer 18	Mark 4
Jul 23	Judg 6	Acts 10	Jer 19	Mark 5
Jul 24	Judg 7	Acts 11	Jer 20	Mark 6
Jul 25	Judg 8	Acts 12	Jer 21	Mark 7
Jul 26	Judg 9	Acts 13	Jer 22	Mark 8
Jul 27	Judg 10	Acts 14	Jer 23	Mark 9
Jul 28	Judg 11	Acts 15	Jer 24	Mark 10
Jul 29	Judg 12	Acts 16	Jer 25	Mark 11
Jul 30	Judg 13	Acts 17	Jer 26	Mark 12
Jul 31	Judg 14	Acts 18	Jer 27	Mark 13

M'Cheyne Chart of Daily Bible Readings

DATE	FAMILY	FAMILY	PRIVATE	PRIVATE
Aug 1	Judg 15	Acts 19	Jer 28	Mark 14
Aug 2	Judg 16	Acts 20	Jer 29	Mark 15
Aug 3	Judg 17	Acts 21	Jer 30-31	Mark 16
Aug 4	Judg 18	Acts 22	Jer 32	Ps 1-2
Aug 5	Judg 19	Acts 23	Jer 33	Ps 3-4
Aug 6	Judg 20	Acts 24	Jer 34	Ps 5-6
Aug 7	Judg 21	Acts 25	Jer 35	Ps 7-8
Aug 8	Ruth 1	Acts 26	Jer 36, 45	Ps 9
Aug 9	Ruth 2	Acts 27	Jer 37	Ps 10
Aug 10	Ruth 3-4	Acts 28	Jer 38	Ps 11-12
Aug 11	1 Sam 1	Rom 1	Jer 39	Ps 13-14
Aug 12	1 Sam 2	Rom 2	Jer 40	Ps 15-16
Aug 13	1 Sam 3	Rom 3	Jer 41	Ps 17
Aug 14	1 Sam 4	Rom 4	Jer 42	Ps 18
Aug 15	1 Sam 5-6	Rom 5	Jer 43	Ps 19
Aug 16	1 Sam 7-8	Rom 6	Jer 44	Ps 20-21
Aug 17	1 Sam 9	Rom 7	Jer 46	Ps 22
Aug 18	1 Sam 10	Rom 8	Jer 47	Ps 23-24
Aug 19	1 Sam 11	Rom 9	Jer 48	Ps 25
Aug 20	1 Sam 12	Rom 10	Jer 49	Ps 26-27
Aug 21	1 Sam 13	Rom 11	Jer 50	Ps 28-29
Aug 22	1 Sam 14	Rom 12	Jer 51	Ps 30
Aug 23	1 Sam 15	Rom 13	Jer 52	Ps 31
Aug 24	1 Sam 16	Rom 14	Lam 1	Ps 32
Aug 25	1 Sam 17	Rom 15	Lam 2	Ps 33
Aug 26	1 Sam 18	Rom 16	Lam 3	Ps 34
Aug 27	1 Sam 19	1 Cor 1	Lam 4	Ps 35
Aug 28	1 Sam 20	1 Cor 2	Lam 5	Ps 36
Aug 29	1 Sam 21-22	1 Cor 3	Ezek 1	Ps 37
Aug 30	1 Sam 23	1 Cor 4	Ezek 2	Ps 38
Aug 31	1 Sam 24	1 Cor 5	Ezek 3	Ps 39

M'Cheyne Chart of Daily Bible Readings

DATE	FAMILY	FAMILY	PRIVATE	PRIVATE
Sep 1	1 Sam 25	1 Cor 6	Ezek 4	Ps 40-41
Sep 2	1 Sam 26	1 Cor 7	Ezek 5	Ps 42-43
Sep 3	1 Sam 27	1 Cor 8	Ezek 6	Ps 44
Sep 4	1 Sam 28	1 Cor 9	Ezek 7	Ps 45
Sep 5	1 Sam 29-30	1 Cor 10	Ezek 8	Ps 46-47
Sep 6	1 Sam 31	1 Cor 11	Ezek 9	Ps 48
Sep 7	2 Sam 1	1 Cor 12	Ezek 10	Ps 49
Sep 8	2 Sam 2	1 Cor 13	Ezek 11	Ps 50
Sep 9	2 Sam 3	1 Cor 14	Ezek 12	Ps 51
Sep 10	2 Sam 4-5	1 Cor 15	Ezek 13	Ps 52-54
Sep 11	2 Sam 6	1 Cor 16	Ezek 14	Ps 55
Sep 12	2 Sam 7	2 Cor 1	Ezek 15	Ps 56-57
Sep 13	2 Sam 8-9	2 Cor 2	Ezek 16	Ps 58-59
Sep 14	2 Sam 10	2 Cor 3	Ezek 17	Ps 60-61
Sep 15	2 Sam 11	2 Cor 4	Ezek 18	Ps 62-63
Sep 16	2 Sam 12	2 Cor 5	Ezek 19	Ps 64-65
Sep 17	2 Sam 13	2 Cor 6	Ezek 20	Ps 66-67
Sep 18	2 Sam 14	2 Cor 7	Ezek 21	Ps 68
Sep 19	2 Sam 15	2 Cor 8	Ezek 22	Ps 69
Sep 20	2 Sam 16	2 Cor 9	Ezek 23	Ps 70-71
Sep 21	2 Sam 17	2 Cor 10	Ezek 24	Ps 72
Sep 22	2 Sam 18	2 Cor 11	Ezek 25	Ps 73
Sep 23	2 Sam 19	2 Cor 12	Ezek 26	Ps 74
Sep 24	2 Sam 20	2 Cor 13	Ezek 27	Ps 75-76
Sep 25	2 Sam 21	Gal 1	Ezek 28	Ps 77
Sep 26	2 Sam 22	Gal 2	Ezek 29	Ps 78:1-39
Sep 27	2 Sam 23	Gal 3	Ezek 30	Ps 78:40-72
Sep 28	2 Sam 24	Gal 4	Ezek 31	Ps 79
Sep 29	1 Ki 1	Gal 5	Ezek 32	Ps 80
Sep 30	1 Ki 2	Gal 6	Ezek 33	Ps 81-82

M'Cheyne Chart of Daily Bible Readings

DATE	FAMILY	FAMILY	PRIVATE	PRIVATE
Oct 1	1 Ki 3	Eph 1	Ezek 34	Ps 83-84
Oct 2	1 Ki 4-5	Eph 2	Ezek 35	Ps 85
Oct 3	1 Ki 6	Eph 3	Ezek 36	Ps 86
Oct 4	1 Ki 7	Eph 4	Ezek 37	Ps 87-88
Oct 5	1 Ki 8	Eph 5	Ezek 38	Ps 89
Oct 6	1 Ki 9	Eph 6	Ezek 39	Ps 90
Oct 7	1 Ki 10	Phil 1	Ezek 40	Ps 91
Oct 8	1 Ki 11	Phil 2	Ezek 41	Ps 92-93
Oct 9	1 Ki 12	Phil 3	Ezek 42	Ps 94
Oct 10	1 Ki 13	Phil 4	Ezek 43	Ps 95-96
Oct 11	1 Ki 14	Col 1	Ezek 44	Ps 97-98
Oct 12	1 Ki 15	Col 2	Ezek 45	Ps 99-101
Oct 13	1 Ki 16	Col 3	Ezek 46	Ps 102
Oct 14	1 Ki 17	Col 4	Ezek 47	Ps 103
Oct 15	1 Ki 18	1 Thess 1	Ezek 48	Ps 104
Oct 16	1 Ki 19	1 Thess 2	Dan 1	Ps 105
Oct 17	1 Ki 20	1 Thess 3	Dan 2	Ps 106
Oct 18	1 Ki 21	1 Thess 4	Dan 3	Ps 107
Oct 19	1 Ki 22	1 Thess 5	Dan 4	Ps 108-109
Oct 20	2 Ki 1	2 Thess 1	Dan 5	Ps 110-111
Oct 21	2 Ki 2	2 Thess 2	Dan 6	Ps 112-113
Oct 22	2 Ki 3	2 Thess 3	Dan 7	Ps 114-115
Oct 23	2 Ki 4	1 Tim 1	Dan 8	Ps 116
Oct 24	2 Ki 5	1 Tim 2	Dan 9	Ps 117-118
Oct 25	2 Ki 6	1 Tim 3	Dan 10	Ps 119:1-24
Oct 26	2 Ki 7	1 Tim 4	Dan 11	Ps 119:25-48
Oct 27	2 Ki 8	1 Tim 5	Dan 12	Ps 119:49-72
Oct 28	2 Ki 9	1 Tim 6	Hosea 1	Ps 119:73-96
Oct 29	2 Ki 10-11	2 Tim 1	Hosea 2	Ps 119:97-120
Oct 30	2 Ki 12	2 Tim 2	Hosea 3-4	Ps 119:121-144
Oct 31	2 Ki 13	2 Tim 3	Hosea 5-6	Ps 119:145-176

M'Cheyne Chart of Daily Bible Readings

DATE	FAMILY	FAMILY	PRIVATE	PRIVATE
Nov 1	2 Ki 14	2 Tim 4	Hosea 7	Ps 120-122
Nov 2	2 Ki 15	Titus 1	Hosea 8	Ps 123-125
Nov 3	2 Ki 16	Titus 2	Hosea 9	Ps 126-128
Nov 4	2 Ki 17	Titus 3	Hosea 10	Ps 129-131
Nov 5	2 Ki 18	Philem	Hosea 11	Ps 132-134
Nov 6	2 Ki 19	Heb 1	Hosea 12	Ps 135-136
Nov 7	2 Ki 20	Heb 2	Hosea 13	Ps 137-138
Nov 8	2 Ki 21	Heb 3	Hosea 14	Ps 139
Nov 9	2 Ki 22	Heb 4	Joel 1	Ps 140-141
Nov 10	2 Ki 23	Heb 5	Joel 2	Ps 142
Nov 11	2 Ki 24	Heb 6	Joel 3	Ps 143
Nov 12	2 Ki 25	Heb 7	Amos 1	Ps 144
Nov 13	1 Chr 1-2	Heb 8	Amos 2	Ps 145
Nov 14	1 Chr 3-4	Heb 9	Amos 3	Ps 146-147
Nov 15	1 Chr 5-6	Heb 10	Amos 4	Ps 148-150
Nov 16	1 Chr 7-8	Heb 11	Amos 5	Lu 1:1-38
Nov 17	1 Chr 9-10	Heb 12	Amos 6	Lu 1:39-80
Nov 18	1 Chr 11-12	Heb 13	Amos 7	Lu 2
Nov 19	1 Chr 13-14	James 1	Amos 8	Lu 3
Nov 20	1 Chr 15	James 2	Amos 9	Lu 4
Nov 21	1 Chr 16	James 3	Obadiah	Lu 5
Nov 22	1 Chr 17	James 4	Jonah 1	Lu 6
Nov 23	1 Chr 18	James 5	Jonah 2	Lu 7
Nov 24	1 Chr 19-20	1 Peter 1	Jonah 3	Lu 8
Nov 25	1 Chr 21	1 Peter 2	Jonah 4	Lu 9
Nov 26	1 Chr 22	1 Peter 3	Micah 1	Lu 10
Nov 27	1 Chr 23	1 Peter 4	Micah 2	Lu 11
Nov 28	1 Chr 24-25	1 Peter 5	Micah 3	Lu 12
Nov 29	1 Chr 26-27	2 Peter 1	Micah 4	Lu 13
Nov 30	1 Chr 28	2 Peter 2	Micah 5	Lu 14

M'Cheyne Chart of Daily Bible Readings

DATE	FAMILY	FAMILY	PRIVATE	PRIVATE
Dec 1	1 Chr 29	2 Peter 3	Micah 6	Lu 15
Dec 2	2 Chr 1	1 John 1	Micah 7	Lu 16
Dec 3	2 Chr 2	1 John 2	Nahum 1	Lu 17
Dec 4	2 Chr 3-4	1 John 3	Nahum 2	Lu 18
Dec 5	2 Chr 5:1-6:11	1 John 4	Nahum 3	Lu 19
Dec 6	2 Chr 6:12- 42	1 John 5	Hab 1	Lu 20
Dec 7	2 Chr 7	2 John	Hab 2	Lu 21
Dec 8	2 Chr 8	3 John	Hab 3	Lu 22
Dec 9	2 Chr 9	Jude	Zeph 1	Lu 23
Dec 10	2 Chr 10	Rev 1	Zeph 2	Lu 24
Dec 11	2 Chr 11-12	Rev 2	Zeph 3	John 1
Dec 12	2 Chr 13	Rev 3	Hag 1	John 2
Dec 13	2 Chr 14-15	Rev 4	Hag 2	John 3
Dec 14	2 Chr 16	Rev 5	Zech 1	John 4
Dec 15	2 Chr 17	Rev 6	Zech 2	John 5
Dec 16	2 Chr 18	Rev 7	Zech 3	John 6
Dec 17	2 Chr 19-20	Rev 8	Zech 4	John 7
Dec 18	2 Chr 21	Rev 9	Zech 5	John 8
Dec 19	2 Chr 22-23	Rev 10	Zech 6	John 9
Dec 20	2 Chr 24	Rev 11	Zech 7	John 10
Dec 21	2 Chr 25	Rev 12	Zech 8	John 11
Dec 22	2 Chr 26	Rev 13	Zech 9	John 12
Dec 23	2 Chr 27-28	Rev 14	Zech 10	John 13
Dec 24	2 Chr 29	Rev 15	Zech 11	John 14
Dec 25	2 Chr 30	Rev 16	Zech 12:1-13:1	John 15
Dec 26	2 Chr 31	Rev 17	Zech 13:2-9	John 16
Dec 27	2 Chr 32	Rev 18	Zech 14	John 17
Dec 28	2 Chr 33	Rev 19	Mal 1	John 18
Dec 29	2 Chr 34	Rev 20	Mal 2	John 19
Dec 30	2 Chr 35	Rev 21	Mal 3	John 20
Dec 31	2 Chr 36	Rev 22	Mal 4	John 21

Genesis 1; Matthew 1; Ezra 1; Acts 1

∾

ALL FOUR OF THESE CHAPTERS DEPICT NEW BEGINNINGS, but the first reading—
Genesis 1—portrays the beginning of everything in this created universe.

On the face of it, this chapter, and the lines of thought it develops, establish
that God is different from the universe that he creates, and therefore pantheism
is ruled out; that the original creation was entirely good, and therefore dualism is
ruled out; that human beings, male and female together, are alone declared to be
made in the image of God, and therefore forms of reductionism that claim we are
part of the animal kingdom *and no more* must be ruled out; that God is a talking
God, and therefore all notions of an impersonal God must be ruled out; that this
God has sovereignly made all things, including all people, and therefore concep-
tions of merely tribal deities must be ruled out.

Some of these and other matters are put positively by later writers of Scripture
who, reflecting on the doctrine of creation, offer a host of invaluable conclusions.
The sheer glory of the created order bears telling witness to the glory of its Maker
(Ps. 19). The universe came into being by the will of God, and for this, God is
incessantly worshiped (Rev. 4:11). That God has made everything speaks of his
transcendence, i.e., he is above this created order, above time and space, and
therefore cannot be domesticated by anything in it (Acts 17:24-25). That he made
all things and continues to rule over all, means that both racism and tribalism are
to be rejected (Acts 17:26). Further, if we ourselves have been made in his image,
it is preposterous to think that God can properly be pictured by some image that
we can concoct (Acts 17:29). These notions and more are teased out by later
Scriptures.

One of the most important entailments of the doctrine of creation is this: it
grounds all human responsibility. The theme repeatedly recurs in the Bible,
sometimes explicitly, sometimes by implication. To take but one example, John's
gospel opens by declaring that everything that was created came into being by the
agency of God's "Word," the Word that became flesh in Jesus Christ (John 1:2-3,
14). But this observation sets the stage for a devastating indictment: when this
Word came into the world, *and even though the world was made through him*, the
world did not recognize him (John 1:10). God made us to "image" himself; he
made us for his own glory. For us to imagine ourselves autonomous is, far from
being a measure of our maturity, the supreme mark of our rebellion, the flag of
our suppression of the truth (Rom. 1).

∾

Genesis 2; Matthew 2; Ezra 2; Acts 2

WHAT A STRANGE WAY, we might think, to end this account of Creation: "The man and his wife were both naked, and they felt no shame" (**Gen. 2:25**). Hollywood would love it: what an excuse for sexual titillation if someone tries to place the scene on the big screen. We hurry on, chasing the narrative.

Yet the verse is strategically placed. It links the account of the creation of woman and the establishment of marriage (Gen. 2:18-24) with the account of the Fall (Gen. 3). On the one hand, the Bible tells us that woman was taken from man, made by God to be "a helper suitable for him" (2:18), yet doubly one with him: she is bone of his bones and flesh of his flesh (2:23), and now the two are united as one in marriage, one flesh (2:24), the paradigm of marriages to come, of new homes and new families. On the other hand, in the next chapter we read of the Fall, the wretched rebellion that introduces death and the curse. Part of that account, as we glean from tomorrow's reading, finds the man and the woman hiding from the presence of the Lord, because their rebellion opened their eyes to their nakedness (3:7, 10). Far from being unashamed, their instinct is to hide.

This was not how it was supposed to be. In the beginning, "the man and his wife were both naked, and they felt no shame." The sexual arena stands to the fore, of course; yet there is a symbol-laden depth to the pronouncement. It is a way of saying that there was no guilt; there was nothing to be ashamed of. This happy innocence meant openness, utter candor. There was nothing to hide, whether from God or from each other.

How different after the Fall. The man and the woman hide from God, and blame others. The candor has gone, the innocence has dissipated, the openness has closed. These are the immediate effects of the first sin.

How much more dire are the same effects worked into the psyche of a fallen race, worked into individuals like you and me with so much to hide. Would you want your spouse or your best friend to know the full dimensions of each of your thoughts? Would you want your motives placarded for public display? Have we not done things of which we are so ashamed that we want as few people as possible to know about them? Even the person whose conscience is said to be "seared" (e.g., 1 Tim. 4:2) and who therefore boasts of his sin does so only in some arenas, but not in others.

What astonishing dimensions characterize the salvation that addresses problems as deep as these.

Genesis 3; Matthew 3; Ezra 3; Acts 3

∾

IN ANY DOMAIN, we are unlikely to agree as to what the solution of a problem is, unless we agree as to the nature of the problem.

The religions of the world offer an enormous range of solutions to human problems. Some promulgate various forms of religious self-help exercises; some advocate a kind of faithful fatalism; others urge tapping into an impersonal energy or force in the universe; still others claim that mystical experiences are available to those who pursue them, experiences that relativize all evil. One of the critical questions to ask is this: What constitutes the irreducible heart of human problems?

The Bible insists that the heart of all human problems is rebellion against the God who is our Maker, whose image we bear, and whose rule we seek to over-throw. All of our problems, without exception, can be traced to this fundamental source: our rebellion and the just curse of God that we have attracted by our rebellion.

This must not be (mis)understood in some simplistic sense. It is not necessarily the case that the greatest rebels in this world suffer the greatest pain in this world, on some simple tit-for-tat scheme. But whether we are perpetrators (as in hate, jealousy, lust, or theft) or victims (as in rape, battery, or indiscriminate bombing), our plight is tied to sin—ours or that of others. Further, whether our misery is the result of explicit human malice or the fruit of a "natural" disaster, **Genesis 3** insists that this is a disordered world, a broken world—and that this state of affairs has come about because of human rebellion.

God's curses on the human pair are striking. The first (Gen. 3:16), which promises pain in childbearing and disordered marriages, is the disruption of the first designated task human beings were assigned before the Fall: male and female, in the blessing of God, being fruitful and increasing in number (1:27-28). The second (Gen. 3:17-19), which promises painful toil, a disordered ecology, and certain death, is the disruption of the second designated task human beings were assigned before the Fall: God's image-bearers ruling over the created order and living in harmony with it (1:28-30).

With perfect justice God might have destroyed this rebel breed instantly. He can no more ignore such rebellion than he can deny his own deity. Yet in mercy he clothes them, suspends part of the sentence (death itself)—and foretells a time when the offspring of the woman will crush the serpent who led the first couple astray. One reads Revelation 12 with relief, and grasps that Genesis 3 defines the problem that only Christ can meet.

∾

Genesis 4; Matthew 4; Ezra 4; Acts 4

∾

IT TOOK ONLY ONE GENERATION for the human race to produce its first murderer (**Gen. 4**). Two reflections:

(1) *In the Bible, there are many motives behind murder.* Jehu killed for political advantage (2 Kings 9–10); David killed to cover up his adultery (2 Sam. 11); Joab murdered out of revenge, and out of the fear of having his privileged position usurped (2 Sam. 3); some of the men of Gibeah in Benjamin killed out of unbridled lust (Judg. 19). It would be easy to enlarge the list. On the occasion of the first murder, the motive was sibling rivalry out of control. Cain could not bear to think that his brother Abel's offering was acceptable to God, while his own was not. Instead of seeking God so as to improve his own sacrifice, he killed the man he saw as his rival.

What is common to all these motives is the assumption entertained by the murderer that he or she is at the center of the universe. Even God must approve what I do; if not, since I cannot kill God, I will kill those whom God approves. Instead of the glorious situation that obtained before the Fall, when in the minds of God's image-bearers, God himself was at the center, and loved and cherished as our good and wise Maker and Ruler, now each individual wants to be the center of the universe, as if saying, "Even God must serve me. If he does not, perhaps it is time to invent new gods. . . ."

Among the shocking elements in the murder of Cain is the stark fact that Cain's nose is out of joint *because he does not have God's approval.* The fatal sibling rivalry lies in this instance in the domain of religion. No matter: once I insist on being number one, I must be number one in every domain. Sad to tell, if the constraints of culture and fear of the penal system restrain me from outright murder, they are unlikely to restrain me from the kind of hate that the Lord Jesus insists is of the same moral order as murder (Matt. 5:21-26). So while the motives for murder are superficially many, at heart they become one: I wish to be god. And that is the supreme idolatry.

(2) *In the Bible, the innocent are sometimes murdered.* In this account, Abel is the righteous brother, yet he is the one who is murdered. From this fact we must reflect on two things. First, the Bible is utterly realistic about the horrible cruelty and unfairness of sin. Second, already by way of anticipation, we quietly recognize that if ultimate redress and justice are possible, God must intervene—and the books can only finally be squared after death.

∾

Genesis 5; Matthew 5; Ezra 5; Acts 5

∾

AGAIN AND AGAIN IN THE FIFTH CHAPTER OF GENESIS, one finds the refrain, "and then he died." So-and-so lived so many years, *and then he died . . . and then he died . . . and then he died. . . .* Why the repetition?

From the beginning, God's intention had been that the intercourse between himself and his image-bearers would be eternal: Adam and Eve were to experience eternal life with God. Their rebellion put an end to this trajectory (Gen. 3:21-22). Even if death did not fall on them immediately (Adam lived to the age of 930, according to Gen. 5:5), it was inevitable. The chapter before this table of deaths records the first murder—another death. And the three succeeding chapters (Gen. 6–8) record the Flood, in which the human race dies, save only Noah and his family. Whether by murder or by immediate divine judgment or by old age, the result is always the same: "and then he died." As the wry contemporary expression puts it, "Life is hard, and then you die."

In fact, by God's just decree, death is taking hold of the human race. The life spans in Genesis 5 are extraordinary. They cannot last: more years means more evil. By Genesis 6:3, God determines to cut short the life span of his rebellious image-bearers. This decision is implemented gradually but firmly, so that by Genesis 11 the recorded ages have declined considerably, and in later records very few live longer than 120 years. But whatever the age, the final result is the same: "and then he died."

Contemporary Western thought finds death so frightening that in polite conversation it is the last taboo. Nowadays one can chatter on about sex and finances, and never raise an eyebrow; mention death, and most people are uncomfortable at best. Even many Christians think of their faith almost exclusively in terms of what it does for them *now*, rather than in terms of preparing them for eternity such that it transforms how they live now.

God does not want us to shut our eyes to the effects of our sin, to the inevitability of death. Nevertheless, this chapter includes one bright exception: "Enoch walked with God; then he was no more, because God took him away" (Gen. 5:24). It is almost as if God is showing that death is not ontologically necessary; that those who walk with God one day escape death; that even for those who die, there is hope—in God's grace—of life beyond our inevitable death. But it is tied to a walk with God. It will take the rest of the Bible to unpack what that means.

∾

Genesis 6; Matthew 6; Ezra 6; Acts 6

∽

THE FIRST THREE SECTIONS OF **MATTHEW 6** (which itself is the central chapter of the Sermon on the Mount) deal with three fundamental acts of piety in Judaism: giving to the needy (traditionally called "alms-giving"), prayer, and fasting (Matt. 6:1-18). The common link is striking: Jesus recognizes how easy it is for sinners to engage in worthy, philanthropic and even religious activities, less in order to do what is right than to be admired for doing what is right. If being thought generous is more important than being generous, if gaining a reputation for prayerfulness is more important to us than praying when no one but God is listening, if fasting is something in which we engage only if we can disingenuously talk about it, then these acts of piety become acts of impiety.

The fundamental way to check out how sound we are in each of these areas is to perform these acts so quietly that none but God knows we are doing them. So be generous, but tell no one what you are giving (6:1-4). Insist that even the recipients be silent. Pray far more in secret than you do in public (6:5-8). By all means, fast—but tell no one you are doing so (6:16-18). As for the middle item in these three traditional acts of piety, there is a further test: do not bother to ask your heavenly Father for forgiveness where you yourself are unwilling to forgive (6:14-15).

In each of these three traditional acts of piety, genuine Christian living is characterized by a simple yet profound desire to please God, and not by the ostentation that is in reality more interested in generating the impression among our peers that we are pleasing God.

The last two sections of the chapter continue this probing of our innermost motives. (1) In the first, Jesus tells us to store up treasure in heaven, for our hearts will inevitably pursue our treasure. What we ultimately value will tug at our "hearts"—our personalities, our dreams, our time, our imaginations, our inmost beings—and we will pursue it. That thing becomes our god. If what we value is merely material, our god is materialism. But if all we cherish most belongs to the eternal realm, then our whole being will pursue what is of transcendent significance. (2) In the second, Jesus tells us that a true and faithful relationship with God refuses to indulge in endless, needless fretting. We can trust God—his wisdom, his goodness, his providential ordering of things—even in this broken, evil world. Not to trust him betrays the pagan character of our hearts.

In short: seek first God's kingdom and righteousness (6:33).

∽

Genesis 7; Matthew 7; Ezra 7; Acts 7

THERE WAS A TIME WHEN scarcely a person in the Anglo-Saxon world would not have been able to cite John 3:16. Doubtless it was the best known verse in the entire Bible. It may still hold pride of place today—I am uncertain. But if it does, the percentage of people who know it is considerably smaller, and continues to decline as biblical illiteracy rises in the West.

Meanwhile there is another verse that is (perhaps more) frequently quoted, almost as a defiant gesture, by some people who do not know their Bibles very well, but who think it authorizes their biases. It is **Matthew 7:1**: "Do not judge, or you too will be judged." In an age when philosophical pluralism is on the ascendancy, these nine words might almost be taken as *the* public confession.

Three things must be said. *First,* it is striking that today's readings include not only Matthew 7 but also Genesis 7. There the sweeping judgment of the Flood is enacted: "Every living thing on the face of the earth was wiped out; men and animals and the creatures that move along the ground and the birds of the air were wiped from the earth. Only Noah was left, and those with him in the ark" (Gen. 7:23). The same God stands behind both passages, so we should not be too hasty in understanding Matthew 7:1 to mean that all judgment is intrinsically evil.

Second, this is not an instance where something practiced in the Old Testament is somehow abolished in the New. It is not as if judgment was possible in Genesis but is now abolished in Matthew. After all, Matthew 7:6 demands that we make judgments about who are "dogs" and "pigs," and the paragraphs at the end of this chapter warn against false prophets (and tell us how we are to discern who is true and who is false), and who is truly a follower of Jesus and who is not. Moreover, not only does this chapter speak of a terrible judgment no less final than the flood (Matt. 7:13, 19, 23), but there are many passages in the New Testament that are equally uncompromising.

Third, we must not only expose false interpretations of Matthew 7:1, we must understand what it does say and appropriate it. The verb *judge* has a wide range of meanings, and the context (7:1-5) is decisive in giving it its color in this passage. People who pursue righteousness (6:33) are easily prone to self-righteousness, arrogance, condescension toward others, an ugly holier-than-thou stance, hypocrisy. Not all are like that, of course, but the sin of "*judg*mentalism" is common enough. Jesus won't have it.

Genesis 8; Matthew 8; Ezra 8; Acts 8

∽

WHY DOES JESUS FIND the faith of the centurion so astonishing (**Matt. 8:5-13**)? The centurion assures Jesus that as far as he is concerned it is unnecessary for the Master to visit his home in order to heal the paralyzed servant. He understands that Jesus need only say the word, and the servant will be healed. "For," the centurion explains, "I myself am a man under authority, with soldiers under me. I tell this one, 'Go,' and he goes; and that one, 'Come,' and he comes. I say to my servant, 'Do this,' and he does it" (8:9). Why is this such an astonishing evidence of faith?

Three factors stand out. The *first* is that in an age of not a little superstition, the centurion believed that Jesus' healing power did not lie in hocus-pocus, or even in his personal presence, but in his word. It was not *necessary* for Jesus to touch or handle the servant, or even be present; he needed only to say the word, and it would be done.

The *second* is that he came to such confident assertions despite the fact that he was not steeped in Scripture. He was a Gentile. What grasp of Scripture he had we cannot say, but it was certainly less than that enjoyed by many of the learned in Israel. Yet his faith was purer, simpler, more penetrating, more Christ-honoring than theirs.

The *third* astonishing element in this man's faith is the analogy he draws. He recognizes that he himself is a man under authority, and therefore he has authority when he speaks in the context of that relationship. When he tells a Roman soldier under him to come or go or do something, he is not speaking merely as one man to another man. The centurion speaks with the authority of his senior officer, the tribune, who in turn speaks, finally, with the authority of Caesar, with the authority of the mighty Roman Empire. That authority belongs to the centurion, not because he is in fact as powerful as Caesar in every dimension, but because he is a man under authority: the chain of command means that when the centurion speaks to the foot soldier, Rome speaks. Implicitly, the centurion is saying that he recognizes in Jesus an analogous relationship: Jesus so stands in relationship to God, and under God's authority, that when Jesus speaks, God speaks. The centurion, of course, was not speaking within the framework of a mature Christian doctrine of Christ, but the eyes of faith had enabled him to penetrate very far indeed.

This is the faith we need. It trusts Jesus' word, reflects a simple profundity, and believes that when Jesus speaks, God speaks.

∽

Genesis 9—10; Matthew 9; Ezra 9; Acts 9

DESPITE THE COMPREHENSIVENESS of the punishment it meted out, the Flood did not change human nature. God well knows that murder, first committed by Cain, will happen again. Now he prescribes capital punishment (**Gen. 9:6**), not as a deterrent—deterrence is not discussed—but as a signal that murder is in a class by itself, in that it kills a being made in the image of God. But there are other signs that sin continues. The promise God makes, sealed by the rainbow, not to destroy the race in this fashion again (9:12-17), is relevant not because the race has somehow been shocked into compliance, but precisely because God recognizes that the same degradation will occur again and again. And Noah himself, who with reference to his pre-Flood days can rightly be called a "preacher of righteousness" (2 Peter 2:5), is now depicted as a drunk, with family relationships already breaking down.

But there is another parallel between these chapters of Genesis and what took place before the Flood. Before the Flood, despite the grip of sin, there are individuals like Abel, whose sacrifice pleases God (Gen. 4); there are people who recognize their great need of God, and call upon the name of the Lord (4:26); there is Enoch, the seventh from Adam, who walked with God (5:22). In other words, there is a race within the race, a smaller race, not intrinsically superior to the other, but so relating to the living God that it heads in a quite different direction. Writing at the beginning of the fifth century A.D., Augustine of Hippo in North Africa traces back to these earliest chapters the beginning of two humanities, two cities—the city of God and the city of man. (See also the meditation for December 27.) That contrast develops and grows in various ways throughout the Bible, until the book of Revelation contrasts "Babylon" and the "new Jerusalem." Empirically, believers find they are citizens of both; in terms of allegiance, they belong to one or the other.

The same distinctions re-form after the Flood. The race soon demonstrates that the problems of rebellion and sin are deep-seated; they constitute part of our nature. Yet distinctions also begin to appear. While this covenant that God makes not to destroy the earth the same way again is between God and *all* living things (9:16), Noah's sons divide, much as Adam's had. The wearisome cycle begins again, but it is not without hope: the city of God never falls into utter abeyance, but anticipates the more explicit covenantal distinctions to come, now just around the corner, and the glorious climax to come at the end of redemptive history.

Genesis 11; Matthew 10; Ezra 10; Acts 10

∾

MOVED BY COMPASSION when the crowds remind him of sheep without a shepherd, Jesus instructs his disciples, "Ask the Lord of the harvest, therefore, to send out workers into his harvest field" (Matt. 9:38)—and then he organizes a trainee mission for the twelve who constitute his inner circle (**Matt. 10**). There are many wonderful things to learn from this chapter, which, judging by the language (e.g., 10:18), Jesus takes to be a kind of forerunner of a lifelong mission. Here I must focus on just one element.

That element is the degree of conflict that Jesus anticipates in this evangelistic enterprise. Some entire communities will reject Jesus' followers (10:11-14). In later years, although their witness will reach to the highest levels of government, those very governments will sometimes impose harsh sanctions (10:17-19). The priorities of the Gospel will split families so severely that some family members will betray other family members (10:21, 35). At its worst, persecution will hound Christian witnesses from one center to another (10:22-23). In some instances this persecution will end in martyrdom (10:28).

Anyone with the slightest familiarity with history knows how frequently and chillingly these prophecies have been fulfilled. The fact that many in the West have for so long been largely exempt from the worst features of such persecution has let us lower our guard—even Christians may think that a hassle-free life is something that society owes us. But as the Judeo-Christian heritage of the West weakens, we may one day be caught up in realities that missions specialists know but that the rest of us sometimes ignore: the last century and a half have seen more converts, *and more martyrs,* than the first eighteen centuries combined.

What will stabilize us in such times? This chapter mentions several precious supports: the recognition that Jesus our Master was hated before us (10:24-25); assurance that in the end justice will be done and will be seen to be done (10:26-27); recognition that a proper fear of God reduces fear of human beings (10:28); quiet confidence in the sovereignty of God, even in these circumstances (10:29-31); encouraging recognition that those who do receive us receive Christ, and therefore receive God (10:40); Christ's own promise that the rewards of eternity cannot fail (10:41-42).

In any case, a fundamental principle is at stake: This is the way Christians view things; indeed, it is bound up with being a Christian. "Anyone who does not take his cross and follow me is not worthy of me. Whoever finds his life will lose it, and whoever loses his life for my sake will find it" (10:38-39).

∾

Genesis 12; Matthew 11; Nehemiah 1; Acts 11

THIS PASSAGE, **Genesis 12,** marks a turning point in God's unfolding plan of redemption. From now on, the focus of God's dealings is not scattered individuals, but a race, a nation. This is the turning point that makes the Old Testament documents so profoundly Jewish. And ultimately, out of this race come law, priests, wisdom, patterns of relationships between God and his covenant people, oracles, prophecies, laments, psalms—a rich array of institutions and texts that point forward, in ways that become increasingly clear, to a new covenant foretold by Israel's prophets.

Even in this initial covenant with Abram, God includes a promise that already expands the horizons beyond Israel, a promise that repeatedly surfaces in the Bible. God tells Abraham, "All peoples on earth will be blessed through you" (12:3). Lest we miss its importance, the book of Genesis repeats it (18:18; 22:18; 26:4; 28:14). A millennium later, the same promise is refocused not on the nation as a whole, but on one of Israel's great kings: "May his name endure forever; may it continue as long as the sun. All nations will be blessed through him, and they will call him blessed" (Ps. 72:17). The "evangelical prophet" often articulates the same breadth of vision (e.g., Isa. 19:23-25). The earliest preaching in the church, after the resurrection of Jesus, understood that the salvation Jesus had introduced was a fulfillment of this promise to Abraham (Acts 3:25). The apostle Paul makes the same connection (Gal. 3:8).

Even when the passage in Genesis is not explicitly cited, the same stance— that God's ultimate intentions were from the beginning to bring men and women from every race into the new humanity he was forming—surfaces in a hundred ways. In fact, quite apart from this passage, two of the three remaining passages in today's readings point in the same direction. In Matthew 11:20-24, Jesus makes it clear, in disturbing language, that on the last day pagan cities, though punished, may be punished less severely than the cities of Israel who enjoyed the unfathomable privilege of hearing Jesus for themselves, and seeing his miracles, but who made nothing of it. His own invitation is broad: "Come to me, all you who are weary and burdened, and I will give you rest" (Matt. 11:28). And in Acts 11, Peter recounts his experiences with Cornelius and his household to the church in Jerusalem, leading them to conclude, "So then, God has granted even the Gentiles repentance unto life" (Acts 11:18).

Christ receives the unrestrained praise of heaven, because with his blood he purchased people for God "from every tribe and language and people and nation" (Rev. 5:9; see meditation for December 15).

Genesis 13; Matthew 12; Nehemiah 2; Acts 12

∽

THE PICTURE IS A LOVELY ONE. Jesus is so tender and gentle that when he finds a "bruised reed" (**Matt. 12:20**), instead of snapping it off thoughtlessly, he binds it up in the hope that it will rejuvenate itself. If the wick of a candle has been reduced to a smoldering ember, instead of snuffing it out—thereby extinguishing it completely—Jesus fans it back into flame. He will act this way, we are told, "till he leads justice to victory. In his name the nations will put their hope" (12:20-21).

The words are drawn from Isaiah 42:1-4, one of the "Suffering Servant" passages of Isaiah. Many people expected a Messiah who would come with decisive and irresistible power and bring justice to the earth, or at least to Israel. But it appears unlikely that many people linked the coming King with Isaiah's promised servant. That is why the notion of a kingdom that dawned in the context of meekness and blessing, and restrained in the matter of climactic judgment, was so unexpected. Yet here was Jesus, healing the sick among the people—and then warning them not to tell people who he was (12:15-16). Small wonder Matthew sees in such conduct a direct fulfillment of Isaiah's lovely words.

Even the surrounding verses betray something of the same theme. While Jesus is healing someone on the Sabbath, his opponents try to kill him for ostensibly breaking the Sabbath (12:9-14); while Jesus casts out demons from a poor victim, his opponents are ready to write Jesus off as the devil himself (12:22-28). Their very harshness, in the name of an alleged orthodoxy, contrasts sharply with his gentleness.

In addition to the great christological implications, this passage discloses something of the nature of the kingdom into which Christians have been drawn, and therefore of the conduct that is demanded of us. On the one hand, as Matthew has made clear in the previous chapter, Jesus' witnesses are called to a holy and courageous boldness, a firm fidelity to the Gospel that is willing to endure ostracism and even persecution. But we are not to display the kind of "strength" that is hard and harsh, the kind of uprightness that is angry and condescending, the kind of courage that is merely ruthless, the kind of witness that rants and manipulates. We follow the Lord Jesus, who tells his followers, "Take my yoke upon you and learn from me, for I am gentle and humble in heart" (11:29). That means that we too, while we proclaim "justice to the nations" (12:18), resolve not to quarrel or cry out, clanging cymbals in the streets.

∽

Genesis 14; Matthew 13; Nehemiah 3; Acts 13

∿

IF ONE WERE TO READ through the book of Genesis without knowing the content of any other book of the Bible, one of the most enigmatic sections would certainly be these few verses about Melchizedek (**Gen. 14:18-20**). After all, how does he contribute in any substantial way to the plotline of the book?

His presence is precipitated by the decision (recorded in Gen. 13) of Abram and Lot to separate in order to stop the wrangling that was breaking out between their respective herdsmen. Lot opts for the plains of Sodom and Gomorrah. That means he and his family and wealth are taken captive when Kedorlaomer and the petty kings aligned with him attack the twin towns and escape with considerable plunder. Abram and his sizable number of fighting men go after the attackers. The skirmish ends in the release of Lot and his family, and the restoration of the people and goods that had been carried off. In the verses that follow, Abram refuses to accept any reward from the king of Sodom, a city already proverbial for wickedness, but he gladly accepts the blessing of the king of Salem (which possibly equals Jerusalem?) and in return pays him an honorific tithe.

Historically, Melchizedek (his name means "king of righteousness") appears to be the king of the city-state of Salem (a name meaning "peace" or "well-being"). He functions not only as Salem's king, but as "priest of God Most High" (14:18). Indeed, it is in the name of God Most High that he blesses Abram. And Abram so respects him, apparently knowing him from previous dealings, that he honors him in return.

We need not think that Abram was the only person on earth who retained knowledge of the living God. Melchizedek was another, and Abram finds in him a kindred spirit. In a book that provides the exact genealogy of virtually everyone who is important to the storyline, rather strikingly Melchizedek simply appears and disappears—we are told neither who his parents were nor when and how he died. He and his city are a foil to Sodom and its king. Once again, there are two cities: the city of God and the city of man (as Augustine would label them).

Melchizedek is mentioned in only two other places in the Bible. The first is Psalm 110 (see meditation for June 17); the other is Hebrews, where the writer recognizes that the inclusion of Melchizedek in the plotline of Genesis is no accident, but a symbol-laden event with extraordinary significance (especially Heb. 7). God is preparing the way for the ultimate priest-king, not only in verbal prophecies but in models (or *types*) that provide the categories and shape the expectations of the people of God.

∿

Genesis 15; Matthew 14; Nehemiah 4; Acts 14

∾

GOD'S TIME SCALE is so different from ours. Abram wants a son, and feels his time is running out; God envisages a race with countless millions of descendants. Abram feels his life is approaching its termination with nothing very much settled as to God's purpose in calling him out of Ur of the Chaldeans; God sees the entire course of redemptive history.

What God does in **Genesis 15** is promise Abraham that his offspring will constitute a vast number. At one level, God's promise is enough: "Abram believed the LORD, and he credited it to him as righteousness" (Gen. 15:6). Abram's faith is simple and profound: he believed God's promises, taking God at his word. And that faith, in God's eyes, was credited as righteousness. This does not mean that Abram earned brownie points for deploying such a righteous faith. Rather, the idea is that what God demands of his image-bearers, what he has always demanded, is righteousness—but in this sinful race what he accepts, crediting it as righteousness, is faith, faith that acknowledges our dependence upon God and takes God at his word. This faith of Abram is what makes him the "father" of those who believe (Rom. 4; Gal. 3).

Yet however genuine this faith, some of the details of God's promise Abram has trouble imagining. God tells him of a time when his descendants will possess all the land around him, and Abram wavers and asks for a sign (Gen. 15:8). Graciously, God provides one: in a vision, Abram is enabled to see God entering into a covenant with him. Probably the pieces of the animals between which "a smoking firepot with a blazing torch" (Gen. 15:17) passes represent a way of saying, "May those who enter into this covenant similarly be torn apart if they break the terms of this covenant." What is a visionary act of kindness to anchor Abram's faith is also an instance of God's long-range plans, his vast frame of reference: he is establishing his covenant with Abram and his offspring, a covenant relation into which Christians enter today (Gal. 3:6-9).

There is one more strand in this chapter that depicts God's long-term view of things. One reason why Abram cannot begin to take over the Promised Land immediately is that "the sin of the Amorites has not yet reached its full measure" (Gen. 15:16). God's sovereign timing so matches his moral sensibilities that by the time the children of Abraham are ready to take over the Promised Land, the inhabitants of that land will have so sunk in degradation that judgment must be meted out. That time, God says, is coming, but in this chapter it has not yet arrived.

∾

Genesis 16; Matthew 15; Nehemiah 5; Acts 15

IN ALL OF ANCIENT NEAR EASTERN LITERATURE, so far as I am aware, Hagar is the only woman whom Deity directly addresses by name (**Gen. 16:8; 21:17**). The woman in question is not one of the great matriarchs of the Old Testament—Sarah, perhaps, or Rachel, or Rebekah—but a slave who resents her mistress and flees. Yet God addresses her, tells her to submit to Sarai (16:9), promises that the child she is carrying in her womb will be a son, and later tells her that that son will be the progenitor of a great nation (21:18).

The account has many interwoven layers to think about. Placed after God's covenant with Abram in Genesis 15, this incident reflects well on neither Abram nor Sarai. Desperate for children, they think they have the right to bring God's purposes—and their own desires!—to pass by legal but shady means. The result is not only tension in their household for years to come—tension that spills over into the next generation (Gen. 21, 25), but the beginnings of the Arab peoples, who frequently find themselves locked in hostility with Israel to this day. One of the great features of the Bible is its sheer honesty: great men and women are portrayed with all their warts. This remains a broken world, and the very best are fallen. This should warn us against untamed hero-worship.

Yet there is another connection with the previous chapters. God had promised Abram that all peoples on earth would be blessed through him (12:3). The election of Abram is a means to that end. However focused on Abram's offspring his purposes will be, God remains the sovereign Lord of all. In the book of Genesis, the account of Abram is nestled into the broader account of the creation of all, and the Fall of all. And so here, at the very beginning of the history of the nation of Israel, God displays his concern for the despised and the outcast, people who are not organically connected with the promised line.

We may detect the same concern in the Lord Jesus. In **Matthew 15:21-28**, Jesus well knows that during the days of his flesh his mission is in the first instance directed to "the lost sheep of Israel" (15:24). There is a redemptive-historical primacy to the ancient covenant people of God. But this does not prevent him from acknowledging the remarkable faith of yet another woman, a Canaanite, who wisely changes her plea. She no longer addresses Christ as "Son of David" (15:22), on whom she can make no direct claim, and simply pleads for mercy (15:27). Another "Hagar" finds that mercy abundant, as countless people do today.

Genesis 17; Matthew 16; Nehemiah 6; Acts 16

∾

WE ARE NOT TO THINK that God disclosed himself to Abram every day: the decisive moments take place over considerable time. Putting the chronological hints together, Genesis 12 occurs when Abram is seventy-five; Genesis 15 is undated, but occurs during the following decade. Now he is ninety-nine, and Ishmael is already thirteen (**Gen. 17:1, 25**). God's opening words on this occasion must have been a great comfort, pulling together as they do some of the themes already introduced: "I am God Almighty; walk before me and be blameless. I will confirm my covenant between me and you and will greatly increase your numbers" (17:1-2).

In the following verses, there is initial emphasis on the covenant, on the promise of the land, and on the fact that Abram will be "the father of many nations" (17:4-5). The latter takes pride of place, but there are three new elements that carry the history of redemption forward.

First, both Abram and Sarai are given new names. If Abram means "exalted father," Abraham means "father of many," i.e., "the father of many nations," which implicitly announces that however important his role as head of the fledgling Hebrew nation, Abraham will be greater still in his foundational role as the one through whom all the peoples on the earth will be blessed (12:3). Sarah "will be the mother of nations" (17:16).

Second, God introduces circumcision as the initiatory sign of the covenant. Circumcision was practiced by several ancient Near Eastern peoples. Here, however, it has a distinctive role: a rite that is not unknown in Abraham's world is picked up by God and assigned distinctive significance in the history of the covenant God enters into with his people. Abraham loses no time in complying (17:23-27). This is a social "boundary marker" which across the course of history increasingly marks the Hebrews out as different; but it is more than that. It is so definitively established as the unique sign of the everlasting covenant that failure to comply means one is cut off from the people of God (17:13-14). Even before there is a great quantity of stipulation in the covenant, its framework, its boundary, and its symbolism are being established.

Third, Abraham's understandable but unhappy skepticism that he will bring forth a son of Sarah at this late stage in their marriage leads him to propose Ishmael as the one through whom God will fulfill his promises (17:17-18). But God will have none of it. Ishmael will sire great numbers, but the covenant line goes through Isaac (17:19-21). The history of the covenant people is thus decisively shaped by God's sovereign choice.

∾

Genesis 18; Matthew 17; Nehemiah 7; Acts 17

∿

ONE OF THE GREAT FAILURES into which even believers sometimes fall is the tendency to underestimate Jesus (**Matt. 17:1-8**).

Jesus takes the inner three of his twelve disciples—Peter, James, and John—to a high mountain, just the four of them. "There he was transfigured before them. His face shone like the sun, and his clothes became as white as the light" (17:2). Suddenly Moses and Elijah appeared, "talking with Jesus" (17:3). It is as if the ultimate identity of the eternal Son is allowed to peep through; the three disciples become "eyewitnesses of his majesty" (2 Peter 1:16). It is hard not to see here also a foretaste of the glory of the exalted Son (cf. Rev. 1:12-16), of the Jesus before whom every knee will bow, in heaven and on earth and under the earth, every tongue confessing "that Jesus Christ is Lord, to the glory of God the Father" (Phil. 2:10-11).

But Peter misunderstands. He rightly recognizes that it is an enormous privilege to be present on this occasion: "Lord," he says, "it is good for us to be here" (17:4). Then he puts his foot in his mouth: "If you wish, I will put up three shelters—one for you, one for Moses and one for Elijah." He entirely misunderstands the significance of the presence of Moses and Elijah. He thinks that Jesus is being elevated to their great stature, the stature of the mediator of the Sinai covenant and of the first of the great biblical prophets.

He is utterly mistaken. Their presence signified, rather, that the law and the prophets bore witness to him (cf. 5:17-18; 11:13). God himself sets the record straight. In a terrifying display, God thunders from an enveloping cloud, "This is my Son, whom I love; with him I am well pleased. Listen to him!" (17:5). By the time the three disciples recover from their prostrate terror, it is all over: "When they looked up, they saw no one except Jesus" (17:8)—a pregnant conclusion to the account.

Jesus brooks no rivals. There have been, there are, many religious leaders. In an age of postmodern sensibilities and a deep cultural commitment to philosophical pluralism, it is desperately easy to relativize Jesus in countless ways. But there is only one Person of whom it can be said that he made us, and then became one of us; that he is the Lord of glory, and a human being; that he died in ignominy and shame on the odious cross, yet is now seated on the right hand of the Majesty on high, having returned to the glory he shared with the Father before the world began.

∿

Genesis 19; Matthew 18; Nehemiah 8; Acts 18

IF A PERSON ISN'T CAREFUL, it is fairly easy to distort an analogy. The reason is obvious. When one thing is an analogy of another, inevitably there are points where the two things are parallel, and other points where they are quite different. If they were parallel at every point, then their relationship would not be analogical: the two would instead be identical. What makes an analogical relationship so fruitful and insightful lies precisely in the fact that the two things are *not* identical. But that is also what sometimes makes them a little tricky to understand.

This point is critical to the understanding of the analogy Jesus draws in **Matthew 18:1-6.** When his disciples begin to argue over who is the greatest in the kingdom of heaven, Jesus calls a little child and insists that unless they "change and become like little children" they will "never enter the kingdom of heaven" (18:3). Indeed, "whoever humbles himself like this child is the greatest in the kingdom of heaven" (18:4). To welcome a little child in Jesus' name is to welcome Jesus (18:5); to cause one of these little ones who believe in Jesus to sin is to commit so grievous an offense it would be better never to have been born (18:6).

It is important to notice what the analogy does *not* establish. There is no suggestion that children are innocent or sinless, no hint that their faith is intrinsically pure, no sentimental illusion that children have a better understanding of God than do adults. The primary point of the analogy is established by the context of the disciples' argument. While they fret over who is greatest in the kingdom, Jesus is at pains to draw attention to members of society whom no one would think great. Children are such dependent creatures. They are not strong, wise, or sophisticated. They are relatively transparent. Proud adults, then, must humble themselves so that they may approach God as do little children: simply, in unselfconscious dependence, without any hope of being the greatest in the kingdom.

Moreover, if such children trust Jesus—doubtless without much sophistication, but with a transparent simplicity—those who corrupt them and lead them astray are pathetically and profoundly evil.

Here, then, is an image of greatness in the kingdom that shatters our pretensions, abases our pride, shames our selfish aspirations. If we must not draw the wrong conclusions from this analogy, there are plenty of correct ones to think through and put into practice.

Those who aspire to ecclesiastical heights and great reputations need to reflect at length on these words: "Therefore, whoever humbles himself like this child is the greatest in the kingdom of heaven."

Genesis 20; Matthew 19; Nehemiah 9; Acts 19

∾

AFTER JESUS' INTERVIEW with the rich young man, he says to his disciples, "I tell you the truth, it is hard for a rich man to enter the kingdom of heaven. Again I tell you, it is easier for a camel to go through the eye of a needle than for a rich man to enter the kingdom of God" (**Matt. 19:23-24**). The disciples, we are told, "were greatly astonished." They exclaimed, "Who then can be saved?" (19:25).

Their question betrays a great deal. It is as if the disciples thought that if anyone could be saved, it would surely be the kind of moral, upright, and frankly wealthy young man who had just turned away from Jesus in some sadness. If even he could not be saved, then who in the world could be? Perhaps they thought that his wealth showed him to be blessed by God, while his publicly upright character confirmed their judgment.

Thus they betray how poorly they understood Jesus' pronouncement. His point was that wealth easily becomes a surrogate god. It is extraordinarily difficult for a person who is attached to riches, not least riches that he or she has accumulated and therefore feels proud about, to approach God as a child might approach (19:13-15), and simply ask for help and receive grace. The disciples look on these things precisely the wrong way. Possessions are blessings, they reason, and come from God. If a person enjoys possessions, those blessings must find their origin in God. So, surely a person with many blessings has a greater likelihood of being saved than others who can boast of fewer blessings.

Jesus does not argue the toss. If at this point he were to talk about the greater or lesser likelihood of someone being saved, he would be supporting the legitimacy of their question, which is in fact singularly ill conceived. That is simply not the way to look at the matter. Take the group that the disciples think are closest to the kingdom: Shall they be saved? "With man this is impossible," Jesus insists (19:26). And that means, of course, that from the disciple's perspective, if the most fortunate can't get in, then no one can get in. That's the point: "With man this is impossible."

Yet this impossibility can be reversed, for we serve a God who does many things that we humans cannot possibly do. Who shall be saved? "With God all things are possible" (19:26). That is where our hope lies: with a God who takes the most unlikely subjects, rich and poor alike, and writes his law on their hearts. Apart from God's intervening grace, there is no hope for any of us.

∾

Genesis 21; Matthew 20; Nehemiah 10; Acts 20

∿

IN THE NINETEENTH CENTURY, Lord Acton wrote that all power corrupts, and absolute power corrupts absolutely. The founding fathers of the American Republic would not have disagreed. That is one of the reasons why they constructed a government with checks and balances—they did not want any one branch to have too much power, because they knew that sooner or later it would be corrupted. That is also a primary reason why they wanted constitutionally mandated democratic voting. It was not because they trusted the wisdom of people as a collective—their writings show that they were very nervous about giving too much power to popular vote. But they wanted a mechanism for voting people out of office, replacing them with others. That way, no one in power could unceasingly accumulate power: sooner or later the people could turf them out, and without bloodshed.

Jesus understands the nature of power in all governmental hierarchy: "You know that the rulers of the Gentiles lord it over them, and their high officials exercise authority over them" (**Matt. 20:25**). Sad to say, ecclesiastical power can be equally corrupting. That is why Jesus sets out a radically different paradigm: "Not so with you. Instead, whoever wants to become great among you must be your servant, and whoever wants to be first must be your slave" (20:26-27).

It is of vital importance to the health of the church that we understand this passage aright. Three reflections may focus its meaning.

First, the ultimate model in this respect is the Lord Jesus himself, who "did not come to be served, but to serve, and to give his life as a ransom for many" (20:28). This is not only a great text about the substitutionary nature of the atonement Jesus achieved when he died on the cross (cf. 20:17-19), but powerful insistence that the life and death of Jesus are to constitute the measure of Christian leadership.

Second, becoming a slave of all most emphatically does not mean that leaders must become servile, stupid, ignorant, or merely nice—any more than Jesus' leadership and sacrifice were characterized by such incompetence.

Third, what it does mean is that Christian leadership is profoundly self-denying for the sake of others, like Christ's ultimate example of self-denial for the sake of others. So the church must not elevate people to places of leadership who have many of the gifts necessary to high office, but who lack this one. To lead or teach, for example, you must have the gift of leadership or teaching (Rom. 12:6-8). But you must also be profoundly committed to principled self-denial for the sake of brothers and sisters in Christ, or you are disqualified.

∿

Genesis 22; Matthew 21; Nehemiah 11; Acts 21

∾

THE DRAMATIC POWER of the testing of Abraham by the offering of Isaac (**Gen. 22**) is well known. The very terseness of the account calls forth our wonder. When he tells his servant that *we* (22:5—i.e., both Abraham and Isaac) will come back after worshiping on Mount Moriah, was Abraham speculating that God would raise his son back from the grave? Did he hope that God would intervene in some unforeseen way? What conceivable explanation could Abraham give his son when he bound him and laid him on the prepared altar?

A trifle earlier, Abraham's reply to Isaac's question about the lamb is a masterstroke: "God himself will provide the lamb for the burnt offering, my son" (22:8). There is no suggestion that Abraham foresaw the cross. Judging by the way he was prepared to go through with the sacrifice (22:10-11), it is not even clear that he expected that God would provide a literal animal. One might even guess that this was a pious answer for the boy until the dreadful truth could no longer be concealed. Yet in the framework of the story, Abraham spoke better than he knew: God did provide the lamb, a substitute for Isaac (22:13-14). In fact, like other biblical figures (e.g., Caiaphas in John 11:49-53), Abraham spoke *much* better than he knew: God would provide not only the animal that served as a substitute in this case, but the ultimate substitute, the Lamb of God, who alone could bear our sin and bring to pass all of God's wonderful purposes for redemption and judgment (Rev. 4—5; 21:22).

"The LORD will provide" (22:14): that much Abraham clearly understood. One can only imagine how much the same lesson was embedded in young Isaac's mind as well, and to his heirs beyond him. God himself connects this episode with the covenantal promise: Abraham's faith here issues in such stellar obedience that he does not elevate even his own cherished son to the place where he might dethrone God. God reiterates the covenant: "I will surely bless you and make your descendants as numerous as the stars in the sky and as the sand on the seashore. Your descendants will take possession of the cities of their enemies, and through your offspring all nations on earth will be blessed, because you have obeyed me" (22:17-18). On this point, God swears by himself (22:16), not because otherwise he might lie, but because there is no one greater by whom to swear, and the oath itself would be a great stabilizing anchor to Abraham's faith and to the faith of all who follow in his train (cf. Heb. 6:13-20).

∾

Genesis 23; Matthew 22; Nehemiah 12; Acts 22

෬

THE CLOSING VERSES OF Matthew 22 (**Matt. 22:41-46**) contain one of the most intriguing exchanges in the Gospels. After successfully fending off a series of tricky questions designed rather more to trap him or demean him than to elicit the wise answers he actually gives, Jesus poses a question of his own: "What do you think about the Christ [i.e., the Messiah]? Whose son is he?" (22:42). Some Jews thought there would be two Messiahs—one from David's line (the tribe of Judah) and one from the tribe of Levi. But not surprisingly, the Pharisees here give the right answer: "The son of David" (22:42). Now Jesus drops his bombshell: "How is it then that David, speaking by the Spirit, calls him 'Lord'? For he says, 'The Lord said to my Lord: "Sit at my right hand until I put your enemies under your feet"'" (22:43-44).

Jesus is citing Psalm 110, identified by the superscription as a psalm of David. If a mere courtier had written the psalm, then when he wrote "The LORD says to my Lord," he would have been understood to mean "The Lord [God] said to my Lord [the King]." In fact, that is the way many liberal scholars interpret the psalm—which means, of course, that they must ignore what the superscription says. But if *David* wrote the psalm, then the "my Lord" whom he addresses must be someone other than himself. The explanation offered by many students of the Bible, both Jewish and Christian, over the centuries, is correct: David, "speaking by the Spirit" (22:43), writing what is called an oracular psalm (i.e., an oracle, a prophecy immediately prompted by the Spirit), is referring to the Messiah who was to come: "The LORD [God] said to my Lord [the Messiah]." And what he said, in the rest of the psalm, establishes him as both universal king and perfect priest.

In days when family hierarchies meant that the son was always viewed as in some ways inferior to the father, Jesus drives home the point he is making: "If then David calls him [i.e., the Messiah] 'Lord,' how can he be his son?" (22:45).

The implications are staggering. The Messiah from the line of David would, on the one hand, doubtless be David's son, removed by a millennium from David but nevertheless in the throne succession. But on the other hand, he would be so great that even David must address him as "my Lord." Any other conception of the Messiah is too small, too reductionistic. The Old Testament texts pointed in the right direction generations earlier. But there will always be people who prefer the simplifications of reductionism to the profundities of the revelation in the whole Bible.

෬

Genesis 24; Matthew 23; Nehemiah 13; Acts 23

෨

THE LANGUAGE IN **Matthew 23** is frankly shocking. Jesus repeatedly pronounces his "woe" on the Pharisees and teachers of the law, labeling them "hypocrites," calling them "blind guides" and "blind fools," likening them to "whitewashed tombs that "look beautiful on the outside but on the inside are full of dead men's bones and everything unclean." They are "sons of hell," a "brood of vipers." What calls forth such intemperate language from the Lord Jesus?

There are three primary characteristics in these people that arouse Jesus' ire.

The *first* is the loss of perspective that, with respect to the revelation of God, focuses on the minors and sacrifices the majors. They are ever so punctilious about tithing, even putting aside a tenth of the herbs grown in the garden, while somehow remaining unconcerned about the massive issues of "justice, mercy and faithfulness" (23:23). Jesus carefully says that he is not dismissing the *relatively* minor matters: his interlocutors should not neglect them, for these prescriptions were, after all, mandated by God. But to focus on them to the exclusion of the weightier matters is akin to straining out a gnat and swallowing a camel. Similarly, carefully crafted rules about when it is important to tell the truth and when and how one can get away with a lie (23:16-22) not only overlook that truth-telling is of fundamental importance, but implicitly deny that this entire universe is God's, and all our promises and pledges are before him.

The *second* is love for the outward forms of religion with very little experience of a transformed nature. To be greeted as a religious teacher, to be honored by the community, to be thought holy and religious, while inwardly seething with greed, self-indulgence, bitterness, rivalry, and hate is profoundly evil (23:5-12, 25-32).

The *third* damning indictment is that because they have a major teaching role, these leaders spread their poison and contaminate others, whether by precept or example. Not only do they fail to enter the kingdom themselves, they effectively close it down to others (23:13-15).

How many evangelical leaders spend most of their energy on peripheral, incidental matters, and far too little on the massive issues of justice, mercy, and faithfulness—in our homes, our churches, the workplace, in all our relationships, in the nation? How many are more concerned to be thought wise and holy than to be wise and holy? How many therefore end up damning their hearers by their own bad example and by their drifting away from the Gospel and its entailments?

Our only hope is in this Jesus who, though he denounces this appalling guilt with such fierceness, weeps over the city (Matt. 23:37-39; Luke 19:41-44).

෨

Genesis 25; Matthew 24; Esther 1; Acts 24

∾

IN TUMULTUOUS TIMES, Christians have often been tempted to set dates as to when the Lord would return—almost always saying that he would return within a generation of the one making the prediction. In **Matthew 24:36-44**, however, Jesus insists that the time is hidden. We cannot know it, and we should not try to know it.

More precisely, the passage emphasizes two things.

First, not only is the hour of the end a secret preserved by the Father for himself alone, but when the judgment falls it will be unexpected, sudden, and irreversible. That is the point Jesus is making when he draws a comparison with the sudden onset of the deluge: "As it was in the days of Noah, so it will be at the coming of the Son of Man" (24:37). The point is not that the people at the end of the ages will be as wicked as people were in the days of Noah. That may or may not be true, but it is not what Jesus says. Jesus draws attention to the sheer normality of life in Noah's day before the Flood: "People were eating and drinking, marrying and giving in marriage, up to the day Noah entered the ark" (24:38). The Flood took them by surprise, and utterly destroyed them. "That is how it will be at the coming of the Son of Man" (24:39). Two men or two women will be laboring together in some joint task, and the judgment will snatch one away and leave the other (24:40-41). The end of the age will be sudden and unexpected.

Second, it follows ("Therefore," 24:42) that faithful servants will always be ready. Obviously a homeowner in a dicey neighborhood doesn't know when a thief will turn up. Rather, he takes such precautions that he is always prepared. The point is not that Jesus' return at the end of the age is sneaky—like the approach of the thief—brutal, or exploitative. The point, rather, is that although the timing of his return cannot be predicted, he will come, and his people should be as prepared for it as the homeowner in the insecure neighborhood is prepared for the arrival of the thief (whose timing is equally unpredictable). "So you also must be ready, because the Son of Man will come at an hour when you do not expect him" (24:44).

What would you like to be doing, saying, thinking, or planning when Jesus comes again? What would you *not* like to be doing, saying, thinking, or planning when Jesus comes again? Jesus tells you always to "keep watch, because you do not know on what day your Lord will come" (24:42).

∾

Genesis 26; Matthew 25; Esther 2; Acts 25

∾

THE PARABLE OF THE sheep and the goats (**Matt. 25:31-46**) focuses attention on the hungry, the thirsty, the naked, the sick, and those in prison. It speaks volumes to us in a culture where the poor, the wretched, and the unfortunate can easily be ignored or swept aside to the periphery of our vision. Here Jesus, the Son of Man and the King, declares, "I tell you the truth, whatever you did for one of the least of these brothers of mine, you did for me" (25:40; cf. v. 45). Doesn't this mean that somehow when we serve the wretched we serve Christ? Doesn't this then become a distinguishing mark—perhaps even *the* distinguishing mark—of true followers of Jesus Christ?

That, at least, is how this parable is usually interpreted. At one level I am loath to challenge it, because it is always important for those who know and follow the living God to show their life in God in the realms of compassion, service, and self-abnegation. Certainly elsewhere the Bible has a great deal to say about caring for the poor.

But it is rather unlikely that that is the focus of this parable. Another ancient stream of interpretation has much more plausibility. Two elements in the text clarify matters. *First,* Jesus insists that what was done by the "sheep," or not done by the "goats," was done "for one of the least of these brothers of mine" (25:40; cf. v. 45). There is overwhelming evidence that this expression does not refer to everyone who is suffering, but to Jesus' followers who are suffering. The emphasis is not on generic compassion (as important as that is elsewhere), but on who has shown compassion to the followers of Jesus who are hungry, thirsty, unclothed, sick, or in prison.

Second, both the sheep and the goats (25:37, 41, 44) are surprised when Jesus pronounces his verdict in terms of the way they have treated "the least of these brothers of mine." If what Jesus is referring to was compassion of a generic sort, it is hard to see how anyone would be all that surprised. The point is that it is *Jesus' identification* with these people who have (or have not) been helped that is critical—and that is a constant feature of biblical religion. For example, when Saul (Paul) persecutes Christians, he is persecuting *Jesus* (Acts 9:4). Real followers of Jesus will go out of their way to help other followers of Jesus, not least the weakest and most despised of them; others will have no special inclination along these lines. That is what separates sheep and goats (25:32-33).

So how do you treat other Christians, even the least of Jesus' brothers?

∾

Genesis 27; Matthew 26; Esther 3; Acts 26

∾

ALL FOUR OF THE PASSAGES contribute to the theme of the providence of God.

Genesis 27 is in many ways a pathetic, grubby account. Earlier Esau had despised his birthright (25:34); now Jacob swindles him out of it. In this Jacob is guided by his mother Rebekah, who thus shows favoritism among her children and disloyalty to her husband. Esau throws a tantrum and takes no responsibility for his actions at all. Indeed, he nurses his bitterness and plots the assassination of his brother. The family that constitutes the promised line is not doing very well.

Yet those who read the passage in the flow of the entire book remember that God himself had told Rebekah, before the twin brothers were born, that the older would serve the younger (25:23). Perhaps that is one of the reasons why she acted as she did: apparently she felt that God needed a little help in keeping his prediction, even immoral help. Yet behind these grubby and evil actions God is mysteriously working out his purposes to bring the promised line to the end he has determined. Certainly God could have arranged to have Jacob born first, if that was the man he wanted to carry on the line. Instead, Esau is born first, but Jacob is chosen, as if to say that the line is important, but God's sovereign, intervening choosing is more important than mere human seniority, than mere primogeniture.

In **Matthew 26**, the authorities hatch a nasty plot to corrupt justice and sort out a political problem; Judas, one of Jesus' intimates, sells his master; Jesus is in agony in Gethsemane; he is arrested and betrayed by a kiss; the Sanhedrin condemns and brutalizes its prisoner; Peter disowns Jesus. Yet who can doubt, in the flow of the book, that God remains in sovereign control to bring about the desired end? Jesus will give his life "as a ransom for many" (20:28), and all the failures, pain, and sin in this chapter issue in redemption.

The book of **Esther** does not even use the word *God,* but here too, even Haman's gross government-sanctioned genocide is heading toward God's salvation. And Paul (**Acts 26**) apparently would have been acquitted if he had not appealed to Caesar—yet that very appeal brings him in the end to declare the Gospel at the heart of the Empire.

Providence is mysterious. It must never be used to justify wrong actions or to mitigate sin: Isaac and his family are more than a little sleazy, Judas is a deceitful wretch, Haman is vile, and the Roman court trying Paul is more than a little corrupt. Yet God sovereignly rules, behind the scenes, bringing glory out of gore and honor out of shame.

∾

Genesis 28; Matthew 27; Esther 4; Acts 27

∾

THE NAME *BETHEL* MEANS "house of God." I wonder how many churches, houses, Bible colleges and seminaries, Christian shelters, and other institutions have chosen this name to grace their signs and their letterheads.

Yet the event that gave rise to the name (**Gen. 28**) was a mixed bag. There is Jacob, scurrying across the miles to the home of his uncle Laban. Ostensibly he is looking for a godly wife—but this reason nests more comfortably in Isaac's mind than in Jacob's. In reality he is running for his life, as the previous chapter makes clear: he wishes to escape being assassinated by his own brother in the wake of his own tawdry act of betrayal and deceit. Judging by the requests he makes to God, he is in danger of having too little food and inadequate clothing, and he is already missing his own family (28:20-21). Yet here God meets him in a dream so vivid that Jacob declares, "How awesome is this place! This is none other than the house of God; this is the gate of heaven" (28:17).

For his part, God reiterates the substance of the Abrahamic Covenant to this grandson of Abraham. The vision of the ladder opens up the prospect of access to God, of God's immediate contact with a man who up to this point seems more driven by expedience than principle. God promises that his descendants will multiply and be given this land. The ultimate expansion is also repeated: "All peoples on earth will be blessed through you and your offspring" (28:14). Even at the personal level, Jacob will not be abandoned, for God declares, "I am with you and will watch over you wherever you go, and I will bring you back to this land. I will not leave you until I have done what I have promised you" (28:15).

Awakened from his dream, Jacob erects an altar and calls the place Bethel. But in large measure he is still the same wheeler-dealer. He utters a vow: If God will do this and that and the other, if I get all that I want and hope for out of this deal, "then the LORD will be my God" (28:20-21).

And God does not strike him down! The story moves on: God does all that he promised, and more. All of Jacob's conditions are met. One of the great themes of Scripture is how God meets us where we are: in our insecurities, in our conditional obedience, in our mixture of faith and doubt, in our fusion of awe and self-interest, in our understanding and foolishness. God does not disclose himself only to the greatest and most stalwart, but to us, at *our* Bethel, the house of God.

∾

Genesis 29; Matthew 28; Esther 5; Acts 28

∾

THE CLOSING SENTENCE OF **Matthew 28** is striking: "And surely I am with you always, to the very end of the age" (28:20). Of course, this is a grand promise from the resurrected Christ to his people, on the verge of his ascension. But the context discloses that it is not some generalized assurance and nothing more. It is contextually linked to the Great Commission. What is the nature of this link? Or, to tease the question out, why is Jesus' promise to be with his disciples to the very end of the age tacked on to his assertion of his own authority, and of his command to make disciples of all people everywhere?

We should recognize that these words are not cast as a raw condition, bordering on a threat. Jesus does *not* say, in effect, "*If* you disciple all nations, I shall be with you always, to the very end of the age"; still less, "If you do *not* disciple all nations, I shall *not* be with you always, to the very end of the age." Yet some kind of link is presupposed. What is it?

The link is so general that I suspect we are meant to think that the presence of Jesus with us is the matrix in which we obey the Great Commission—that is, simultaneously the experience of those who obey the commission, and the framework out of which we obey it. We know and experience the presence of Jesus, in accordance with his promise, and we bear witness to this, even as we proclaim who he is and what he has done and what he commands. As objective as is the truth of the Gospel that we proclaim, we proclaim it not only because it is truth, but because we ourselves have experienced its saving and transforming power. We therefore not only herald its truth, we also bear personal witness to it, to Jesus himself. We are not merely dispassionate heralds to certain objective events, we are disciples committed to making other disciples.

It is not surprising that as we discharge this commission, the promised presence of Jesus is cherished all the more. Because we know him and his transforming presence in our own lives, we evangelize, baptize, instruct, disciple—and know him all the better, and experience all the more his transforming presence in our own lives. His promise to be with us to the end of the age is thus the matrix out of which we obey the Great Commission, simultaneously the ground and the goal, the basis and the reward. How could it be otherwise? We serve him because we love him and long to hear his blessed "Well done!" at the end of our course.

∾

Genesis 30; Mark 1; Esther 6; Romans 1

WHEN I WAS A CHILD IN SUNDAY SCHOOL, I learned the names of the twelve tribes of Israel by singing a simple chorus: "These are the names of Jacob's sons: / Gad and Asher and Simeon, / Reuben, Issachar, Levi, / Judah, Dan, and Naphtali— / Twelve in all, but never a twin— / Zebulun, Joseph, and Benjamin."

But many more years passed before I grasped how important are the twelve tribes in the Bible's storyline. Many of the dynamics of the rest of Genesis turn on their relationships. The organization of the nation of Israel depends on setting aside one tribe, the Levites, as priests. From another son, Judah, springs the Davidic dynasty that leads to the Messiah. Over the centuries, the tribe of Joseph would be divided into Ephraim and Manasseh; in substantial measure, Benjamin would merge with Judah. By the last book in the Bible, Revelation, the twelve tribes of the old covenant constitute the counterpoint to the twelve apostles of the new covenant: this twelve by twelve matrix (i.e., 144, in the symbolism of this apocalyptic literature) embraces in principle the whole people of God.

But what tawdry beginnings they have in **Genesis 30**. The deceit of Laban in Genesis 29, which resulted in Jacob's marrying both Leah and Rachel, now issues in one of the most unhealthy instances of sibling rivalry in holy Scripture. Each of these women from this family is so eager to outshine the other that she gives her handmaid to her husband rather than allow the other to get ahead in the race to bear children. So self-centered and impetuous are the relationships that another time Rachel is prepared to sell her husband's sex time to her sister Leah for a few mandrakes. Polygamy has taken hold, and with it a mess of distorted relationships.

From these painful and frankly dysfunctional family relationships spring eleven sons and one daughter (the birth of the last son, Benjamin, is reported in chap. 35). Here are the origins of the twelve tribes of Israel, the foundation of the Israelite nation. Their origins are not worse than those of others; they are merely typical. But already it is becoming clear that God does not deal with this family because they are consistently a cut above other families. No, he uses them to keep his covenantal promises to Abraham, Isaac, and Jacob. He graciously perseveres with them to bring about his grand, redemptive purposes. The tawdry family dynamics, the sort of thing that might generate a B-grade movie, cannot possibly prevent the universe's Sovereign from keeping his covenantal vows.

Genesis 31; Mark 2; Esther 7; Romans 2

∽

THE THREE MOST COMMON ACTS of piety amongst many Jews were prayer, fasting, and alms-giving (i.e., giving money to the poor). So when Jesus' disciples seemed a little indifferent to the second, it was bound to provoke interest. The Pharisees fasted; the disciples of John the Baptist fasted. But fasting was not *characteristic* of Jesus' disciples. Why not? (**Mark 2:18-22.**)

Jesus' response is stunning: "How can the guests of the bridegroom fast while he is with them? They cannot, so long as they have him with them. But the time will come when the bridegroom will be taken from them, and on that day they will fast" (2:19-20). Here is Jesus, profoundly self-aware, deeply conscious that he himself is the messianic bridegroom, *and that in his immediate presence the proper response is joy.* The kingdom was dawning; the king was already present; the day of promised blessings was breaking out. This was not a time for mourning, signaled by fasting.

Yet when Jesus went on to speak of the bridegroom being taken away from his disciples, and that this event would provoke mourning, it is very doubtful if anyone, at the time, grasped the significance of the utterance. After all, when the Messiah came, there would be righteousness and the triumph of God. Who could speak of the Messiah being taken away? The entire analogy of the bridegroom was becoming opaque.

But after Jesus' death and resurrection, after his exaltation to glory, and after the promise of his return at the end of the age, the pieces would fit together. The disciples would experience terrible sorrow during the three days of the tomb, before Jesus' glorious resurrection forever shattered their despair. And in an attenuated sense, Jesus' disciples would experience cycles of suffering that would call forth days of fasting as they faced the assaults of the Evil One while waiting for their Master's blessed return. But not now. Right now, sorrow and fasting were frankly incongruous. The promised Messiah, the heavenly Bridegroom, was among them.

The truth, Jesus says, is that with the dawning of the kingdom, the traditional structures of life and forms of piety would change. It would be inappropriate to graft the new onto the old, as if the old were the supporting structure—in precisely the same way that it is inappropriate to repair a large rent in an old garment by using new, unshrunk cloth, or use old and brittle wineskins to contain new wine still fermenting, whose gases will doubtless explode the old skin. The old does not support the new; it points to it, prepares for it, and then gives way to it. Thus Jesus prepares his disciples for the massive changes that were dawning.

∽

Genesis 32; Mark 3; Esther 8; Romans 3

WHAT A TRANSFORMATION IN JACOB (**Gen. 32**)! Superficially, of course, not much has changed. He left Beersheba for Paddan Aram because he was afraid for his life; his brother Esau had reason enough, according to his own light, to kill him. Now he is returning home, and Jacob is still frightened half to death of his brother. No less superficially, one might argue that much has changed; Jacob fled the tents of his parents a single man, taking almost nothing with him, while here he returns home a rich, married man with many children.

But the deepest differences between the two journeys are reflected in Jacob's changed attitude toward God. On the outbound trip, Jacob takes no initiative in matters divine. He simply goes to sleep (Gen. 28). It is God who intervenes with a remarkable vision of a ladder reaching up to heaven. When Jacob awakens, he acknowledges that what he experienced was some sort of visitation from God (28:16-17), but his response is to barter with God: if God will grant him security, safety, prosperity, and ultimately a happy return home, Jacob for his part will acknowledge God and offer him a tithe.

Now it is rather different. True, God again takes the initiative: Jacob meets angelic messengers (32:1-2). Jacob decides to act prudently. He sends some of his people ahead to announce to Esau that his brother is returning. This spawns devastating news: Esau is coming to meet him, but with four hundred men.

On the one hand, Jacob sets in motion a carefully orchestrated plan: successive waves of gifts for his brother are sent on ahead, with each of the messengers carefully instructed to speak to Esau with the utmost courtesy and respect. On the other hand, Jacob admits that matters are out of his control. Bartering is gone; in "great fear and distress" (32:7) Jacob takes action, and then prays, begging for help. He reminds God of his covenantal promises, he pleads his own unworthiness, he acknowledges how many undeserved blessings he has received, he confesses his own terror (32:9-12). And then, in the darkest hours, he wrestles with this strange manifestation of God himself (32:22-30).

Twenty years or so have passed since Jacob's outward-bound journey. Some people learn nothing in twenty years. Jacob has learned humility, tenacity, godly fear, reliance upon God's covenantal promises, and how to pray. None of this means he is so paralyzed by fear that he does nothing but retreat into prayer. Rather, it means he does what he can, while believing utterly that salvation is of the Lord.

By the time the sun rises, he may walk with a limp, but he is a stronger and better man.

Genesis 33; Mark 4; Esther 9—10; Romans 4

THE SO-CALLED PARABLE OF THE SOWER (**Mark 4:1-20**) might better be called the parable of the soils, for the variable that gives the parable life and depth is the variation in the land onto which the seed is thrown.

Because Jesus provides the interpretation of his own story, its primary emphases should not be in doubt. The seed is the "word," i.e., the word of God, which here is equivalent to the Gospel, the good news of the kingdom. Like a farmer scattering seed by hand in the ancient world, this word is scattered widely. Inevitably, some of the seed falls on ground that for one reason or another is inhospitable: perhaps it is the hard-packed dirt of the path, or perhaps birds come and eat the seed before it settles into the plowed ground and germinates, or perhaps it grows in the shadow of thornbushes that squeeze the life out of it, or perhaps it germinates in shallow soil with limestone bedrock just beneath the surface, such that the roots cannot go down very far to absorb the necessary moisture. The parallels with the way people hear the word are obvious. Some are hard and repel any entry of the word; others are soon distracted by the playthings Satan quickly casts up; others find that worries and wealth—the terrible Ws— squeeze out all concern for spiritual matters; still others hear the word with joy and seem to be the most promising of the crop, but never sink the deep roots necessary to sustain life. But thank God for the soil that produces fruit, sometimes even abundant fruit.

So much is clear enough. But two other features of this parable deserve reflection.

The *first* is that this parable, like many others, adjusts the commonly held perspective that when the Messiah came there would be a climactic and decisive break: the guilty and the dirty would all be condemned, and the righteous and the clean would enjoy a transforming rule. That is what the final kingdom would be like. But Jesus pictures the dawning of the kingdom a little differently. In the parable of the mustard seed (4:30-32), for example, the kingdom is like a tree that starts from small beginnings and grows into something substantial; here is growth, not apocalyptic climax. So also the parable of the sower: for the time being, the word is going to be scattered widely, and people will respond to it in different ways, with widely divergent yields.

The *second* is that not all of those who show initial signs of kingdom life actually take root and bear fruit. That truth deserves meditation and calls for self-examination.

Genesis 34; Mark 5; Job 1; Romans 5

∾

REVENGE MOVIES AND REVENGE BOOKS are so endemic to popular culture that we rarely think about the ambiguous, corrosive nature of sin. There are only good guys and bad guys. But in the real world, it is far from uncommon for sin to corrupt not only those who do evil but also those who respond to it with self-righteous indignation. The only persons not blamed in this horrible account of rape and pillage (**Gen. 34**) are the victims—Dinah herself, of course, and the Shechemites who, though unconnected with the guilt of Hamor's son or the corruption of Hamor, are either slaughtered or enslaved.

Certainly Shechem son of Hamor is guilty. In the light of his rape of Dinah, his efforts to pay the bridal price and to secure the agreement of the other males to be circumcised appear less like noble atonement than determined, willful selfishness, a kind of ongoing rape by other means. The reasoning of Hamor and his son, both in approaching Jacob's family and in approaching their own people, is motivated by self-interest and characterized by half-truths. They neither acknowledge wrongdoing nor speak candidly, and they try to sway their own people by stirring up greed.

The "grief and fury" of Dinah's brothers (34:7) may be understandable, but their subsequent actions are indefensible. With extraordinary duplicity, they use the central religious rite of their faith as a means to incapacitate the men of the village (the word *city* refers to a community of any size), then slaughter them and take their wives, children, and wealth as plunder. Does any of this honor Dinah? Does any of it please God?

Even Jacob's role is at best ambiguous. His initial silence (34:5) may have been nothing more than political expedience, but it sounds neither noble nor principled. His final conclusion (34:30) is doubtless an accurate assessment of the political dangers, but offers neither justice nor an alternative.

What does this chapter contribute to the book of Genesis, or, for that matter, to the canon?

Many things. For a start, the chapter reminds us of a recurrent pattern. Just because God has once again graciously intervened and helped his people in a crisis (as he does in Gen. 32—33) does not mean there is no longer any moral danger of drift toward corruption. Further, once again it is clear that the promised line is not chosen because of its intrinsic superiority; implicitly, this chapter argues for the primacy of grace. Apparently the crisis at Shechem is what brings the family back to Bethel (Gen. 35:1, 5), which brings closure to Jacob's movements and, more importantly, reminds the reader that "the house of God" is more important than all merely human habitation.

∾

Genesis 35—36; Mark 6; Job 2; Romans 6

∿

IN MARK'S ACCOUNT of the feeding of the five thousand and of Jesus' subsequent walk on the water (**Mark 6**), one finds a small aside that stirs up profitable reflection. As soon as Jesus climbed into the boat in the midst of the raging storm, the wind died down. The disciples, Mark comments, "were completely amazed, for they had not understood about the loaves; their hearts were hardened" (6:51-52).

The *first* observation is the most obvious: the astonishment of the disciples betrays the dismal fact that they have reflected very little on the spectacular miracle Jesus performed just a few hours earlier. On the face of it, the person who can so control nature as to be able to take a few scraps of food and feed thousands of people can doubtless handle nature well enough to subdue a storm. Yet lest we become too smug in our condemnation of the disciples, we ought to reflect on how easily we forget the Lord's gracious dealings in our own lives, and are frankly (and shamefacedly) surprised when he intervenes once again.

The *second* observation lies a little deeper. If Jesus truly is the promised Messiah, if he enjoys the powers he has already displayed, can any responsible disciple think that he is losing control? Can any responsible member of the Twelve imagine that this sort of Messiah could call disciples to himself, and then lose them all in a boating accident? This is not to suggest that accidents cannot happen to followers of Jesus today. Of course they can—this is a fallen world, and Jesus' followers are not exempt from all of the tragic and vicious entanglements of its fallenness. But even we must learn in difficult and frightening circumstances to trust God's wise providence. Here the disciples must surely learn something more—their own peculiar service as the inner core of disciples is so bound up with the ministry of Jesus that it is unthinkable that they could be "accidentally" killed.

And *third,* one cannot help but reflect on Mark's conclusion, "their hearts were hardened." This does not mean they were stupid. Nor does it mean that while their minds were all right, their affections were twisted, as if *heart* refers to the center of affections alone. In the symbolism of biblical anthropology, *heart* refers to the seat of human personality, not too far removed from what we mean by *mind* (although that is perhaps too restrictively cerebral). Their entire orientation was still too restricted, too focused on the immediacy of their fears, too limited by their inability to penetrate to the full mystery of who Jesus is and why he came.

This side of the cross and resurrection, we have still less excuse than they.

∿

Genesis 37; Mark 7; Job 3; Romans 7

∾

MANY PROTESTANTS ARE suspicious of "traditions." In popular polemic, Protestants have often portrayed Roman Catholics as embracing the Bible plus traditions, while we ourselves simply hold to the Bible. There are several matters that need clarification before we can hear aright what **Mark 7** says about traditions.

The *first* is a historical observation. There is very good evidence that until the Reformation the Roman Catholic Church had not yet formulated the clear-cut distinction that prevailed after the Reformation. Even when the Catholic Church was propounding fairly innovative doctrine, it tried hard to tie that doctrine to Scripture in some way, perhaps through a series of inferences. But confronted by the Reformation's *sola Scriptura* ("Scripture alone"), the Catholic Church argued for a view of revelation that insisted that truth was given as a deposit to the church itself, and part of this was the deposit found in holy Scripture and part lay in other traditions that the church guarded and passed on. In this kind of formulation, then, tradition is set over against Scripture as something additional to it.

That brings us to the *second* observation, one that touches on the text of the New Testament. Here, one can find the word *tradition* or *traditions* used in either a positive or a negative way. The word *tradition* simply refers to what is handed on. If what is handed on is apostolic teaching, then *traditions* are a very good thing (e.g., 1 Cor. 11:2); if what is handed on conflicts with what God says, then *traditions* are unhelpful and dangerous (as here in Mark 7).

This distinction between different kinds of *tradition* is not the same as one that we commonly draw today. We distinguish traditions that are intrinsically neutral but nevertheless helpful in building families or communities—family traditions, or interesting cultural or ecclesiastical traditions—and those that are repressive, restrictive, or stifling. In short, we make distinctions on the basis of the social effect of traditions, not on the basis of whether or not they are true. But in the New Testament, traditions are praised or criticized not on the basis of their social function but in the light of their conformity to or departure from the Word of God. Here in Mark 7:1-13, the traditions that Jesus condemns are those that allow people to sidestep what the Scripture clearly says.

In the *third* place, we must recognize that confessing evangelicals who nominally eschew tradition sometimes embrace traditions that effectively domesticate the Word of God. These may be traditional interpretations of Scripture, or traditional ecclesiastical practices, or traditional forms of conduct that are "allowed" in our circles but that are a long way from holy Scripture. In every case, fidelity to Christ mandates reformation by the Word of God.

∾

Genesis 38; Mark 8; Job 4; Romans 8

UNDER QUESTIONING, the disciples confess who Jesus is (**Mark 8:27-30**). *Christ* is the Greek form of *Messiah,* which has a Hebrew background. This confession triggers a flood of fresh revelation from the Lord Jesus (8:31-38). Now he teaches that the Son of Man "must suffer many things and be rejected by the elders, chief priests and teachers of the law, and that he must be killed and after three days rise again" (8:31). As Mark points out, Jesus "spoke plainly about this" (8:32). Apparently earlier comment on the subject was far more veiled.

Living as we do on this side of the cross, it is easy for us to be a bit condescending about Peter's reaction and rebuke of the Master (8:32). From Peter's perspective, Jesus simply had to be wrong on this subject. After all, messiahs don't get killed: they win. And how could a God-anointed, miracle-working Messiah like Jesus lose? Peter was wrong, of course, profoundly wrong. For even the disciples had not yet grasped that Jesus the Messiah was simultaneously conquering King *and Suffering Servant.*

But there was more to come. Not only did Jesus insist that he himself was going to suffer and die and rise again, but he also insisted that each of his followers "must deny himself and take up his cross and follow me" (8:34). To a first-century ear, such language was shocking. "To take up your cross" did not mean putting up with a toothache, job loss, or personal disability. Crucifixion was universally viewed as the most barbaric of Roman forms of execution, scarcely to be mentioned in polite company. The condemned criminal "picked up his cross," i.e., picked up the cross-member and carried it to the place of execution. If it was your lot to pick up your cross, there was no hope for you. There was only an ignominious and excruciating death.

Yet that is the language Jesus uses. For what all of his disciples must learn is that to be a follower of Jesus entails a painful renunciation of self-interest and a wholehearted turn to Jesus' interests. Yet Jesus' blunt language is not an invitation to spiritual masochism, but to life and bounty. For it is an infallible rule of the kingdom that self-focus issues in death, while "whoever loses his life for me and for the gospel will save it" (8:35). Only for a few will this commitment entail loss of physical life; for all of us it means death to self, discipleship to Jesus. And that includes a glad confession of Jesus, and principled refusal to be ashamed of Jesus and his words in this adulterous and sinful generation (8:38).

Genesis 39; Mark 9; Job 5; Romans 9

∿

IT IS ENTIRELY APPROPRIATE to read **Genesis 39** as a lesson in moral courage, a case study of a God-fearing man who rightly perceives that an attractive temptation is in reality an invitation to sin against God (39:9), and who therefore cares more for his purity than his prospects.

Nevertheless, Genesis 39 must also be read in several broader dimensions, each with important lessons.

First, this chapter begins and ends very much the same way. This literary "inclusion" signals that the themes in the opening and the closing control the entire chapter. At the beginning, Joseph is sold into the service of Potiphar. God is so very much with him that in due course he becomes the head slave of this substantial household. We must not think this took place overnight; the chronology suggests eight or ten years elapsed. During this time Joseph would have had to learn the language and work his way up from the bottom. But all of this was tied to the blessing of God on Joseph's life, and Joseph's consequent integrity. At the end of the chapter, Joseph has been thrown into prison on a false charge, but even here God is with him and grants him favor in the eyes of the warden, and in due course becomes a prisoner-trustee. Thus the chapter as a whole demonstrates that sometimes God chooses to bless us and make us people of integrity in the midst of abominable circumstances, rather than change our circumstances.

Second, Genesis 39 serves as a foil to Genesis 38. Judah is a free and prosperous man, but when he is bereaved of his wife he ends up sleeping with his daughter-in-law. He deploys a double standard and shames himself and his family. (The fact that initially he wants Tamar executed for a sin he himself has also committed shows that he is less interested in punishing the guilty as a matter of principle than in punishing those who are caught.) Joseph is a slave, yet under the blessing of God retains his sexual purity and his integrity. Which one is happier in the eyes of the world? Which one is happier in the light of eternity?

Third, Genesis 39 is part of the march toward Joseph's elevation to leadership in Egypt. By the wretched means described in Genesis 37, 39—40, Joseph eventually becomes "prime minister" of Egypt and saves many from starvation—including his own extended family, *and therefore the messianic line.* But Joseph could not know how all of that would work out as he was going through his misery. The most he knew were the stories passed down from Abraham, and his own youthful dreams (Gen. 37). But Joseph walks by faith and not by sight.

∿

Genesis 40; Mark 10; Job 6; Romans 10

∾

TRUSTING GOD'S PROVIDENCE is not to be confused with succumbing to fatalism. It is not a resigned sigh of *Que sera, sera*—"What will be, will be." This Joseph understood (**Gen. 40**).

The account of Pharaoh's cupbearer and baker does not tell us which of the two, if either, was actually guilty of something; it only tells us which of the two Pharaoh decided was guilty. Even then, we are not told the nature of the crime. The focus, rather, is on their respective dreams, and the fact that only Joseph, of those in prison, is able to interpret their dreams. The interpretations are so dramatic, and so precisely fulfilled, that their accuracy cannot be questioned.

Joseph himself is under no illusion as to the source of his powers. "Do not interpretations belong to God?" he asks (40:8). Even before Pharaoh, where he might have been expected to slant his explanations just a little so as to enhance his own reputation, Joseph will later insist even more emphatically that he cannot himself interpret dreams; God alone can do it (41:16, 25).

Yet despite this unswerving loyalty to God, despite this candid confession of his own limitations, despite the sheer tenacity and integrity of his conduct under unjust suffering, Joseph does not confuse God's providence with fatalism. The point is demonstrated in this chapter in two ways.

First, Joseph is quite prepared to tell his predicament to the cupbearer (the servant who will be released in three days and restored to the court) in the hope that he might be released (40:14-15). Joseph's faith in God does not mean that he becomes entirely passive. He takes open action to effect improvement in his circumstances, provided that action is stamped with integrity.

Second, when he briefly describes the circumstances that brought him into prison, Joseph does not hide the sheer evil that was done. He insists he "was forcibly carried off from the land of the Hebrews" (40:15). The point was important, for most slaves became such because of economic circumstances. For example, when people fell into bankruptcy, they sold themselves into slavery. But that was not what had happened to Joseph, and he wanted Pharaoh to know it. He was a victim. Further, even during his life as a slave in Egypt he did "nothing to deserve being put in a dungeon"—which of course means he was incarcerated unjustly. Thus Joseph does not confuse God's providential rule with God's moral approbation.

Fatalism and pantheism have no easy way of distinguishing what is from what ought to be. Robust biblical theism encourages us to trust the goodness of the sovereign, providential God, while confronting and opposing the evil that takes place in this fallen world.

Genesis 41; Mark 11; Job 7; Romans 11

∾

THE EXCHANGE BETWEEN Jesus and some of his opponents, reported in **Mark 11:27-33**, is one of the strangest in the four Gospels. Jesus ducks their crucial question by asking one of his own, one that they cannot answer for political reasons. Why doesn't Jesus respond in a straightforward manner? Doesn't this sound a little like brinkmanship, or, worse, a petty jockeying for power and one-upmanship?

At one level, the question of the chief priests, the teachers of the law, and the elders was entirely legitimate. By what authority does Jesus clear the temple courts, accept the accolades of countless thousands as he is ushered into Jerusalem on a donkey, and preach with robust confidence? His is not the authority of the rabbinic schools, nor of those who hold high ecclesiastical and political office. So what kind of authority is it?

How might Jesus have responded? If he said he was simply doing these things on his own, he would sound presumptuous and arrogant. He could not name an adequate *earthly* authority. If he insisted that everything he said and did were the words and deeds of God, they could have had him up on a blasphemy charge. It is not obvious what true answer he might have given them that would have simultaneously satisfied them and preserved his own safety.

So Jesus tells them, in effect, that he will answer their question if they will answer one of his: "John's baptism—was it from heaven, or from men? Tell me!" (11:30). His interlocutors weigh their possible answers on the basis of political expediency. If they say, "From heaven," they reflect, he will condemn them for not becoming disciples of John. Worse, they cannot fail to see that this is also a setup for the answer to *their* question. For after all, John the Baptist pointed to Jesus. If they acknowledge that John's ministry is anchored in heaven, and John pointed to Jesus, then Jesus *has* answered their question; his ministry, too, must have heaven's sanction behind it. But if they say, "From men," they will lose face with the people who cherished John. So they say nothing, and forfeit their right to hear an answer from Jesus (11:31).

A pair of pastoral implications flow from this exchange. The *first* is that some people cannot penetrate to Jesus' true identity and ministry, even when they ask questions that seem to be penetrating, because in reality their minds are made up, and all they are really looking for is ammunition to destroy him. The *second* is that sometimes a wise answer is an indirect one that avoids traps while exposing the two-faced perversity of the interlocutor. While Christians should normally be forthright, we should never be naive.

∾

Genesis 42; Mark 12; Job 8; Romans 12

∾

THE EXCHANGE BETWEEN Jesus and some of his opponents in **Mark 12:13-17** is full of interest. Mark says that Jesus' interlocutors set out "to catch him in his words" (12:13). Doubtless that is why they begin with some pretty condescending flattery about how principled a teacher he is, utterly unwilling to be swayed by popular opinion. It is all a setup. "Is it right to pay taxes to Caesar or not?" they ask. "Should we pay or shouldn't we?" (12:14-15).

They thought they had him. If he answered "No," then he would be in trouble with the Roman authorities, who certainly were not going to allow a popular religious preacher in a volatile country like this one go around advocating nonpayment of taxes. Jesus might even be executed for treason. But if he answered "Yes," then he would lose the confidence of the people and therefore diminish his popularity. Many ordinary Jews not only felt the ordinary human resentment of taxes, but raised theological objections. How could conscientious Jews pay in coins that had the image of the emperor on them, especially coins that ascribed titles of deity to him? Besides, if Jews were really righteous, would not God come down and deliver his people again, this time from the Roman superpower? Does not principled fidelity to God demand nonpayment of taxes?

Whatever answer Jesus gave, he would be a loser. But he refuses to yield. Instead, he asks for a coin, asks whose image is on it, and argues that it is right to give to Caesar what is Caesar's and to God what is God's. Jesus thereby neatly escapes their snare, and his interlocutors are amazed.

But there are layers of implications here. Under a strict theocracy, Jesus' words would be incoherent: the rule of God is mediated by the king, so that their domains are not so easily separable. Moreover, the old covenant structure was, on paper, tightly bound to theocratic rule. Yet here is Jesus announcing that a distinction must be made between Caesar's claims and the claims of the living God.

Of course, this does not mean that Caesar's domain is entirely independent of God's domain, nor that God does not remain in providential control. But it is hard to avoid the conclusion that Jesus is announcing a fundamental change in the administration of the covenant community. The locus of the community is no longer a theocratic kingdom; it is now an assembly of churches from around the world, living under many "kings" and "Caesars," and offering worship to none of them. And that is why many Christians around the world trace the history of the non-establishment of a particular religion to this utterance of the Lord Jesus himself.

∾

Genesis 43; Mark 13; Job 9; Romans 13

∾

CHRISTIANS HAVE OFTEN DISAGREED over the precise interpretation of **Mark 13**. But whatever disagreements prevail, we cannot fail to note the stunning contrast between the perspectives of the disciples when they look around the temple complex and the perspectives of Jesus himself.

The disciples are impressed by the "massive stones" and by the "magnificent buildings" (13:1). What draws their attention is the architecture, the product of human creativity and ingenuity. But Jesus thinks on another plane. He evaluates the patterns of evil in this world, the false religious pretensions, the persecution of his disciples, the judgment that will fall. As for the stones and the buildings, he foresees judgment: "Not one stone here will be left on another; every one will be thrown down" (13:2). A mere forty years elapse before this prediction is literally fulfilled.

This passage is reminiscent of another. In Acts 17:16ff., Paul finds himself in Athens. What is striking is his reaction to the city. Luke does not say that Paul was impressed by the spectacular architecture, by the history of sheer learning, by the literature that its citizens had produced, or by the glory of her heritage. Far from it. Paul looked around this venerable old city and was "greatly distressed to see that the city was full of idols" (17:16).

In neither case, then—neither in Jesus' estimate of Jerusalem, nor in Paul's estimate of Athens—was the analysis superficial. In both cases, the evaluation looked at things from God's perspective. Those who are impressed by mighty buildings and spectacular human accomplishments could profitably think through the account of the tower of Babel (Gen. 11). Doubtless there were some then who were impressed by the edifice. But God, looking at the human heart and the reasons for the building, saw it as one more evidence of insufferable hubris.

In much the same way, we too are called to understand and evaluate our culture from God's perspective. Because human beings are made in the image of God, there is much that we can do that is worthy and admirable. Theologically speaking, this is the product of "common grace." But it is possible to be far too impressed by wealth, power, architecture, fame, learning, physical prowess, and technology, with the result that we do not think through the moral and spiritual dimensions of the world around us. We may see the glory, and overlook the shame; we may detect human accomplishments, and neglect the undergirding idolatry; in short, we may be impressed by all that impresses God's fallen image-bearers, but fail to assess these realities in the light of the cross and in the light of eternity. We would do far better to follow the examples of Jesus and Paul.

∾

Genesis 44; Mark 14; Job 10; Romans 14

∿

UP TO THIS POINT IN THE NARRATIVE (**Gen. 44**), Judah has not appeared in a very good light. When Joseph's brothers first declare their intention to kill him (Gen. 37:19-20), two of them offer alternatives. Reuben suggests that Joseph should simply be thrown into a pit from which he could not escape (37:21-22). This proposal had two advantages. First, murder could not then be *directly* ascribed to the brothers, and second, Reuben hoped to come back later, in secret, and rescue his kid brother. Reuben was devastated when his plan did not work out (37:29-30). The other brother with an independent proposal was Judah. He argued that there was no profit in mere murder. It would be better to sell Joseph into slavery (37:25-27)—and his view prevailed.

Judah reappears in the next chapter, sleeping with his daughter-in-law (Gen. 38), and, initially at least, deploying a double standard (see meditation for February 6).

Yet here in Genesis 44, Judah cuts a more heroic figure. Joseph manipulates things to have Benjamin and his brothers arrested for theft, and insists that only Benjamin will have to remain in Egypt as a slave. Perhaps Joseph's ploy was designed to test his older brothers to see if they still resented the youngest, if they were still so hard that they could throw one of their number into slavery and chuckle that at least they themselves were free. It is Judah who intervenes, and pleads, of all things, the special love his father has for Benjamin. He even refers to Jacob's belief that Joseph was killed by wild animals (44:28), as if the sheer deceit and wickedness of it all had been preying on his mind for the previous quarter of a century. Judah explains how he himself promised to bring the boy back safely, and emotionally pleads, "Now then, please let your servant remain here as my lord's slave in the place of the boy, and let the boy return with his brothers. How can I go back to my father if the boy is not with me? No! Do not let me see the misery that would come upon my father" (44:33-34).

This is the high point in what we know of Judah's pilgrimage. He offers his life in substitution for another. Perhaps in part he was motivated by a guilty conscience; if so, the genuine heroism grew out of genuine shame. He could not know that in less than two millennia, his most illustrious descendant, in no way prompted by shame but only by obedience to his heavenly Father and by love for guilty rebels, would offer himself as a substitute for them (**Mark 14**).

∿

Genesis 45; Mark 15; Job 11; Romans 15

∽

IN MARK 15 PEOPLE SPEAK better than they know.

"What shall I do, then," Pilate asks, "with the one you call the king of the Jews?" (15:12). Of course, he utters the expression "king of the Jews" with a certain sneering contempt. When the crowd replies, "Crucify him!" (15:13, 14), the politically motivated think this is the end of another messianic pretender. They do not know that this king *has* to die, that his reign turns on his death, that he is simultaneously King and Suffering Servant.

The soldiers twist together a crown of thorns and jam it on his head. They hit him and spit on him, and then fall on their knees in mock homage, crying, "Hail, king of the Jews!" (15:18). In fact, he is more than the King of the Jews (though certainly not less). One day, each of those soldiers, and everyone else, will bow down before the resurrected man they mocked and crucified, and confess that he is Lord (Phil. 2:9-11).

Those who passed by could not resist hurling insults: "So! You who are going to destroy the temple and build it in three days, come down from the cross and save yourself!" (15:29-30). The dismissive mockery hid the truth they could not see: earlier Jesus had indeed taught that he himself was the real temple, the antitype of the building in Jerusalem, the ultimate meeting-place between God and human beings (John 2:19-22). Indeed, Jesus not only insisted that he is himself the temple, but that this is so by virtue of the fact that this temple must be destroyed and brought back to life in three days. If he had "come down from the cross" and saved himself, as his mockers put it, he could not have become the destroyed and rebuilt "temple" that reconciles men and women to God.

"He saved others but he can't save himself" (15:31). Wrong again—and right again. This is the man who *voluntarily* goes to the cross (14:36; cf. John 10:18). To say "he can't save himself" is ridiculously limiting. Yet he couldn't save himself *and* save others. He saves others by *not* saving himself.

"Let this Christ, this King of Israel, come down now from the cross, that we may see and believe" (15:32). But what kind of Christ would they then have believed in? A powerful king, doubtless—but not the Redeemer, not the Sacrifice, not the Suffering Servant. They could not long have believed in him, for the basis of this transformation in them was the very cross-work they were taunting him to abandon.

"Surely this man was the Son of God" (15:39). Yes; more than they knew.

∽

Genesis 46; Mark 16; Job 12; Romans 16

ONE OF THE MOST DIFFICULT THINGS to grasp is that the God of the Bible is both personal—interacting with other persons—and transcendent (i.e., above space and time—the domain in which all our *personal* interactions with God take place). As the transcendent Sovereign, he rules over everything without exception; as the personal Creator, he interacts in personal ways with those who bear his image, disclosing himself to be not only personal but flawlessly good. How to put those elements together is finally beyond us, however frequently they are simply assumed in Scripture.

When Jacob hears that Joseph is alive, he offers sacrifices to God, who graciously discloses himself to Jacob once again: "I am God, the God of your father. Do not be afraid to go down to Egypt, for I will make you into a great nation there. I will go down to Egypt with you, and I will surely bring you back again. And Joseph's own hand will close your eyes" (**Gen. 46:3-4**).

The book of Genesis makes it clear that Jacob knew that God's covenant with Abraham included the promise that the land where they were now settled would one day be given to him and to his descendants. That is why Jacob needed this direct disclosure from God to induce him to leave the land. Jacob was reassured on three fronts: (a) God would make his descendants multiply into a "great nation" during their sojourn in Egypt; (b) God would eventually bring them out of Egypt; (c) at the personal level, Jacob is comforted to learn that his long-lost son Joseph will attend his father's death.

All of this provides personal comfort. It also discloses something of the mysteries of God's providential sovereignty, for readers of the Pentateuch know that this sojourn in Egypt will issue in slavery, that God will then be said to "hear" the cries of his people, that in the course of time he will raise up Moses, who will be God's agent in the ten plagues, the crossing of the Red Sea, the granting of the Sinai covenant and the giving of the law, the wilderness wanderings, and the (re)entry into the Promised Land. The sovereign God who brings Joseph down to Egypt to prepare the way for this small community of seventy persons has a lot of complex plans in store. These are designed to bring his people to the next stage of redemptive history, and finally to teach them that God's words are more important than food (Deut. 8).

One can no more detach God's sovereign transcendence from his personhood, or vice versa, than one can safely detach one wing from an airplane and still expect it to fly.

Genesis 47; Luke 1:1-38; Job 13; 1 Corinthians 1

∾

HOW DID THE CANONICAL Gospels come down to us?

At one level, it is enough to be assured that God provided them. But normally God operates through identifiable means. At no point do the canonical Gospels give the impression that they were handed down from heaven on golden plates, or transcribed by apostles attentive to divine dictation.

Luke provides the most detail as to how he went about his task (**Luke 1:1-4**). He tells us that "many" had already "undertaken to draw up an account" of Jesus' life and ministry, in line with what was "handed down to us by those who from the first were eyewitnesses and servants of the word" (1:1-2). From this we can infer two things: (a) Luke does not himself claim to be an eyewitness of Jesus. He does claim to be in touch with what the original "eyewitnesses and servants of the word" handed down. (b) By the time he writes, Luke knows that already there are many written reports circulating. This is not surprising. The Jews were a literate race. Every boy learned to read and write. It is inconceivable that no one committed anything to paper in the first years after Jesus' death, resurrection, and exaltation.

Then Luke tells us he himself "carefully investigated everything from the beginning." The words suggest that he read the sources, talked with all the principals he could find, and evaluated the reports. We can glimpse at least a little of his method when we read his second volume, the book of Acts. There, by following his movements, we discover that he can be placed in all the early major Christian centers, where he would have the opportunity to talk to all of the earliest Christian leaders, and to read all of the earliest reports and archives. It is not too much of a leap, then, to infer that if Luke the doctor (see Col. 4:14) has some extra information about Mary's unique pregnancy (Luke 1:26ff.), it is because he looked her up and had some long chats. In due course, then, he chose to write "an orderly account" (1:3).

Two things follow. First, however much the Spirit of God superintended the production of this gospel, such divine superintendence did not obviate the need for strenuous research and careful work. Second, this method of bringing a canonical book into being is entirely in line with its subject matter: God himself brought the messianic Son of David, the Son of God, into *this* world (1:35), the eternal invading the temporal, forever assuring that one could talk of him as a witness speaks of what is observed. The transmission of Christian truth necessarily rests, in part, not on mysticism, but on witness.

∾

Genesis 48; Luke 1:39-80; Job 14; 1 Corinthians 2

∾

SOMETIMES BAD THEOLOGY BREEDS reactionary bad theology. Because Roman Catholicism has gradually added more titles and myths to Mary, Protestants have sometimes reacted by remaining silent about her astonishing character. Neither approach fares very well when tested by this passage (**Luke 1:39-80**) and a few others we shall have occasion to think about.

Catholics have added titles such as "Mother of God" and "Queen of Heaven" to Mary, neither of which is found in the Bible. The view that Mary was immaculately conceived (and was therefore born sinless), and that she, like Enoch, was transported to heaven bodily, thereby escaping death, are equally unsupported. The latter became a dogma for Roman Catholics as recently as 1950. According to news reports, the current Pope is weighing whether he should establish, as something that *must* be confessed, another title conservative Catholics apply to Mary, viz. "Co-Redemptrix."

But Luke's witness points in another direction. In Mary's song (1:46-55), traditionally called the *Magnificat* (from the Latin word for *magnifies*: "My soul *magnifies* [NIV—*glorifies*] the Lord"), Jesus' mother says that her spirit rejoices in "God my Savior"—which certainly sounds as if she thought of herself as needing a Savior, which would be odd for one immaculately conceived. Indeed, a rapid scan of the Gospels discloses that during Jesus' ministry, Mary had no special access to her famous son, sometimes failed to understand the nature of his mission (e.g., 2:48-50), and never helped someone obtain some favor from Jesus that he or she could not otherwise obtain. Indeed, the unanimous testimony of Scripture is that people should come to Jesus: "Come to *me*, all you who are weary and burdened, and *I* will give you rest" (Matt. 11:28), Jesus says—not, "Come to my mother." He alone is the true mediator between God and human beings.

Nevertheless, Mary is wholly admirable, a model of many virtues (as is also, e.g., Joseph in Gen. 37—50). She accepts her astonishing role with submissiveness and equanimity, considering what it must have initially done to her reputation (1:34-38). Elizabeth twice calls her "blessed" (1:42, 45), i.e., approved by God; the supernatural recognition of the superiority of Mary's Son over Elizabeth's son (1:41-45) was doubtless one of the things that Mary pondered in her heart (2:19). But none of this goes to Mary's head: she herself recognizes that her "blessedness" is not based on intrinsic superiority, but on God's (the "Mighty One's") mindfulness of her "humble state" and his choice to do "great things" for her (1:48-49). Her focus in the *Magnificat*, as ours must be, is on the faithfulness of God in bringing about the deliverance so long promised (1:50-55).

∾

Genesis 49; Luke 2; Job 15; 1 Corinthians 3

∾

JESUS GREW UP A THOROUGHLY Jewish boy. Not only was his lineage Jewish, it was Davidic: legally, he belonged to the suppressed royal house (**Luke 2:4**). Imperial politics were divinely manipulated to ensure that Jesus would be born in the ancient town of David (2:1-4, 11). On the eighth day of his life, he was circumcised (2:21). At the appropriate time, Mary and Joseph offered a sacrifice in keeping with the Law's prescription of what was required of every firstborn male (2:22-24). "Joseph and Mary," we are told, did "everything required by the Law of the Lord" (2:39). In the first days of Jesus' life, Simeon prophetically addressed God in prayer, declaring that the coming of Jesus was "for glory to your people Israel" (2:32); aged Anna "gave thanks to God and spoke about the child to all who were looking forward to the redemption of Jerusalem" (2:38). Every year, Joseph and Mary traveled the long miles from Nazareth to Jerusalem to participate in the Feast of Passover, "according to the custom" (2:41-42), joining tens of thousands of other pilgrims; and of course, Jesus went along, witnessed the slaughter of thousands of Passover lambs, heard the temple choirs, and recited the ancient Scriptures. At the age of twelve, Jesus' constant exposure to the heritage of his people and the content of their Scriptures led to the extraordinary exchanges he enjoyed with the temple teachers (2:41-52).

We cannot begin to grasp the categories in which Jesus spoke and acted, the categories in which his life and ministry, his death and resurrection, have significance, unless we find them in the ancient Hebrew Bible.

Yet that is not all there is to say. That same Bible does not *begin* with Abraham and the origins of the Israelites. It begins with God, the origin of the universe, the creation of human beings bearing God's image, the wretched rebellion of the Fall, the first cycles of judgment and forgiveness, the first promises of redemption to come. Certainly Paul understood that the Bible's long story of the Jews must be set *within* the still longer story of the human race, and that even the first calling of the man who is the ancestor of all Jews specifies that through him all the nations of the earth will be blessed (Gal. 3; cf. Gen. 12). Here at the beginning of Jesus' life, the same framework peeps through. Simeon praises the Sovereign Lord for allowing him to live to see this baby: "For my eyes have seen your salvation, which you have prepared in the sight of *all people,* a light for revelation *to the Gentiles* and for glory to your people Israel" (2:31-32).

∾

Genesis 50; Luke 3; Job 16—17; 1 Corinthians 4

∾

THE LAST CHAPTER OF GENESIS includes a section that is both pathetic and glorious (**Gen. 50:15-21**).

Everything that is sad and flawed in this family resurfaces when Jacob dies. Joseph's brothers fear that their illustrious sibling may have suppressed vengeful resentment only until the death of the old man. Why did they think like this? Was it because they were still lashed with guilt feelings? Were they merely projecting onto Joseph what they would have done had they been in his place?

Their strategy involves them in fresh sin: they lie about what their father said, in the hope that an appeal from Jacob would at least tug at Joseph's heartstrings. In this light, their abject submission ("We are your slaves," 50:18) sounds less like loyal homage than desperate manipulation.

By contrast, Joseph weeps (50:17). He cannot help but see that these groveling lies betray how little he is loved or trusted, even after seventeen years (47:28) of nominal reconciliation. His verbal response displays not only pastoral gentleness—"he reassured them and spoke kindly to them," promising to provide for them and their families (50:21)—it also reflects a man who has thought deeply about the mysteries of providence, about God's sovereignty and human responsibility. "Don't be afraid," he tells them. "Am I in the place of God? You intended to harm me, but God intended it for good to accomplish what is now being done, the saving of many lives" (50:19-20).

The profundity of this reasoning comes into focus as we reflect on what Joseph does *not* say. He does not say that during a momentary lapse on God's part, Joseph's brothers sold him into slavery, but that God, being a superb chess player, turned the game around and in due course made Joseph prime minister of Egypt. Still less does he say that God's intention had been to send Joseph down to Egypt in a well-appointed chariot, but unfortunately Joseph's brothers rather mucked up the divine plan, forcing God to respond with clever countermoves to bring about his own good purposes. Rather, *in the one event*—the selling of Joseph into slavery—there were two parties, and two quite different intentions. On the one hand, Joseph's brothers acted, and their intentions were evil; on the other, God acted, and his intentions were good. Both acted to bring about this event, but while the evil in it must be traced back to the brothers and no farther, the good in it must be traced to God.

This is a common stance in Scripture. It generates many complex, philosophical discussions. But the basic notion is simple. God is sovereign, and invariably good; we are morally responsible, and frequently evil.

∾

Exodus 1; Luke 4; Job 18; 1 Corinthians 5

❧

"THEN A NEW KING, who did not know about Joseph, came to power in Egypt" (**Ex. 1:8**). Those who learn nothing from history are destined to repeat all its mistakes, we are told; or, alternatively, the only thing that history teaches is that nothing is learned from history. Whimsical aphorisms aside, one cannot long read Scripture without pondering the sad role played by *forgetting*.

Examples abound. One might have expected, after the Flood, that so sweeping a judgment would frighten postdiluvial human beings into avoiding the wrath of God, but that is not what happens. God leads Israel out of bondage, deploying spectacular plagues and the crossing of the Red Sea, but mere weeks elapse before the Israelites are prepared to ascribe their rescue to a god represented by a golden calf. The book of Judges describes the wretched pattern of sin, judgment, rescue, righteousness, followed by sin, judgment, rescue, righteousness—the wearisome cycle spiraling downward. One might have thought that under the Davidic dynasty, kings in the royal line would remember the lessons their fathers learned, and be careful to seek the blessing of God by faithful obedience; but that is scarcely what occurred. After the catastrophic destruction of the northern kingdom and the removal of its leaders and artisans to exile under the Assyrians, why did not the southern kingdom take note and preserve covenantal fidelity? In fact, a bare century-and-a-half later the Babylonians subject them to a similar fate. Appalling forgetfulness is not hard to find in some of the New Testament churches as well.

So the forgetfulness of Egypt's rulers, aided by a change of dynasty, is scarcely surprising. A few hundred years is a long time. How many Christians in the West have really absorbed the lessons of the evangelical awakening, let alone of the magisterial Reformation?

Not far from where I am writing these lines is a church that draws five or six thousand on a Sunday morning. Its leaders have forgotten that it began as a church plant a mere two decades ago. They now want to withdraw from the denomination that founded them, not because they disagree theologically with that denomination, not because of some moral flaw in it, but simply because they are so impressed by their own bigness and importance that they are too arrogant to be grateful. One thinks of seminaries that have abandoned their doctrinal roots within one generation, of individuals, not the least scholars, who are so impressed by novelty that clever originality ranks more highly with them than godly fidelity. Nations, churches, and individuals change, at each step thinking themselves more "advanced" than all who went before.

To our shame, we forget all the things we should remember.

❧

Exodus 2; Luke 5; Job 19; 1 Corinthians 6

∾

IN THE MOST CRUCIAL EVENTS IN REDEMPTIVE HISTORY, God takes considerable pains to ensure that no one can properly conclude that these events have been brought about by human resolve or wit. They have been brought about by God himself—on his timing, according to his plan, by his means, for his glory—yet in interaction with his people. All of this falls out of **Exodus 2:11-25.**

The account is brief. It does not tell us how Moses' mother managed to instill in him a profound sense of identity with his own people before he was brought up in the royal household. Perhaps he enjoyed ongoing contact with his birth mother; perhaps as a young man he delved into his past, and thoroughly investigated the status and subjugation of his own people. We are introduced to Moses when he has already so identified with the enslaved Israelites that he is prepared to murder a brutal Egyptian slave overlord. When he discovers that the murder he committed has become public knowledge, he must flee for his life.

Yet one cannot help reflecting on the place of this episode in the plotline that leads to Moses' leadership of the Exodus some decades later. By God's own judicial action, many Egyptians would then die. So why doesn't God use Moses now, while he is still a young man, full of zeal and eagerness to serve and emancipate his people?

It simply isn't God's way. God wants Moses to learn meekness and humility, to rely on God's powerful and spectacular intervention, to await God's timing. He acts in such a way that no one will be able to say that the real hero is Moses, the great visionary. By the time he is eighty, Moses does not want to serve in this way; he is no longer an idealistic, fiery visionary. He is an old man whom God almost cajoles (Ex. 3) and even threatens (Ex. 4:14) into obedience. There is therefore no hero but God, and no glory for anyone other than God.

The chapter ends by recording that "the Israelites groaned in their slavery and cried out, and their cry for help because of their slavery went up to God. God heard their groaning and he remembered his covenant with Abraham" (2:23-24). This does not mean that God had forgotten his covenant. We have already seen that God explicitly told Jacob to descend into Egypt and foretold that God would one day bring out the covenantal plan. The same God who sovereignly arranges these matters and solemnly predicts what he will do, chooses to bring about the fulfillment of these promises by personally interacting with his covenantal people in their distress, responding to their cry.

∾

Exodus 3; Luke 6; Job 20; 1 Corinthians 7

∽

TWO ELEMENTS IN **Exodus 3** demand attention.

The *first* is the dramatic introduction of "the angel of the LORD" (3:2). Initially, at least, Moses does not perceive an "angel." The text reads, "There the angel of the LORD appeared to him in flames of fire from within a bush"—but this cannot mean that an angelic being appeared within the flames, differentiable from the flames, for what draws Moses' attention is the bush itself which, though apparently burning, was never consumed. The manifestation of "the angel of the LORD," then, was apparently in the miraculous flames themselves. Strikingly, when the voice speaks to Moses out of the burning bush, it is not the voice of the angel but the voice of God: "*God* called to him from within the bush, 'Moses! Moses!'" (3:4). The ensuing discussion is between God and Moses; there is no further mention of "the angel of the LORD."

On the face of it, then, this "angel of the LORD" is some manifestation of God himself. We shall have occasion to think through other Old Testament passages where the angel of the Lord appears—sometimes in human form, sometimes not even explicitly called an "angel" (recall the "man" who wrestles with Jacob in Gen. 32), always hauntingly "other," and always identified in some way with God himself.

We might well ask if, when the text before us records that "God said," it really means no more than that God spoke through this angelic messenger: after all, if the messenger speaks the words of God, then in a sense it is God himself who is speaking. But the biblical manifestations of "the angel of the LORD" do not easily fit into so neat and simplistic an explanation. It is almost as if the biblical writers want to stipulate that God himself appeared, while distancing this transcendent God from any mere appearance. The angel of the Lord remains an enigmatic figure who is identified with God, yet separable from him—an early announcement, as it were, of the eternal Word who became flesh, simultaneously God's own fellow and God's own self (John 1:1, 14).

The *second* element is even more important, though I can assign it only the briefest comment here. The name of God (3:13-14) may be rendered "I AM WHO I AM," as it is in the NIV, or "I will be what I will be." In Hebrew, the abbreviated form "I am" is related in some fashion to YHWH, often spelled out as *Yahweh* (and commonly rendered "LORD," in capital letters; the same Hebrew letters stand behind English *Jehovah*). The least that this name suggests is that God is self-existent, eternal, completely independent, and utterly sovereign: God is what he is, dependent on no one and nothing.

∽

Exodus 4; Luke 7; Job 21; 1 Corinthians 8

∽

IN EXODUS 4 two elements introduce complex developments that stretch forward to the rest of the Bible.

The *first* is the reason God gives as to why Pharaoh will not be impressed by the miracles that Moses performs. God declares, "I will harden his heart so that he will not let the people go" (4:21). During the succeeding chapters, the form of expression varies: not only "I will harden Pharaoh's heart" (7:3), but also "Pharaoh's heart became hard" or "was hard" (7:13, 22; 8:19, etc.) and "he hardened his heart" (8:15, 32, etc.). No simple pattern is discernible in these references. On the one hand, we cannot say that the pattern works up from "Pharaoh hardened his heart" to "Pharaoh's heart was hardened" to "God hardened Pharaoh's heart" (as if God's hardening were nothing more than the divine judicial confirmation of a pattern the man had chosen for himself); on the other hand, we cannot say that the pattern simply works down from "God hardened Pharaoh's heart" to "Pharaoh's heart was hardened" to "Pharaoh hardened his heart" (as if Pharaoh's self-imposed hardening was nothing more than the inevitable outworking of the divine decree).

Three observations may shed some light on these texts. (a) Granted the Bible's storyline so far, the assumption is that Pharaoh is already a wicked person. In particular, he has enslaved the covenant people of God. God has not hardened a morally neutral man; he has pronounced judgment on a wicked man. Hell itself is a place where repentance is no longer possible. God's hardening has the effect of imposing that sentence a little earlier than usual. (b) In all human actions, God is never completely passive: this is a *theistic* universe, such that "God hardens Pharaoh's heart" and "Pharaoh hardened his own heart," far from being disjunctive statements, are mutually complementary. (c) This is not the only passage where this sort of thing is said. See, for instance, 1 Kings 22; Ezekiel 14:9; and above all 2 Thessalonians 2:11-12: "For this reason God sends them a powerful delusion so that they will believe the lie and so that all will be condemned who have not believed the truth but have delighted in wickedness."

The *second* forward-looking element is the "son" terminology: "Israel is my firstborn son, and I told you, 'Let my son go, so he may worship me.' But you refused to let him go; so I will kill your firstborn son" (Ex. 4:22-23). This first reference to Israel as the son of God develops into a pulsating typology that embraces the Davidic king as the son *par excellence*, and results in Jesus, the ultimate Son of God, the true Israel and the messianic King.

∽

Exodus 5; Luke 8; Job 22; 1 Corinthians 9

∾

ACCORDING TO **Luke 8:19-21**, "Jesus' mother and brothers came to see him" but were unable to achieve their objective owing to the press of the crowd. Word was passed up to Jesus: "Your mother and brothers are standing outside, wanting to see you"—apparently under the assumption that Jesus himself would make his way to them, or use his authority to ensure that a passage was opened up for them. After all, this was a culture much less individualistic than our own, much more oriented to the family and the extended family.

That is what makes Jesus' answer astonishing: "My mother and brothers are those who hear God's word and put it into practice" (8:21). Four things must be said.

First, this is not an isolated passage. Once Jesus begins his public ministry, on no occasion, until the cross, does he betray any slight preference for his own family members, including his mother. In every instance, he either quietly distances himself from them (as here and 11:27-28), or else gently rebukes them (e.g., John 2:1-11). There is no exception. Those who argue that Mary has an inside track into the affections and blessings that only Jesus can bestow cannot responsibly adduce evidence from these texts.

Second, the reasons for Jesus' conduct are not hard to find. Quite apart from this passage, the Gospels keep drawing attention to Jesus' uniqueness. In the context of Luke, the familial connection is overshadowed by Jesus' virginal conception, which is tied to Jesus' mission and to who he is. Judging by the book of Acts, even Jesus' natural family had to come to terms, after the resurrection, with who this son and brother of theirs really was, and they became part of the Christian community that worshiped him.

Third, not for a moment does this suggest Jesus was callous toward the feelings of his family. One of the most touching moments in the gospel of John pictures Jesus on the cross, almost with his dying breath providing the care and stability needed to his distraught mother (John 19:26-27).

Fourth, the force of the passage before us must not be missed: Jesus insists that those closest to him, those he "owns" as his, those who have ready access to him, those who are part of his real family, are henceforth not his natural relatives, but "those who hear God's word and put it into practice" (8:21). Unlike many rulers, Jesus showed no interest in a natural dynasty. Nor was his ultimate focus on his tribe, clan, or nuclear family. He came to call into permanent being the family of God—and they are characterized by the obedient hearing of God's word.

∾

Exodus 6; Luke 9; Job 23; 1 Corinthians 10

∿

ONE OF THE TASKS IMPOSED ON those who wish to read the canonical Gospels sensitively is to see how the various units are linked. Casual readers remember individual stories about Jesus from their Sunday school days, but do not always reflect on the links that weld these stories into a complete Gospel. Moreover, the individual evangelists did not arrange their material exactly the same way as the others, so the special flavor of each gospel is often lost unless the distinctive links are thoughtfully pondered.

An instructive example is found in **Luke 9:49-50.** The preceding verses (9:46-48) find Jesus' disciples arguing as to which of them would be greatest (in the consummated kingdom, presumably). Knowing their thoughts, Jesus teaches them an embarrassing lesson, employing a little child to make his point. Important people honey up to even more important people. Those who follow Jesus welcome the least powerful members of society—the little children. What Jesus demands is an outlook fundamentally at variance with that of the world: "For he who is least among you all—he is the greatest" (9:48).

It is at this juncture that 9:49-50 comes into play. John comments that he and the others saw a man driving out demons in Jesus' name, "and we tried to stop him, because he is not one of us." Jesus forbids them this course of action, "for whoever is not against you is for you." At first glance this is a somewhat different topic from that of the preceding verses. Then again, maybe not: the connections call for reflection. John's complaints no longer sound like godly concern for orthodoxy, but like power-hungry moaning more concerned that those who preach and heal belong to the right party than that the mission itself be advanced. So this is pathetically tied to the debate over who would be the greatest. Personal aggrandizement will inevitably prove an unstable base for making wise assessments of the ministry of others.

The following verses (9:51-56) find Jesus in Samaria. When the Samaritans prove inhospitable, Jesus' disciples are quite prepared to call fire down upon them. Jesus rebukes them. Since these verses follow the themes already elucidated, the attitude the disciples here betray is clarified. Their passion for judgment against the Samaritans is motivated less by a genuine grasp of and devotion to Christ Jesus, than by a power-hungry self-focus.

The closing verses of the chapter highlight the same contrast (9:57-62). The three who protest the loudest about how eagerly they will follow Jesus are firmly put in their place: they have not counted the cost of discipleship, and so their pious protestations take on the ugly hue of self-love.

∿

Exodus 7; Luke 10; Job 24; 1 Corinthians 11

༁

THE STORY IS TOLD of Dr. Martyn Lloyd-Jones, one of the most influential preachers of the twentieth century. When he was dying of cancer, one of his friends and former associates asked him, in effect, "How are you managing to bear up? You have been accustomed to preaching several times a week. You have begun important Christian enterprises; your influence has extended through tapes and books to Christians on five continents. And now you have been put on the shelf. You are reduced to sitting quietly, sometimes managing a little editing. I am not so much asking therefore how you are coping with the disease itself. Rather, how are you coping with the stress of being out of the swim of things?"

Lloyd-Jones responded in the words of **Luke 10**: "[D]o not rejoice that the spirits submit to you, but rejoice that your names are written in heaven" (10:20—though of course Lloyd-Jones would have cited the King James Version).

The quotation was remarkably apposite. The disciples have just returned from a trainee mission, and marvel that "even the demons submit to us in your name" (10:17). At one level, Jesus encourages them. He assures them that (in some visionary experience?) he has seen Satan fall like lightning from heaven (10:18). Apparently Jesus understands this trainee mission by his disciples as a sign, a way-stage, of Satan's overthrow, accomplished in principle at the cross (cf. Rev. 12:9-12). He tells his disciples that they will witness yet more astonishing things than these (Luke 10:18-19). "However," he adds (and then come the words quoted by Lloyd-Jones), "do not rejoice that the spirits submit to you, but rejoice that your names are written in heaven" (10:20).

It is so easy to rejoice in success. Our self-identity may become entangled with the fruitfulness of our ministry. Of course, that is dangerous when the success turns sour—but that is not the problem here. Things could not be going better for Jesus' disciples. And then the danger, of course, is that it is not God who is being worshiped. Our own wonderful acceptance by God himself no longer moves us, but only our apparent success.

This has been the sin of more than a few "successful" pastors, and of no fewer "successful" lay people. While proud of their orthodoxy and while entrusted with a valid mission, they have surreptitiously turned to idolizing something different: success. Few false gods are so deceitful. When faced with such temptations, it is desperately important to rejoice for the *best* reasons—and there is none better than that our sins are forgiven, and that by God's own gracious initiative our names have been written in heaven.

༁

Exodus 8; Luke 11; Job 25—26; 1 Corinthians 12

ONE OF THE MOST STRIKING PICTURES of what might be called a "partial conversion" is found in **Luke 11:24-26.** Jesus teaches that when an evil spirit comes out of someone, it "goes through arid places seeking rest and does not find it"—apparently looking for some new person in whom to take up residence. Then the spirit contemplates returning to its previous abode. A reconnoiter finds the former residence surprisingly vacant. The spirit rounds up seven cronies who are even more vile, "and they go in and live there. And the final condition of that man is worse than the first."

Apparently the man who has been exorcised of the evil spirit never replaced that spirit with anything else. The Holy Spirit did not take up residence in his life; the man simply remained vacant, as it were.

There are three lessons to learn.

First, "partial conversions" are all too common. A person gets partially cleaned up. He or she is drawn close enough to the Gospel and to the people of God that there is some sort of turning away from godlessness, a preliminary infatuation with holiness, an attraction toward righteousness. But like the person represented by rocky soil in the parable of the sower and the soils (8:4-15), this person may initially seem to be the best of the crop, and yet not endure. There has never been the kind of conversion that spells the takeover of an individual by the living God, a reorientation tied to genuine repentance and enduring faith.

The *second* lesson follows: a little Gospel is a dangerous thing. It gets people to think well of themselves, to sigh with relief that the worst evils have been dissipated, to enjoy a nice sense of belonging. But if a person is not truly justified, regenerated, and transferred from the kingdom of darkness and into the kingdom of God's dear Son, the dollop of religion may serve as little more than an inoculation against the real thing.

The *third* lesson is inferential. This passage is thematically tied to another large strand of Scripture. Evil cannot simply be opposed—that is, it is never enough simply to fight evil, to cast out a demon. Evil must be replaced by good, the evil spirit by the Holy Spirit. We must "overcome evil with good" (Rom. 12:21). For instance, it is difficult to overcome bitterness against someone by simply resolving to stop being bitter; one must replace bitterness by genuine forgiveness and love for that person. It is difficult to overcome greed by simply resolving not to be quite so materialistic; one must fasten one's affections on better treasure (cf. Luke 12:13-21) and learn to be wonderfully and self-sacrificially generous. Overcome evil with good.

Exodus 9; Luke 12; Job 27; 1 Corinthians 13

∾

YOU'VE SEEN THE BUMPER STICKER: "The person with the most toys wins." Wins what? The person with the most toys takes out of this life exactly what everyone else does. A billion years or so into eternity, how many toys we accumulated during our seventy years in this life will not seem too terribly important.

Yet in a materialistic culture, it is horrifying to begin to recognize just how endemic greed is, how it seeps into all kinds of priorities and relationships. In **Luke 12:13-21**, Jesus is confronted by someone who begs him, "Teacher, tell my brother to divide the inheritance with me." We do not know whether this individual had a just complaint or not. From Jesus' perspective, it did not matter, for a more fundamental issue was at stake. For this individual, a share of the inheritance was more important than a godly relationship with his brother. Not only does Jesus insist he did not come to be an arbiter of such minor matters (12:14), he warns, "Watch out! Be on your guard against all kinds of greed; a man's life does not consist in the abundance of his possessions" (12:15). Perhaps the person with the most toys does not win after all.

This precipitates the parable of the rich farmer whose rising stores of grain prompt him to build bigger and bigger barns (12:16-20). In our culture, we might easily substitute *builder* or *software producer* or *real estate agent* for *farmer*. In a culture that fixates on present possessions, it is distressingly easy for believers to get sucked into the same vortex of greed. What starts as an entirely proper commitment to do one's best for Christ's sake degenerates into a selfish competitiveness and a bottomless acquisitiveness. You busily plan your retirement; after all, you tell yourself, you have "plenty of good things laid up for many years" (12:19). Because everyone is telling you how well you are doing, you do not hear the voice of God: "You fool! This very night your life will be demanded from you. Then who will get what you have prepared for yourself?" (12:20).

The problem is not wealth itself. The Bible bears witness to some rich people who used their wealth for God, people who were not so attached to their wealth that it became a surrogate god. Yet one hesitates to point out this fact, for most of us are so good at deceiving ourselves we inevitably think this concession lets us off the hook. Others are greedy or miserly; I am hard working and frugal. Others are materialistic and hedonistic; I am realistic and believe that a merry heart does good like medicine. So meditate on Luke 12:21.

∾

Exodus 10; Luke 13; Job 28; 1 Corinthians 14

PILATE WAS A WEAK, wicked man. Thus the account in **Luke 13:1-5** is entirely credible. The details may be obscure, but the general picture is clear enough. Some Galileans had offered sacrifices: if they were Jews, they must have done so at the temple in Jerusalem. Perhaps they were involved, or were perceived to be involved, in some wing of the nationalistic Zealot movement, and Pilate saw them as a threat. He had them slaughtered, and their blood mingled with the blood of the sacrificial animals they themselves had brought. If the mingling of blood is literal, this means that Pilate had them slaughtered in the temple courts—sacrilege mingling with slaughter.

When this incident is brought up to Jesus for his comment, he launches out in a direction that must have astonished his interlocutors. Perhaps some expected him to denounce Pilate; perhaps others wanted him to comment on the Zealot movement; a few may have hoped he would offer a few waggish denunciations about these rebels getting what they deserved. Jesus opts for none of those paths. "Do you think that these Galileans were worse sinners than all the other Galileans because they suffered this way? I tell you, no! But unless you repent, you too will all perish" (13:2-3).

The point he was making might well been lost in the political sensitivities of this tragedy, so Jesus promptly refers to another disaster, this one stripped of Galileans, Pilate, the temple, sacrifices, and mingled blood. Eighteen people died when a tower collapsed. Jesus insists that they were no more wicked than anyone else in Jerusalem. Rather, the same lesson is to be learned: "unless you repent, you too will all perish" (13:5).

Jesus' surprising analysis makes sense only if three things are true: (a) All of us deserve to perish. If we are spared, that is an act of grace. What *should* surprise us is that so many of us are spared so long. (b) Death comes to all of us. Our world often argues that the worst disaster is for someone to die young. Not so. The real disaster is that we all stand under this sentence of death, and we all die. The age at which we die is only *relatively* better or worse. (c) Death has the last word for all of us—unless we repent, which alone leads us beyond death to the life of the consummated kingdom.

Have you heard of the millions massacred under Pol Pot? Have you heard of the savage butchery in southern Sudan? Have you seen the massed graves in Bosnia? Or the pictures of the Florida swamp where Valujet Flight 592 crashed? I tell you the truth: unless you repent, you too will all perish.

Exodus 11:1—12:20; Luke 14; Job 29; 1 Corinthians 15

∿

THE CRUSHING PLAGUES have followed their ordained sequence. Repeatedly, Pharaoh hardened his heart; yet, however culpable this man was, God sovereignly moved behind the scenes, actually warning Pharaoh, implicitly inviting repentance. For instance, through Moses God had already said to Pharaoh, "I have raised you up for this very purpose, that I might show you my power and that my name might be proclaimed in all the earth. You still set yourself against my people and will not let them go" (9:16-17). Yet now Pharaoh's patience entirely collapses. He warns Moses that he is not to appear in the court again: "The day you see my face you will die" (10:28).

So the stage is set for the last plague, the greatest and worst of all. After the previous nine disasters, one would think that Moses' description of what would happen (**Ex. 11**) would prompt Pharaoh to hesitate. But he refuses to listen (11:9); and all this occurs, God says, "so that my wonders may be multiplied in Egypt" (11:9).

In Exodus 11—12 there is yet another almost incidental description of God's sovereign provision. Exodus 11 tells us, almost parenthetically, that "the LORD made the Egyptians favorably disposed toward the people" (11:3). This is followed in Exodus 12 by the description of the Egyptians urging the Israelites to leave the country (12:33). One can understand the rationale: how many more plagues like this last one could they endure? At the same time, the Israelites ask for clothing and silver and gold. "The LORD had made the Egyptians favorably disposed toward the people, and they gave them what they asked for; so they plundered the Egyptians" (12:36).

Psychologically, it is easy enough, after the event, to explain all this. In addition to the fear the Israelites now incited among the Egyptians, perhaps guilt was also operating: who knows? "We *owe* them something." Psychologically, of course, one could have concocted a quite different scenario: in a fit of rage, the Egyptians massacre the people whose leader and whose God have brought such devastating slaughter among them.

In reality, however, the ultimate reason why things turn out this way is because of the powerful hand of God: the Lord himself made the Egyptians favorably disposed toward the people.

This is the element that is often overlooked by sociologists and others who treat all of culture like a closed system. They forget that God may intervene, and turn the hearts and minds of the people. Massive revival that transforms the value systems of the West is now virtually inconceivable to those enamored with closed systems. But if God graciously intervenes and makes the people "favorably disposed" to the preaching of the Gospel. . . .

Exodus 12:21-51; Luke 15; Job 30; 1 Corinthians 16

THE PASSOVER WAS not only the climax of the ten plagues, it was the beginning of the nation. Doubtless Pharaoh had had enough of Moses; God had had enough of Pharaoh. This last plague wiped out the firstborn of the land, the symbol of strength, the nation's pride and hope. At the same time, by his design it afforded God an opportunity to teach some important lessons, in graphic form, to the Israelites. If the angel of death was to pass through the land, what principle would distinguish the homes that suffered death from those where everyone survived?

God tells the Israelites to gather in houses, each house bringing together enough people to eat one entire year-old lamb. Careful instructions are provided for the preparation of the meal. The strangest of these instructions is that a daub of blood is to be splashed on the top and both sides of the doorframe; "and when I see the blood, I will pass over you" (**Ex. 12:13**). The point is repeated: "When the LORD goes through the land to strike down the Egyptians, he will see the blood on the top and sides of the doorframe and will pass over that doorway, and he will not permit the destroyer to enter your houses and strike you down" (12:23). Because of the blood, the Lord would "pass over" them; thus the Passover was born.

The importance of this event cannot be overestimated. It signaled not only the release of the Israelites from slavery, but the dawning of a new covenant with their Redeemer. At the same time, it constituted a picture: guilty people face death, and the only way to escape that sentence is if a lamb dies instead of those who are sentenced to die. The calendar changes to mark the importance of this turning point (12:2-3), and the Israelites are told to commemorate this feast in perpetuity, not the least as a way of instructing children yet unborn as to what God did for this fledgling nation, and how their own firstborn sons were spared on the night that God redeemed them (12:24-27).

A millennium and a half later, Paul would remind believers in Corinth that Christ Jesus, our Passover Lamb, was sacrificed for us, inaugurating a new covenant (1 Cor. 5:7; 11:25). On the night that he was betrayed, Jesus took bread and wine, and instituted a new commemorative rite—and this too took place on the festival of Passover, as if this new rite connects the old with that to which it points: the death of Christ. The calendar changed again; a new and climactic redemption had been achieved. God still passes over those who are secured by the blood.

Exodus 13; Luke 16; Job 31; 2 Corinthians 1

∾

ON FIRST READING, the parable of the shrewd manager and its unexpected conclusion is one of the strangest stories that Jesus tells (**Luke 16:1-9**).

An inefficient and wasteful manager is called in by the wealthy owner and told he is to be sacked. He must close out the books and pick up his pink slip. Terribly concerned about his future, the manager wonders what he should do. He does not possess the robust physique that would equip him for manual labor, and he really does not want to go on the dole.

So he comes up with a totally unscrupulous plan. While he still enjoys legitimate authority over the owner's goods and accounts, he starts cutting deals with his master's debtors. It is a huge operation, and the sums are enormous. For debtor after debtor, he slashes the amount of their indebtedness, in some cases as much as fifty percent. His reasoning is very simple. In a culture where a gift creates an obligation, he recognizes that all these people will feel obligated to accommodate him when he finds himself without a job and income. With sums like these, he will be able to rely on their hospitality for a very long time. Doubtless the master did not like having his accounts diddled, but he was savvy enough to recognize the shrewdness his manager had shown.

Then comes the startling application: "For the people of this world are more shrewd in dealing with their own kind than are the people of the light. I tell you, use worldly wealth to gain friends for yourselves, so that when it is gone, you will be welcomed into eternal dwellings" (16:8-9). What does this mean?

It cannot mean that Jesus advocates unscrupulous business practices. The point is that the manager used resources under his control (though not properly his) to prepare for his own future. Do the "people of the light" use resources under their control to prepare for *their own* future? What is that future? The shrewd manager wanted to be welcomed into the homes of these debtors; the people of the light are to be "welcomed into eternal dwellings" (16:9). So should we not be investing heavily in heaven, laying up treasures there? If that includes spending money on the right things, so be it: when it is all gone, we still have an eternal dwelling ahead of us. The idea is not that we can buy heaven, but that it is unimaginably irresponsible not to plan for our home, when even the people of this world know enough to prepare for their future homes. Understandably, the next verses (16:10-15) strip away the glamour of possessions in favor of what God highly values.

∾

Exodus 14; Luke 17; Job 32; 2 Corinthians 2

◌

THREE OBSERVATIONS ON the crossing of the Red Sea (**Ex. 14**):

First, the dynamic confrontation between Pharaoh and the sovereign Lord continues. On the one hand, Pharaoh follows his desires, concluding that the Israelites are hemmed in by sea and desert, and therefore easy prey (14:3). Moreover, Pharaoh and his officials now regret they let the people go. Slavery was one of the fundamental strengths of their economic system, certainly the most important resource in their building programs. Perhaps the plagues were horrible flukes, nothing more. The Israelite slaves must be returned.

Yet God is not a passive player as these events unfold, nor simply someone who responds to the initiative of others. He leads the fleeing Israelites away from the route to the northeast, not only so that they may escape confrontation with the Philistines (13:17), but also so that the Egyptians will conclude that the Israelites are trapped (14:3). In fact, God is leading the Egyptians into a trap, and his hardening of the heart of Pharaoh is part of that strategy (14:4, 8, 17). This sweeping, providential sovereignty is what ought to ground the trust of the people of God (14:31). Above all, the Lord is determined that in this confrontation, both the Israelites and the Egyptians will learn who God is. "I will gain glory through Pharaoh and all his army. . . . The Egyptians will know that I am the LORD when I gain glory through Pharaoh, his chariots and his horsemen" (14:17-18). "And when the Israelites saw the great power the LORD displayed against the Egyptians, the people feared the LORD and put their trust in him and in Moses his servant" (14:31).

Second, the "angel of God" reappears (14:19)—not as an angel, but as a pillar of fire by night and a pillar of cloud by day, alternately leading the people and separating them from the pursuing Egyptians. But looked at another way, one may say that "the LORD went ahead of them in a pillar of cloud to guide them on their way and by night in a pillar of fire to give them light" (13:21). The ambiguities we saw earlier (Ex. 3; see meditation for February 20) continue.

Third, whatever means (such as the wind) were ancillary to the parting of the Red Sea, the event, like the plagues, is presented as miraclulous—not the normal providential ordering of everything (which regularity makes science possible), but the intervention of God over against the way he normally does things (which makes miracles unique, and therefore not susceptible to scientific analysis). For people to walk on dry land between walls of water (14:21-22) is something the sovereign God of creation may arrange, but no other.

Exodus 15; Luke 18; Job 33; 2 Corinthians 3

∾

EACH OF THE FIRST FOUR UNITS OF **Luke 18** can easily be misunderstood; each makes abundant sense when read in conjunction with the others.

The *first* (18:1-8) is a parable that Jesus tells his disciples "to show them that they should always pray and not give up" (18:1). An unjust judge is badgered by a persistent widow so that in the end he provides her with the justice she asks for. "And will not God bring about justice for his chosen ones, who cry out to him day and night? Will he keep putting them off?" (18:7). If even this judge eventually puts things right, how much more will God, when his "chosen ones" cry to him? By itself, of course, this parable could be taken to mean that the longer and louder one prays, the more blessings one gets—a kind of tit-for-tat arrangement that Jesus himself elsewhere disavows (Matt. 6:5-15). But the last verse (18:8) focuses the point: "However, when the Son of Man comes, will he find faith on the earth?" The real problem is not with God's unwillingness to answer, but with our faithless and lethargic refusal to ask.

The *second* (18:9-14) parable describes a Pharisee and a tax collector who go up to the temple to pray. Some modern relativists conclude from this story that Jesus accepts everyone, regardless of his or her continuing sins, habits, or lifestyle. He rejects only self-confident religious hypocrites. Certainly Jesus rejects the latter. But the parable does not suggest that the tax collector wished to continue in his sin; rather, he begs for mercy, knowing what he is; he approaches God out of a freely recognized need.

In the *third* unit (18:15-17) Jesus insists that little children be brought to him, "for the kingdom of God belongs to such as these." One must "receive the kingdom of God like a child," or not at all. Yet this does not commend childlike behavior in all respects (e.g., naïveté, short-term thinking, moral immaturity, the cranky "No!" of the "terrible twos"). But little children do have an openness, a refreshing freedom from self-promotion, a simplicity that asks and trusts.

The *fourth* unit (18:18-30) finds Jesus telling a rich ruler to sell all that he has and give to the poor, if he is to have treasure in heaven, and then follow Christ. Does this mean that only penurious asceticism will enjoy the blessings of heaven? Is it not Christ's way of stripping off this particular person's real god, the pathetic ground of his self-confidence, so that he may trust Jesus and follow him wholly?

Can you see what holds these four units together?

∾

Exodus 16; Luke 19; Job 34; 2 Corinthians 4

∿

THE CLOSING VERSES OF Exodus 15 are a harbinger of things to come. Despite the miraculous interventions by God that characterized their escape from Egypt, the people do not really trust him; the first bit of hardship turns to whining and complaining. **Exodus 16** carries the story further, and shows that this muttering is linked, at several levels, to overt defiance of the living God.

We need not imagine that the Israelites were *not* hungry; of course they were. The question is what they did about it. They might have turned to God in prayer and asked him to supply all their needs. As he had effected their rescue so dramatically, would he not also provide for them? But instead they sarcastically romanticize their experience of slavery (!) in Egypt (16:3), and grumble against Moses and Aaron (16:2).

Moses might have felt miffed at the sheer ingratitude of the people. Wisely, he recognizes its real focus and evil. Although they grumble against Moses and Aaron, their real complaint is against God himself (16:7-8): "You are not grumbling against us, but against the LORD."

In all this, the Lord is still forbearing. As he turned the bitter waters of Marah into sweetness (15:22-26), so he now provides them with meat in the form of quail, and with manna. This frankly miraculous provision not only meets their need, but is granted so that they "will see the glory of the LORD" (16:7). "Then you will know that I am the LORD your God" (16:12). Further, the Lord says, "I will test them and see whether they will follow my instructions" (16:4).

Unfortunately, not a few in the community fail the test miserably. They try to hoard manna when they are told not to; they try to gather manna when, on the Sabbath, none is provided. Moses is frankly angry with them (16:20); the Lord himself challenges this chronic disobedience (16:28).

Why should people who have witnessed so spectacular a display of the grace and power of God slip so easily into muttering and complaining and slide so gracelessly into listless disobedience? The answer lies in the fact that many of them see God as existing to serve them. He served them in the Exodus; he served them when he provided clean water. Now he must serve not only their needs but their appetites. Otherwise they are entirely prepared to abandon him. While Moses has been insisting to Pharaoh that the people needed to retreat into the desert in order to serve and worship God, the people themselves think God exists to serve them.

The fundamental question is, "Who is the real God?" New covenant believers face the same choice (1 Cor. 10:10).

∿

Exodus 17; Luke 20; Job 35; 2 Corinthians 5

∾

BY THIS STAGE IN JESUS' MINISTRY, the tensions between him and the authorities have become acute. Some are overtly theological; others have pragmatic overtones and elements of turf protection. Every unit in **Luke 20** reflects some of this increasing tension.

We shall focus on the parable of the tenants (20:9-19). The story becomes more comprehensible to Western minds when we recall that these "tenant farmers" in the first-century culture were not simply employees (in the modern sense), but workers tied to an entire social structure. They *owed* the owner of the vineyard not only a percentage of the produce, but respectful allegiance. Their treatment of the servants he sent was not only harsh and greedy, but shameful. That he should send his son would not be thought of as a stupid act on his part: it would simply be unthinkable for them to kill him. But in the story that Jesus tells, that is just what they do: they kill him, hoping somehow that the land will become theirs now that the rightful heir is dead.

What then will the owner do? Jesus answers his own question: "He will come and kill those tenants and give the vineyard to others" (20:16).

The people grasp the point of the parable. The main lines were clear: God was the vineyard owner, the tenant farmers were Israel, the servants rejected by the farmers were the prophets, and eventually God sends his "son" (doubtless a slightly ambiguous category for them)—and the result is that the land and prosperity that the owner provided are stripped from them and given to others. Small wonder they exclaim, "May this never be!"

That was exactly the response Jesus expected from them. He had set them up for it. But now he looks at them steadily and cites Scripture to prove that that is exactly how things will turn out, exactly how things therefore *must* turn out. For doesn't Scripture say, "The stone the builders rejected has become the capstone" (20:17; Ps. 118:22)? That "stone" finally wins; those who fall on it are broken to pieces, those on whom it falls are crushed. But the fact of the matter is that the stone is initially rejected by the builders.

Doubtless Jesus' hearers did not understand all of the ramifications of this parable. But the scribes and chief priests understood enough to know that they themselves did not figure too well in it: they must be included among the people who beat up on prophets and finally reject God's Son. Politically, this is one more step to the cross; theologically, Jesus teaches his followers what kind of Messiah he is, and how his death is as inevitable as the scriptural prophecies that predict it.

∾

Exodus 18; Luke 21; Job 36; 2 Corinthians 6

∽

ONE CAN ONLY IMAGINE the conversations that Moses had enjoyed with Jethro, his father-in-law, during the decades they spent together in Midian. But clearly, some of the talk was about the Lord God. Called to his extraordinary ministry, Moses temporarily entrusted his wife and sons to his father-in-law's care (**Ex. 18:2**). Perhaps that decision had been precipitated by the extraordinary event described in Exodus 4:24-26, where in the light of this new mission Moses' own sons undergo emergency circumcision to bring Moses' household into compliance with the covenant with Abraham, thereby avoiding the wrath of God.

But now Moses learns that Jethro is coming to see him, restoring to him his wife Zipporah and their sons Gershom and Eliezer. Soon Moses continues the old conversation. This time he gives his father-in-law a blow-by-blow account of all that the Lord had done in rescuing his people from slavery in Egypt. Doubtless some of Jethro's delight (18:9) is bound up with his ties with his son-in-law. But if his final evaluative comment is taken at face value, Jethro has also come to a decisive conclusion: "Now I know that the LORD is greater than all other gods, for he did this to those who had treated Israel arrogantly" (18:11). And he offers sacrifices to the living God (18:12).

All this material is provided as background for what takes place in the rest of the chapter. The next day, Jethro sees Moses attempting to arbitrate every dispute in the fledgling nation. With wisdom and insight he urges on Moses a major administrative overhaul—a rigorous judicial system with most of the decisions being taken at the lowest possible level, only the toughest cases being reserved for Moses himself, the "supreme court." Moses listens carefully to his father-in-law, and puts the entire plan into operation (18:24). The advantages for the people, who are less frustrated by the system, and for Moses, who is no longer run ragged, are beyond calculation. And at the end of the chapter, Jethro returns home.

In some ways, the account is surprising. Major administrative structures are being put into place among the covenant community without any word from God. Why is Jethro, at best on the fringes of the covenant people, allowed to play such an extraordinary role as counselor and confidant of Moses?

The questions answer themselves. God may use the means of "common grace" to instruct and enrich his people. The sovereign goodness and provision of God are displayed as much in bringing Jethro on the scene at this propitious moment as in the parting of the waters of the Red Sea. Are there not contemporary analogies?

∽

Exodus 19; Luke 22; Job 37; 2 Corinthians 7

∾

THE NEW TESTAMENT ACCOUNTS of the "words of institution"—i.e., the words that institute the Lord's Supper as an ongoing rite—vary somewhat, but their commonalities are striking. **Luke 22:7-20** allows us to reflect on some elements of one of those accounts.

All three synoptic Gospels indicate that Jesus ordered his disciples to prepare for a Passover meal; Luke stresses the point (22:1, 7-8, 11, 15). Jesus wants his own actions and words to be understood in the light of that earlier traditional feast. The Passover celebrated not only the release of the Israelites from bondage, but the *way* that release was accomplished: in God's plan, the angel of death "passed over" the houses protected by the sacrificial blood, while all the other homes in Egypt lost their firstborn. Moreover, this miraculous exodus set the stage for the inauguration of the Sinai covenant. So when Jesus now takes bread at a Passover meal and says, "This is my body given for you" (22:19), and when he takes the cup and says, "This cup is the new covenant in my blood, which is poured out for you" (22:20), one hears more than overtones from the old covenant ritual. This side of the cross, one cannot avoid the conclusion that Jesus sees his own death, the shedding of his own blood, as the God-provided sacrifice which averts the wrath of God, that he himself is the Passover Lamb of God *par excellence,* and that his death establishes a covenant with the people of God by releasing them from a darker, deeper slavery.

Someone has said that the four most disputed words in the history of the church are "This is my body." Without entering the lists on all that might be said about this clause, surely we can agree that *one* of its functions, as it is repeated in the ritual that Christ Jesus himself prescribed, is commemorative: "Do this in remembrance of me" (22:19). It is shocking that this should be necessary, in exactly the same way that it is shocking that a commemorative rite like the Passover should have been necessary. But history shows how quickly the people of God drift toward peripheral matters, and end up ignoring or denying the center. By a simple rite, Jesus wants his followers to come back to his death, his shed blood, his broken body, again and again and again.

It is also an anticipatory rite. It looks forward to the consummated kingdom, when the Passover and the Lord's Supper alike find their fulfillment (22:16, 18). We eat and drink as he prescribes "until he comes" (1 Cor. 11:26), when commemoration and proclamation will be swallowed up by the bliss of his presence.

∾

Exodus 20; Luke 23; Job 38; 2 Corinthians 8

✌

THE TEN COMMANDMENTS (**Ex. 20**) were once learned by every child at school in the Western world. They established deeply ingrained principles of right and wrong that contributed to the shaping of Western civilization. They were not viewed as ten recommendations, optional niceties for polite people. Even many of those who did not believe that they were given by God himself ("God spoke all these words," 20:1) nevertheless viewed them as the highest brief summary of the kind of private and public morality needed for the good ordering of society.

Their importance is now fast dissipating in the West. Even many church members cannot recite more than three or four of them. It is unthinkable that a thoughtful Christian would not memorize them.

Yet it is the setting in which they were first given that calls forth this meditation. The Ten Commandments were given by God through Moses to the Israelites in the third month after their rescue from Egypt. Four observations:

(1) The Ten Commandments are, in the first place, the high point of the covenant mediated by Moses (cf. 19:5), delivered by God at Sinai (Horeb). The rest of the covenant makes little sense without them; the Ten Commandments themselves are buttressed by the rest of the covenantal stipulations. However enduring, they are not merely abstract principles, but are cast in the concrete terms of that culture: e.g., the prohibition to covet your neighbor's ox or donkey.

(2) The Ten Commandments are introduced by a reminder that God redeemed this community from slavery: "I am the LORD you God, who brought you out of Egypt, out of the land of slavery" (20:2). They are his people not only because of creation, not only because of the covenant with Abraham, but because God rescued them from Egypt.

(3) God delivered the Ten Commandments in a terrifying display of power. In an age before nuclear holocaust, the most frightening experience of power was nature unleashed. Here, the violence of the storm, the shaking of the earth, the lightning, the noise, the smoke (19:16-19; 20:18) not only solemnized the event, but taught the people reverent fear (20:19-20). The fear of the Lord is not only the beginning of wisdom (Prov. 1:7), but also keeps people from sinning (Ex. 20:20). God wants them to know he had rescued them; he also wants them to know he is not a domesticated deity happily dispensing tribal blessings. He is not only a good God, but a terrifying, awesome God.

(4) Since God is so terrifying, the people themselves insist that Moses should mediate between him and them (20:18-19). And this prepares the way for another, final, Mediator (Deut. 18:15-18).

✌

Exodus 21; Luke 24; Job 39; 2 Corinthians 9

THE FIRST TWO VERSES of the following poem are a meditation on part of **Luke 24:1-8, 13-25**. The last two verses draw on other resurrection accounts (John 20:24-29; Heb. 2:14-15; 1 Cor. 15:50-58). It may be sung to the Londonderry Air ("Danny Boy").

They came alone: some women who remembered him,
Bowed down with spices to anoint his corpse.
Through darkened streets, they wept their way to honor him—
The one whose death had shattered all their hopes.
"Why do you look for life among the sepulchers?
He is not here. He's risen, as he said.
Remember how he told you while in Galilee:
The Son of Man will die—and rise up from the dead."

The two walked home, a study in defeat and loss,
Explaining to a stranger why the gloom—
How Jesus seemed to be the King before his cross,
How all their hopes lay buried in his tomb.
"How slow you are to see Christ's glorious pilgrimage
Ran through the cross"—and then he broke the bread.
Their eyes were opened, and they grasped the Scripture's truth:
The man who taught them had arisen from the dead.

He was a skeptic: not for him that easy faith
That swaps the truth for sentimental sigh.
Unless he saw the nail marks in his hands himself,
And touched his side, he'd not believe the lie.
Then Jesus came, although the doors were shut and locked.
"Repent of doubt, and reach into my side;
Trace out the wounds that nails left in my broken hands.
And understand that I who speaks to you once died."

Long years have passed, and still we face the fear of death,
Which steals our loved ones, leaving us undone,
And still confronts us, beckoning with icy breath,
The final terror when life's course is run.
But this I know: the Savior passed this way before,
His body clothed in immortality.
The sting's been drawn: the power of sin has been destroyed.
We sing: Death has been swallowed up in victory.

Exodus 22; John 1; Job 40; 2 Corinthians 10

∿

WE SHALL DO WELL to reflect on a little of the case law found in the Pentateuch—beginning now with some of the laws of restitution found in **Exodus 22:1-15.**

Thieves must not only pay back what they stole, but something extra as well (22:1, 4). This extra amount is not only a punishment for them, but compensates the victim for the sense of being violated, or for the inconvenience of being deprived of whatever had been stolen. Zacchaeus understood the principle, and his repentance was demonstrated by his resolution to make restitution fourfold, and give generously to the poor (Luke 19:1-10).

If a thief cannot pay back what he has stolen, the law demanded that he be sold into slavery to pay for his theft (22:3). Slavery in this culture had economic roots. There were no modern bankruptcy laws, so a person might sell *himself* into slavery to deal with outstanding debts. But in Israel, slavery was not normally to be open-ended: it was supposed to come to an end in seven-year cycles (21:2-4).

The succeeding verses lay out the restitution to be made for various offenses, with exceptions included to make the law flexible enough to handle the hard cases or delicate cases (e.g., 22:14-15). In some instances, conflicting claims must be brought before a judge, who is charged with discerning who is telling the truth. For instance, if someone gives his neighbor his silver or goods for safekeeping, and then that neighbor claims that they were stolen from him by a thief, a judge must determine whether the neighbor is telling the truth, or is himself a thief. If the thief is caught, he must pay back double. If the judge determines that the neighbor is a liar, the neighbor must himself pay back double the amount (22:7-9).

When the crime is theft, *restitution* most directly preserves the notion of *justice*. Where thieves are simply sent to prison, it will not be long before experts debate whether the purpose of prison is remedial, therapeutic, educational, custodial (for the preservation of society), or vengeful. A sentence directly related to the crime preserves the primacy of *justice*. The same is true, of course, of the much maligned *lex talionis,* the "eye for an eye" statute (21:23-25) that was not an excuse for a personal vendetta but a way of giving the courts punishments that exactly fitted the crime. This sense of justice needing to be satisfied permeates the Old Testament treatments of sin and transgression as well, ultimately preparing the way for an understanding of the cross as the sacrifice that meets the demands of justice (cf. Rom. 3:25-26).

∿

Exodus 23; John 2; Job 41; 2 Corinthians 11

∾

WHEN THE JEWISH LEADERS question Jesus' right to cleanse the temple as he did, and demand that he provide some authority for his action, he replies, "Destroy this temple, and I will raise it again in three days" (**John 2:19**).

Only John's gospel records this early exchange. According to the Synoptics, at Jesus' trial this utterance was vaguely recalled by those who wanted him done away with on the capital charge of temple desecration. That their memories of the event were a little fuzzy accords well with the fact that Jesus uttered these words at the *beginning* of his ministry, perhaps two years and more before his arrest and trial.

But what did Jesus mean by these words? His opponents thought he was referring to the literal temple, and judged his claim ludicrous (2:20). According to John, not even the disciples understood what he was talking about at the time. When John wrote his gospel, of course, he knew, and he records his conclusion: "But the temple he had spoken of was his body" (2:21). But he faithfully records, "After he was raised from the dead, his disciples recalled what he had said. Then they believed the Scripture and the words that Jesus had spoken" (2:22).

Several things follow:

(1) John is often accused of anachronism, of reading back into the time of Jesus events and beliefs that developed only later. This is singularly unlikely. No evangelist is more persistent than John (at least sixteen times) in carefully distinguishing what the disciples understood back *then* (during Jesus' ministry) and what they understood only *later.*

(2) The turning point in their understanding of Jesus' words was the combination of his resurrection from the grave, and a fresh grasp of and belief in the Scripture (2:22). Because Jesus died and rose again, they were forced to think of Jesus the Messiah in more than merely regal or triumphal categories. Both the events and Jesus' own tutelage of them taught them that the Messiah was to be not only the Davidic King, but the Suffering Servant. The old covenant mandate of a priestly system, sacrifices, a day of atonement, a Passover lamb, a peculiar temple constructed to a specific design laid down by God himself—all forced them to recognize that their earlier reading of Scripture (what we call the Old Testament) had been terribly reductionistic. Now they could see that the Old Testament temple, the meeting place between God and his covenant people, pointed to the ultimate "meeting place," the ultimate Mediator. Jesus would occupy this role by virtue of his death and resurrection—the "temple" would be destroyed, and rebuilt.

(3) Jesus himself is the source of this "hermeneutic," this way of reading Old Testament Scripture.

∾

Exodus 24; John 3; Job 42; 2 Corinthians 12

∿

IT IS NOT EASY TO SORT OUT some of the sequence of events in these chapters of Exodus. What is clear is that God graciously provides enough of the revelation of his covenant that the people agree to its terms (**Ex. 24**). More of its stipulations, especially with respect to the tabernacle and priestly arrangements, are spelled out in the next chapters. Moses' long departure on the mountain begins about this time, and precipitates the fickle rebellion that produces the idol of the golden calf (**Ex. 32**), which brings Moses down the mountain, smashing the tablets of the Ten Commandments. We shall reflect on those events in due course.

Here we must think through several elements of this covenant ratification.

(1) The Israelites would have already been familiar with *suzerainty covenants* that were not uncommon in the ancient world. A regional power or a superpower would impose such a treaty on lesser nations. Both sides would agree to certain obligations. The lesser power agreed to abide by the rules set down by the stronger power, pay certain taxes, maintain proper allegiance; the greater power would promise protection, defense, and loyalty. Often there was an introduction that spelled out the past history, and a postscript that threatened curses and judgments on whichever side broke the covenant.

(2) Parts of Exodus and Deuteronomy in particular mirror these covenants. Some elements in this chapter are unique. What is clear, however, is that the people themselves agree to the covenantal stipulations that Moses carefully writes out: "We will do everything the LORD has said; we will obey" (24:7). Thus later rebellion reflects not merely a flighty independent spirit, but the breaking of an oath, the trashing of a covenant. They are thumbing their nose at the treaty of the great King.

(3) To strengthen the allegiance of the covenantal community, God graciously discloses himself not only to Moses but to Aaron and his sons, and to seventy elders. Whenever Old Testament writers say that certain people "saw God" (24:10-11) or the like, inevitably there are qualifications, for as this book says elsewhere, no one can look on the face of God and live (33:20). Thus when we are told that the elders saw the God of Israel, the only description is "something like" a pavement "under his feet" (24:10). God remains distanced. Yet this is a glorious display, graciously given to deepen allegiance, while a special mediating role is preserved for Moses, who alone goes all the way up the mountain.

(4) The covenant is sealed with the shedding of blood (24:4-6).

(5) Throughout the forty days Moses remains on the mountain, the glory of the Lord is visibly displayed (24:15-18). This anticipates developments in later chapters.

∿

Exodus 25; John 4; Proverbs 1; 2 Corinthians 13

EXODUS 25 AND JOHN 4 are canonically tied together.

The former begins the instructions for the construction of the tabernacle and its accoutrements (Ex. 25—30). The tabernacle is the forerunner of the temple, built in Solomon's day. Repeatedly in these chapters God says, "See that you make them according to the pattern shown you on the mountain," (25:40) or "Set up the tabernacle according to the plan shown you on the mountain" (26:30) or the like. The epistle to the Hebrews picks up on this point. The tabernacle and temple were not arbitrary designs; they reflected a heavenly reality. "This is why Moses was warned when he was about to build the tabernacle: 'See to it that you make everything according to the pattern shown you on the mountain'" (Heb. 8:5).

John 4 finds Jesus in discussion with a Samaritan woman. Samaritans believed that the proper place to worship God was not Jerusalem, home of the temple, but on Mounts Gerizim and Ebal, since these were the last places stipulated for such worship when the people entered the land (Deut. 11:29; Josh. 8:33). They did not accept as Scripture the texts concerning the monarchy. The woman wants to know what Jesus thinks: Is the appropriate place for worship these mountains, near where they are standing, or Jerusalem (John 4:20)?

Jesus insists that the time is dawning when neither place will suffice (4:21). This does not mean that Jesus views the Samaritan alternative as enjoying credentials equal to those of Jerusalem. Far from it: he sides with the Jews in this debate, since they are the ones that follow the full sweep of Old Testament Scripture, including the move from the tabernacle to the temple in Jerusalem (4:22). "Yet a time is coming and has now come when the true worshipers will worship the Father in spirit and truth, for they are the kind of worshipers the Father seeks" (4:23).

This means: (1) With the coming of Christ Jesus and the dawning of the new covenant, appropriate worship will no longer be tied to a specific geographic location. Implicitly, this announces the obsolescence of the temple. Worship will be as geographically extensive as the Spirit, as God himself who is spirit (4:24). (2) Worship will not only be "in spirit" but "in truth." In the context of this gospel, this does not mean that worship must be sincere ("true" in that sense); rather, it must be in line with what is ultimately true, the very manifestation of truth, Jesus Christ himself. He is the "true light" (1:9), the true temple (2:19-22), the true bread from heaven (6:25ff.), and more. True worshipers worship in spirit and in truth.

Exodus 26; John 5; Proverbs 2; Galatians 1

∾

ONE OF THE MOST STRIKING biblical passages dealing with what it means to confess that Jesus Christ is the Son of God is **John 5:16-30.**

In a preindustrial culture, the majority of sons do what their father does. A baker's son becomes a baker; a farmer's son becomes a farmer. This stance—like father, like son—enables Jesus on occasion to refer to his own followers as "sons of God." Thus Jesus declares, "Blessed are the peacemakers, for they will be called *sons of God*" (Matt. 5:9). In other words, God himself is the supreme peacemaker; therefore, people who are peacemakers act, in this respect, like God, and therefore can be designated, in this respect, "sons of God."

That is the kind of functional category with which Jesus begins in John 5:17. When challenged about his "working" on the Sabbath, he does not offer a different reading of what "Sabbath" means, or suggest that what he was doing was not "work" but some deed of mercy or necessity; rather, he justifies his "working" by saying that he is only doing what his Father does. His Father works (even on the Sabbath, or providence itself would cease!), and so does he.

His interlocutors perceive that this is an implicit claim to equality with God (5:18). Yet almost certainly they misunderstand Jesus in one respect. They think the claim blasphemous, because it would make Jesus into *another* God—and they are quite right to hold that there is but one God. Jesus responds with two points. *First*, he insists he is functionally dependent on his Father: "the Son can do nothing by himself; he can do only what he sees his Father doing" (5:19). Jesus is not another "God-center": he is functionally subordinate to his Father. Yet *second*, this functional subordination is itself grounded in the fact that *this* Son does *whatever* the Father does (5:19). Christians may be "sons of God" in certain respects; Jesus is the unique Son, in that "whatever the Father does the Son also does." If the Father creates, so does the Son: indeed, the Son is the Father's agent in creation (1:2-3). In the following verses, the Son, like the Father, raises people from the dead, and is the Father's agent in the final judgment.

Muslims with little grasp of Christian theology think the Christian Trinity is made up of God, Mary, and Jesus: God copulated with Mary and produced Jesus. They think the notion bizarre and blasphemous, and they are right. But this is not what we hold, nor what Scripture teaches. I wish they could study John 5.

I believe that Jesus Christ is the Son of God.

∾

Exodus 27; John 6; Proverbs 3; Galatians 2

JESUS DECLARES HIMSELF TO BE the "bread of life" (**John 6:35**), the "bread of God" (6:33).

The language is metaphorical, of course. That is made clear by John 6:35, where the metaphor is unpacked just a little: "I am the bread of life. He who comes to me will never go hungry, and he who believes in me will never be thirsty." One normally *eats* bread; one does not "come" to bread or "believe" in bread. Thus what Jesus means by eating this bread of life must be largely equivalent to what it means to come to Jesus and believe in him.

This "bread of life discourse" (as it is called) follows the feeding of the five thousand (6:1-15). There Jesus provides bread and fish to the hungry masses. These were the staple foods of Galilee; he provided what was needed to sustain life. But in this gospel the evangelist points out that Jesus' miracles are not mere events of power, they are *significant:* they point beyond themselves, like signs. This miracle points to the fact that Jesus not only *provides* bread, but rightly understood he *is* bread. He is the staple apart from which there is no real life at all.

Further, he is the ultimate "manna" (6:30-33). His interlocutors remind him that Moses provided manna, "bread from heaven" (Ex. 16), and they want him to do the same. After all, he had done it the day before in the feeding of the five thousand. If Jesus has performed the miracle once, why not again—and again and again? Isn't that what Moses did?

But Jesus insists the ultimate source of the "bread from heaven" was not Moses but God, and the ultimate "bread from heaven" was not the manna of the wilderness years, but the One who came down from heaven—Jesus himself. After all, everyone who ate the manna in the wilderness died. Those who eat the ultimate bread from heaven, the antitype of the manna, never die.

People in an agrarian culture understand that almost everything they eat is something that has died. We think of food as packaged things. The reality is that when you eat a hamburger, you are eating a dead cow, dead wheat, dead lettuce, dead tomatoes, dead onions, and so forth. The chief exception is the odd mineral, like salt. Jesus' audience, and John's readership, understood that other things die so that we may live; if those other things don't die, we do. Jesus gives his life so that we may live; either he dies, or we do. He is the true bread from heaven who gives his life "for the life of the world" (6:51).

Exodus 28; John 7; Proverbs 4; Galatians 3

THE PRIESTLY GARMENTS God prescribes (**Ex. 28**) are strange and colorful. Perhaps some of the details were not meant to carry symbolic weight, but were part of the purpose of the ensemble as a whole: to give Aaron and his sons "dignity and honor" as they discharge their priestly duties (28:2, 40).

Some of the symbolism is transparent. The breastpiece of the high priest's garment was to carry twelve precious or semi-precious stones, set out in four rows of three, "one for each of the names of the sons of Israel, each engraved like a seal with the name of one of the twelve tribes" (28:21).

The breastpiece is also called "the breastpiece of decision" (28:29). This is probably because it carries the Urim and Thummim. Perhaps they were two stones, one white and one black. They were used in making decisions, but just how they operated no one is quite sure. On important matters, the priest would seek the presence and blessing of God in the temple, and operate the Urim and Thummim, which would come out one way or the other and thus, under God's sovereign care, provide direction. Thus over his heart the priest simultaneously carries the names of the twelve tribes "as a continuing memorial before the LORD," and the Urim and Thummim, "whenever he enters the presence of the LORD," thus always bearing "the means of making decisions for the Israelites over his heart before the LORD" (28:29-30).

On the front of his turban, Aaron is to affix a plate of pure gold. On it will be engraved the words, "HOLY TO THE LORD" (28:36). "It will be on Aaron's forehead, and he will bear the guilt involved in the sacred gifts the Israelites consecrate, whatever their gifts may be. It will be on Aaron's forehead continually so that they will be acceptable to the LORD" (28:38). This assumes that the "sacred gifts the Israelites consecrate" were primarily sin offerings of various sorts, offered to atone for guilt. The priest, even by the symbolism embodied in his garments, conveys this guilt into the presence of the holy God, who alone can deal with it. The text implies that if the priest does not exercise this role, the sacrifices the Israelites offer will *not* be acceptable to the Lord. The priestly/sacrificial/temple structure hangs together as a complete system.

In due course these meditations will reflect on passages that announce the impending obsolescence of this system, which thereby becomes a prophetic announcement of the ultimate priest, the ultimate covenant community, the ultimate authority for giving direction, the ultimate offering, the ultimate temple. There is no limit to his "dignity and honor" (cf. Rev. 1:12-18).

Exodus 29; John 8; Proverbs 5; Galatians 4

∾

TWO COMMENTS on **John 8:12-51.**

(1) Already in John 7:7, Jesus said to his brothers, "The world cannot hate you, but it hates me, because I testify that what it does is evil." Both in his own person and in his uncompromising words, Jesus is so offensive that the world hates him. He is the very embodiment of 3:19-21: "Light has come into the world, but men loved darkness instead of light because their deeds were evil."

John 8 now goes further. Jesus insists that when the Devil lies, "he speaks his native language, for he is a liar and the father of lies" (8:44). Then Jesus adds, "Yet because I tell you the truth, you do not believe me" (8:45).

That is stunning. The first clause is not concessive, as if Jesus had said, "*Although* I tell you the truth, you do not believe me." That would be bad enough. But Jesus says, "*Because* I tell you the truth, you do not believe me." What options does that leave him? Should he tell the smooth lies that comfortable people want to hear? That might get him a hearing, but it is unthinkable that Jesus would follow such a course. So he continues telling the truth, and precisely *because* he tells the truth, he is not believed. To those so blinded, speaking the truth is precisely what hardens their hearts. It ignites the burning hatred that issues in the conflagration of the cross.

(2) Jesus insists that "Abraham rejoiced at the thought of seeing my day" (8:56): probably what Jesus has in mind is the promise God made and renewed to Abraham that in his offspring all the nations of the earth would be blessed (Gen. 12). It is unlikely Jesus is claiming that Abraham had some vision that unfolded the life and times of Jesus in a kind of visionary preview. What he means, rather, is that Abraham knew God, believed God's promises about the offspring, and in faith contemplated the fulfillment of those promises, rejoicing in the prospect of what he could not yet fully grasp: "he saw it and was glad" (8:56). But at very least this means that Jesus is the object and fulfillment of God's promise to Abraham, thus superseding him in importance. More: if the eternal Word (John 1:1) was always with God, and was always God, even Abraham's faith-borne contemplation of God was nothing less than a contemplation of him who became Jesus of Nazareth. "I tell you the truth," Jesus answered, "before Abraham was born, *I am*" —the very covenant name of God (Ex. 3:14).

When his opponents pick up stones to kill Jesus because of this second point, they prove his first point.

∾

Exodus 30; John 9; Proverbs 6; Galatians 5

∾

AS THE FEEDING OF THE FIVE THOUSAND precipitates the bread of life discourse, so Jesus' healing of the congenitally blind man in **John 9** precipitates some briefer comments on the nature of spiritual blindness and sight.

Some of the authorities were finding it difficult to believe that the victim had in fact been born blind. If it were the case, and if Jesus had really healed him, then this would say something about Jesus' power that they did not want to hear. Then as now, there were plenty of "faith healers" in the land, but most of their work was not very impressive: the less gullible could easily dismiss most of the evidence of their success. But to give sight to a *congenitally* blind man—well, that was unheard of in faith-healing circles (9:32-33). Unable to respond to the straightforward testimony of this man, the authorities resort to stereotyping and personal abuse (9:34).

Jesus meets up with him again, discloses more of himself to him, invites his faith, and accepts his worship (9:35-38). Then he makes two important utterances:

(1) "For judgment I have come into this world, so that the blind will see and those who see will become blind" (9:39). In some ways, this is stock reversal, like the account of the rich man and Lazarus (Luke 16:19-31), or the parable of the Pharisee and the tax collector (Luke 18:9-14)—a common theme in the Gospels. But this reversal is in the realm of vision. Those who "see," with all their principles of sophisticated discernment, are blinded by what Jesus says and does; those who are "blind," the moral and spiritual equivalent of the man in this chapter who is born blind, to these Jesus displays wonderful compassion, and even gives sight.

Some Pharisees, overhearing Jesus' comment and priding themselves on their discernment, are shocked into asking if Jesus includes them among the blind. This precipitates his second utterance.

(2) "If you were blind, you would not be guilty of sin; but now that you claim you can see, your guilt remains" (9:41). Of course, Jesus might simply have replied "Yes!" to their question. But that would not have exposed the seriousness of their problem. By subtly changing the metaphor, Jesus drives home his point another way. Instead of insisting his opponents are blind, Jesus points out that they themselves claim to see—better than anyone else, for that matter. But that is the problem: those who are confident of their ability to see do not ask for sight. So (implicitly) they remain blind, with the culpable blindness of smug self-satisfaction. There are none so blind as those who do not know they are blind.

∾

Exodus 31; John 10; Proverbs 7; Galatians 6

IN THE EXTENDED METAPHOR of the shepherd in **John 10,** Jesus keeps revising the dimensions and application of the metaphor as he drives home a variety of points, a few of which we may pick up:

(1) For the biblically literate, it would be difficult not to think of Ezekiel 34. There God denounces the false shepherds of Israel, and repeatedly says that a day is coming when he himself will be the shepherd of his people, feeding them, leading them, disciplining them. Jesus' insistence that, so far as shepherds go, those who came before him "were thieves and robbers" (John 10:8), would call Ezekiel 34 to mind. Then, toward the end of that Old Testament chapter, God says he will place over his flock one shepherd—his servant David. Now the Good Shepherd is here, one with God (1:1), yet from David's line.

(2) In defining himself as the "good shepherd," Jesus says that the "good shepherd lays down his life for the sheep" (10:11). This pushes the metaphor to the wall. In real life, a good shepherd *risks* his life for his sheep, and may *lose* it. But he doesn't voluntarily *sacrifice* his life for the sheep. For a start, who would look after the other sheep? And in any case, it would be inappropriate: risking your life to save the livestock is one thing, but actually choosing to die for them would be disproportionate. A human life is worth more than a flock of sheep.

(3) Yet in case we have not yet absorbed the incongruity of Jesus' claim, he spells it out even more clearly. He is *not* simply risking his life. Nor is he merely the pawn of vicious circumstances: no one can take his life from him. He is laying it down of his own accord (10:18). Indeed, the reason why his Father continues to love him is that the Son is perfectly obedient—and it is the Father's good mandate that this Son lay down his life (10:17; cf. Phil. 2:6-8).

(4) Jesus' sheep respond to his voice; others reject him. The implicit election is ubiquitous in the passage (e.g., 10:27-28).

(5) Jesus' mission includes not only sheep among the Israelites, but other sheep that "are not of this sheep pen" (10:16). But if they are Jesus' sheep, whether Jews or Gentiles, they "will listen to [his] voice, and there shall be one flock and one shepherd" (10:16). Here is the fulfillment of the promise that in Abraham's offspring all the nations of the earth will be blessed. And this is also why, in the last analysis, there can never be more than one head of the church— Jesus Christ himself.

Exodus 32; John 11; Proverbs 8; Ephesians 1

∽

EXODUS 32 IS simultaneously one of the low points and one of the high points in Israel's history.

Only months out of slavery in Egypt, the Israelites prove so fickle that the delay of Moses on the mountain (a mere forty days) provides them with all the excuse they need for a new round of complaining. Moses' delay does not prompt them to pray, but elicits callous ingratitude and disoriented syncretism. Even their tone is sneering: "As for this fellow Moses who brought us up out of Egypt, we don't know what has happened to him" (32:1).

Aaron is revealed as a spineless wimp, unable or unwilling to impose any discipline. He is utterly without theological backbone—not even enough to be a thoroughgoing pagan, as he continues to invoke the name of the Lord even while he himself manufactures a golden calf (32:4-5). He is still a wimp when, challenged by his brother, he insists, rather ridiculously, "Then they gave me the gold, and I threw it into the fire, and out came this calf!" (32:24). Despite the covenantal vows they had made (24:7), many in the nation wanted all the blessings they could get from Yahweh, but gave little thought to the nature of their own sworn obligations to their Maker and Redeemer. It was a low moment of national shame—not the last in their experience, not the last in the confessing church.

The high point? When God threatens to wipe out the nation, Moses intercedes. Not once does he suggest that the people do not deserve to be wiped out, or that they are not as bad as some might think. Rather, he appeals to the glory of God. Why should God act in such a way that the Egyptians might scoff and say that the Lord isn't strong enough to pull off this rescue (32:12)? Besides, isn't God obligated to keep his vows to the patriarchs, Abraham, Isaac, and Israel (32:13)? How could God go back on his solemn promises? His final appeal is simply for forgiveness (32:30-32), and if God cannot extend such mercy, then Moses does not want to begin a new race (as angry as he himself is, 32:19). He prefers to be blotted out with the rest of the people.

Here is an extraordinary mediator, a man whose entire sympathies are with God and his gracious salvation and revelation, a man who makes no excuses for the people he is called to lead, but who nevertheless so identifies with them that if judgment is to fall on them he begs to suffer with them. Here is a man who "stands in the gap" (cf. Ezek. 13:3-5; 22:29-30).

∽

Exodus 33; John 12; Proverbs 9; Ephesians 2

∿

ONE CANNOT UNDERSTAND **Exodus 33** without grasping two things: (1) The tabernacle had not yet been built. The "tent of meeting" pitched outside the camp (33:7) where Moses went to seek the face of God must therefore have been a temporary arrangement. (2) The theme of judgment trails on from the wretched episode of the golden calf. God says he will not go with his people; he will merely send an angel to help them (33:1-3).

So Moses continues with his intercession (33:12-13). While dwelling on the fact that this nation is the Lord's people, Moses now wants to know who will go with him. (Aaron is so terribly compromised.) Moses himself still wants to know and follow God's ways. God replies, "My Presence will go with you, and I will give you rest" (33:14). But how does this square with the Lord's threat to do no more than send an angel, to keep away from the people so that he does not destroy them in his anger? So Moses presses on: "If your Presence does not go with us, do not send us up from here [angel or no!]" (33:15). What else, finally, distinguishes this fledgling nation from all other nations but the presence of the living God (33:16)?

And the Lord promises, "I will do the very thing you have asked, because I am pleased with you and I know you by name" (33:17).

Although Moses continues to pray along these lines in the next chapter (34:9), the glorious fact is that God no longer speaks of abandoning his people. When the tabernacle is built, it is installed in the midst of the twelve tribes.

Three brief reflections: (1) These chapters exemplify the truth that God is a jealous God (Ex. 20:5; 34:14). For one human being to be jealous of another is sinful: we are finite, and we are called to be stewards of what we have received, not jealous of others. But for God *not* to be jealous of his own sovereign glory and right would be a formidable failure: he would be disowning his own unique significance as God, implicitly conceding that his image-bearers have the right to independence. (2) God is said to "relent" about forty times in the Old Testament. Such passages demonstrate his personal interactions with other people. When all forty are read together, several patterns emerge—including the integration of God's "relenting" with his sovereign will. (3) Wonderfully, when Moses asks to see God's glory, God promises to display his goodness (33:18-19). It is no accident that the supreme manifestation of the glory of God in John's gospel is in the cross.

∿

Exodus 34; John 13; Proverbs 10; Ephesians 3

∾

WHEN AT THE END OF THE previous chapter, Moses asks to see the Lord's glory, he is promised (as we have seen) a display of his goodness (33:19). But no one, not even Moses, can gaze at God's face and live (33:20). So the Lord arranges for Moses to glimpse, as it were, the trailing edge of the afterglow of the glory of God—and this remarkable experience is reported in **Exodus 34.**

As the Lord passes by the cleft in the rock where Moses is safely hidden, the Lord intones, "YAHWEH, YAHWEH, the compassionate and gracious God, slow to anger, abounding in love and faithfulness" (34:6). The Hebrew words rendered "love" and "faithfulness" are a common pair in the Old Testament. The former is regularly connected with God's covenantal mercy, his covenantal grace; the latter is grounded in his reliability, his covenantal commitment to keep his word, to do what he promises, to be faithful, to be true.

When John introduces Jesus as the Word of God (John 1:1-18), he tells his readers that when the Word of God became flesh (1:14), he "tabernacled" among us, and we have seen his glory, the glory of the One who came from the Father, full of "grace" and "truth." There are good reasons to think that John has chosen these two words to render the paired expression of the Old Testament. He was clearly thinking of these chapters: Exodus 32—34. Echoing Exodus 33, he reminds us that "no one has ever seen God" (1:18). But now that Jesus Christ has come, this Word-made-flesh has made the Father known, displaying "grace and truth" *par excellence.* The Law was given by Moses—that was wonderful enough, certainly a grace-gift from God. But "grace and truth" in all their unshielded splendor came with Jesus Christ (1:17).

Even the lesser revelation graciously displayed for Moses' benefit brings wonderful results. It precipitates covenant renewal. The Lord responds to Moses' prayer: "I am making a covenant with you. Before all your people I will do wonders never before done in any nation in all the world. The people you live among will see how awesome is the work that I, the LORD, will do for you" (34:10). From God's side, this ensures their entry into the Promised Land, for the Lord himself will drive out the opposition (34:11); from the side of the covenant community, what is required is obedience, including careful separation from the surrounding pagans and paganism. "Do not worship any other god, for the LORD, whose name is Jealous, is a jealous God" (34:14).

How could it be otherwise? This God is gracious, but he is also true.

∾

Exodus 35; John 14; Proverbs 11; Ephesians 4

∾

THE FAREWELL DISCOURSE, beginning in **John 14**, includes some extraordinarily rich material on the Holy Spirit. Some highlights:

(1) In Greek, every noun is grammatically designated masculine, feminine, or neuter. The word for "spirit" is neuter. When a pronoun referring to "spirit" is used, it too should be neuter. In this chapter, however, the pronoun is sometimes masculine, breaking grammatical form, a way of gently affirming that the Holy Spirit is personal.

(2) Among his titles is "Counselor" (14:16), or, in some English versions, "Comforter" or "Helper." When *Comforter* was coined, it drew from Latin words that meant "to strengthen" or "to strengthen along with." Today a comforter is either a thick quilt or someone who helps the bereaved, and is therefore too restrictive to convey what is meant here. The Greek word is capable of a variety of nuances, so some do not translate it but merely transliterate it (i.e., put it into English spelling) as *Paraclete.* He is certainly someone who is called alongside to help and to strengthen. Sometimes the help is legal: he can for instance serve as prosecuting attorney (16:7-11), and he may be our legal "Counselor." (The word should not conjure up pictures of camp counselors or psychological counselors.)

(3) He is, Jesus says, *"another* Counselor" (14:16, italics added). In older Greek, this word for "another" usually had overtones of "another of the same kind." By the time of the New Testament, that meaning is fairly rare; it cannot be assumed, but must be demonstrated from the context. In this case, Jesus is clearly promising to send someone who will stand in his place. Intriguingly, apart from its use in the Farewell Discourse, the word rendered "Counselor" is found in the New Testament only in one other place, viz. 1 John 2:1 (NIV: "one who speaks to the Father in our defense"). So Jesus is the first *Paraclete.* At his impending departure, he promises to send the Holy Spirit, another *Paraclete,* to and for his followers.

(4) He is also called "the Spirit of truth" (14:17). This not only means he tells the truth as opposed to lies, but that he is the true Spirit, the one who mediates the very presence of the Father and the Son to the believers (14:23).

(5) The Spirit, Jesus promises, "will teach you all things and will remind you of everything I have said to you" (14:26). Since the "you" are being *reminded* of what Jesus said, in the first instance they must be the first disciples. The Spirit will enable them to recall Jesus' teaching, and flesh out its significance in the wake of the cross and resurrection. How secure would the links have been without his work?

∾

Exodus 36; John 15; Proverbs 12; Ephesians 5

GOD'S LOVE IS SPOKEN of in a variety of ways in the Bible.

In some passages God's love is directed toward his elect. He loves them and not others (e.g., Deut. 4:37; 7:7-8; Mal. 1:2). But if we think of the love of God as invariably restricted to his elect, we will soon distort other themes: his gracious provision of "common grace" (Is he not the God who sends his rain upon the just and upon the unjust? [Matt. 5:45]), his mighty forbearance (e.g., Rom. 2:4), his pleading with rebels to turn and repent lest they die, for he takes no pleasure in the death of the wicked (e.g., Ezek. 33:11). On the other hand, if this were all that the Bible says about the love of God, God would soon be reduced to an impotent, frustrated lover who has done all he can, poor chap. That will never account for the loving initiative of effective power bound up with the first passages cited, and more like them.

There are yet other ways the Bible speaks of the love of God. One of them dominates in **John 15:9-11.** Here the Father's love for us is conditional upon obedience. Jesus enjoins his disciples to obey him in exactly the same way that he obeys his Father, so that they may remain in his love: "If you obey my commands, you will remain in my love, just as I have obeyed my Father's commands, and remain in his love" (15:10).

The context shows that this is not telling us *how* people become Jesus' followers. Rather, assuming that his hearers *are* his followers, Jesus insists that there is a relational love at stake that must be nurtured and preserved. In exactly the same way, the love of the Father for the Son says nothing about *how* that relation originated (!), it merely reflects the nature of that relationship. The Father's love for the Son is elsewhere said to be demonstrated in his "showing" the Son everything, so that the Son does all the Father does and receives the same honor as the Father (John 5:19-23); the Son's love for the Father is demonstrated in obedience (14:31). As my children remain in my love by obeying me and not defying me, so Jesus' followers remain in his love. Of course, there is a sense in which I shall always love my children, regardless of what they do. But there is a relational element in that love that is contingent upon their obedience.

Thus Jesus mediates the Father's love to us (15:9), and the result of our obedience to him is great joy (15:11). "Keep yourselves in God's love" (Jude 21).

Exodus 37; John 16; Proverbs 13; Ephesians 6

∾

THE COMING OF THE HOLY SPIRIT, the "Counselor" or *Paraclete,* is dependent on Jesus' "going away," i.e., his death by crucifixion, subsequent resurrection, and exaltation (**John 16:7**; cf. 7:37-39). This raises important questions about the relationship between the Spirit's role under the old covenant, before the cross, and his role this side of it. That is worthy of careful probing. Here, however, John's emphasis on the Spirit's work must be made clear.

At the end of John 15, the Counselor, we are told, will bear witness to Jesus, and to this task to which the disciples of Jesus will lend their voices (15:26-27). The prime witness falls to the Spirit. In John 16:8-11, the Counselor convicts the world of sin, righteousness, and judgment. He does so because Jesus is returning to the Father and no longer exercises the role of convicting people himself.

If the Holy Spirit bears witness to Jesus in 15:26-27 and brings conviction to people by continuing the work of Jesus in 16:8-11, in 16:12-15 he brings glory to Jesus by unpacking Christ to those who attended that Last Supper (the "you" in v. 12 cannot easily be taken in any other way, and controls the other instances of "you" in the rest of the paragraph; cf. also 14:26). As Jesus is not independent of his Father, but speaks only what the Father gives him to say (5:16-30), so the Spirit is not independent of the Father and the Son: "He will not speak on his own; he will speak only what he hears" (16:13). His focus is Jesus: "He will bring glory to me by taking from what is mine and making it known to you" (16:14). And of course, even here what belongs to Jesus comes from the Father: "All that belongs to the Father is mine. That is why I said the Spirit will take from what is mine and make it known to you" (16:15).

The reason why Jesus himself has not unpacked everything about himself and his mission to the disciples is that they are not yet ready to bear it (16:12). Even this late in their discipleship, they cannot quite integrate in their own minds the notion of a King-Messiah and the notion of a Suffering Messiah. Until that point is firmly nailed down, the way they read their Scriptures—what we call the Old Testament—will be so skewed by political and royal aspirations that they are not going to get it right.

How much of the Spirit's work focuses on Jesus Christ—bearing witness to him, continuing certain aspects of his ministry, unpacking his significance!

∾

Exodus 38; John 17; Proverbs 14; Philippians 1

∾

JOHN 17 IS CONSTANTLY cited in ecumenical circles. Jesus prays for "those who will believe in me through their message, that all of them may be one, Father, just as you are in me and I am in you . . . to let the world know that you sent me" (17:20-23). The implication is that by supporting the ecumenical movement whole-heartedly one is bringing to pass the fulfillment of Jesus' prayer.

It is an important prayer. But note what else he prays for in this chapter:

(1) Jesus prays that God will protect his first disciples from "the evil one," especially now that he himself is being removed from the scene (17:11, 15). Perhaps he is especially thinking of the terrible blows to their faith as their Master is crucified and buried.

(2) Jesus prays that his disciples will be sanctified by the truth—understanding well that God's word is truth, and that the very purpose of his own sanctification (i.e., he "sanctifies" himself—sets himself apart for his Father's holy purposes—by obeying his Father and going to the cross) is that they may be sanctified (17:17-18).

(3) Jesus prays that both these first disciples and those who will ultimately believe through their message will be "in us [i.e., 'in' the Father and the Son] so that the world may believe that you have sent me" (17:21).

(4) Jesus declares he wants all those the Father has given him to be where he is, and finally to see his glory, the very glory the Father gave him because the Father loved him from "before the creation of the world" (17:24).

In addition, of course, Jesus prays that his disciples may all be one. It would be nice if all those who emphasize this petition emphasized the other petitions no less—or, for that matter, that all those who emphasize, say, the second petition in the list above also emphasized the prayer for unity.

The question to ask, however, is whether Jesus' prayers are answered. Does not Jesus elsewhere attest that he knows full well that the Father *always* "hears" him (11:42)? Certainly the Father protected all of the earliest disciples, except, of course, for Judas Iscariot, whom even Jesus in his prayer acknowledges is "doomed to destruction" (17:12). The other petitions are likewise being answered, and will be finally answered at the consummation. This is true also of Jesus' prayer for unity: real Christians attest a profound unity, a real unity, regardless of hierarchical structures and often in defiance of ecumenical initiatives, in answer to Jesus' prayer. This often attracts others to the Gospel. We must hunger and strive for the fulfillment of all of Jesus' petitions.

∾

Exodus 39; John 18; Proverbs 15; Philippians 2

∾

WHEN PILATE ASKS JESUS whether or not he is "the king of the Jews" (**John 18:33**), what interests him is whether or not Jesus presents some sort of political threat. Is he one of these nationalistic, self-proclaimed "messiahs" who are intent on wresting authority from the Roman superpower? If so, he must suffer a capital sentence.

When Jesus finally replies, his answer is like none that Pilate ever heard: "My kingdom is not of this world. If it were, my servants would fight to prevent my arrest by the Jews. But now my kingdom is from another place" (John 18:36).

One might profitably spend a lot of time pondering this response. We shall focus on four points:

(1) The meaning of *kingdom* here cannot have the static sense of *realm*, as in "the kingdom of Jordan" or "the kingdom of Saudi Arabia." It means something closer to the dynamic sense of *kingdominion*, of kingly rule, for Jesus focuses on what his "kingdom" is "of" or "from," i.e., what is the source of his kingly rule. This does not mean there is no domain to this *kingdominion*, no realm connected with it; there is, as we shall see. But it is not the focus of the use of the term here.

(2) Jesus says his kingdom is "not of this world"; it is "from another place." In other words, all the kingdoms and centers of political strength that human beings construct trace their authority to realities in this world. Not Jesus. His kingdom, his ruling authority, is "from another place"—and readers of this gospel know that that means from heaven, from God himself.

(3) That is why his servants will not fight. His kingdom does not advance and become an empire the way the empires of this world achieve success, viz. inevitably with a great deal of military drive. The kingdom of God does not advance by human armies and literal warrior-saints. One wishes that those who stirred up the Crusades had meditated a little longer on this text. Apparently Pilate believed at least this part of what Jesus was saying, and therefore saw him as no political threat (18:38).

(4) But this does not mean that Jesus is making no claim whatsoever with respect to the kingdoms of this world. He insists he is King Jesus, even if his source of authority is not in this world, and his servants will not defend him by resorting to arms. Nevertheless the time will come when all will acknowledge that he alone is Lord of lords and King of kings (Rev. 17:14; 19:16), and all the kingdoms of this world are destined to become his (Rev. 11:15).

∾

Exodus 40; John 19; Proverbs 16; Philippians 3

∾

THE CLOSING LINES OF **Exodus 40** tie together several important themes already introduced, and anticipate several others. Here the construction of the tabernacle is complete, along with the vestments and accoutrements for priestly service. "Then the cloud covered the Tent of Meeting, and the glory of the LORD filled the tabernacle" (40:34).

This must be the pillar of cloud (during the day) and the pillar of fire (during the night) that had accompanied them from the beginning. It signaled the very presence of God, and gave them direction as to when and where to move. Now that cloud rests over the newly constructed tabernacle or Tent of Meeting, settling in it, filling it. Indeed, in this inaugural filling, the presence of the Lord is so intense that not even Moses, let alone any other, can enter (40:35). Moreover, from now on the cloud of glory rests upon the tabernacle when the people are to stay put, and rises and leads the people when they are to move on (40:36-38). Six observations:

(1) For the pillar of cloud and fire to rest on the tabernacle is to link this structure with the visible symbol of the ongoing, guiding, powerful presence of God.

(2) At one point, after the wretched rebellion that resulted in the construction of a golden calf, God had refused to go up in the midst of his covenant community. Moses interceded (Ex. 32—34). Here is the fruit of his prayers. The tabernacle is now built, the presence of God hovers over it in the symbolic form with which the people have become familiar, and all of this right in the midst of the twelve tribes.

(3) This focus on the tabernacle at the end of Exodus prepares the way for the opening chapters of Leviticus, viz. the specification of the sacrifices and offerings to be performed in connection with tabernacle service.

(4) That tabernacle anticipates the temple. In fact, it is a kind of mobile temple. In the days of Solomon, when the permanent structure is complete, the glory of God likewise descends there, establishing the link with the tabernacle and with the pillar of cloud and fire of the wilderness years.

(5) To anticipate the future: nothing more powerfully symbolizes the impending destruction of Jerusalem than the vision of the departure of the glory of God (Ezek. 10—11).

(6) Nothing more powerfully attests the unique revelatory and mediating role of Jesus Christ than the insistence that he is the true temple (John 2:19-22); and nothing more powerfully portrays the sheer glory of heaven than the assertion that there is no temple there, for the Lord God Almighty and the Lamb are its temple (Rev. 21:22).

∾

Leviticus 1; John 20; Proverbs 17; Philippians 4

∿

THOMAS GETS A LOT OF BAD PRESS—"Doubting Thomas," we call him. Yet the reason he doubts that Jesus has risen from the dead may have more to do with the fact that he was not present when Jesus first appeared to the apostolic band (**John 20:19-25**). Is it entirely obvious that any of the others would have fared any better if they had been absent on the critical day?

Certainly Thomas does not lack courage. When Jesus purposes to return from Galilee to Judah to raise Lazarus from the dead, and the disciples, understanding the political climate, recognize how dangerous such a course of action will be, it is Thomas who quietly encourages his colleagues: "Let us also go, that we may die with him" (11:16). On occasion Thomas articulates the question the entire band is wanting to ask. Thus, when Jesus insists he is going away, and that by now they really do know the way, Thomas is not just speaking for himself when he quietly protests, "Lord, we don't know where you are going, so how can we know the way?" (14:5).

But here in John 20, if he is the one caught out by his absence, at the second appearance of the resurrected Jesus to the apostolic band Thomas also triggers some dialogue of stellar importance. When Jesus shows up, through locked doors, he specifically turns to Thomas and displays the scars of his wounds: "Put your finger here; see my hands. Reach out your hand and put it into my side. Stop doubting and believe" (20:27). Thomas asks no further evidence. He erupts with one of the great christological confessions of the New Testament: "My Lord and my God!" (20:28).

Jesus responds with an utterance that illuminates the nature of Christian witness today: "Because you have seen me, you have believed; blessed are those who have not seen and yet have believed" (20:29). Jesus here casts his shadow forward down the meadows of history, envisaging the countless millions who will trust him without ever having seen him in the flesh, without ever having traced out the scars on his hands, feet, and side. Their faith is not inferior. Indeed, in the peculiar providence of God, the report of Thomas's experience is one of the things the Spirit of God will use to bring them to faith. Jesus graciously provides the visual and tangible evidence to the one, so that the written report of Thomas's faith and confession will spur to conversion those who have access only to text. Both Thomas and his successors believe in Jesus and have life in his name (20:30-31).

∿

Leviticus 2—3; John 21; Proverbs 18; Colossians 1

∿

AFTER THE REMARKABLE EXCHANGE that reinstates Peter, Jesus quietly tells him that this discipleship will someday cost him his life: "When you are old you will stretch out your hands, and someone else will dress you and lead you where you do not want to go" (**John 21:18**). If the prediction itself has some ambiguity, by the time John records it here all ambiguities had disappeared: "Jesus said this to indicate the kind of death by which Peter would glorify God" (21:19). Tradition has it, probably rightly, that Peter was martyred in Rome, about the same time that Paul was executed, both under the Emperor Nero, in the first half of the 60s.

Peter observes "the disciple whom Jesus loved"—none other than John the evangelist—following them as he and Jesus stroll along the beach (20:20). The designation "the disciple whom Jesus loved" should not be taken to mean that Jesus played a nasty game of arbitrary favorites. Small indications suggest that many people who followed Jesus felt specially loved by him. Thus when Lazarus lay seriously ill, his sisters, Mary and Martha, sent a message to Jesus saying, "Lord, the one you love is sick" (11:3). Even after the resurrection and ascension, Jesus' followers have delighted in his love, his *personal* love for *them*. Thus Paul needs only to mention Jesus and the cross, and he may burst into spontaneous praise with an additional subordinate clause: "who loved me and gave himself for me" (Gal. 2:20).

In this case, however, there is still something of the old Peter left. Doubtless he was glad to be reinstated, to be charged with feeding Jesus' lambs and sheep (John 21:15-17). On the other hand, the prospect of an ignominious death was less appealing. So when Peter sees John, he asks, "Lord, what about him?" (21:21).

We are in no position to criticize Peter. Most of us are constantly comparing service records. Green is a not uncommon color among ministers of the Gospel. Someone else has it a little easier, so we can explain away his or her superior fruitfulness. Their kids turn out better, their church is a little more prosperous, their evangelism more effective. Alternatively, we achieve a certain amount of "success" and find ourselves looking over our shoulders at those coming behind, making snide remarks about those who will soon displace us. But after all, they've had more advantages than we, haven't they?

It is all so pathetic, so self-focused, so sinful. Jesus tells Peter, "If I want him to remain alive until I return, what is that to you? You must follow me" (21:22). The diversity of gifts and graces is enormous; the only Master we must please is Jesus.

∿

Leviticus 4; Psalms 1—2; Proverbs 19; Colossians 2

THE FIRST PSALM IS sometimes designated a wisdom psalm. In large part this designation springs from the fact that it offers two ways, and only two ways—the way of the righteous (**Ps. 1:1-3**) and the way of the wicked (1:4-5), with a final summarizing contrast (1:6).

The first three verses, describing the righteous person, fall naturally into three steps. In verse 1, the righteous person is described negatively, in verse 2 positively, and in verse 3 metaphorically. The negative description in verse 1 establishes what the "blessed" man is *not* like. He does *not* "walk in the counsel of the wicked"; he does *not* "stand in the way of sinners"; he does *not* "sit in the seat of mockers."

The wicked man, then, is grinding to a halt (walk/stand/sit). He begins by walking in the counsel of the wicked: he picks up the advice, perspectives, values, and worldview of the ungodly. If he does this long enough, he sinks to the next level: he "stands in the way of sinners." This translation gives the wrong impression. To "stand in someone's way" in English is to hinder them. One thinks of Robin Hood and Little John on the bridge: each stands in the other's way, and one of them ends in the stream. But "to stand in someone's way" in Hebrew means something like "to stand in his moccasins": to do what he does, to adopt his lifestyle, his habits, his patterns of conduct. If he pursues this course long enough, he is likely to descend to the abyss and "sit in the seat of mockers." He not only participates in much that is godless, but sneers at those who don't. At this point, someone has said, a person receives his master's in worthlessness and his doctorate in damnation. The psalmist insists, "Blessed is the man who does *not* walk in the counsel of the wicked, or stand in the way of sinners, or sit in the seat of mockers" (italics added). The righteous person is described negatively.

One might have expected the second verse to respond with contrasting parallelism: "Blessed, rather, is the man who walks in the counsel of the righteous, who stands in the way of the obedient, who sits in the seat of the grateful"—or something of that order. Instead, there is one positive criterion, and it is enough: "But his delight is in the law of the LORD, and on his law he meditates day and night" (1:2).

Where one delights in the Word of God, constantly meditating on it, there one learns good counsel, there one's conduct is shaped by revelation, there one nurtures the grace of gratitude and praise. That is a sufficient criterion.

Leviticus 5; Psalms 3—4; Proverbs 20; Colossians 3

∿

IMAGINE A COMPLEX, WELL-ORDERED SOCIETY such that in every area of life there are actions that make a person dirty and further prescribed actions that make that person clean. When you get up in the morning, you wear clothes of certain kinds of fabric, but not others. There are clean foods and unclean foods. If a spot of mold appears on the wall of your house, there are procedures for treating it. Men must adopt a certain course after a wet dream, women in connection with their periods. Some unclean things must not even be touched. In addition there is a complex religious and sacrificial system each person is supposed to observe, and failure to observe it at any point brings its own uncleanness. And all of this fits into a still broader set of constraints that include what we normally call *moral* categories: how we speak, truth-telling, how we treat others, questions of property, sexual integrity, neighborly actions, judicial impartiality, and so forth. Understand, too, that in this society the rules have been laid down by God himself. They are not the results of some elected Congress or Parliament, easily overturned by a fickle or frustrated public eager for something else. To ignore or defy these rules is to defy the living God. What kinds of lessons would be learned in such a society?

Welcome to the world of Leviticus. This, too, is part of the heritage from Mount Sinai, part of the Mosaic Covenant. Here the people of God are to learn that God prescribes what is right and wrong, and that he has a right to do so; that holiness embraces all of life; that there is a distinction between the conduct of the people of God and the conduct of the surrounding pagans, not merely a difference in abstract beliefs. Here the Lord himself prescribes what sacrifices are necessary, along with confession of sin (Lev. 5:5), when a person falls into uncleanness; and even that the system itself is no final answer, since one is constantly falling under another taboo and returning to offer sacrifices one has offered before. One begins to wonder if there will ever be one final sacrifice for sins.

But that is down the road. Here in **Leviticus 5,** Christian readers delight to observe that while God trains up his covenant people in elementary religious thought, he provides means such that even the poorest in society may regain cleanness. The person who cannot afford a sacrificial lamb may bring a pair of doves or a pair of pigeons; the person who cannot afford these may bring a small amount of flour. The lessons continue; always there is hope and a way of escape from the punishment that rebellion attracts.

∿

Leviticus 6; Psalms 5—6; Proverbs 21; Colossians 4

∽

AT THE BEGINNING OF LEVITICUS 6, the Lord lays down through Moses what must take place when someone in the covenant community has lied to a neighbor about something entrusted to him, has cheated him, has lied about recovered property so that he can keep it, or has committed perjury or a range of other sins. Two observations will clarify what these verses (6:1-7) contribute to the unfolding legal and moral structure.

(1) Readers of Leviticus, not least of the NIV, have by now become familiar with the distinction between *unintentional* sins (e.g., much of Lev. 4) and intentional sins. Some interpreters have argued that there are no sacrificial offerings to pay for intentional sins. Those who sin intentionally are to be excluded from the community.

Part of the problem is with our rendering of *intentional* and *unintentional*. *Intentional* commonly reflects a Hebrew expression meaning "with a high hand"; *unintentional* renders "not with a high hand." That background is important as we think through Leviticus 6:1-7. The sins described here are all *intentional* in the modern sense: one cannot lie, cheat, or commit perjury without intending to do so. There are God-given steps to be followed: restitution where possible (following the principles laid out in Ex. 22), and prescribed confession and sacrifices.

Of course, some *unintentional* guilt is gained when one is unaware of committing an offense (as in 5:3); there is still guilt, for the action is prohibited, even though the offender may not have been personally aware of committing an offense. Other *unintentional* guilt does not refer to guilt accumulated unknowingly, but to guilt consciously accumulated even though the offense was not committed "with a high hand." Many is the sin committed because one is attracted on the instant to it, or because one has been nurturing resentments, or because it seems less risky to lie than to tell the truth. This is still not the yet more appalling sin "with a high hand," where the sinner looks at the sin directly, self-consciously reflects that this defies God, and openly and brazenly opts for the sin in order to defy God. As far as I can see, the old covenant does not prescribe atonement for such defiance, but judgment.

(2) Even the sins mentioned in this passage—all sins against some other human party—are treated first of all in relation *to God*: "If anyone sins and is *unfaithful to the LORD* by deceiving his neighbor" (6:2, italics added). The guilt offering is brought to the priest; the offender must not only provide restitution to the offended human, but must seek *the Lord's* forgiveness. Defiance of God is what makes wrongdoing sin, what makes sin odious.

∽

Leviticus 7; Psalms 7—8; Proverbs 22; 1 Thessalonians 1

PSALM 7 IS THE SECOND OF FOURTEEN PSALMS that are linked in the title to some historical event (the first is Ps. 3). We cannot know the details, but clearly David felt terribly betrayed when he was falsely charged by someone close to him who should have known better. We shall focus on the last four verses (7:15-17):

> *He who is pregnant with evil and conceives trouble gives birth to disillusionment.*
> *He who digs a hole and scoops it out falls into the pit he has made.*
> *The trouble he causes recoils on himself; his violence comes down on his own head.*
> *I will give thanks to the LORD because of his righteousness*
> *and will sing praise to the name of the LORD Most High.*

The colorful language makes the point tellingly. Here is someone carefully digging a pit to serve as a trap for someone else—but the digger falls in himself. The first line pictures someone "pregnant with evil" and "conceiv[ing] trouble," but giving birth not to the trouble they intended to produce, but to (their own) disillusionment. The psalmist then expresses his conviction more straightforwardly in verse 16: "The trouble he causes recoils on himself; his violence comes down on his own head."

David's conviction is grounded neither in some impersonal force ("right wins out in the end") nor in some Pollyanna-like optimism ("I'm sure it will turn out all right"), but in the righteousness of God: "I will give thanks to the LORD because of his righteousness and will sing praise to the name of the LORD Most High" (7:17). David is not blind to the injustices of the world, but he lives in a theistic universe where right will finally prevail because God is just.

If we cast our minds more broadly through the pages of Scripture (not to mention our own experience), it is easy to think of instances where the tricks and traps set by evil people recoiled on themselves before they could do any real damage. Haman hangs on the gallows he has prepared for Mordecai. But in many cases judgment falls on the perpetrator in this life, only after he or she has succeeded in doing enormous damage. David could not help but know this: he had been caught himself. He succeeded in sleeping with Bathsheba and murdering her husband Uriah before he was caught, and had to face judgment himself. Judas Iscariot's life ended horribly, but not before he had betrayed his Master. Ahab faced prophetic wrath, but only after his wicked queen Jezebel had managed to malign Naboth and had him killed in order to steal his vineyard.

But the ultimate sanction is at the last judgment, without which there is no final justice in this universe.

Leviticus 8; Psalm 9; Proverbs 23; 1 Thessalonians 2

∾

AT THE BEGINNING OF THE AMERICAN EXPERIMENT in democracy, the Founding Fathers adopted several stances, accepted by few today, that were deeply indebted to the Judeo-Christian heritage. This is not to say that the Founding Fathers were all Christians. Many weren't; they were vague deists. But among these biblical assumptions was the belief that human beings are not naturally good and have potential for enormous evil.

For that reason, when the Fathers constructed their political system, they never appealed to "the wisdom of the American people" or similar slogans common today. Frankly, they were a little nervous about giving too much power to the masses. That is why there was no direct election of the president: there was an intervening "college." Only (white) men with a stake in the country could vote. Even then, the branches of government were to be limited by a system of checks and balances, because for the Fathers, populist demagoguery was as frightening as absolute monarchy (as we saw in another connection on January 20).

Certainly one of the great advantages of almost any system of genuine democracy (*genuine* in this context presupposes a viable opposition, freedom of the press, and largely uncorrupted voting) is that it provides the masses with the power to turf out leaders who disillusion us. In that sense, democracy still works: government must be by the consent of the governed. Yet the primitive heritage has so dissipated today that politicians from all sides appeal to the wisdom of the people. Manipulated by the media, voting their pocketbooks, supporting sectional interests or monofocal issues, voters in America and other Western democracies do not show very great signs of transcendent wisdom. Worse, we labor under the delusion (indeed, we foster the delusion) that somehow things will be all right provided lots of people vote. Our system of government is our new Tower of Babel: it is supposed to make us impregnable. The Soviet empire totters; other nations crumble into the dust, Balkanized, destroyed by civil war, tribal genocide, grinding poverty, endemic corruption, Marxist or some other ideology. Not us. We belong to a democracy, "rule by the people."

Not for a moment should we depreciate the relative good of living in a country with a relatively high level of income, a stable government, and some accountability. But such blessings do not guarantee righteousness. "The LORD reigns forever; he has established his throne for judgment. He will judge the world in righteousness; he will govern the peoples with justice" (**Ps. 9:7-8**).

Hear the voice of Scripture: "Arise, O LORD, let not man triumph; let the nations be judged in your presence. Strike them with terror, O LORD; let the nations know they are but men" (Ps. 9:19-20).

∾

Leviticus 9; Psalm 10; Proverbs 24; 1 Thessalonians 3

ᕤ

PSALM 10 CONTINUES THE THEME of the justice and judgment of God, now slanted away from the more immediate and personal issue of justice for David when he feels betrayed by his enemies and toward a more general treatment. Where is God when evil people triumph? "Why, O LORD, do you stand far off? Why do you hide yourself in times of trouble?" (10:1).

In Psalm 10:2-11, the wicked man is described in a composite picture. He arrogantly preys on weaker people (10:2). Far from showing any self-restraint, he boasts of his appetites "and reviles the Lord" (10:3). The sad fact of the matter is that "in all his thoughts there is no room for God" (10:4). Yet it is not difficult to find wicked people who are extraordinarily prosperous, even while they defy all the laws of God (10:5). The wicked man's explosive arrogance seems to put him above lesser mortals, and he is touted in the papers as the one who gleefully pronounces to himself, "Nothing will shake me; I'll always be happy and never have trouble" (10:6). Nevertheless he curses his opponents, and spreads lies and malice with his tongue (10:8). In the worst cases he stoops to murder, whether directly as in gang warfare, mob violence, and terrorist attack, or indirectly through ruthless schemes that crush the helpless (10:9-10). And what does he think of God? "God has forgotten; he covers his face and never sees" (10:11).

The psalmist now addresses God directly (10:12-15): "Arise, LORD! Lift up your hand, O God. Do not forget the helpless" (10:11). He reminds himself that God *does* see all the trouble and grief that befall this broken race; he *does* consider it; in his own time, he *does* take it in hand (10:14). That is why the victim and the orphan wisely commit themselves "to you" (10:14). So much evil is done in secret and will not be exposed by the ordinary judicial process. The psalmist therefore calls to God for justice: "Break the arm of the wicked and evil man; call him to account for his wickedness *that would not be found out*" (10:15, italics added).

The closing verses (10:16-18) find the psalmist reminding himself that God's scale of timing is less urgent than ours: "The LORD is King for ever and ever; the nations will perish from his land" (10:16). The scale that anticipates the dissolution of nations is not meant to dispel confidence that God also concerns himself with the minuscule scale of individual calamity. Rather, it is another way of saying that "the wheels of God's justice grind exceeding slow, but they grind exceeding fine."

ᕤ

Leviticus 10; Psalms 11—12; Proverbs 25; 1 Thessalonians 4

∾

IN LEVITICUS 8, AARON AND HIS SONS, under a ritual prescribed by God, are ordained as priests. In Leviticus 9, they begin their ministry. Here in **Leviticus 10**, still within the seven days of their ordination rites, two of Aaron's sons, Nadab and Abihu, put coals in their censers and add incense, apparently thinking that they will add something to the ceremonies and rituals God laid down. But "fire came out from the presence of the LORD and consumed them, and they died before the LORD" (10:2). Before Aaron can protest, Moses pronounces an oracle from God: "'Among those who approach me I will show myself holy; in the sight of all the people I will be honored.' Aaron remained silent" (10:3).

That is not all. Moses insists that Aaron and his remaining sons, Eleazar and Ithamar, must not break the sacred cycle of ordination to participate in the public mourning for Nadab and Abihu. They are not to leave the tabernacle while "the LORD's anointing oil" is on them (10:7). First cousins once removed will look after the bodies and discharge family obligations (10:4-5).

What are we to think? A cynic might say that this is elevating ritual above people. Isn't God a bit insensitive when he cuts down two fine sons who are simply trying to jazz up the worship service a little?

I cannot claim to know all the answers. But consider:

(1) God has repeatedly said that everything connected with the service of the tabernacle must be done exactly according to the pattern provided on the mountain. He has already shown himself to be a God who brooks no rivals, and who expects to be obeyed. At issue is whether God is God.

(2) Throughout the Bible, the closer the people are to times and situations of revelation or revival, the more immediate the divine sanction against those who defy him. Uzzah puts out his hand to steady the ark and is killed; Ananias and Sapphira are killed because of their lies. In colder, more rebellious times, God seems to let the people go to extraordinary lengths of evil before reining them in. Yet *the former periods bring greater blessing*: more of the immediate presence of God, more disciplined zeal among the people.

(3) In context, Nadab and Abihu almost certainly had defiant, willful motives. For when Aaron makes a different adjustment in the ritual, *with the best of motives*, surprising flexibility is sanctioned (10:16-20).

(4) This firm lesson prepared the priests for the other major component in their ministry: "You must distinguish between the holy and the common, between the unclean and the clean, *and you must teach the Israelites all the decrees the LORD has given them through Moses*" (10:10-11, italics added).

∾

Leviticus 11—12; Psalms 13—14; Proverbs 26; 1 Thessalonians 5

IN THIS MEDITATION I want to bring two passages together: "I am the LORD your God; consecrate yourselves and be holy, because I am holy. Do not make yourselves unclean by any creature that moves about on the ground. I am the LORD who brought you up out of Egypt to be your God; therefore be holy, because I am holy" (**Lev. 11:44-45**); "The fool says in his heart, 'There is no God'" (**Ps. 14:1**).

What does *holy* mean? When the angels cry "Holy, holy, holy is the LORD Almighty" (Isa. 6:3; cf. Rev. 4:8), do they mean "Moral, moral, moral is the LORD Almighty"? Or "Separate, separate, separate is the LORD Almighty"? Just to ask such questions demonstrates how inadequate such common definitions of *holy* really are.

At its core, *holy* is almost an adjective corresponding to the noun *God*. God is God; God is holy. He is unique; there is no other. Then, derivatively, that which belongs exclusively to him is designated *holy*. These may be things as easily as people: certain censers are holy; certain priestly garments are holy; certain accouterments are holy, not because they are moral, and certainly not because they are themselves divine, but because in this derivative sense they are restricted in their use to God and his purposes, and thus are *separate* from other use. When people are holy, they are holy for the same reason: they belong to God, serve him and function with respect to his purposes. (Occasionally in the Old Testament there is a further extension of the term to refer to the realm of the sacred, such that even pagan priests can in this sense be called *holy*. But this further extension does not concern us here.)

If people conduct themselves in a certain way because they belong to God, we *may* say that their conduct is moral. When Peter quotes these words, "Be holy, because I am holy" (1 Peter 1:16), the entailment, in his context, is a turning away from "evil desires" (1:14) and living life "in reverent fear" (1:17). But it is no accident that these words in Leviticus 11 are found not in a context of *moral* commands and prohibitions but of *ceremonial* restrictions dealing with clean and unclean foods. For belonging to God, living on his terms, reserving ourselves for him, delighting in him, obeying him, honoring him—these are more *fundamental* than the specifics of obedience that we label *moral* or *ceremonial*.

Indeed, this stance is so basic in God's universe that only the fool says, "There is no God" (Ps. 14:1). This is the precise opposite of holiness, the most conspicuous and fundamental demonstration, "They are corrupt, their deeds are vile" (14:1).

Leviticus 13; Psalms 15—16; Proverbs 27; 2 Thessalonians 1

OBSERVE THE PATTERN OF CAPITAL LETTERS: "I said to the LORD, 'You are my Lord; apart from you I have no good thing'" (**Ps. 16:2**). In other words, addressing Yahweh ("LORD"), David confesses him "Lord," his Master; then he adds, "Apart from you I have no good thing."

(1) Looked at one way, these words delimit what is good, and thereby almost define the good. Nothing is ultimately good if it is abstracted from God. It may be good in a relative sense, of course. The Lord made the sun and pronounced it good, and good it is: it provides all of this world's energy. Yet abstracted from the knowledge of God, it became an object of worship among many ancient peoples (called Ra in Egypt—and the covenant community itself could get caught up in syncretistic sun worship, Ezek. 8:16), and attracts a different kind of sun worshiper today. We may enjoy reasonably good health; surely that is a good thing. But suppose we use our energy to do what is selfish or evil, or deploy the blessings the Lord entrusts to us simply to order our lives as autonomously as possible? Apart from the Lord, we "have no good thing."

(2) Looked at another way, the text is literally true. Since God is the Creator of all, then no good thing that we enjoy has come to us apart from him. "Every good and perfect gift is from above," James writes (1:17). Paul asks, "What do you have that you did not receive? And if you did receive it, why do you boast as though you did not?" (1 Cor. 4:7). So our first order of business ought to be gratitude. Apart from the Lord, we "have no good thing."

(3) Yet the text is certainly more visceral than that. Its tone is closer to the words of Asaph: "Whom have I in heaven but you? And earth has nothing I desire besides you. My flesh and my heart may fail, but God is the strength of my heart and my portion forever" (Ps. 73:25-26). In comparison with knowledge of our Maker and Redeemer, nothing else is worth very much, whether in this life or in the life to come. Apart from the Lord, we "have no good thing."

(4) The text will trigger in some minds other "apart from" passages. Perhaps the best known is John 15:5, where Jesus says, "I am the vine; you are the branches. If a man remains in me and I in him, he will bear much fruit; *apart from me* you can do nothing" (italics added). Apart from the vine, we branches bear no fruit; and apart from him we "have no good thing."

Leviticus 14; Psalm 17; Proverbs 28; 2 Thessalonians 2

∾

PSALM 17 IS A PRAYER FOR VINDICATION. Certainly David knows that he is not always righteous (see Ps. 51!). But in particular circumstances, the believing man or woman may well be certain that he or she has acted with utter integrity, with transparent righteousness. That is the case with David here. If in such instances opponents lie about you or set up a whisper campaign, if like a lion on the prowl they try to hunt you down (17:10-12), what are the righteous to do?

The first thing necessary is a humble pursuit of the God who vindicates. Indeed, David hopes not only for ultimate vindication, but for something more immediate: "Rise up, O LORD, confront them, bring them down; rescue me from the wicked by your sword" (17:13). Even so, he recognizes that to ask for vindication from this sort of God places him on the side of those who do *not* simply belong to this world: "O LORD, by your hand save me from such men, *from men of this world* whose reward is in this life" (17:14, italics added).

Since God remains sovereign, vindication can only finally come from God: "May my vindication come from you; may your eyes see what is right" (17:2). Indeed, David appeals to God's faithful love for his own: "Show the wonder of your great love, you who save by your right hand those who take refuge in you from their foes" (17:7).

These are all important lessons, repeated, in whole or in part, many times in the Bible. Thus we find the apostle Paul telling the Roman believers, "Do not repay anyone evil for evil. Be careful to do what is right in the eyes of everybody. If it is possible, as far as it depends on you, live at peace with everyone. *Do not take revenge, my friends, but leave room for God's wrath, for it is written: 'It is mine to avenge; I will repay'* [Deut. 32:35], says the Lord" (Rom. 12:17-19, italics added).

This is a lesson believers must constantly relearn and apply to themselves. It is easy enough to absorb it when things are going well. But when church members are unfairly attacking your ministry, when gossips are undermining your position in the company for their own advantage, when colleagues in the university department invariably attach the ugliest motives to everything you say and do—that is the test for leaving things in the hands of the God whose care for his own and whose passion for justice ensure final vindication.

And such faith brings us relief from stress: "And I—in righteousness I will see your face; when I awake, I will be satisfied with seeing your likeness" (17:15).

∾

Leviticus 15; Psalm 18; Proverbs 29; 2 Thessalonians 3

∽

DAVID WROTE PSALM 18 after the Lord had delivered him from the hand of Saul and all his enemies. It is a joyous, grateful psalm. Some of the same themes we found in Psalms 16 and 17 are repeated here. But among the new elements in this psalm are the following.

First, the language of this psalm abounds in colorful nature metaphors (especially in vv. 7-15)—a fairly common feature of Hebrew poetry. When God answered, "the earth trembled and quaked, and the foundations of the mountains shook"; "smoke rose from his nostrils," and fire from his mouth. "He parted the heavens and came down; dark clouds were under his feet" (18:7-9); alternatively, "He mounted the cherubim and flew; he soared on the wings of the wind" (18:10). "The LORD thundered from heaven," his voice resounded; "he shot his arrows . . . great bolts of lightning." The "valleys of the sea were exposed" at the blast from the Lord's nostrils (18:13-14).

This is marvelous. Just because these are not the metaphors we commonly use today does not mean we cannot appreciate them, or grasp what the psalmist is telling us. God's power is ineffable; he controls even nature itself, which simply does his bidding; the most terrifying displays of power in nature are nothing more than the results of his commands. The metaphorical language can extend to how the Lord rescued David: "he drew me out of deep waters" (18:16)—though of course David was not in danger of literal drowning. But it must have felt like it more than once, when Saul and the army were hot on his trail.

Second, while many lines in this psalm describe in wonderful, sometimes metaphorical language how God has helped David, others picture God strengthening David to enable him to do what he had to do. "With your help I can advance against a troop; with my God I can scale a wall" (18:29). "It is God who arms me with strength and makes my way perfect. He makes my feet like the feet of a deer; he enables me to stand on the heights. He trains my hands for battle; my arms can bend a bow of bronze. You give me your shield of victory, and your right hand sustains me; you stoop down to make me great" (18:32-35).

Perhaps God does not strengthen *us* to make war. But in a theistic universe, we confess God gives us strength to write computer programs, to sort out administrative problems, to change yet another diaper, to study the Greek text of the New Testament, to bear up under insult.

"The LORD lives! Praise be to my Rock! Exalted be God my Savior!" (18:46).

∽

Leviticus 16; Psalm 19; Proverbs 30; 1 Timothy 1

GOD IS SO WONDERFULLY GENEROUS in his self-disclosure. He has not revealed himself to this race of rebels in some stinting way, but in nature, by his Spirit, in his Word, in great events in redemptive history, in institutions that he ordained to unveil his purposes and his nature, even in our very makeup. (We bear the *imago Dei.*) **Psalm 19** depicts two of these avenues of divine self-disclosure.

The *first* is nature, or more precisely, one part of nature, the heavenly host observed and enjoyed by all of us. "The heavens declare the glory of God; the skies proclaim the work of his hands. Day after day they pour forth speech; night after night they display knowledge" (19:1-2). But just as ancient peoples manufactured complex myths to explain the sun, the moon, and the stars, the shame of our culture is that we manufacture complex "scientific" myths to explain them as well. Of course, our knowledge of how things really are is more advanced and accurate than theirs. But our deep-seated philosophical commitment to the notion of random, purposeless, mindless, accidental, "steady-state" origination of everything is horribly perverse—anything to avoid the far more obvious conclusion of a supremely intelligent God capable of spectacularly wonderful design. The evidence is there; the celestial host "pour forth speech; night after night they display knowledge."

The *second* is "the law of the LORD": perfect, trustworthy, right, pure, righteous, radiant, reviving the soul, making wise the simple, giving joy to the heart, enduring forever, more precious than gold, sweeter than honey, warning, promising great reward (19:7-11). Here too we manage to trim and silence what God has revealed. Great scholars invest wasted lives in undermining its credibility. Many people choose snippets and themes that soon constitute a grid for eliminating the rest. Cultural drift constructs new epistemologies that relativize God's words so that they are no more revelatory than the source documents of any other religion. Worst of all, Christians invest so little time and energy in learning what they claim to be the Word of God that it falls away by default. Yet it remains an unimaginably glorious revelation.

Leviticus 16 depicts another avenue of revelation. God graciously instituted an annual ritual under the old covenant that depicted fundamental principles of what he is like and what is acceptable to him. Guilty sinners may approach him through a mediator and a blood sacrifice that he prescribes: the Day of Atonement is both ritual and prophecy (cf. Heb. 9:11—10:18).

Respond with the psalmist: "May the words of my mouth and the meditation of my heart be pleasing in your sight, O LORD, my Rock and my Redeemer" (19:14).

Leviticus 17; Psalms 20—21; Proverbs 31; 1 Timothy 2

∾

TWO SPECIFICATIONS IN LEVITICUS 17 constrained the ancient Israelite who wished to remain faithful to the covenant.

The *first* (17:1-9) limited sacrifices to what the Mosaic Covenant mandates and sanctions. Apparently some Israelites were offering sacrifices in the open fields, wherever they happened to be (17:5). Doubtless some of these were genuinely offered up to the Lord; others easily slid into syncretistic offerings devoted to local pagan deities (17:7). To bring sacrificial practice under the discipline of the tabernacle (and later the temple) was designed simultaneously to eliminate syncretism and to train up the people in the theological structures inherent in the Mosaic Covenant. Out there in the field it was all too easy to assume that these religious observances would win the favor of God (or the gods!), thereby securing good crops and nice kids. The tabernacle/temple system ideally brought the people under the tutelage of the Levites, teaching the people a better way. God himself had mandated this system. Only prescribed mediators and sacrifices were acceptable. The entire structure was designed to enhance the transcendence of God, to establish and clarify the sheer ugliness and vileness of sin, to demonstrate that a person could be accepted by God only if that sin were atoned for. Moreover, the system had two further advantages. It brought the people together for the thrice-annual festivals in Jerusalem, securing the cohesion of the covenant people; and it prepared the way for the supreme sacrifice in annual sacrifices that trained generations of believers that sin must be paid for in the way God himself prescribes, or there is no hope for any of us.

The *second* constraint imposed by this chapter (17:10-16) is the prohibition against eating blood. The reason given is specific: "For the life of a creature is in the blood, and I have given it to you to make atonement for yourselves on the altar; it is the blood that makes atonement for one's life" (17:11). The passage does not ascribe magical powers to blood. After all, the life is not in the blood *apart* from the rest of the body, and the strong prohibition against eating blood could never be *perfectly* carried out (since no matter how carefully you drain the blood from an animal there is always a little left). The point is that there is no life in the body where there is no blood; it is the obvious physical element for symbolizing the life itself. To teach the people how only the sacrifice of *life* could atone for sin—since the punishment of sin is death—it is difficult to imagine a more effective prohibition. We recall its significance every time we participate in the Lord's Table.

∾

Leviticus 18; Psalm 22; Ecclesiastes 1; 1 Timothy 3

∾

THE BEGINNING OF THE SO-CALLED "HOLINESS CODE" (**Lev. 18**) is full of interest. We should take note of at least four things:

(1) Just because this is the first time that some prohibitions have been articulated in the Bible does not necessarily mean that this is the first time anyone thought of them, or condemned the practices in question. Before murder is actually prohibited as such, Cain commits it, is condemned for it, and is punished. The same is true for many actions treated in the Law of Moses. Much of the Law of God is written on the human conscience, so that societies without Scripture erect moral structures which, however different from the values of Scripture, overlap with Scripture in important and revealing ways. Similarly, many of the prohibitions of sexual alignments listed here were doubtless already frowned upon; now their prohibition is codified.

(2) As usual, the commandments in this chapter are tied to the person and character of God (18:2-4, 21, 30), the Exodus (18:3), and the sanctions of the covenant (18:29).

(3) Many prohibitions in this chapter establish barriers in sexual relations: a man is not to have sexual relations with his mother or stepmother, sister or half sister, granddaughter, aunt, daughter-in-law, sister-in-law, and so forth. Homosexuality is "detestable" (18:22); bestiality is "a perversion" (18:23). Tied to this list is the prohibition against sacrificing any of your children to the horrible god Molech, who demanded that some be burned in sacrifice (18:21); perhaps the common point is family integrity. Another striking element in this chapter is the fact that the perversions are prohibited in Israel so that this fledgling nation does not become as debauched as those they are about to displace—lest they head in that same direction and are vomited out of the land (18:24-30). The shadow of the exile hangs over the horizon before the people even enter the land.

(4) Intriguingly, Leviticus 18:5 is cited in Romans 10:5 and Galatians 3:10. The general point in both passages is the same. The "Law," i.e., the law-covenant, is grounded in demand: keep God's decrees and laws, and live. This is not to say that faith isn't required, still less that the Old Testament covenant is not characterized by grace (not least in the sacrificial system, such that those who breached the covenant had a recourse to find a way back). But its heartbeat is demand. By contrast, the heartbeat of the new covenant, like the covenant with Abraham, is above all characterized by faith (whatever its demands). Whatever the overlap, the distinctive heartbeat of the two covenants must not be confused.

∾

Leviticus 19; Psalms 23—24; Ecclesiastes 2; 1 Timothy 4

ॐ

PERHAPS THE MOST STRIKING FEATURE OF LEVITICUS 19 is the repeated clause, "I am the LORD." In each case, it provides the *reason why* the Israelites are to obey the particular command.

Each must respect his mother and father, and must obey God's Sabbaths: "I am the LORD" (19:3). They are not to succumb to idolatry: "I am the LORD" (19:4). When they harvest, they are to leave enough of the produce behind that the poor may find something to eat: "I am the LORD" (19:10). They are not to swear falsely using the name of God: "I am the LORD" (19:12). They are not to play foul jokes on the handicapped, such as cursing the deaf or putting a stumbling block in front of the blind: "I am the LORD" (19:14). They are not to take any action that endangers a neighbor's life: "I am the LORD" (19:16). They are neither to seek revenge nor bear a grudge against a neighbor, but each is to love his neighbor as himself: "I am the LORD" (19:18). Upon entering the Promised Land, after planting any fruit tree they are not to eat its fruit for three years, and then must offer all the fruit to the Lord in the fourth year, before eating the fruit from the fifth year onward: "I am the LORD" (19:23-25). They are not to mutilate or tattoo their bodies: "I am the LORD" (19:28). They are to observe God's Sabbaths and have reverence for his sanctuary: "I am the LORD" (19:30). They are not to resort to mediums or spiritists: "I am the LORD" (19:31). They are to rise in the presence of the aged, show respect for the elderly, and revere God: "I am the LORD" (19:32). Foreigners resident in the land must be treated as one of the native-born: "I am the LORD" (19:33-34). Business standards must be aboveboard: "I am the LORD" (19:35-36).

Although some of the commandments and prohibitions in this chapter do *not* end with this formula, they are nevertheless blessed with the same motive, for the closing verse wraps the chapter up: "Keep all my decrees and all my laws and follow them. I am the LORD" (19:37).

Moreover, judging by the opening verse of the chapter, the formula "I am the LORD" is in fact a reminder of something longer: "Speak to the entire assembly of Israel and say to them: 'Be holy because I, the LORD your God, am holy'" (19:1). We have already meditated a little on what *holy* means (cf. April 8). Here, what is striking is that many of these commandments are social in their effect (honesty, generosity, integrity, and so forth); yet the Lord's holiness is the fundamental warrant for them. For the covenant people of God, the highest motives are bound up with pleasing him and fearing his sanctions.

ॐ

Leviticus 20; Psalm 25; Ecclesiastes 3; 1 Timothy 5

ONE OF THE STARTLING FEATURES OF **PSALM 25** is the diversity of needs David asks the Lord to address.

David is in danger of being overwhelmed by enemies and thereby put to shame (Ps. 25:2). He wishes to learn the ways and paths of God, to be taught God's truth (25:4-5). He begs that God will forget the sins of his rebellious youth (25:7); moreover, he recognizes that there are times when his iniquity is great, and needs to be forgiven (25:11). David confesses that he is lonely and afflicted, full of anguish (25:16-17). He speaks afresh of his affliction and distress, alludes once again to his sins, and feels threatened by the increase of the enemies who hate him (25:18-19). Moreover, judging by the last verse (25:22), it is quite possible that David recognized that his own crises and failures had a bearing on the well-being of the people he served as king; so his prayer embraces them as well.

It is of course important to reflect on how the Lord God graciously helps his covenant people in an extraordinary diversity of ways. Yet here I wish to point out something a little different, viz. how so many of the ills and crises that afflict us are bound up with each other. The various things that David mentions are not discreet items on a list. They are tied together in various ways.

For example, when David prays that his enemies will not put him to shame, he recognizes that God alone is the final arbiter, so that in the end all will be put to shame who are "treacherous without excuse" (25:3). But that means that David himself must learn God's ways and God's truth; he needs his own sins forgiven. He must in humility keep the covenant (25:9-10), properly fearing the Lord (25:12, 14). Because of the trouble he is suffering, he is not only afflicted but lonely (25:16)—anguish in one arena so often breeds a sense of desperate isolation, even alienation. Yet the final petitions of the psalm do not descend into a wallowing self-pity, but sum up the connections already made: David needs release from his enemies, forgiveness for his sins, relief from his affliction, and personal integrity and uprightness, all bound up with the protection of the Lord God himself.

Here is a wholesome self-awareness. Sometimes our prayers for relief from loneliness are steeped in self-love; sometimes our requests for justice fail to recognize how endemic sin really is, so that we remain unconcerned about our own iniquity. Yet here is a man who not only knew God and how to pray, but knew himself.

Leviticus 21; Psalms 26—27; Ecclesiastes 4; 1 Timothy 6

"ONE THING I ASK OF THE LORD, this is what I seek: that I may dwell in the house of the LORD all the days of my life, to gaze upon the beauty of the LORD and to seek him in his temple" (**Ps. 27:4**). This glorious stance finds parallels elsewhere. Thus in Psalm 84:10-11 the psalmist declares, "Better is one day in your courts than a thousand elsewhere; I would rather be a doorkeeper in the house of my God than dwell in the tents of the wicked. For the LORD God is a sun and shield; the Lord bestows favor and honor; no good thing does he withhold from those whose walk is blameless."

This is not quite the same as saying that the psalmist wants to spend all his time in church. The temple was more than a church building, and synagogue buildings had not yet been invented. This was a way of saying that the psalmist wanted to spend all his time in the presence and blessing of the living God of the covenant, the God who supremely manifested himself in the city he had designated and the temple whose essential design he had stipulated. This necessarily included all the temple liturgy and rites, but it wasn't a fine sense of religious aesthetics that drove the psalmist. It is nothing less than an overwhelming sense of the sheer beauty of the Lord.

But there are two further connections to be observed:

(1) The psalmist's longing is expressed in terms of intentional choice: "this is what *I seek*" (27:4, italics added); "*Better* is one day in your courts than a thousand elsewhere; I would *rather* be a doorkeeper in the house of my God than dwell in the tents of the wicked" (84:10, italics added). The psalmist expresses his desire and his preference, and in both cases his focus is God himself. We will not really understand him unless, in God's grace, we share that focus.

(2) The psalmist recognizes that there is in this stance abundant security for him. While it is good to worship God and delight in his presence simply because God is God, and he is good and glorious; yet at the same time it is also right to recognize that our own security is bound up with resting in this God. David wishes "to gaze upon the beauty of the LORD and to seek him in his temple," *for* "in the day of trouble he will keep me safe in his dwelling; he will hide me in the shelter of his tabernacle and set me high upon a rock" (27:4-5). "I would rather be a doorkeeper in the house of my God," we read, *for* "the LORD God is a sun and shield" (84:10-11).

Leviticus 22; Psalms 28—29; Ecclesiastes 5; 2 Timothy 1

∾

THE OPENING VERSES OF **PSALM 29** SUGGEST that a great part of what it means to "worship the LORD in the splendor of his holiness" is to ascribe to him the praise that is his due: ascribe to him glory and strength, "the glory due his name" (29:1-2).

In this light, the central section of the psalm (29:3-9) is remarkable, for it focuses on just one element in God's activity, viz. the voice of the Lord. "The voice of the LORD is over the waters"—possibly an allusion both to the original creation, when God simply "spoke" and the universe came into being and took form, and to the spectacular deliverance when God parted the Red Sea, but also to every storm-swept current; "the God of glory thunders, the LORD thunders over the mighty waters." The voice of the Lord is both powerful and majestic. It "breaks in pieces the cedars of Lebanon," proverbial for their size and strength—an allusion to the unleashed storms that God's voice calls forth. Indeed, this is nothing to him, for nations and mountains alike perform his bidding, and all of them hear the thunder of his voice in the storm that traverses from Lebanon in the north to Kadesh in the south.

The secularist looks at a storm and thinks exclusively of the physical properties that have brought it about. The believer understands that those properties have been built into the material world by its Creator, and that God himself speaks in thunder and lightning. The only proper response is to gather in his temple, and in a spirit of mingled awe and humility cry, *Glory!*" (29:9).

Small wonder that the psalm ends (29:10-11) by focusing on the universal reign of God: "the LORD is enthroned as King forever," whether at the time of the deluge (the Hebrew word for "flood" in this passage is found only here and in Gen. 6—11)—the very deluge that most powerfully demonstrated God's power to deploy the forces of "nature" as he sees fit—or in the perpetual blessings and strength God confers on his people.

Isaiah foresees the day when the "Root of Jesse will stand as a banner for the peoples," when the nations will rally to him and his place of rest will be, literally, *"the glory"* (Isa. 11:10). When Stephen, the first Christian martyr, was about to be sent into eternity by the furious mob, his eyes were opened, and he looked up to heaven and saw *"the glory* of God, and Jesus standing at the right hand of God" (Acts 7:55).

His is the final voice of God; he is the Word of God. "Ascribe to the LORD glory and strength" (29:1). Let all cry, "Glory!"

∾

Leviticus 23; Psalm 30; Ecclesiastes 6; 2 Timothy 2

LEVITICUS 23 PROVIDES A description of the principal "appointed feasts" (23:2). These include the Sabbath, which of course could not be observed by taking a pilgrimage to Jerusalem. The remaining feasts mentioned, however, are bound up with the temple in Jerusalem. There are three such feasts, along with the related celebrations tied to the principal three. (In later times Jews added a fourth feast.)

Apart from the Sabbath itself, the *first* "appointed feast" (or pair of appointed feasts) was the Passover coupled with the Feast of Unleavened Bread. The "Lord's Passover" began at dusk on the fourteenth day of the first Jewish month (Nisan), when the Passover meal was actually eaten, and the people gathered to remember the Lord's spectacular rescue of them from Egypt. The next day began the weeklong Feast of Unleavened Bread, a reminder not only of the rapid flight from Egypt, but of the Lord's injunction to put aside all yeast for that period of time—a symbol of putting aside all evil. The first and seventh days were to be free from work and solemnized by sacred assemblies.

The Firstfruits festival (23:9-14), followed by the Feast of Weeks (23:15-22)—the seven weeks immediately after Firstfruits, culminating on the fiftieth day by a sacred assembly—was a powerful way, especially in a highly agrarian society, to remember that God alone provides us with all we need to live. It was a way of publicly bearing witness to our dependence on God, of expressing our individual and corporate thanksgiving to our Maker and Sustainer. There are slight analogues in countries like England and Canada in "Harvest Sunday" festivals and Canadian Thanksgiving. (The American Thanksgiving is partly a harvest festival, but is freighted with substantial symbolism to do with finding freedom in a new land.) But no festival of thanksgiving can be more valuable than the quality and extent of the thankfulness of the people who participate.

On the first day of the seventh Jewish month, another sacred assembly, the Feast of Trumpets, commemorated with trumpet blasts (23:23-25), anticipated *Yom Kippur*—the Day of Atonement (23:26-33)—which fell on the tenth day of the seventh month. This was the day the high priest entered the Most Holy Place, with the prescribed blood, to cover both his own sins and the sins of the people (cf. comments on April 12). The fifteenth day of that month began the eight-day Feast of Booths (23:33-36), when the people were to live in "booths" or "tabernacles," huts and tents, to remind themselves of the pilgrimage years before they entered into the Promised Land.

How should the people of the new covenant remember and commemorate the provisions of our great covenantal God?

Leviticus 24; Psalm 31; Ecclesiastes 7; 2 Timothy 3

DAVID WAS IN DEEP TROUBLE. The exact circumstances may be obscure to us, as we who live three thousand years later probe the details. But we do know that David was shut up in a besieged city (**Ps. 31:21**) and felt trapped. He was so threatened that he flirted with despair. And that is when he felt abandoned by God himself: "In my alarm I said, 'I am cut off from your sight!'" (31:22).

That is the worst despair of all—to feel that God has abandoned you. It was part of Job's torment. Job felt he could mount a case in his own defense, if only he could find God long enough to argue with him. But the heavens were silent, and the silence multiplied his despair.

We have already reflected on the fact that it was fear of being abandoned by God that kept Jacob wrestling with the unknown man in the darkness (Gen. 32:22-32) and kept Moses pressing God to abandon his threat to remain outside the camp of the rebellious Israelites (Ex. 32—34). In a theistic universe, there can be nothing worse than being truly abandoned by God himself. The worst of hell's torments is that men and women are truly abandoned by God. "Abandon hope, all ye who enter here."

Yet the sad reality is that we who bear God's image oscillate between fearing abandonment by God, and wanting to escape from his presence. The same David who wrote this psalm was not particularly eager to delight in the presence of God when he was lusting after Bathsheba and plotting to murder her husband. Too often we would like God to look the other way when we hanker to thumb our noses at him and insist on following our own paths, and we would like God to demonstrate his presence and his glory to us, and certainly get us out of trouble, when we find ourselves in desperate straits.

What an incalculable blessing that God is better than our fears. He does not owe us succor, relief, or rescue. Even our cries of alarm—"I am cut off from your sight!"—may have more to do with desperate unbelief than with candid pleas for help. But David's experience may prove an encouragement to us, for he quickly pens two more lines: "Yet you heard my cry for mercy when I called to you for help" (31:22).

> Love the LORD, all his saints!
> The LORD preserves the faithful,
> but the proud he pays back in full.
> Be strong and take heart,
> all you who hope in the LORD. (Ps. 31:23-24)

Leviticus 25; Psalm 32; Ecclesiastes 8; 2 Timothy 4

∿

"BLESSED IS HE WHOSE TRANSGRESSIONS ARE FORGIVEN, whose sins are covered. Blessed is the man whose sin the LORD does not count against him and in whose spirit is no deceit" (**Ps. 32:1-2**). In a theistic universe where God keeps the books, it is difficult to imagine any greater blessedness.

The sad tragedy is that when many people reflect on this brute fact—that we must give an account to him, and there is no escaping his justice—almost instinctively they do the wrong thing. They resolve to take the path of self-improvement, they turn over a new leaf, they conceal or even deny the sins of frivolous youth. Thus they add to their guilt something additional—the sin of deceit.

We dare not ask for justice—we would be crushed. But how can we hide from the God who sees everything? That is self-delusion. There is only one way forward that does not destroy us: we must be *forgiven*. "Blessed is he whose transgressions are *forgiven*." And what is bound up with such forgiveness? For a start, such a person will not pretend there are no sins to forgive: blessed is the man "in whose spirit is no deceit."

That is why the ensuing verses speak so candidly of confession (32:3-5). It was when David "kept silent" (i.e., about his sins) that his "bones wasted away"; his anguish was so overwhelming it brought wretched physical pain. David writhed under the sense that God himself was against him: "For day and night your hand was heavy upon me; my strength was sapped as in the heat of summer" (32:4).

The glorious solution? "Then I acknowledged my sin to you and did not cover up my iniquity. I said, 'I will confess my trangressions to the LORD'—and you forgave the guilt of my sin" (32:5).

The New Testament writer closest to saying the same thing is John in his first letter (1 John 1:8-9). Writing to believers, John says, "If we claim to be without sin, we deceive ourselves and the truth is not in us." There it is again: the self-deception bound up with denying our sinfulness. "If we confess our sins, he is faithful and just and will forgive us our sins and purify us from all unrighteousness." There it is again: the only remedy to human guilt. This God forgives us, not because he is indulgent or too lazy to be careful, but because we have confessed our sin, and above all, because he is "faithful and just": "faithful" to the covenant he has established, "just" so as not to condemn us when Jesus himself is the propitiation for our sins (2:2).

∿

Leviticus 26; Psalm 33; Ecclesiastes 9; Titus 1

∾

ONE OF THE COMMON FEATURES of ancient suzerainty treaties—treaties between some regional superpower and a vassal state (see March 13)—was some section near the end that spelled out the advantages of compliance and the dangers of noncompliance. Inevitably, these blessings and curses were primarily promised the vassal states.

In many respects, **Leviticus 26** mirrors this ancient pattern, promising blessings for obedience (i.e., for compliance with the covenant) and punishment for disobedience (i.e., for noncompliance with the covenant). The pattern is repeated, somewhat modified, for the covenant renewal in Deuteronomy (see especially Deut. 27—30).

We must not think of the alternatives offered in this chapter as promises made to mere individuals, still less as a simple scheme for acquiring eternal life. That the promises are not individualistic is demonstrated by the nature of many of the blessings and curses. When God sends rain, for instance, he does not send it on discrete individuals, but on regions, in this case on the nation, the covenant community; and similarly when God sends plague, or sends his people into exile. The same evidence shows that what is at stake is not in the first instance the acquiring of eternal life, but the well-being of the covenant community in terms of the blessings promised them.

Nevertheless, we may reflect on two of the many parallels between these old covenant sanctions and what still pertains under the new covenant.

First, obedience is still required under the new covenant, even though some of the stipulations to be obeyed have changed. It is therefore not surprising that John 3:36 contrasts the person who *believes* in the Son with the one who *disobeys* (NIV: *rejects*) him. Those who persist in gross sin are specifically said to be excluded from the kingdom (1 Cor. 6:9-11). The Apocalypse repeatedly contrasts those who "overcome" (i.e., in fidelity to Christ Jesus) with those who are cowardly, unbelieving, vile (e.g., Rev. 21:7-8). The undergirding reason is that the new covenant provides for a new nature. Though we do not achieve perfection until the consummation, an utter lack of transformation under the terms of such a covenant is unthinkable. The result is that judgment is spelled out on both unbelief and disobedience; the two hang together.

Second, one of the striking features of the punishments listed in Leviticus 26 is how God gradually ratchets them up, culminating finally in exile. Disease, drought, military reverses, plague, the dreadful famine of siege conditions (26:29), and even a sovereignly induced fearfulness (26:36) all take their toll. The Lord's forbearance with covenant-breakers, over generations of delayed judgment, is massive. But the only real solution is confession of sin and renewal of the covenant (26:40-42).

∾

Leviticus 27; Psalm 34; Ecclesiastes 10; Titus 2

∾

ONE OF THE INEVITABLE CHARACTERISTICS of those who genuinely praise the Lord is that they want others to join with them in their praise. They recognize that if God is the sort of God their praises say he is, then he *ought* to be recognized by others. Moreover, one of the reasons for praising the Lord is to thank him for the help he has provided. If then we see others in need of the same sort of help, isn't it natural for us to share our own experience of God's provision, in the hope that others will seek God's help? And will this not result in an enlarging circle of praise?

It is wonderful to hear David say, "I will extol the LORD at all times; his praise will always be on my lips" (**Ps. 34:1**). But he also invites others, first to share the Lord's goodness, and then to participate in praise. Hence we read, first, "My soul will boast in the LORD; let the afflicted hear and rejoice" (34:2). The afflicted need to learn from the answers to prayer that David has experienced, and which he will shortly detail. And second, the broad invitation to expand the circle of praise follows: "Glorify the LORD with me; let us exalt his name together" (34:3).

The next lines find David testifying to his own experience of God's grace (34:4-7). The succeeding section is an earnest exhortation to others to trust and follow this same God (34:8-14), and the remainder of the psalm is devoted to extolling the Lord's righteousness, which ensures he is attentive to the cries of the righteous and sets his face against those who do evil (34:15-22).

God, David insists, did actually save him "out of all his troubles" (34:6). That is objective fact. Whether he can be seen or not, the "angel of the LORD encamps around those who fear him, and he delivers them" (34:7). But in addition to the troubles through which we pass, sometimes more threatening, certainly no less damaging, are the fears that attend them. Fear makes us lose perspective, doubt God's faithfulness, question the value of the fight. Fear induces stress, bitterness, cowardice, and folly. But David's testimony is a wonderful encouragement: "I sought the LORD and he answered me; he delivered me from all my fears" (34:4). True, the word *fears* could refer to his own psychological terror, or to the things that made him afraid: doubtless the Lord delivered David from both. But that his own outlook was transformed is made clear by the next verse: "Those who look to him are radiant; their faces are never covered with shame" (34:5).

∾

Numbers 1; Psalm 35; Ecclesiastes 11; Titus 3

∾

PSALM 35 IS ONE OF THE PSALMS GIVEN OVER to the theme of vindication (see also the meditation of April 10). They make many Christians uncomfortable. The line between vindication and vindictiveness sometimes seems a little thin. How can the line of reasoning in this psalm ever be made to square with the teaching of the Lord Jesus about turning the other cheek (Matt. 5:38-42)? Isn't there an edge of, say, *nastiness* about the whole thing? After all, David does not just ask that he himself be saved from the ravages of those who are unjustly attacking him (e.g., 35:17, 22-23), he explicitly asks that his enemies "be disgraced and put to shame" (35:4), that they be ruined and ensnared by the very nets they have laid for others (35:8).

Two reflections:

(1) On some occasions David is not speaking only out of a sense of being threatened as an individual, but also out of a sense of his responsibilities as king, as the Lord's anointed servant. If he is being faithful to the covenant, then surely it is the Lord's name that is on the line when God's "son," the Lord's appointed king, is jeopardized. For the Lord "delights in the well-being of his servant" (35:27), and David recognizes that his own preservation is bound up with the well-being of "those who live quietly in the land" (35:20). At issue, then, is public justice, not personal vendetta, against which the Lord Jesus so powerfully contends in the words already quoted.

(2) More importantly, although Christians turn the other cheek, this does not mean they are slack regarding justice. We hold that God is perfectly just, and he is the One who says, "It is mine to avenge; I will repay" (Deut. 32:35). That is why we are to "leave room for God's wrath" (Rom. 12:19). He is the only One who can finally settle the books accurately, and to think otherwise is to pretend that we can take the place of God. All David is asking is that God perform what he himself says he will ultimately do: execute justice, vindicate the righteous, defend the covenantally faithful.

The last chapter of Job is not an anticlimax for just this reason: Job was vindicated. The sufferings of the Lord Jesus fall into the same pattern. He made himself a nobody and suffered the odium of the cross, in obedience to his Father (Phil. 2:6-8), and was supremely vindicated (Phil. 2:9-11). We, too, may suffer injustice and cry for the forgiveness of our tormentors, as Jesus did—even as we also cry that justice may prevail, that God be glorified, that his people be vindicated. This is God's will, and David had it right.

∾

Numbers 2; Psalm 36; Ecclesiastes 12; Philemon

∿

AMONG THE INSIGHTS the Psalms convey, some of the most penetrating deal with the nature of wickedness and of wicked people. Rarely are these put into abstract categories. They are almost always functional and relational.

What lies at the heart of the "sinfulness of the wicked"? "There is no fear of God before his eyes" (**Ps. 36:1**). This means something more than that the wicked person is foolishly unafraid of the punishment that God will finally mete out (though it does not mean less than that). It means that the wicked are so blind that they do not see the ultimate realities. They either do not see God at all, or, scarcely less horribly, they do not see God as he is.

All appropriate behavior and outlook for human beings made in the image of God find their reference point and measure in God himself. The fear of the Lord is the beginning of both knowledge (Prov. 1:7) and wisdom (Prov. 9:10), for "knowledge of the Holy One is understanding" (Prov. 9:10). The converse is utter folly: "fools despise wisdom and discipline" (Prov. 1:7). Small wonder the psalmist insists that it is the fool who says, "There is no God" (Ps. 14:1). Scarcely less foolish is the conjuring up of domesticated gods we can manage, or of savage gods that are brutal and immoral, or of impersonal gods that depersonalize God's image-bearers. When one is blind to the true God, including his glorious holiness that must rightly instill fear in image-bearers as rebellious as we, there is no stopping place in our descent into the abyss of folly.

The blindness of the wicked extends to their assessment of themselves. "For in his own eyes he flatters himself too much to detect or hate his sin" (Ps. 36:2). If he could see well enough to detect his sin, to see it for what it is—rebellion against the living God—and hate it for its sheer vileness and utter arrogance before the majestic holiness of his Maker, inevitably he would also fear God. The twin blindnesses are one.

This, of course, is why philosophical debates about the existence of God can never be resolved by reason alone. It is not that God is unreasonable, still less that he has left himself without witness. Rather, the tragedy and ignominy of human sin leave us, apart from God's grace, horribly blind. Yet this blindness is *culpable* blindness: the *wicked* have no fear of God before their eyes. Paul understands the point so well that he makes this the culminating proof-text in his proof of human lostness (Rom. 3:18). Thank God for the next thirteen verses the apostle pens.

∿

Numbers 3; Psalm 37; Song of Songs 1; Hebrews 1

∾

FROM SINAI ON, the Levites are treated differently from the other tribes: they alone handle the tabernacle and its accoutrements, from them come the priests, they are not given a separate allotment of land but are dispersed throughout the nation, and so forth. But here in **Numbers 3**, one of the most startling distinctives is portrayed.

All the males one month of age and up from the tribe of Levi were counted. Their total was 22,000 (3:39). Then all the *firstborn* males one month of age and up from the rest of the Israelites were counted. Their total was 22,273 (3:43): the differential between the two figures is 273. God declares that because he spared all the Israelite firstborn at the first Passover in Egypt, the firstborn are peculiarly his (3:13). The assumption, of course, is that at one level they too should have died: they were not intrinsically better than the Egyptians who did. They had been protected by the blood of the Passover lamb God had prescribed. Clearly God was not now going to demand the life of all the Israelite firstborn. Instead, he insists that they are all his in a peculiar way—but that he will accept, instead of all the firstborn males of all Israel, all the males of the tribe of Levi. Since the two totals do not exactly coincide, the 273 extra firstborn males from Israel must be redeemed some other way, and so a redemption tax is applied (3:46-48).

There are some lessons to be learned. One of them is intrinsic to the narrative and already noted: the Israelites were not intrinsically superior to the Egyptians, not intrinsically exempt from the wrath of the destroying angel. More importantly, those saved by the blood belong to the Lord in some peculiar way. If God has accepted the blood that was shed in their place, he does not demand that they die: he demands that they live for him and his service. Owing to the covenantal requirements of the Sinai code, a substitution is accepted: the Levites substitute for all the Israelites who should have come under the sweep of the Passover requirement.

The fulfillment of these patterns under the terms of the new covenant is not hard to find. We are saved from death by the death of the supreme Passover Lamb (1 Cor. 5:7). Those saved by his blood belong to the Lord in a peculiar way, i.e., not only by virtue of creation but by virtue of redemption (1 Cor. 6:20). He demands that we live for him and his service, and in this we constitute a nation of priests (1 Peter 2:5-6; Rev. 1:6).

∾

Numbers 4; Psalm 38; Song of Songs 2; Hebrews 2

∾

ONE OF THE MOST ATTRACTIVE FEATURES of David is his candor. At his best he is transparently honest. That means, among other things, that when there is an array of things going wrong in his life he does not collapse them into a single problem.

Nothing could be clearer from **Psalm 38**. Commentators sometimes try to squeeze the diverse elements in this psalm into a single situation, but most such re-creations seem a trifle forced. It is worth identifying some of the most striking components of David's misery.

(1) He is facing God's wrath (38:1), and (2) suffering from an array of physical ailments (38:3-8). (3) As a result he is full of frustrated sighing and has sunk into depression (38:9-10). (4) His friends have abandoned him (38:11). (5) Meanwhile he still faces the plots and deception of his standard (political) enemies (38:12). (6) He is so enfeebled that he is like a deaf mute (38:13-14), unable to speak, for his enemies are numerous and vigorous (38:19). (7) Meanwhile he is painfully troubled by his own iniquity (38:18).

One can imagine various ways to tie these points together, but a fair bit of speculation is necessary. What stands out in this psalm is that even while David is asking for vindication against his enemies, he does so in the context of confessing his own sin, of facing, himself, the wrath of God. It is quite possible that he understands both his physical suffering and even the loss of his friends and the opposition of evil opponents to be expressions of God's wrath—which intrinsically he admits to deserving. In this psalm David does not ask for vindication grounded in his own covenantal fidelity. He frankly confesses his sin (38:18), waits for the Lord (38:15), begs God not to forsake him (38:21), entreats God to help him (38:22) and not to rebuke him in anger and wrath (38:1). In short, David appeals for mercy.

This is another face of the vindication theme (see the meditation for April 24). Yes, we want God to display his justice. In circumstances where we have been frankly wronged, it is comforting to recall that God's justice will ultimately triumph. But what about the times when we are guilty ourselves? Will justice alone suffice? If all we want from God is justice, what human being will survive the divine holocaust?

While pleading for vindication, it is urgently important that we confess our own sin, and entreat God for mercy. For the God of justice is also the God of grace. If this be not so, there is no hope for any of us.

∾

Numbers 5; Psalm 39; Song of Songs 3; Hebrews 3

∾

SELF-DISCIPLINE IS NORMALLY A GOOD THING. Indeed, Christians believe that God has given them "a spirit of power, of love and of self-discipline" (2 Tim. 1:7). But certain forms of self-discipline are ignoble, even dangerous.

For example, the Stoics in the days of the apostle Paul thought that it was the part of wisdom to live in harmony with the way things are in the world, and that this entailed living apart from the "passions," in perfect accord with reason. Motivated by high moral principles, they prided themselves in living above the emotions, above deep personal commitments that could bring suffering. At one level, such "stoicism" is admirable. But it is a long way from the personal commitments that the Gospel mandates, complete with the vulnerability and suffering that are a part of this fallen order. In fact, that is the problem with the Stoic worldview: its view of the world and what is wrong with it is so far removed from what the Bible says that it defines what is good in ways that owe more to a certain kind of pantheism than to anything else. So from a Christian perspective, even if there is something admirable to Stoic self-discipline, it can never be judged genuinely good. Some self-discipline merely puffs people up with the pride of resolution.

Another kind of questionable self-discipline occurs in the opening verses of **Psalm 39**. David has resolved not to speak. It is not entirely clear whether his self-disciplined resolution not to say anything, especially in the presence of the wicked (39:1), is motivated by fear that otherwise he is in danger of joining them, or more likely out of fear that if he speaks he will let slip something that might be dangerous in this company, or simply out of some misplaced conviction that it is enough to keep silent and not lend them support. Clearly, however, it was a moral resolve, in some ways commendable—and wholly inadequate. For as he kept silent, he did not even say anything good (39:2). One way or another he was trying to beat sin by disciplined silence.

David learned a better way. He speaks—but in his speech he addresses God (39:4ff.). He is aware of life's fleeting passage, and concludes that, in the end, we have nothing to look for except to put our hope in the Lord (39:7). God alone can save us from our transgressions and enable us to escape the snares of opponents (39:8). Resolute silence in the face of the mystery of providence is no way forward (39:9); it is a false self-discipline, an ugly defiance rather than a cheerful submission to God's "discipline" (39:11).

∾

Numbers 6; Psalms 40—41; Song of Songs 4; Hebrews 4

∾

THE NAZIRITE VOW (**Num. 6**) could be taken by any man or woman (i.e., not just a Levite) and was entirely voluntary. It was normally undertaken for an extended period of time, and culminated in certain prescribed offerings and sacrifices (6:13-21).

The vow itself was designed to separate someone out for the Lord (6:2, 5-8), a kind of voluntary self-sacrifice. Perhaps it was marked by special service or meditation, but that was not the formal, observable side of the Nazirite vow. The Nazirite was to mark out his or her vow by three abstinences. (1) For the duration of the vow, his or her hair was not to be cut. This was so much a mark of the individual's separation to God that when the vow came to an end, the hair that had grown throughout the duration of the vow was to be cut off and burned in the fellowship offering (6:18). (2) The Nazirite was to keep out of contact with corpses. That could mean real hardship if, for instance, a relative died during the period of the vow. If someone suddenly died in the presence of a Nazirite, the inevitable defilement, which could be construed as defiling the hair that he had dedicated (6:9), had to be removed by prescribed ritual and sacrifice, including shaving off the defiled hair (6:9-12). (3) In addition, the Nazirite was to abstain from all alcohol until the termination of the vow (6:3, 20). This too was something of a privation, for wine was a common drink, not least at the great festivals. (It was common to "cut" wine with water, from between three parts water to one part wine, to ten parts water to one part wine, which made it about the strength of beer.)

The symbolism is reasonably transparent. (1) That which is holy belongs exclusively to the Lord and his use (like the laver or the ephod). The symbol was the hair, dedicated to the Lord and therefore not cut until it was offered in sacrifice. (2) That which is holy belongs to the living God, not to the realm of death and decay, which arise from the horror of sin. So the Nazirites were to abstain from coming into contact with dead persons. (3) That which is holy finds its center and delight in God. It does not need the artificial "high" of alcohol; still less does it want to be controlled by anyone or anything other than God himself.

How, then, shall members of the new covenant, in their call to be holy, dedicate themselves wholly to God, avoid all that belongs to the realm of death, and be slaves to no one and nothing save Jesus?

∾

Numbers 7; Psalms 42—43; Song of Songs 5; Hebrews 5

MILLIONS OF CHRISTIANS HAVE SUNG the words as a chorus. Millions more have meditated on them in their own quiet reading of Scripture: "As the deer pants for streams of water, so my soul pants for you, O God" (**Ps. 42:1**).

It is a haunting image. One pictures the buck or the doe, descending through the forest's perimeter in the half-light of dusk, to slake the thirst of a hot day in the cool waters of a crystal stream. When Christians have applied the image to themselves, they have conjured up a plethora of diverse personal circumstances: semi-mystical longings for a feeling of the transcendent, courageous God-centeredness that flies in the face of cultural opposition, a lonely longing for a sense of God's presence when the heavens seem as bronze, a placid contentment with our own religious experience, and more.

But whatever the possible applications of this haunting image, the situation of the deer—and of the psalmist, too, as we shall see—is full of enormous stress. The deer is not sidling up to the stream for the regular supply of refreshment; it is panting for water. The metrical psalter adds the words, "when heated by the chase"; but there is no hint of that here, and the application the psalmist makes would fit less well than another possibility. The psalmist is thinking of a deer panting for refreshing streams of water during a season of drought and famine (as in Joel 1:20). In the same way, he is hungry for the Lord, famished for the presence of God, and in particular hungry to be back in Jerusalem enjoying temple worship, "leading the procession to the house of God, with shouts of joy and thanksgiving among the festive throng" (42:4). Instead, he finds himself "downcast" (42:5) because he is way up the Jordan Valley, somewhere near the heights of Hermon, in the far north of the country.

Here the psalmist must contend with foes who taunt him, not least regarding his faith. They sneer all day long, "Where is your God?" (42:10). The only thing that will satisfy the psalmist is not, finally, Jerusalem and the temple, but God himself. Wherever he finds himself, the psalmist can still declare, "By day the LORD directs his love, at night his song is with me—a prayer to the God of my life" (42:8). So he encourages himself with these reflections: "Why are you downcast, O my soul? Why so disturbed within me? Put your hope in God, for I will yet praise him, my Savior and my God" (42:11).

Sing the chorus, repeat the ancient lines. And draw comfort when you are fighting the bleak bog of despair, and God seems far away.

Numbers 8; Psalm 44; Song of Songs 6; Hebrews 6

∽

BEFORE THEY BEGAN THEIR DUTIES FOR THE FIRST TIME, the Levites were set apart by a ritual God himself established to "make them ceremonially clean" (**Num. 8:5-14**). The details need not concern us here. What we shall reflect on is the theological reasoning God gives for ordering things this way.

Part of it we have heard before: this is by way of review. God himself has "taken them as my own" (8:16), i.e., he has selected the Levites "from among the other Israelites" (8:6) to be peculiarly his, "in place of the firstborn, the first male offspring from every Israelite woman" (8:16). The rationale is reviewed: this stems from the Exodus, from the first Passover, when the firstborn of the Egyptians were struck down but not the firstborn sons of Israel (8:17-18).

But now a new element is introduced. God has "taken" the Levites to be peculiarly his, and, having "taken" them, he has also "given" them as "gifts" to Aaron and his sons, the chief priests, "to do the work at the Tent of Meeting on behalf of the Israelites and to make atonement for them so that no plague will strike the Israelites when they go near the sanctuary" (8:19). So God has "taken" them and then "given" them to his people.

Formally, of course, God has "given" them to Aaron and his sons, but since the work the Levites do is for the benefit of all Israel, there is a sense in which God has given the Levites to the entire nation. The pattern is spelled out again ten chapters later (Num. 18:5-7). God says to Aaron, "I myself have selected your fellow Levites from among the Israelites as a gift to you" (18:6).

The closest New Testament parallel is found in Ephesians 4. By his death and resurrection, Christ Jesus "led captives in his train and gave gifts to men" (Eph. 4:8). The words are ostensibly quoted from Psalm 68:18, where the Hebrew text says that God *received* gifts *from* men. But it has been argued, rightly, that Psalm 68 assumes such themes as those in Numbers 8 and 18, and that in any case Paul is melding together both Numbers and Psalm 68 to make a point. Under the new covenant, Christ Jesus by his triumph has captured us, and to *each one of us* (Eph. 4:7) he has apportioned grace and then poured us back on the church as his "gifts to men."

That is how we are to think of ourselves. We are Christ's captives, captured from the race of rebellious image-bearers and now poured out as God's "gifts to men." That invests all our service with unimaginable dignity.

∽

Numbers 9; Psalm 45; Song of Songs 7; Hebrews 7

∾

TWO THEMES CONTROL NUMBERS 9. The *second* is the descent of the pillar of cloud and fire onto the tabernacle, the "Tent of the Testimony," the first day it was set up (9:15-23). This pillar had guided and protected the people from the time of their first departure from Egypt. It was the visible sign of God's presence—and from now on it is associated with the tabernacle (and later with the temple). Thus the storyline of the manifestation of the presence of God continues.

But the *first* theme is the celebration of the Passover on the first anniversary of the original Passover (9:1-14). The original Passover, described in Exodus 12, was not only bound up with the Exodus, but was to be commemorated, according to the Mosaic covenant, in well-defined ways (see Ex. 12; Lev. 23:5-8; Deut. 16:1-8). God's instructions to Moses are that the people are to celebrate the Passover "in accordance with all its rules and regulations" (Num. 9:3). But this stipulation precipitates a crisis. Because some of the people had become ceremonially unclean by coming into contact with a dead body (for instance, if a member of their family had died), strictly speaking they could not participate in the Passover feast until they had become ceremonially clean—and that took enough time that they would be unable to celebrate on the prescribed day, the fourteenth of Abib (called Nisan after the exile), the first month in the Jewish calendar.

So Moses consults the Lord. The Lord's answer is that such ceremonially unclean people may postpone their celebration of Passover until the fourteenth of the *second* month. But this postponement, the Lord insists, is *only* for those unable, for ceremonial reasons, to celebrate at the prescribed time. Those who opt for postponement for reasons of personal expediency are to be cut off from the people.

There are many lessons to be learned from this episode, but one of them is sometimes overlooked. In any complex system of laws, sooner or later different laws will lay down competing or even conflicting claims. The result is that such laws must be laid out in some hierarchy of importance. Here the *month* is considered less critical than ceremonial cleanliness or the Passover celebration itself. Jesus himself recognizes the general point. The Law forbids regular work on the Sabbath, and it says a male child should be circumcised on the eighth day. Suppose the eighth day is a Sabbath (John 7:23)? Which takes precedence?

Minds that think *only* on the legal plane may not grasp the direction in which laws point. Organize them aright, Jesus says (and Paul elsewhere makes the same point in other ways), and you discover that they point to him (John 7:24).

∾

Numbers 10; Psalms 46—47; Song of Songs 8; Hebrews 8

∾

A COMMON THEME OF **PSALMS 46** AND **47** is the sovereign authority of God over all the nations. He is not some mere tribal deity. He is the Most High (46:4). Nations may be in an uproar; kingdoms rise and fall. But God needs only to lift his voice, and the earth itself melts away (46:6). By his authority desolation works its catastrophic judgment; by his authority wars cease (46:8-9). The Lord Most High is "the great King over all the earth" (47:2, 7). "God reigns over the nations; God is seated on his holy throne" (47:8).

This ensures the security of the covenant community. The surrounding pagan nations may threaten, but if God is in charge, the covenant people of God can testify, "The LORD Almighty is with us; the God of Jacob is our fortress" (46:7). "He subdued nations under us, peoples under our feet" (47:3). Indeed, as for Jerusalem, the "place where the Most High dwells": "God is within her, she will not fall; God will help her at break of day" (46:4-5).

The psalmist sees at least two further entailments. *First,* sooner or later God "will be exalted among the nations" (46:10). "For God is the King of all the earth" (47:7). These last two references *could* be understood as a threat rather than a promise of blessing: God will be exalted among these pagan nations in exactly the same way he was exalted by destroying the Egyptian army at the Red Sea. But in the light of Psalm 47:9 we would probably be unwise to insist on so negative a reading: "The nobles of the nations assemble as the people of the God of Abraham, for the kings of the earth belong to God; he is greatly exalted." In other words, one of the entailments of monotheism is that God is the God of all, whether acknowledged as such or not. And one day he will be acknowledged by all; in many cases such acknowledgment will be accompanied by worship and adoration, as the nobles of the nations assemble before God exactly as do the people of the God of Abraham. To use Paul's categories, here is the inclusion of Gentiles as Abraham's sons (cf. Rom. 4:11; Gal. 3:7-9). "Be still, and know that I am God; I will be exalted among the nations, I will be exalted in the earth" (46:10).

The *second* entailment is praise. "Come and see the works of the LORD" (Ps. 46:8). "Clap your hands, all you nations; shout to God with cries of joy. How awesome is the LORD Most High, the great King over all the earth!" (47:1-2). "Sing praises to God, sing praises; sing praises to our King, sing praises" (47:6).

∾

Numbers 11; Psalm 48; Isaiah 1; Hebrews 9

∽

ONE OF THE WAYS GOD TALKS ABOUT THE FUTURE IS . . . well, by simply talking about the future. There are places in the Bible where God predicts, in words, what will happen: he *talks* about the future. But he also provides pictures, patterns, types, and models. In these cases he establishes an institution, or a rite, or a pattern of relationships. Then he drops hints, pretty soon a cascade of hints, that these pictures or patterns or types or models are not ends in themselves, but are ways of anticipating something even better. In these cases, then, God talks about the future in pictures.

Christians who read their Bibles a lot ponder the connections between the Davidic kingship and Jesus' kingship, between the Passover lamb and Jesus as "Passover Lamb," between Melchizedek and Jesus, between the Sabbath rest and the rest Jesus gives, between the high priest's role and Jesus' priestly role, between the temple the old covenant priest entered and the heavenly "holy of holies" that Jesus entered, and much more. Of course, for those who lived under the old covenant stipulations, covenantal fidelity *meant* adherence to the institutions and rites God laid down, even while those same institutions and rites, on the broader canonical scale, looked forward to something even better. Through these pictures, God talked about the future. Once a Christian grasps this point, parts of the Bible come alive in fresh ways.

One of these picture-models is Jerusalem itself, sometimes referred to as Zion (the historic stronghold). Jerusalem was bound up not only with the fact that from David on, it was the capital city (even after the division into Israel and Judah, it was the capital of the southern kingdom), but also with the fact that from Solomon on it was the site of the temple, and therefore of the focus of God's self-disclosure.

So for the psalmist, "the city of our God, his holy mountain" is not only "beautiful" but "the joy of the whole earth" (**Ps. 48:1-2**). It is not only the center of armed security (48:4-8), but the locus where God's people meditate on his unfailing love (48:9), the center of praise (48:10). Yet the psalmist looks beyond the city to God himself: *he* is the one who "makes her secure forever" (48:8), whose praise reaches to the end of the earth, for ever and ever (48:10, 14).

As rooted as they are in historic Jerusalem, the writers of the new covenant look to a "Jerusalem that is above" (Gal. 4:26), to "Mount Zion," to "the heavenly Jerusalem, the city of the living God" (Heb. 12:22), to the "new Jerusalem" (Rev. 21:2). Reflect long and often on the connections.

∽

Numbers 12—13; Psalm 49; Isaiah 2; Hebrews 10

∾

REBELLION HAS many faces.

Numbers 12—13 reports two quite different and complex forms of rebellion. The *first* finds Aaron and Miriam bad-mouthing their brother Moses. The presenting problem is that because the Lord has spoken through them as well as through Moses, they feel they have the right to share whatever authority he enjoys. But other layers lie hidden: they are upset with Moses because of his marriage to a Cushite. Human motives are often convoluted.

Inevitably, the protest sounds reasonable and sensible, even (to our ears) democratic. Further, it is calculated to put Moses into a horrible position. If he insists that he alone is the leader whom God has peculiarly called to this task, he could be accused by the envious and the skeptical as guilty of self-promoting turf-protection. What saves him, in part, is that, like the Savior who followed him, Moses is an extraordinarily humble man (12:3; cf. Matt. 11:29).

God himself intervenes and designates who the leader is. Moses is unique, for the immediacy of the revelation he receives and transmits is beyond that of all other prophets; further, Moses has proved faithful in all God's household (12:6-8). Miriam faces dreadful judgment. Why Miriam is so afflicted and not Aaron is unclear: perhaps in this rebellion she was the leader, or perhaps God did not want to undermine the legitimate authority Aaron possessed as high priest. What is clear is that even when Miriam, owing to Moses' intercessory intervention, is forgiven, she faces a week of disgrace and illness outside the camp, to teach both her and the nation that the rebellion that manifests itself in lust for power deserves judgment from the living God.

The *second* rebellion, reported in Numbers 13, begins with the fears of ten of the twelve spies commissioned to reconnoiter the Promised Land. They could not fail to report its lush fertility, but they focused on the obstacles. In this they had forgotten, or willfully ignored, all that God had miraculously performed to bring them this far. But their rebellion is worse yet. As leaders they were charged not only with accurate reporting but also with forming the opinion of the people. As leaders of the people of God, they should have presented the features of the land as they found them, and then focused attention on the faithful, covenantal God, reminding the people of the plagues, the Passover, the Exodus, the supply of food and safety in the desert, and God's self-disclosure at Sinai. But in fact, they succeed only in fomenting a major mutiny (see chap. 14), primarily by fostering fear and unbelief.

In what ways does rebellion manifest itself among the people of God today?

∾

Numbers 14; Psalm 50; Isaiah 3—4; Hebrews 11

∾

ANOTHER DAY THINKING ABOUT REBELLION—this time the rebellion displayed by the people at Kadesh Barnea, when they forfeited the opportunity to enter the Promised Land because of their sin (**Num. 14**).

(1) Just as in the previous chapter the ten spies who gave a negative report were responsible for discouraging the people, so the people are responsible to decide to whom they will give heed. They simply go with the majority. If they had adhered to the covenant to which they had pledged themselves, if they had remembered what God had already done for them, they would have sided with Caleb and Joshua. Those who side with the majority voice and not with the word of God are always wrong and are courting disaster.

(2) To doubt the covenantal faithfulness of God, not the least his ability and his will to save his own people and to do what he has said he will do, is to treat God with contempt (14:11, 23). Virtually all perpetual grumbling partakes of such contempt. This is a great evil.

(3) People often hide their own lack of faith, their blatant unbelief, by erecting a pious front. Here they express their concern that their wives and children will be taken as plunder (14:3). Instead of admitting they are scared to death and turning to God for help, implicitly they blame God for being less concerned for their wives and children than they are themselves.

(4) The punishment exacted therefore precisely suits the crime: that adult generation, with a couple of exceptions, dies out in the desert before their children (the very children about whom they profess such concern) inherit the land almost forty years later (14:20-35).

(5) There is a kind of repentance that grieves over past failures but is not resolved to submit to the word of God. The Israelites grieve—and decide to take over the Promised Land, even though God has now told them not to attempt it, since he will no longer be their bulwark and strength. Moses rightly sees that this is nothing other than further disobedience (14:41). Inevitably they are beaten up for their pains (14:44-45).

These five characteristics of this terrible rebellion are not unknown today: a popular adherence to majority religious opinion with very little concern to know and obey the word of God, an indifferent dismissal of God with contempt stemming from rank unbelief, pious excuses that mask fear and unbelief, temporal judgments that kill any possibility of courageous Christian work, and a faulty and superficial "repentance" that leaves a meeting determined to make things right, and yet is still unwilling to listen to the Word of God and obey him. God help us all.

∾

Numbers 15; Psalm 51; Isaiah 5; Hebrews 12

∾

GUILT. What a horrendous burden.

Sometimes people carry a tremendous weight of subjective guilt—i.e., of felt guilt—when they are not really guilty. Far worse is the situation where they carry a tremendous weight of objective guilt—i.e., they really are guilty of some odious sin in the eyes of the living God—and are so hardened that they do not know it.

The superscription of **Psalm 51** discloses that as David writes he consciously carries both objective and subjective guilt. Objectively, he has committed adultery with Bathsheba and has arranged the murder of her husband Uriah; subjectively, Nathan's parable (2 Sam. 12; see the meditation for September 16) has driven home to David's conscience something of the proportion of his own sin, and he writes in shame.

(1) David confesses his sin and cries for mercy (51:1-2). There is no echo of the cries for vindication that mark some of the earlier psalms. When we are guilty, and know we are guilty, no other course is possible, and only this course is helpful.

(2) David frankly recognizes that his offense is primarily against God (51:4), not against Uriah, Bathsheba, the child that was conceived, or even the covenant people who bear some of the judgment. God sets the standards. When we break them, we are defying him. Further, David knows that he sits on the throne out of God's sheer elective grace. To betray the covenant from a position of God-appointed trust is doubly appalling.

(3) David is honest enough to recognize that this sequence of sins, though particularly vile, does not stand alone. It is a display of what is in the heart, of the sin nature that we inherit from our parents. Nothing avails if we are not finally cleansed inwardly, if we are not granted a pure heart and a steadfast spirit (51:5-6, 10).

(4) For David this is not some merely cerebral or cool theological process. Objective guilt and subjective recognition of it so merge that David feels oppressed: his bones are crushed (51:8), he cannot escape the specter of his own sin (51:3), and the joy of his salvation has dissolved (51:12). The transparent honesty and passion of David's prayer disclose that he seeks no blasé or formulaic cleansing.

(5) David recognizes the testimonial value of being forgiven, and uses it as an argument before God as to why he should be forgiven (51:12-15). Implicitly, of course, this is an appeal for God's glory.

(6) Steeped as he is in the sacrificial system of the Mosaic covenant, David nevertheless adopts more fundamental priorities. The prescribed sacrifices mean nothing apart from the sacrifice of a broken spirit, a broken and a contrite heart (51:16-19).

∾

Numbers 16; Psalms 52—54; Isaiah 6; Hebrews 13

∽

TWO MORE WRETCHED EPISODES of rebellion now blemish the history of the Israelites in the wilderness (**Num. 16**).

The *first* is the plot engineered by Korah, Dathan, and Abiram. They stir up trouble not among the riffraff, but among a sizable number of community leaders, about 250 of them. The heart of their criticism against Moses is twofold: (a) They think he has taken too much on himself. "The whole community is holy, every one of them, and the LORD is with them" (16:3). Moses has no right to set himself above "the LORD's assembly" (16:3). (b) The track record of Moses' ministry is so sullied by failure that he cannot be trusted. He brought them out of "a land flowing with milk and honey" (16:13), promising them much, but in reality leading them into the desert. So why on earth should he "lord it over" the people? (16:13)?

Their reasoning would have a certain believability among those who focused on their hardships, who resented all authority, who had short memories of how they had been rescued from Egypt, who did not value all that God had carefully revealed, and who were swayed by the instant appeal of rhetoric but who did not value their own solemn covenantal vows. Their descendants are numerous today. In the name of the priesthood of all believers and of the truth that the whole Christian community is holy, other things that God has *said* about Christian leaders are rapidly skirted. Behind these pretensions of fairness lies, very often, naked lust for power, nurtured by resentments.

Of course, not every leader in the Christian church is to be treated with equal deference: some are self-promoted upstarts that the church is to get rid of (e.g., 2 Cor. 10—13). Nor are all who protest cursed with the judgment that fell on Korah and his friends: some, like Luther and Calvin, like Whitefield and Wesley, and like Paul and Amos before them, are genuine reformers. But in an anti-authoritarian age like ours, one should always check to see if the would-be reformers are shaped by passionate devotion to the words of God, or simply manipulate those words for their own selfish ends.

In the *second* rebellion, the "whole Israelite community" (16:41), fed by pathetic resentments, mutters against Moses and Aaron, accusing them of having killed the rebels the day before—as if they could have opened the ground to swallow them up. Thousands perish because the community as a whole still has not come to grips with God's holiness, the exclusiveness of his claims, the inevitability of his wrath against rebels, his just refusal to be treated with contempt.

And why should our generation be spared?

∽

Numbers 17—18; Psalm 55; Isaiah 7; James 1

∿

AT ONE LEVEL, THE BRIEF ACCOUNT IN NUMBERS 17 wraps up the report of the rebellions in the previous chapter. God wishes to rid himself of the constant grumbling of the Israelites as they challenge Aaron's priestly authority (17:5). So the staff of the ancestral leader of each tribe is carefully labeled and then secreted by Moses, as directed, in the tabernacle, the "Tent of Testimony." God declares, in advance, that the staff belonging to the man he chooses will sprout.

Moses does as he is told. The next morning he fetches the twelve staffs. Aaron's staff, and only his staff, has budded—indeed, it has budded, blossomed, and produced almonds. This staff, by God's instruction, is preserved for posterity. As for the Israelites, it dawns on them that their rebellion was not just against a couple of men, Aaron and Moses, but against the living God. Now they cry, "We will die! We are lost, we are all lost! Anyone who even comes near the tabernacle of the LORD will die. Are we all going to die?" (17:12-13).

What shall we make of this account?

(1) The response of the Israelites is partly good, but is still horribly deficient. It is good in that this event, at least for the time being, prompts them to see that their rebellion was not against Moses and Aaron alone, but against the living God. Fear of God can be a good thing. Yet this sounds more like the cringing fear of people who do not know God very well. They are afraid of being destroyed, but they are not in consequence more devoted to God. In Numbers 20 and 21, the people are whining and grumbling again; this miraculous display of the staff that budded settled nothing for very long. That, too, is horribly realistic: the church has a long history of powerful revivals that have been dissipated or prostituted within a short space of time.

(2) One must ask why God attaches so much importance to the fact that only the designated high priest may perform the priestly duties. We must not infer that this is the way we should defer to all Christian leaders. Within the canonical framework, much more than this is at stake in the account of Aaron's rod that budded. The point is that *only* God's prescribed high priest is acceptable to God for discharging the priestly office. As the opening lines of Numbers 18 make clear, only Aaron and his sons are to "bear the responsibility for offenses against the sanctuary and . . . priesthood." The New Testament insists, "No one takes this honor upon himself; he must be called by God, just as Aaron was" (Heb. 5:4). *So also Christ* (Heb. 5:5)! Only God's appointed priest will do.

∿

Numbers 19; Psalms 56—57; Isaiah 8:1—9:7; James 2

∾

AMERICAN COINS have the words "In God we trust." In our pluralistic age, it is not unreasonable to respond, "Which God?" Even if the answer to that were unambiguously the God of the Bible, most people, I suspect, would think of this trust in God in fairly privatized or mystical ways. It is distressingly easy to think of trust in God as a kind of religious intuition, a pious sensibility, with only the vaguest perception of what this trust entails.

David is under no such delusions. Twice in **Psalm 56** his description of the God in whom he trusts implicitly gives some substance to the nature of trust. David writes, "When I am afraid, I will trust in you. In God, *whose word I praise*, in God I trust; I will not be afraid. What can mortal man do to me?" (56:3-4, emphasis added). Again: "In God, *whose word I praise*, in the LORD, *whose word I praise*—in God I trust; I will not be afraid. What can man do to me?" (56:10-11, emphasis added).

In both passages, David grasps that trust in God is the only solution to his fear: "*When I am afraid*, I will trust in you . . . in God I trust; *I will not be afraid* . . . in God I trust; *I will not be afraid. What can man do to me?*" The superscription of the psalm shows that David wrote it shortly after his horrible experience in Gath (1 Sam. 21:10-15). While fleeing Saul, David hid out in Philistine territory and came within a whisker of being killed. He escaped by feigning madness. Doubtless he had been very afraid, and in his fear he trusted God, and found the strength to pull off a remarkable act that saved his life.

But for our purposes, the striking element in David's confession of his trust is his repetition of one clause. Three times he mentions the Lord God *whose word I praise*. In this context, the specific word that calls forth this description probably has something to do with *why* David could trust him so fully under these circumstances. The most likely candidate for what this "word" is that David praises is God's promise to give him the kingdom and to establish him as the head of a dynasty. His current circumstances are so dire that unbelief might seem more obviously warranted. But David trusts the Lord *whose word I praise*.

What we need is faith in the speaking God, faith in God that is firmly grounded in what this speaking God has said. Then, in the midst of even appalling circumstances, we can find deep rest in the God who does not go back on his word. Transparently, such faith is grounded in God's revelatory words.

∾

Numbers 20; Psalms 58—59; Isaiah 9:8—10:4; James 3

THERE ARE FEW PASSAGES in the Pentateuch which on first reading are more discouraging than the outcome of **Numbers 20:1-13.**

Yet the account carries some subtle complexities. It begins with more of the usual griping. The need of the people is real: they are thirsty (20:2). But instead of humbly seeking the Lord in joyous confidence that he would provide for his own people, they quarrel with Moses and charge him with the usual: they were better off in slavery, their current life in the desert is unbearable, and so forth.

Moses and Aaron seek the Lord's face. The glory of God appears to them (20:6). God specifically says, "Speak to that rock before their eyes and it will pour out its water" (20:8). But Moses has had it. He assembles the crowd and cries, "Listen, you rebels, must we bring you water out of this rock?" (20:10)—which rhetorical question, at its face value, is more than a little pretentious. Then he strikes the rock twice, and water gushes out. But the Lord tells Moses and Aaron, "Because you did not trust in me enough to honor me as holy in the sight of the Israelites, you will not bring this community into the land I give them" (20:12).

Three observations:

(1) God does not say, "Because you did not *obey* me enough . . ." but "Because you did not *trust* in me enough to honor me as holy. . . ." There was, of course, formal disobedience: God said to speak, and Moses struck the rock. But God perceives that the problem is deeper yet. The people have worn Moses down, and Moses responds in kind. His response is not only the striking of the rock, it is the answer of a man who under pressure has become bitter and pretentious (which is certainly not to say that any of us would have done any better!). What has evaporated is transparent trust in God: God is not being honored as holy.

(2) Read the Pentateuch as a whole: the final point is that Moses does not enter the land. Read the first seven books of the Old Testament: one cannot fail to see that the old covenant had not transformed the people. Canonically, that is an important lesson: *the Law was never adequate to save and transform.*

(3) In light of 1 Corinthians 10:4, which shows Christ to be the antitype of the rock, it is hard to resist the conclusion that the reason God had insisted the rock be struck in Exodus 17:1-7, and forbids it here, is that he perceives a wonderful opportunity to make a symbol-laden point: the ultimate Rock, from whom life-giving streams flow, is struck once, and no more.

Numbers 21; Psalms 60—61; Isaiah 10:5-34; James 4

∽

THE BRIEF ACCOUNT OF THE BRONZE SNAKE (**Num. 21:4-9**) is probably better known than other Old Testament accounts of similar brevity, owing to the fact that it is referred to by Jesus himself in John 3:14-15: "Just as Moses lifted up the snake in the desert, so the Son of Man must be lifted up, that everyone who believes in him may have eternal life." What is the nature of the parallel that Jesus is drawing?

In the Numbers account, we are told that as the people continue their God-directed route through the desert, they "grew impatient on the way; they spoke against God and against Moses" (21:4-5). They even whine against the food that God has been providing for them, the daily provision of manna: "We detest this miserable food" (21:5). In consequence the Lord sends judgment in the form of a plague of venomous snakes. Many die. Under the lash of punishment, the people confess to Moses, "We sinned when we spoke against the LORD and against you" (21:7). They beg Moses to intercede with God. God instructs Moses to make a snake and put it on a pole; "anyone who is bitten can look at it and live" (21:8). So Moses casts a bronze snake and places it on a pole, and it has just the effect that God had ordained.

So here we have an ungrateful people, standing in judgment of what God has done, questioning their leader. They face the judgment of God, and the only release from that judgment is a provision that God himself makes, which they receive by simply looking to the bronze serpent.

The situation of Nicodemus is not so very different in John 3. His opening remarks suggest that he sees himself as capable of standing in judgment of Jesus (John 3:1-2), when in fact he really has very little understanding of what Jesus is talking about (3:4, 10). The world is condemned and perishing. Its only hope is in the provision that God makes—in something else that is lifted up on a pole, or more precisely, in some*one* who is lifted up on a cross. This is the first occurrence of "lifted up" in John's gospel. As the chapters unwind, it becomes almost a technical expression for Jesus' crucifixion. The only remedy, the only escape from God's judgment, depends on looking to this provision God has made: We must believe in the Son of Man who is "lifted up" if we are to have eternal life.

That word still comes to us. Massive muttering is a sign of culpable unbelief. Sooner or later we will answer to God for it. Our only hope is to look to the One who was hoisted on a pole.

∽

Numbers 22; Psalms 62—63; Isaiah 11—12; James 5

RECENTLY I WAS PHONED BY A MAN who told me he wanted to put me on a retainer as his private theologian. Then, when he phoned or wrote again, I would try to answer his questions.

I did not bother asking what figure he had in mind. Nor do I want to question his motives: he may well have meant to help me or even honor me, or simply to pay his way. But knowing how easily my own motives can be corrupted, I told him that I could not possibly enter into that sort of arrangement with him. Preachers should not see themselves as being *paid* for what they do. Rather, they are supported by the people of God so that they are free to serve. If he wrote or called and asked questions, I would happily do my best to answer, using the criteria I use for whether or not I answer the countless numbers of questions I receive each year.

Numbers 22 begins the account of Balaam. His checkered life teaches us much, but the lesson that stands out in this first chapter is how dangerous it is for a preacher, or a prophet, to sacrifice independence on the altar of material prosperity. Sooner or later a love of money will corrupt ministry.

That Balaam was a prophet of God shows that there were still people around who retained some genuine knowledge of the one true God. The call of Abraham and the rise of the Israelite nation do not mean that there were no others who knew the one sovereign Creator: witness Melchizedek (Gen. 14). Moreover, Balaam clearly enjoyed some powerful prophetic gift: on occasion he spoke genuine oracles from God. He knew enough about this mysterious gift to grasp that it could not be turned on and off, and that if he was transmitting a genuine oracle he himself could not control its content. He could speak only what God gave him to say.

But that did not stop him from lusting after Balak's offer of money. Balak saw Balaam as some sort of semi-magical character akin to a voodoo practitioner, someone to come and put a curse on the hated Israelites. God unambiguously forbids Balaam to go with Balak, for he has blessed the people Balak wants cursed. Balaam nags God; God relents and lets Balaam go, but only on condition that he does only what God tells him (22:20). At the same time, God stands against Balaam in judgment, for his going is driven by a greedy heart. Only the miraculous incident with the donkey instills sufficient fear in him that he will indeed guard his tongue (22:32-38).

Never stoop to become a peddler of the Word of God.

Numbers 23; Psalms 64—65; Isaiah 13; 1 Peter 1

∾

BALAAM RECOGNIZES THAT he cannot control the oracles he receives (**Num. 23**). He cannot even be sure that an oracle will be given him: "Perhaps the LORD will come to meet with me," he explains (23:3).

"The LORD put a message in Balaam's mouth" (23:5), and this message is reported in the oracle of vv. 7-10. (1) Cast in poetic form, it stakes out the independence of the true prophet. Although Balak is the one who summoned him, Balaam asks, "How can I curse those whom God has not cursed? How can I denounce those whom the LORD has not denounced?" (23:8). (2) The last part of this first oracle reflects on the Israelites themselves. They consider themselves different from the other nations—after all, they are the covenant people of God—and therefore they will not be assimilated (23:9). Not only will their numbers vastly increase ("Who can count the dust of Jacob or number the fourth part of Israel?"), but they are declared to be righteous, the kind of people who ultimately meet a glorious end (23:10).

Balak does not give up easily, and in due course the Lord gives Balaam a second oracle (23:18-24). Here the same themes are repeated and strengthened. (1) Balaam can pronounce only blessing on Israel. After all, God is not going to change his mind just because Balak wants Balaam to take another shot at it. "God is not a man, that he should lie, nor a son of man, that he should change his mind" (23:19). In any case, not only has Balaam "received a command to bless," but even if Balaam disobeyed the command, he frankly admits, God "has blessed, and I cannot change it" (23:20). "There is no sorcery against Jacob, no divination against Israel" (23:23). (2) As for Israel, no misfortune or misery is observed there, for "the LORD their God is with them" (23:21). Since the God of the Exodus is their God, they have the strength of a wild ox, and will triumph over their enemies (23:22, 24).

Two observations: (1) Balak represents the kind of approach to religion cherished by superstitious people. For them, religion serves to crank up blessings and call down curses. The gods serve me, and I am angry and frustrated if they can't be tamed. (2) After the succession of reports of the dreary rebellions of the Israelites, it is astonishing to hear them praised so highly. But the reason, of course, is because it is *God* who sustains and strengthens them. If God blesses his people, no curse against them can stand. And *since God is the source of this oracle,* this is *God's* view of things—and our great ground of confidence and hope.

∾

Numbers 24; Psalms 66—67; Isaiah 14; 1 Peter 2

IN AN AGE OF MANY "PRAISE CHORUSES," people are tempted to think that our generation is especially rich in praise. Surely we know more about praise than our stuffy parents and grandparents in their somber suits and staid services, busily singing their old-fashioned hymns.

It does not help clarity of thought on these matters to evaluate in stereotypes. Despite the suspicions of some older people, not all contemporary expressions of praise are frivolous and shallow; despite the suspicions of some young people, not all forms of praise from an earlier generation are to be abandoned in favor of the immediate and the contemporary.

But there are two elements expressed in the praise of **Psalm 66** that are almost never heard today, and that badly need to be reincorporated both into our praise and into our thinking.

The *first* is found in 66:8-12. There the psalmist begins by inviting the peoples of the world to listen in on the people of God as they praise him because "he has preserved our lives and kept our feet from slipping." Then the psalmist directly addresses God, and mentions *the context* in which the Lord God preserved them: "For you, O God, tested us; you refined us like silver. You brought us into prison and laid burdens on our backs. You let men ride over our heads; we went through fire and water, but you brought us to a place of abundance" (66:10-12).

This is stunning. The psalmist thanks God for testing his covenant people, for refining them under the pressure of some extraordinarily difficult circumstances and for sustaining them through that experience. This is the response of perceptive, godly faith. It is not heard on the lips of those who thank God only when they *escape* trial or are feeling happy.

The *second* connects the psalmist's desperate cry with righteousness: "I cried out to him with my mouth; his praise was on my tongue. *If I had cherished sin in my heart, the Lord would not have listened; but God has surely listened* and heard my voice in prayer" (66:17-19, emphasis added). This is not to say that the Lord answers us because we have merited his favor by our righteous endeavor. Rather, because we have entered into a personal and covenantal relationship with God, we owe him our allegiance, our faith, our obedience. If instead we nurture sin in our inmost being, and then turn to God for help, why should he not respond with the judgment and chastisement that we urgently deserve? He may turn away, and sovereignly let sin take its ugly course.

Our generation desperately needs to connect praise with righteousness, worship with obedience, and the Lord's response with a clean heart.

Numbers 25; Psalm 68; Isaiah 15; 1 Peter 3

～

THERE IS MORE THAN ONE WAY to defeat the people of God.

Balak wanted Balaam to curse the Israelites (Num. 22—24). Under threat of divine sanction, Balaam stood fast and proclaimed only what God gave him to say. But here in **Numbers 25** we discover a quite different tactic. Some of the Moabite women invited some of the Israelite men over for visits. Some of these visits were to the festivals and sacrifices of their gods. Liaisons sprang up. Soon there was both sexual immorality and blatant worship of these pagan gods (25:1-2), in particular the Baal (lit. *Lord*) of Peor (25:3). "And the LORD's anger burned against them" (25:3).

The result is inevitable. Now the Israelites face not the wrath of Moab but the wrath of Almighty God. A plague drives through the camp and kills 24,000 people (25:9). Phinehas takes the most drastic action (25:7-8). If we evaluate it under the conditions of contemporary pluralism, or even against the nature of the sanctions that the church is authorized to impose (e.g., 1 Cor. 5), Phinehas's execution of this man and woman will evoke horror and charges of primitive barbarism. But if we recall that under the agreed covenant of this theocratic nation, the stipulated sanction for both blatant adultery and for idolatry was capital punishment, and if we perceive that by obeying the terms of this covenant (to which the people had pledged themselves) Phinehas saved countless thousands of lives by turning aside the plague, his action appears more principled than barbaric. Certainly this judgment, as severe as it is, is nothing compared with the judgment to come.

But I shall focus on two further observations.

First, Moab had found a way to destroy Israel by enticing the people to perform actions that would draw the judgment of God. Israel was strong only because God is strong. If God abandoned the nation, the people would be capable of little. According to Balaam's oracles, the Israelites were to be "a people who live apart and do not consider themselves one of the nations" (23:9). The evil in this occurrence of covenant-breaking is that they now wish to be indifferentiable from the pagan nations.

What temptations entice the church in the West to conduct that will inevitably draw the angry judgment of God upon us?

Second, later passages disclose that these developments were not casual "boy-meets-girl" larks, but official policy *arising from Balaam's advice* (31:16; cf. 2 Peter 2:16; Rev. 2:14). We are treated to the wretched spectacle of a compromised prophet who preserves fidelity on formal occasions and on the side offers vile advice, especially if there is hope of personal gain.

～

Numbers 26; Psalm 69; Isaiah 16; 1 Peter 4

AT ONE LEVEL, **Psalm 69** finds David pouring his heart out to God, begging for help as he faces extraordinary pressures and opponents. We may not be able to reconstruct all the circumstances that are presented here in poetic form, but David has been betrayed by people close to him, and his anguish is palpable.

At another level, this psalm is a rich repository of texts quoted or paraphrased by New Testament writers: "Those who hate me without reason outnumber the hairs of my head" (69:4; see John 15:25); "I am a stranger to my brothers, an alien to my own mother's sons" (69:8; cf. John 7:5); "for zeal for your house consumes me" (69:9; see John 2:17); "and the insults of those who insult you fall on me" (69:9; see Rom. 15:3); "but I pray to you, O LORD, in the time of your favor; in your great love, O God, answer me with your sure salvation" (69:13; cf. Isa. 49:8; 2 Cor. 6:2); "they put gall in my food and gave me vinegar" (69:21; see Matt. 27:48; Mark 15:36; Luke 23:36); "they . . . gave me vinegar *for my thirst*" (69:21; see Matt. 27:34; Mark 15:23; John 19:28-30); "may their place be deserted; let there be no one to dwell in their tents" (69:25; see Matt. 23:38; Acts 1:20); "may they be blotted out of the book of life" (69:28; cf. Luke 10:20).

For the sheer concentration of such citations and allusions in one chapter, this psalm is remarkable. Of course, they are not all of the same sort, and this brief meditation cannot possibly probe them all. But several of them fall into one important pattern. This is a psalm written by David. (There is no good reason to doubt this attribution from the superscription.) David is not only the head of the dynasty that issues in "great David's greater Son" (as the hymn writer puts it), but in many ways he becomes a model for the king who is to come, a pattern for him—a type, if you will.

That is the reasoning of the New Testament authors. It is easy enough to demonstrate that the reasoning is well grounded. Here it is enough to glimpse something of the result. If King David could endure scorn for God's sake (69:7), how much more the ultimate King—who certainly also suffers rejection by his brothers for God's sake (69:8). If David is zealous for the house of the Lord, how could Jesus' disciples possibly fail to see in his cleansing of the temple and related utterances something of his own zeal (John 2:17)? Indeed, in the minds of the New Testament authors, such passages link with the "Suffering Servant" theme that surfaces in Isaiah 53—and is here tied to King David and his ultimate heir and Lord.

Numbers 27; Psalms 70—71; Isaiah 17—18; 1 Peter 5

∿

MOST CHRISTIANS HAVE listened to testimonies that relate how some man or woman lived a life of fruitlessness and open degradation, or at least of quiet desperation, before becoming a Christian. Genuine faith in the Lord Christ brought about a personal revolution: old habits destroyed, new friends and commitments established, a new direction to give meaning and orientation. Where there was despair, there is now joy; where there was turmoil, there is now peace; where there was anxiety, there is now some measure of serenity. And some of us who were reared in Christian homes have secretly wondered if perhaps it might have been better if we had been converted out of some rotten background.

That is not the psalmist's view. "For you have been my hope, O Sovereign LORD, my confidence since my youth. From birth I have relied on you; you brought me forth from my mother's womb" (**Ps. 71:5-6**). "Since my youth, O God, you have taught me, and to this day I declare your marvelous deeds" (71:17). Indeed, because of this background, the psalmist calmly looks over the intervening years and petitions God for persevering grace into old age: "Do not cast me away when I am old; do not forsake me when my strength is gone" (71:9). "But as for me, I will always have hope; I will praise you more and more" (71:14). "Even when I am old and gray, do not forsake me, O God, till I declare your power to the next generation, your might to all who are to come" (71:18).

Doubtless particular circumstances were used by God to elicit these words from the psalmist's pen. Nevertheless, the stance itself is invaluable. The most thoughtful of those who are converted later in life wish they had not wasted so many of their early years. Now that they have found the pearl of great price, their only regret is that they did not find it sooner. More importantly, those who are reared in godly Christian homes are steeped in Scripture from their youth. There is plenty in Scripture and in personal experience to disclose to them the perversity of their own hearts; they do not have to be sociopaths to discover what depravity means. They will be sufficiently ashamed of the sins they *have* committed, despite their backgrounds, that instead of wishing they could have had a worse background (!), they sometimes hang their head in shame that they have done so little with their advantages, and frankly recognize that apart from the grace of God, there is no crime and sin to which they could not sink.

It is best, by far, to be grateful for a godly heritage and to petition God himself for grace that will see you through old age.

∿

Numbers 28; Psalm 72; Isaiah 19—20; 2 Peter 1

❧

ONE OF THE FEATURES OF THE PSALMS that describe the enthronement of a Davidic king, or the reign of a Davidic king, is how often the language goes "over the top." This feature combines with the built-in Davidic typology to give these psalms a twin focus. On the one hand, they can be read as somewhat extravagant descriptions of one of the Davidic kings (in this case Solomon, according to the superscription); on the other, they invite the reader to anticipate something more than a David or a Solomon or a Josiah.

So it is in **Psalm 72**. On the one hand, the Davidic monarch was to rule in justice, and it is entirely appropriate that so much of the psalm is devoted to this theme. In particular, he is to take the part of the afflicted, "the children of the needy" (Ps. 72:4), those "who have no one to help" (72:12). He is to oppose the oppressor and the victimizer, establishing justice and stability, and rescuing those who would otherwise suffer oppression and violence (72:14). His reign is to be characterized by prosperity, which is itself "the fruit of righteousness" (72:3—a point the West is rapidly forgetting). Gold will flow into the country; the people will pray for their monarch; grain will abound throughout the land (72:15-16).

On the other hand, some of the language is wonderfully extravagant. Some of this is in line with the way other ancient Near Eastern kings were extolled. Nevertheless, combined with the Davidic typology and the rising messianic expectation, it is difficult not to overhear something more specific. "He will endure as long as the sun, as long as the moon, through all generations" (72:5)—which may be true of the dynasty, or may be an extravagant wish for some purely human Davidic king, but is literally true of only one Davidic king. "He will rule from sea to sea and from the River [i.e., the Euphrates] to the ends of the earth" (72:8)— which contains a lovely ambiguity. Are the "seas" no more than the Mediterranean and Galilee? Should the Hebrew be translated (as it might be) more conservatively to read "the end of the land"? But surely not. For not only will "the desert tribes" (i.e., from adjacent lands) bow before him, but the kings of Tarshish—Spain!— and of other distant lands will bring tribute to him (72:9-10). Moreover: "All kings will bow down to him and all nations will serve him" (72:11). "All nations will be blessed through him, and they will call him blessed" (72:17)—as clear an echo of the Abrahamic covenant as one can imagine (Gen. 12:2-3).

One greater than Solomon has come (Matt. 12:42).

❧

Numbers 29; Psalm 73; Isaiah 21; 2 Peter 2

FEW PSALMS HAVE PROVIDED greater succor to people who are troubled by the frequent, transparent prosperity of the wicked than **Psalm 73**.

Asaph begins with a provocative pair of lines: "Surely God is good to Israel, to those who are pure in heart." Does the parallelism hint that the people of Israel *are* the pure in heart? Scarcely; that accords neither with history nor with this psalm. The second line, then, must be a restriction on the first. Should those who are *not* pure in heart be equated with the wicked so richly described in this psalm? Well, perhaps, but what is striking is that the next lines depict not the evil of the wicked but the sin of Asaph's own heart. His own heart was not pure as he contemplated "the prosperity of the wicked" (73:3). He envied them. Apparently this envy ate at him until he was in danger of losing his entire moral and religious balance: his "feet had almost slipped" (73:2).

What attracted Asaph to the wicked was the way so many of them seem to be the very picture of serenity, good health, and happiness (73:4-12). Even their arrogance has its attractions: it seems to place them above others. Their wealth and power make them popular. At their worst, they ignore God with apparent total immunity from fear. They seem "always carefree, they increase in wealth" (73:12).

So perhaps righteousness doesn't pay: "Surely in vain have I kept my heart pure; in vain have I washed my hands in innocence" (73:13). Asaph could not quite bring himself to this step: he recognized that it would have meant a terrible betrayal of "your children" (73:15)—apparently the people of God to whom Asaph felt loyalty and for whom, as a leader, he sensed a burden of responsibility. But all his reflections were "oppressive" to him (73:16), until three profound realizations dawned on him.

First, on the long haul the wicked will be swept away. As Asaph entered the sanctuary, he reflected on the "final destiny" (73:17-19, 27) of those he had begun to envy, and he envied them no more.

Second, Asaph himself, in concert with all who truly know God and walk in submission to him, possesses so much more than the wicked—both in this life and in the life to come. "I am always with you," Asaph exults; "you hold me by my right hand. You guide me with your counsel, and afterward you will take me into glory" (73:23-24).

Third, Asaph now sees his bitterness for the ugly sin it is (73:21-22), and resolves instead to draw near to God and to make known all God's deeds (73:28).

Numbers 30; Psalm 74; Isaiah 22; 2 Peter 3

A FEW YEARS AGO I spent some time in a certain so-called "third world" country, well known for its abject poverty. What struck me most forcibly about the culture of that country, however, was not its poverty, nor the gap between the very wealthy and the very poor—I had read up enough on these points that I was not surprised, and I had witnessed similar tragedies elsewhere—but its ubiquitous, endemic corruption.

Here in the West, we are not well placed to wag a finger. Doubtless we have less overt bribery; doubtless we have published prices for many government services that make bribes and kickbacks a little more difficult to institutionalize; doubtless there is still enough Christian heritage that at least on paper we avow that honesty is a good thing, that a man or woman's word should be his or her bond, that greed is evil—though very often such values are nowadays honored rather more in the breech than in reality. Even so, we are by far the most litigious nation in the world. We produce far more lawyers than engineers (the reverse of Japan). The simplest agreement nowadays must be surrounded by mounds of legalese protecting the participants. A fair bit of this stems from the fact that many individuals and companies will not keep their word, will not try to do the right thing, and will try to rip off the other party if they can get away with it. A lie is embarrassing only if you are caught. Promises and pledges become devices to get what you want, rather than commitments to truth. Solemn marriage vows are discarded on a whim, or dissolved in the heat of lust. And of course, if we easily abandon marriage covenants, business covenants, and personal covenants, it is equally easy to abandon the covenant with God.

Telling the truth and keeping one's promises in one domain of life spill over into other domains; conversely, infidelity in one arena commonly spills over into other arenas. So, nestled within the Mosaic covenant are these words: "This is what the LORD commands: When a man makes a vow to the LORD or takes an oath to obligate himself by a pledge, he must not break his word but must do everything he said" (**Num. 30:1-2**). The rest of the chapter recognizes that such oaths by individuals may not be merely individual matters; there may be spousal or family entailments. So for the right ordering of the culture, God himself sets forth who, under this covenant, is permitted to ratify or set aside a pledge; that pattern says something about headship and responsibility in the family. But the fundamental issue is one of truth-telling and fidelity.

Numbers 31; Psalms 75—76; Isaiah 23; 1 John 1

∾

ONE OF THE IMPORTANT FUNCTIONS of corporate worship is recital, that is, a "re-telling" of the wonderful things that God has done. Hence Psalm 78:2-4: "I will utter hidden things, things from of old—what we have heard and known, what our fathers have told us. We will not hide them from their children; we will tell the next generation the praiseworthy deeds of the LORD, his power, and the wonders he has done." Similarly, if more briefly, **Psalm 75:1**: "We give thanks to you, O God, we give thanks, for your Name is near; men tell of your wonderful deeds." In fact, the *New English Bible* is a little closer to the Hebrew: "Thy name is brought very near to us in the story of thy wonderful deeds." God's "name" is part of his gracious self-disclosure. It is a revelation of who he is (Ex. 3:14; 34:5-7, 14). God's "name," then, is brought very near us in the story of his wonderful deeds: that is, who God is is disclosed in the accounts of what he has done.

Thus the recital of what God has done is a means of grace to bring God near to his people. Believers who spend no time reviewing and pondering in their minds what God has done, whether they are alone and reading their Bibles or joining with other believers in corporate adoration, should not be surprised if they rarely sense that God is near.

The emphasis this psalm makes regarding God is that he is the sovereign disposer, the "disposer supreme" (as one commentator puts it). It is wonderfully stabilizing to us to rest in such a God. He declares, "I choose the appointed time; it is I who judge uprightly" (75:2). It is hard to imagine a category more suggestive of God's firm control than "the appointed time." Yet mere control without justice would be fatalism. This God, however, not only sets the appointed times, but judges uprightly (75:2). Further, in this broken world there are cataclysmic events that seem to threaten the entire social order. Elsewhere David ponders, "When the foundations are being destroyed, what can the righteous do?" (11:3). But here we are reassured, for God himself declares, "When the earth and all its people quake, it is I who hold its pillars firm" (75:3). So the arrogant who may think themselves to be the pillars of society are duly warned: "Boast no more" (75:4). To the wicked, God says, "Do not lift your horns against heaven [like a ram tossing its head about in bold confidence]; do not speak with outstretched neck" (75:5).

Retell God's wonderful deeds and bring near his name.

∾

Numbers 32; Psalm 77; Isaiah 24; 1 John 2

∾

ASAPH MUST HAVE GIVEN A LOT of thought to the question of what believers should remember. Psalm 75, we saw yesterday, commends the power of godly "recital"— a retelling of what God has done so as to bring near God's "name." The importance of remembering and retelling is at the heart of Psalm 78. And here in **Psalm 77**, Asaph highlights yet another element in this theme.

Asaph finds himself in great distress (77:1). Its causes we do not know, but most of us have passed through "dark nights of the soul" when it seems that either God is dead or he does not care. Asaph was so despondent he could not sleep; indeed, he charges God with keeping him from sleep (77:4). Memories of other times when circumstances were so bright that he sang with joy in the night hours (77:6) serve only to depress him further. Bitterness tinges his list of rhetorical questions: "Will the Lord reject forever? Will he never show his favor again? Has his unfailing love vanished forever? Has his promise failed for all time? Has God forgotten to be merciful? Has he in anger withheld his compassion?" (77:7-9).

What Asaph resolves to focus on is all the ways God has disclosed himself in power in the past. He writes: "To this I will appeal: the years of the right hand of the Most High" (77:10)—in other words, he appeals to all the displays of strength, of the deeds of God's "right hand," across the years. "I will remember the deeds of the LORD; yes, I will remember your miracles of long ago. I will meditate on all your works and consider all your mighty deeds" (77:11-12). So in the rest of the psalm, Asaph switches to the second person, addressing God directly, remembering some of the countless deeds of grace and power that have characterized God's dealings with the covenant people of God. He remembers the plagues, the Exodus, the crossing of the Red Sea, the way God led his people "by the hand of Moses and Aaron" (77:13-20).

Christians have all the more to remember. As Asaph "remembered" the Exodus by reading Scripture, so we have even more Scripture. We remember not only all that Asaph remembered, but things he did not know: the Exile, the return from exile, the long years of waiting for the coming of the Messiah. We remember the Incarnation, the years of Jesus' life and ministry, his words and mighty deeds. Above all, we remember his death and resurrection, and the powerful work of the Spirit at Pentecost and beyond.

And as we remember, our faith is strengthened, our vision of God is renewed, and the despair lifts.

∾

Numbers 33; Psalm 78:1-39; Isaiah 25; 1 John 3

∾

THE OPENING FEW VERSES OF **Psalm 78** initially elicit a little puzzlement. Asaph invites his readers (and if this is sung, his hearers) to hear his teaching, to listen to the words of his mouth (78:1). Then he announces, "I will open my mouth in parables, I will utter hidden things, things from of old" (78:2). Anticipation builds; it sounds as if we shall hear brand-new things that have been hidden before Asaph came on the scene. Then he further describes these "hidden things, things from of old": they are "what we have heard and known, what our fathers have told us" (78:3). So, is he embarking on some new revelation, previously hidden, or is he simply reviewing the common heritage of the Israelites? And why add at this point that at least part of his purpose is to disclose these things to the new generation that is coming along (78:4)?

Three observations:

First, the word rendered "parables" has a wide range of meaning. It can refer to narrative parables, wisdom sayings, aphorisms, and several other forms. Here, Asaph seems to mean no more than that he will say what he has to say in the poetic structures and wise comparisons that characterize this psalm.

Second, the content of this psalm is both old—"what we have heard and known, what our fathers have told us"—and new, "hidden things." This psalm is one of a group of "historical psalms," that is, psalms that review some of the experiences of the people of God with their God. For most of its length its chief focus is the Exodus and the events that surrounded it, including the plagues, the crossing of the Red Sea, the provision of manna, and so forth. The psalm brings us down to the reign of David (which, incidentally, shows that Asaph himself lived in David's day or later). Yet this psalm is not a mere review of the bare facts of that history. The recital is designed to draw certain lessons from that history, lessons that might be missed if attention were not drawn to them. These lessons include the sorry patterns of rebellion, God's self-restraint in his rising anger, his graciousness in saving them again and again, and more. These lessons are "hidden" in the bare text, but they are there, and Asaph brings them out.

Third, Asaph understands (1) that deep knowledge of Scripture and of the ways of God means more than knowing facts, but also grasping the unfolding patterns to see what God is doing; (2) that at any time the covenant people of God are never more than one generation from extinction, so it is utterly vital to pass on this accumulating insight to the next generation.

∾

Numbers 34; Psalm 78:40-72; Isaiah 26; 1 John 4

"HOW OFTEN THEY REBELLED against him in the desert and grieved him in the wasteland! Again and again they put God to the test; they vexed the Holy One of Israel" (**Ps. 78:40-41**). Thus Asaph pauses in the course of his recital to summarize one of his main points in this psalm. In fact, one could outline some of the dramatic points Asaph makes as follows:

(1) The repeated rebellion of the people of God is presented not merely as disobedience, but as putting God to the test. That is one of the elements in rebellion that is so gross, so odious. A heavy dose of "in your face" marks this rebellion, an ugly pattern of unbelief that implicitly charges God with powerlessness, with cruelty, with selfishness, with thoughtlessness, with foolishness. Chronic and repeated unbelief "with attitude" always has this element of putting God to the test. What will God do about it? Small wonder that the apostle Paul identifies the same pattern in the conduct of the people during the wilderness years and warns Christians in his day, "We should not test the Lord, as some of them did—and were killed by snakes. And do not grumble, as some of them did—and were killed by the destroying angel. These things happened to them as examples and were written down as warnings for us" (1 Cor. 10:9-11).

(2) Although the first part of the chapter notes God's wrath replying to the pattern of the people's rebellion, it also insists that time after time God "restrained his anger and did not stir up his full wrath" (78:38). But the pattern now becomes grimmer. Eventually the idolatry was so gross that God "was very angry; he rejected Israel completely" (78:59). The context shows that what Asaph has in mind is the judgment of God on the people when he permitted the ark of the Lord to be captured by the Philistines: "He sent the ark of his might into captivity, his splendor into the hands of the enemy" (78:61; cf. 1 Sam. 4:5-11), with the entailment that the people faced terrible destruction at the hand of their enemies.

(3) The closing verses (78:65-72) focus on the gracious choice of Judah and of David as God's answer to the wretched years of the wilderness, of the judges, of the reign of Saul. "And David shepherded them with integrity of heart; with skillful hands he led them" (78:72). Living this side of the Incarnation, Christians are especially grateful for David's line.

(4) Christians know how the storyline of Psalm 78 develops. David's dynasty descends into corruption; God's wrath is greater yet, and the Exile ensues. But worse wrath, and more glorious love, were yet to be displayed in the cross.

Numbers 35; Psalm 79; Isaiah 27; 1 John 5

∽

WHEN PLANS WERE BEING LAID to parcel out the Promised Land to the twelve tribes, Levi was excluded. The Levites were told that God was their inheritance: they would not receive tribal territory, but would be supported by the tithes collected from the rest of the Israelites (Num. 18:20-26). Even so, they needed somewhere to live. So God ordained that each tribe would set aside some towns for the Levites, along with the surrounding pasturelands for their livestock (**Num. 35:1-5**). Since the Levites were to teach the people the law of God, in addition to their tabernacle duties, these land arrangements had the added advantage of scattering the Levites among the people where they could do the most good. Moreover, their scattered lands were never to pass out of Levitical hands (Lev. 25:32-34).

The other peculiar land arrangement established in this chapter is the designation of six "cities of refuge" (35:6-34). These were to be drawn from the forty-eight towns allotted to the Levites, three on one side of the Jordan, and three on the other. A person who killed another, whether intentionally or accidentally, could flee to one of those cities and be preserved against the wrath of family avengers. At a time when blood feuds were not unknown, this had the effect of cooling the atmosphere until the official justice system could establish the guilt or innocence of the killer. If found guilty on compelling evidence (35:30), the murderer was to be executed. One recalls the principle laid down in Genesis 9:6: those who murder human beings, who are made in the image of God, have done something so vile that the ultimate sanction is mandated. The logic is not one of deterrence, but of values (cf. Num. 35:31-33).

On the other hand, if the killing was accidental and the killer therefore innocent of murder, he cannot simply be discharged and sent home, but must remain in the city of refuge until the death of the high priest (35:25-28). Only at that point could the killer return to his ancestral property and resume a normal life. Waiting for the high priest to die could be a matter of days or of decades. If the time was substantial, it might serve to cool down the avengers from the victim's family. But no such rationale is provided in the text.

Probably two reasons account for this stipulation that the slayer must remain in the city of refuge until the death of the high priest. (1) His death marked the end of an era, the beginning of another. (2) More importantly, it may be his death symbolized that someone had to die to pay for the death of one of God's image-bearers. Christians know where that reasoning leads.

∽

Numbers 36; Psalm 80; Isaiah 28; 2 John

∾

WE ARE FIRST INTRODUCED TO Zelophehad and his daughters in Numbers 27:1-11. Normally inheritance descended through the sons. But Zelophehad had no sons, only five daughters named Mahlah, Noah, Hoglah, Milcah, and Tirzah. Zelophehad belonged to the generation that passed away in the desert. Why, the daughters asked Moses, should his family line be prohibited from inheriting just because his progeny were all female? Moses, we are told, "brought their case before the LORD" (27:5). The Lord not only ruled in favor of the daughters' petition, but provided a statute that regularized this decision for similar cases throughout Israel (27:8-11).

But a new wrinkle on this ruling turns up in **Numbers 36.** The family heads of Manasseh, to which the Zelophehad family belongs, ask what will happen if the daughters marry Israelites outside their tribe. They bring their inheritance with them to the marriage, and it would get passed on to *their* sons, but their sons would belong to the tribe of their father—and so over the centuries there could be massive redistribution of tribal lands, and potentially major inequities among the tribes. On this point, too, the Lord himself rules (36:5). "No inheritance may pass from tribe to tribe, for each Israelite tribe is to keep the land it inherits" (36:9). The way forward, then, was for the Zelophehad daughters to marry men from their own tribe—a ruling with which the Zelophehad daughters happily comply (36:10-12).

If this offends our sensibilities, we ought to consider why.

(1) Pragmatically, even we *cannot* marry *anyone*: we almost always marry within our own highly limited circles of friends and acquaintances. So in Israel: most people would *want* to marry within their tribes.

(2) More importantly, we have inherited Western biases in favor of individualism ("I'll marry whomever I please") and of falling in love ("We couldn't help it; it just happened, and we fell in love"). Doubtless there are advantages to these social conventions, but that is what they are: mere social conventions. For the majority of the world's people, marriages are either arranged by the parents or, more likely, at very least worked out with far more family approval operating than in the West. At what point does our love of freedom dissolve into individualistic self-centeredness, with little concern for the extended family and culture—or in this case for God's gracious covenantal structure that provided equitable distribution of land?

We live in our own culture, of course, and under a new covenant. And we, too, have biblical restrictions imposed on whom we marry (e.g., 1 Cor. 7:39). More importantly, we must eschew the abominable idolatry of thinking that the universe must dance to our tune.

∾

Deuteronomy 1; Psalms 81—82; Isaiah 29; 3 John

∽

"OPEN WIDE YOUR MOUTH and I will fill it" (**Ps. 81:10**): the symbolism is transparent. God is perfectly willing and able to satisfy all our deepest needs and longings. Implicitly, the problem is that we will not even open our mouths to enjoy the food he provides. The symbolism returns in the last verse: while the wicked will face punishment that lasts forever, "you would be fed with the finest of wheat; with honey from the rock I would satisfy you" (81:16).

Of course, God is talking about more than physical food (though scarcely less). The setting is a common one both in the Psalms and in the narrative parts of the Pentateuch. God graciously and spectacularly rescued the people from their slavery in Egypt, responding to their own cries of distress. "I removed the burden from their shoulders," God says. "In your distress you called and I rescued you" (81:6-7). Then comes the passage that leads to the line quoted at the beginning of this meditation:

> Hear, O my people, and I will warn you—
>   if you would but listen to me, O Israel!
> You shall have no foreign god among you;
>   you shall not bow down to an alien god.
> I am the LORD your God, who brought you up out of Egypt.
> Open wide your mouth and I will fill it (81:8-10).

Historically, of course, the response of the people was disappointing: "my people would not listen to me; Israel would not submit to me" (81:11). In that case, they were not promised the satisfaction symbolized by full mouths. Far from it. God says, "So I gave them over to their stubborn hearts to follow their own devices" (81:12).

Of course, the nature of the idolatry changes from age to age. I recently read some lines from John Piper: "The greatest enemy of hunger for God is not poison but apple pie. It is not the banquet of the wicked that dulls our appetite for heaven, but endless nibbling at the table of the world. It is not the X-rated video, but the prime-time dribble of triviality we drink in every night. For all the ill that Satan can do, when God describes what keeps us from the banquet table of his love, it is a piece of land, a yoke of oxen, and a wife (Luke 14:18-20). The greatest adversary of love to God is not his enemies but his gifts. And the most deadly appetites are not for the poison of evil, but for the simple pleasures of earth. For when these replace an appetite for God himself, the idolatry is scarcely recognizable, and almost incurable" (*A Hunger for God* [Wheaton: Crossway, 1997], 14).

"Open wide your mouth and I will fill it."

∽

Deuteronomy 2; Psalms 83—84; Isaiah 30; Jude

∽

"FOR THE LORD GOD is a sun and a shield: the LORD bestows favor and honor; no good thing does he withhold from those whose walk is blameless. O LORD Almighty, blessed is the man who trusts in you" (**Ps. 84:11-12**).

Much of this psalm exults in the sheer privilege and delight of abiding in the presence of God, which for the children of the old covenant meant living in the shadow of the temple. "My soul yearns, even faints, for the courts of the LORD; my heart and my flesh cry out for the living God" (84:2). To have a place "near your altar" is to have a home, in exactly the same way that a sparrow finds a home or a swallow builds a nest (84:3). "Blessed are those who dwell in your house; they are ever praising you" (84:4; see also the meditation for April 17).

But what about the last two verses of this psalm? Don't they go over the top, promising too much? The psalmist insists that God withholds "no good thing" from those whose walk is blameless. Well, since we all sin, I suppose there is an escape clause: who is blameless? Isn't it obvious that God withholds lots of good things from lots of people whose walk is about as blameless as walks can get, this side of the new heaven and the new earth?

Consider Eric Liddell, the famous Scottish Olympian celebrated in the film *Chariots of Fire.* Liddell became a missionary in China. For ten years he taught in a school, and then went farther inland to do frontline evangelism. The work was not only challenging but dangerous, not the least because the Japanese were making increasing inroads. Eventually he was interned with many other Westerners. In the squalid camp, Liddell was a shining light of service and good cheer, a lodestar for the many children there who had not seen their parents for years, a self-sacrificing leader. But a few months before they were released, Liddell died of a brain tumor. He was forty-three. In this life he never saw the youngest of his three daughters: his wife and children had returned to Canada before the Japanese sweep that rounded up the foreigners. Didn't the Lord withhold from him a long life, years of fruitful service, the joy of rearing his own children?

Perhaps the best response lies in Liddell's favorite hymn:

> *Be still, my soul! the Lord is on thy side;*
> *Bear patiently the cross of grief or pain.*
> *Leave to thy God to order and provide;*
> *In every change, He faithful will remain.*
> *Be still, my soul! thy best, thy heav'nly Friend*
> *Through thorny ways leads to a joyful end.*

∽

Deuteronomy 3; Psalm 85; Isaiah 31; Revelation 1

IT IS A WONDERFUL PAIRING: "Love and faithfulness meet together." Then another pairing: "righteousness and peace kiss each other" (**Ps. 85:10**). Older readers may remember the first of these two lines in the King James Version: "Mercy and truth" meet together.

In English, "mercy and truth" are pretty distinguishable from the NIV's "love and faithfulness." But the underlying Hebrew, a very common pairing (as in 86:15 or Ex. 34:6—see the meditation for March 23), could be rendered either way. The first word commonly refers to God's covenantal love, his covenantal mercy—his sheer covenantal goodness or grace, poured out on his undeserving people. The second word varies in its English translation, depending on what is being referred to. When the Queen of Sheba tells Solomon that all that she had heard of him was "true," literally "the truth" (1 Kings 10)—that is, that the propositional reports corresponded to reality—she uses the word here rendered "faithfulness." A "true" report is a "faithful" report; when truth is embodied in character, it is faithfulness.

As deployed in this psalm, the categories are used evocatively. When you read the first pairing, "Love and faithfulness meet together," it is natural to read them as descriptions of God: God is the God of covenantal grace or love and of utterly reliable fidelity. The second pairing might be taken the same way: God is both unqualifiedly righteous and the well of all well-being. In him, righteousness and peace kiss each other. But in the next verse, the second word from the first pairing and the first word from the second pairing are picked up and put together to introduce a new thought: "*Faithfulness* springs forth from the earth, and *righteousness* looks down from heaven" (85:11). In the context of the whole psalm, the people's faithfulness is apparently being linked with the Lord's righteousness: the former springs from the earth, while the latter looks down from heaven. It is not absolutely necessary to take things that way, but the psalmist implicitly recognizes the links earlier in his poem: "You forgave the iniquity of your people. . . . Restore us again, O God our Savior. . . . Show us your unfailing love, O LORD . . . he promises peace to his people, his saints—*but let them not return to folly*" (85:2-8, italics added).

However we align these pairings, it is vital to remember that love and faithfulness both belong to God, that righteousness and peace meet and kiss in him. Because of this, God can be both just and the One who justifies the ungodly by graciously giving his Son (Rom. 3:25-26). Should it be surprising to discover that among his image-bearers, love and faithfulness and righteousness and peace go hand in hand, standing together or falling together?

Deuteronomy 4; Psalms 86—87; Isaiah 32; Revelation 2

THE STRUCTURE OF THE BOOK OF Deuteronomy has many detailed parallels with ancient covenants or treaties that regional powers made with their vassal states. One of the components of such treaties was a kind of historical prolegomenon— a brief and selective recapitulation of the historical circumstances that had brought both parties to this point. That is the kind of thing one finds in Deuteronomy 1—3. As the covenant people of God make their second approach to the Promised Land, forty years after the Exodus itself (1:3) and with an entire generation gone, Moses urgently impresses upon the assembly the nature of the covenant, the greatness of the rescue that was now their heritage, the sorry history of rebellion, and above all the sheer majesty and glory of the God with whom they are linked in this spectacularly generous covenantal relationship.

The three chapters of selective history prepare the way for **Deuteronomy 4.** Here the historical survey is largely over; now the primary lessons from that history are driven home. Always review and remember what God has done. God does not owe you this amazing salvation. Far from it: "Because he loved your forefathers and chose their descendants after them, he brought you out of Egypt by his Presence and his great strength" (4:37). But there are entailments. "You were shown these things so that you might know that the LORD is God; besides him there is no other" (4:35). "Acknowledge and take to heart this day that the LORD is God in heaven above and on the earth below. There is no other" (4:39). "Be careful not to forget the covenant of the LORD your God that he made with you; do not make for yourselves an idol in the form of anything the LORD your God has forbidden. For the LORD your God is a consuming fire, a jealous God" (4:23-24). In other words, they are to serve God; but he alone is God. Every generation of believers must reckon with this truth, or face God's wrath.

Of the many lessons that spring from this historical recital, one relatively minor point—painful to Moses and important for us—quietly emerges. Moses repeatedly reminds the people that he himself will not be permitted to enter the land. He is referring to the time he struck the rock instead of speaking to it (Num. 20; see also the meditation for May 9). But now he points out, truthfully, that his sin and punishment took place, he says, "because of you" (Deut. 1:37; 3:23-27; 4:21-22). Of course, Moses was responsible for his own action. But he would not have been tempted had the people been godly. Their persistent unbelief and whining wore him down.

Meditate on a New Testament articulation of this principle: Hebrews 13:17.

Deuteronomy 5; Psalm 88; Isaiah 33; Revelation 3

∾

WHAT IS MOST STRIKING ABOUT **Psalm 88** is that there is no relief. Heman begins the psalm by crying to the Lord, disclosing his discouragement in various ways, and he ends in gloom and despair. Most psalms that deal with discouragement and despair begin in gloom and end in light. This one begins in gloom and ends in deeper gloom.

When Heman begins, although he cries to the Lord, "the God who saves me" (the only note of hope in the entire poem), he plaintively observes that he cries out before God "day and night" (88:1). He frankly feels he is not being heard (88:2, 14). He is not only in difficulty but feels he is near death: "For my soul is full of trouble and my life draws near the grave" (88:3). Indeed, Heman insists that others treat him as if he is doomed (88:4-5). The only explanation is that he is under divine wrath: "Your wrath lies heavily upon me; you have overwhelmed me with all your waves" (88:7; cf. 88:16). Not the least of his miseries is the loss of all his friends (88:8).

Worse yet, Heman is convinced his whole life has been lived under the shadow of death: "From my youth I have been afflicted and close to death," he writes (88:15). Did he, perhaps, suffer from one of the many ugly, chronic, progressive diseases? "I have suffered your terrors and am in despair. Your wrath has swept over me; your terrors have destroyed me. All day long they surround me like a flood; they have completely engulfed me" (88:15-17).

But what makes the psalm utterly grim is the closing line. Not only does Heman charge God with taking away his companions and loved ones, but in the last analysis, "the darkness is my closest friend" (88:18). Not God; the darkness.

One of the few attractive features of this psalm is its sheer honesty. It is never wise to be dishonest with God, of course; he knows exactly what we think anyway, and would rather hear our honest cries of hurt, outrage, and accusation than false cries of praise. Of course, better yet that we learn to understand, reflect, and sympathize with his own perspective. But in any case it is always the course of wisdom to be honest with God.

That brings up the most important element in this psalm. The cries and hurts penned here are not the cheap and thoughtless rage of people who use their darker moments to denounce God from afar, the smug critique of supercilious agnosticism or arrogant atheism. These cries actively engage with God, fully aware of the only real source of help.

∾

Deuteronomy 6; Psalm 89; Isaiah 34; Revelation 4

∽

WE HAVE COME ACROSS other passages dealing with the importance of passing on the heritage of biblical truth to the next generation. That theme lies at the heart of **Deuteronomy 6.** Fresh points that are especially underlined include:

(1) The ancient Israelites were to teach the next generation *to fear* the God of the covenant. Moses teaches the people "so that you, your children and their children after them may fear the LORD your God as long as you live" (6:2). When in the future a son asks his father what the laws mean, the father is to explain the background, the Exodus, and the covenant: "The LORD commanded us to obey all these decrees and to fear the LORD our God, so that we might always prosper and be kept alive, as is the case today" (6:24). We might well ask ourselves what steps we take to teach our children *to fear* the Lord our God, not with the cringing terror that is frightened of whimsical malice but with the profound conviction that this God is perfectly just and does not play around with sin.

(2) Moses underscores *the constancy* with which the next generation is to be taught. The commandments Moses passes on are to remain on the "hearts" of the people (6:6; we would probably say *minds*). Out of this abundance, the next words follow: "Impress them on your children. Talk about them when you sit at home and when you walk along the road, when you lie down and when you get up" (6:7). Even what they wore and how they decorated their houses should serve as reminders of the law of God (6:8-9). We might well ask ourselves how constantly we teach our children the content of Scripture. In ancient Israel children usually learned their vocational skills from their parents, spending countless hours with them, which provided many opportunities to pass on the blessings of the covenant. Our more fragmented culture means we must *make* opportunities.

(3) Above all, the older generation was *to model* utter loyalty to God (6:13-19). This consistent modeling was to include an utter repudiation of idolatry, obedience to the demands of the covenant, revering the name of the Lord God, doing "what is right and good in the LORD's sight" (6:18). How faithfully have we, by our own living, commended serious God-centeredness to our children?

(4) There must be a sensitive awareness of the opportunities *to answer questions* our children raise (6:20-25). Never bluff. If you do not know the answer, find out, or find someone who does. We must ask ourselves if we make maximum use of the questions our children raise.

∽

Deuteronomy 7; Psalm 90; Isaiah 35; Revelation 5

∾

SEVERAL COMPLEX THEMES intertwine in **Deuteronomy 7**. Here I want to reflect on two of them.

The *first* is the emphasis on election. "For you are a people holy to the LORD your God. The LORD your God has chosen you out of all the peoples on the face of the earth to be his people, his treasured possession" (7:6). Why so? Was it on the ground of some intrinsic superiority, some greater intelligence, some moral superiority, or some military prowess that the Lord made his choice? Not so. "The LORD did not set his affection on you and choose you because you were more numerous than other peoples, for you were the fewest of all peoples. But it was because the LORD loved you and kept the oath he swore to your forefathers that he brought you out with a mighty hand and redeemed you from the land of slavery, from the power of Pharaoh king of Egypt" (7:7-8).

Three observations: (1) In the Bible, God's utter sovereignty does not diminish human responsibility; conversely, human beings are moral agents who choose, believe, obey, disbelieve, and disobey, and this fact does not make God's sovereignty finally contingent. That is clear from the way God's sovereignty manifests itself in this chapter, that is, in election, even while the chapter bristles with the responsibilities laid on the people. People who do not believe both truths—that God is sovereign and human beings are responsible—sooner or later introduce some intolerable wobbles into the structure of their faith. (2) Here God's love is selective. God chooses Israel because he sets his affection on them, and not for anything in themselves. The thought recurs elsewhere (e.g., Mal. 1:2-3). But this is not the only way that the Bible speaks of the love of God (e.g., John 3:16).

The *second* theme is the encouragement God gives his people not to fear the people they will have to fight as they take over the Promised Land (7:17-22). The reason is the Exodus. Any God that could produce the plagues, divide the Red Sea, and free his people from a regional superpower like Egypt is not the kind of God who is going to have trouble with a few pagan and immoral Canaanites. Fear is the opposite of faith. The Israelites are encouraged not to be afraid, not because they are stronger or better, but because they are the people of God, and God is unbeatable.

These two themes—and several others—intertwine in this chapter. The God who chooses people is strong enough to accomplish all his purposes in them; the people chosen by God ought to respond not only with grateful obedience, but with unshakable trust.

∾

Deuteronomy 8; Psalm 91; Isaiah 36; Revelation 6

∾

DEUTERONOMY 8 PROVIDES AN important theological perspective on the forty years of wandering in the wilderness. Because God is a personal God, one can tell the story of those years in terms of the interaction between God and his people: he meets their need, they rebel, he responds in judgment, they repent—and then the cycle repeats itself. On the other hand, one can look at the whole account from the perspective of God's transcendent and faithful sovereignty. He remains in charge. That is the vantage offered here.

Of course, God *could have* given them everything they wanted before they had even bothered to articulate their desires. He *could have* spoiled them rotten. Instead, his intention was to humble them, to test them, even to let them hunger before eventually feeding them with manna (8:2-3). The purpose of this latter exercise, Moses insists, was that God might teach them "that man does not live on bread alone but on every word that comes from the mouth of the LORD" (8:3). More generally: "Know then in your heart that as a man disciplines his son, so the LORD your God disciplines you" (8:5).

Why all this discipline? The sad reality is that fallen people like you and me readily fixate on God's gifts and ignore their Giver. At some point, this degenerates into worshiping the created thing rather than the Creator (cf. Rom. 1:25). God knows that is Israel's danger. He is bringing them into a land with agricultural promise, adequate water, and mineral wealth (8:6-9). What likelihood would there be *at that point* of learning that "man does not live on bread alone but on every word that comes from the mouth of the LORD"?

Even after these forty years of discipline, the dangers will prove enormous. So Moses spells the lessons out to them. Once the people have settled in the Promised Land and are enjoying its considerable wealth, the dangers will begin. "Be careful that you do not forget the LORD your God, failing to observe his commands, his laws and his decrees" (8:11). With wealth will come the temptation to arrogance, prompting the people to forget the Lord who brought them out of slavery (8:12-14). In the end, not only will they value the wealth above the words of God, they may even justify themselves, proudly declaiming, "My power and the strength of my hands have produced this wealth for me" (8:17)—conveniently forgetting that even the ability to produce wealth is a gracious gift from God (8:18).

In what ways does your life show you cherish every word that comes from the mouth of God, above all the blessings and even the necessities of this life?

∾

Deuteronomy 9; Psalms 92—93; Isaiah 37; Revelation 7

∽

IF DEUTERONOMY 8 REMINDS THE Israelites that God is the One who gave them all their material blessings, not least the ability to work and produce wealth, **Deuteronomy 9** insists he is also the One who will enable them to take over the Promised Land and vanquish their opponents. Before the struggle, the Israelites are still fighting their fears. God graciously reassures them: "But be assured today that the LORD your God is the one who goes across ahead of you like a devouring fire. He will destroy them; he will subdue them before you" (9:3). But *after* the struggle, the temptation of the Israelites will be quite different. Then they will be tempted to think that, whatever their fears before the event, it was their own intrinsic superiority that enabled them to accomplish the feat. So Moses warns them:

> *After the Lord your God has driven them out before you do not say to yourself, "The Lord has brought me here to take possession of this land because of my righteousness." No, it is on account of the wickedness of these nations that the Lord is going to drive them out before you. It is not because of your righteousness or your integrity that you are going in to take possession of their land; but on account of the wickedness of these nations . . . to accomplish what he swore to your fathers, to Abraham, Isaac and Jacob. Understand, then, that it is not because of your righteousness that the Lord your God is giving you this good land to possess, for you are a stiff-necked people. (9:4-6)*

And the evidence for this last point? Moses reminds them of their sorry rebellions during the wilderness years, starting from the wretched incident of the golden calf (9:4-29).

What shall we learn? (1) Although the annihilation of the Canaanites fills us with embarrassed horror, there is a sense in which (dare I say it?) we had better get used to it. It is of a piece with the Flood, with the destruction of several empires, with hell itself. The proper response is Luke 13:1-5: unless we repent, we shall all likewise perish. (2) It may be true to say that the Israelites won because the Canaanites were so evil. It does not follow that the Canaanites lost because the Israelites were so good. God was working to improve the Israelites out of his own covenantal faithfulness. But they were extremely foolish if they thought, after the event, that they had earned their triumph. (3) Our temptations, like Israel's, vary with our circumstances: faithless fear in one circumstance, arrogant pride in another. Only the closest walk with God affords us the self-criticism that abominates both.

∽

Deuteronomy 10; Psalm 94; Isaiah 38; Revelation 8

∾

INTERSPERSED WITH THE HISTORICAL RECITAL that makes up much of the early chapters of Deuteronomy are bursts of exhortation. One of the most moving is found in **Deuteronomy 10:12-22.** Its magnificent themes include:

(1) A sheer God-centeredness that embraces both *fearing* God and *loving* God (10:12-13). In our confused and blinded world, fearing God without loving him will dissolve into terror, and thence into taboos, magic, incantations, rites; loving God without obeying him will dissolve into sentimentalism without strong affection, pretensions of godliness without moral vigor, unbridled lust for power without any sense of impropriety, nostalgic yearnings for relationships without any passion for holiness. Neither pattern squares with what the Bible says: "And now, O Israel, what does the LORD your God ask of you but to fear the LORD your God, to walk in all his ways, to love him . . . ?" (10:12).

(2) A sheer God-centeredness that pictures election as a gracious act. God owns the whole show—"the heavens, even the highest heavens, the earth and everything in it" (10:14). He can do with it as he wishes. What he has in fact done is "set his affection" on the patriarchs, loving them, and in turn choosing their descendants (10:15; cf. 4:37).

(3) A sheer God-centeredness that is never satisfied with the mere rites and show of religion: it demands the heart (10:16). That is why physical circumcision could never be seen as an end in itself, not even in the Old Testament. It symbolized something deeper: circumcision of the heart. What God wants is not merely an outward sign that certain people belong to him, but an inward disposition of heart and mind that orient us to God continually.

(4) A sheer God-centeredness that recognizes his impartiality, and therefore his justice—and acts accordingly (10:17-20). He is "God of gods and Lord of lords, the great God, mighty and awesome" (10:17). Small wonder then that he accepts no bribes and shows no partiality. (Never confuse election with partiality. Partiality is favoritism that is corrupted by a willingness to pervert justice for the sake of the favored few; election chooses certain people out of God's free decision and nothing else, and even then justice is not perverted: hence the cross.) And he expects his people to conduct themselves accordingly.

(5) A sheer God-centeredness that is displayed in his people's praise (10:20-22). "He is your praise; he is your God" (10:21). Those who focus much on God have much for which to praise. Those whose vision is merely terrestrial or self-centered dry up inside like desiccated prunes. God is your praise!

∾

Deuteronomy 11; Psalms 95—96; Isaiah 39; Revelation 9

∽

MY PARENTS WERE RATHER POOR—not with the poverty one finds in the worst of the world's slums, but poor by North American standards. My Dad was a pastor. Before I was born, still at the end of the Great Depression, Dad took around a little wagon of food that had been collected one Christmas for the poor, and then came home to the flat my parents rented, where the only food for Christmas dinner was a can of beans. My parents gave thanks to God for that—and then even as they were doing so, they were invited out for a meal. I can remember many instances, as I was growing up, when our family prayed that God would meet our needs—huge medical bills when we could afford no insurance, for example—and he always did. When I left home to go to university, my parents scrimped and saved; that year they sent me ten dollars. For them it was a lot of money; for myself, I was financially on my own, and worked and studied. Many times I went two or three days without food, drinking lots of water to keep my stomach from rumbling, asking the Lord to meet my needs, fearful I would have to put the studies aside. God always met them, sometimes in simple ways, sometimes in astonishing displays.

Today I look at my children, and recognize that although they face new sets of trials and temptations, so far they have never had to face anything resembling deprivation (not getting everything they want doesn't count!). Then I read **Deuteronomy 11,** where Moses makes a generational distinction: "Remember today that your children were not the ones who saw and experienced the discipline of the LORD your God: his majesty, his mighty hand, his outstretched arm; the signs he performed and the things he did in the heart of Egypt, both to Pharaoh king of Egypt and to his whole country" (11:2-3; see 11:5). No, it wasn't the children. "But it was your own eyes that saw all these great things the LORD has done" (11:7).

What then does Moses infer from this generational distinction? (1) The older generation should be quick to obey, because of all that they have had the opportunity to learn (11:8). Here I am, wondering about my children's limited experience, when the first thing God says is that I am the one with no excuse. (2) The older generation must systematically pass on what they have learned to their children (11:19-21); again, the prime responsibility is mine, not theirs. (3) More broadly, God's provision to the people of the blessings of the covenant, here focused on the land and its bounty, depends on the first two points.

∽

Deuteronomy 12; Psalms 97—98; Isaiah 40; Revelation 9

∾

ALTHOUGH THE BOOK OF Deuteronomy constantly looks backward to the Exodus and years of wilderness wanderings, it also looks forward: the people are about to enter the Promised Land, and certain things will change. In times of transition, one must grasp the distinction between what should change and what should not.

Yesterday's chapter includes the word *today*: "Remember *today* that your children were not the ones . . ." (Deut. 11:2). That word is important throughout this book. A proper grasp of the past prepares the way for the changes *today*, on the verge of entry into the Promised Land. In **Deuteronomy 12**, the biggest change that is envisaged is the establishment within the land of a place where God will choose "to put his Name" and establish his dwelling (12:5, 11). In other words, the chapter anticipates the time when neither independent sacrifices offered wherever the worshiper happens to be (12:8), nor the mobile tabernacle of the years of pilgrimage, will be acceptable; rather, God will establish a stable center in the land. "To that place you must go; there bring your burnt offerings and sacrifices, your tithes and special gifts. . . . There, in the presence of the LORD your God, you and your families shall eat and shall rejoice in everything you have put your hand to, because the LORD your God has blessed you" (12:5-7). In due course the tabernacle was situated at Shiloh, Bethel, and finally at Jerusalem, where it was replaced by the temple in the days of Solomon.

The changed circumstances bring points of both continuity and discontinuity. Moses insists that then, as now, there will be no tolerance for the pagan worship practices of the surrounding nations and of those they purge from the land (12:29-31). But the sheer distance that most people will live from the central sanctuary means that they cannot be expected to have all meat slaughtered in its precincts, nor to observe the fine distinctions between what is the priest's part and what is their part. Now it will be entirely appropriate to slaughter their animals and eat them as they would wild game killed in the field (12:15-22). Even so, three points continue in full force. (1) They must not forget to provide for the Levites (many of whom depended on the service of the tabernacle/temple for their sustenance—12:19); (2) they must not eat the blood of the animals they slaughter (12:23-25); (3) they are still expected to offer the consecrated sacrifices at the central shrine on the high feast days, when every family is expected to present itself to the Lord (12:26-28).

Other transitions follow in the history of redemption and demand our thoughtful meditation (e.g., Ps. 95:7-11; Mark 7:19; John 16:5-11; Heb. 3:7—4:11).

∾

Deuteronomy 13—14; Psalms 99—101; Isaiah 41; Revelation 11

∾

THREE QUESTIONS:

(1) How can you spot a false prophet? The Bible offers several complementary criteria. For instance, in Deuteronomy 18:22 we are told that if an ostensible prophet predicts something and that thing does not take place, the prophet is false. Of course, that criterion does not help very much if what the prophet has predicted is far into the future. Moreover, here in **Deuteronomy 13** we are warned that the inverse does not prove the prophet *is* trustworthy. If what the ostensible prophet predicts takes place, or if he manages to perform some sort of miraculous sign or wonder, another criterion must be brought to bear. Is this prophet's message enticing people to worship some god other than the Lord who brought the people out of Egypt?

What this criterion presupposes is a thorough grasp of antecedent revelation. You have to know what God *has* revealed about himself before you can determine whether or not the prophet is leading you to a false god. For the false god may still be given the biblical names of God (as in, say, Mormonism, or the christology of Jehovah's Witnesses). John's first epistle offers this same criterion: if what an ostensible prophet (1 John 4:1-6) teaches cannot be squared with what the believers have heard "from the beginning" (1 John 2:7; 2 John 9), it is not of God (so also Paul in Gal. 1:8-9).

(2) Why are false prophets dangerous? Apart from the obvious reason, viz. that they teach false doctrine that leads people astray from the living God and therefore ultimately attracts his judgment, there are two reasons. *First,* their very description—"false prophet"—discloses the core problem. They profess to speak the word of God, and this can be seductive. If they came along and said, "Let us sin disgustingly," most would not be attracted. The seduction of false prophecy is its ostensible spirituality and truthfulness. *Second,* although false prophets may enter a community from outside (e.g., Acts 20:29—and if it is the "right" outside, this makes them very attractive), they may arise from *within* the community (e.g., Acts 20:30), as here—for example, a family member (13:6). I know of more than one Christian institution that went bad doctrinally because of nepotism.

(3) What should be done about them? Three things. *First,* recognize that these testing events do not escape the bounds of God's sovereignty. Allegiance is all the more called for (13:3-4). *Second,* learn the truth, learn it well, or you will always lack discernment. *Third,* purge the community of false prophets (a process that takes a different form under the new covenant: e.g., 2 Cor. 10—13; 1 John 4:1-6), or they will gradually win credence and do enormous damage.

∾

Deuteronomy 15; Psalm 102; Isaiah 42: Revelation 12

∽

ONE OF THE STRIKING features of the many passages in Deuteronomy that describe what life should be like once the people enter the Promised Land is a tension between what is held out as the ideal and what will in fact prove the reality.

Thus, on the one hand, the people are told that "there should be no poor among you, for in the land the LORD your God is giving you to possess as your inheritance, he will richly bless you, if only you fully obey the LORD your God and are careful to follow all these commands I am giving you today" (**Deut. 15:4-5**). On the other hand, the same chapter frankly acknowledges, "There will always be poor people in the land. Therefore I command you to be openhanded toward your brothers and toward the poor and needy in your land" (15:11).

The former passage, that "there should be no poor among you," is grounded in two things: the sheer abundance of the land (a sign of covenantal blessing), and the civil laws God wants imposed so as to avoid any form of the wretched "poverty trap." The latter include the canceling of debts every seven years—a shocking proposal to our ears (15:1-11). There is even a warning about harboring the "wicked thought," once the seventh year was impending, of planning stinginess (15:8-10).

The extent to which these idealistic statutes were ever enacted is disputed. There is very little evidence that they became widely observed public law in the Promised Land. Thus the second passage, that "there will always be poor people in the land," is inevitable. It reflects the grim reality that *no* economic system can guarantee the abolition of poverty, because human beings operate it, human beings are greedy, human beings will keep tweaking and eventually perverting the system for personal advantage. This is not to suggest that all economic systems are equally good or equally bad: transparently, that is not so. Nor is it to suggest that legislators should not constantly work to correct a system and fill loopholes that encourage corruption. But it is to suggest that the Bible is painfully realistic about the impossibility of any utopia, economic or otherwise, in this fallen world. Moreover, on occasion the Israelites would become so corrupt, both within the economic arena and beyond it, that God would withhold his blessing from the land; for instance, the rain might be withheld (as in the days of Elijah). And then the land itself would not be able to support all the people living there.

Thus the insistence that there will always be poor people (a point Jesus reiterates, Matt. 26:11) is not a surreptitious fatalism, but an appeal for openhanded generosity.

∽

Deuteronomy 16; Psalm 103; Isaiah 43; Revelation 13

∾

IT IS DIFFICULT TO IMAGINE a lovelier psalm than **Psalm 103**. When our children were growing up, the price they "paid" for their first leather-bound Bibles was memorizing Psalm 103. Across the centuries, countless believers have turned to these lines to find their spirits lifted, a renewed commitment to praise and gratitude, an incentive to prayer, a restoration of a God-centered worldview. This psalm could easily claim our meditations for the rest of the month, for the rest of the year. Instead, we focus on three of its features.

(1) The psalm is bracketed by exhortations to praise. At the front end, David exhorts himself, and, by his example, his readers: "Praise the LORD, O my soul; all my inmost being, praise his holy name" (103:1). Implicitly David recognizes that it is distressingly easy to preserve the externals of praise, with nothing erupting from within the heart of God's image-bearers. This will not do: "*all my inmost being*, praise his holy name." By the end of the psalm, however honest and profound this individual's worship, the framework for praising such a God is too small, for after all, God's kingdom rules over all (103:19): "Praise the LORD, you his angels, you mighty ones who do his bidding, who obey his word. Praise the LORD, all his heavenly hosts, you his servants who do his will. Praise the LORD, all his works, everywhere in his dominion. Praise the LORD, O my soul" (103:20-22). Now the psalmist's praise is one with the praise of heaven, with the praise of the entire created order.

(2) When David starts to enumerate "all his benefits" (103:2), he begins with the forgiveness of sins (103:3). Here is a man who understands what is of greatest importance. If we have everything but God's forgiveness, we have nothing of worth; if we have God's forgiveness, everything else of value is also promised (cf. Rom. 8:32).

(3) David soon moves from the blessings he enjoys as an individual believer to the Lord's public justice (103:6), to his gracious self-disclosure to Moses and the Israelites (103:7-18). Here he stays the longest time, turning over and over in his mind the greatest blessings the Lord has granted to his people. Above all, he focuses once again on the sheer privilege of having sins forgiven, removed, forgotten. All of this, David perceives, stems from the character of God. "The LORD is compassionate and gracious, slow to anger, abounding in love" (103:8). He deals with our sin—but compassionately, fully bearing in mind our weak frames. We may be creatures of time, but "from everlasting to everlasting the LORD's love is with those who fear him" (103:17).

∾

Deuteronomy 17; Psalm 104; Isaiah 44; Revelation 14

∽

MOSES ENVISAGES A TIME when the Israelite nation will choose a king (**Deut. 17:14-20**). He could not know that centuries later, when the Israelites would first ask for a king, they would do so for all the wrong motives—primarily so that they could be like the pagan nations around them. The result was Saul. But that is another story.

If the people are to have a king, what sort of king should he be? (1) He must be the Lord's own choice (17:15). (2) He must be an Israelite, drawn "from among your own brothers" (17:15), not some foreigner. (3) He must not acquire for himself great numbers of horses, i.e., amass great personal wealth and military might, and especially not if it means some sort of alliance with a power such as Egypt (17:16). (4) He must not take many wives (17:17). The issue was not simply polygamy. In the ancient Near East, the more powerful the king the more wives he had. This prohibition is therefore simultaneously a limit on the king's power, and a warning that many wives will likely lead his heart astray (17:17). This is not because wives are intrinsically evil; rather, a king on the hunt for many wives is likely to marry princesses and nobility from surrounding countries, and they will bring their paganism with them. Within that framework, the king's heart will be led astray. That is exactly what happened to Solomon. (5) Upon accession to the throne, the first thing the king must do is write out for himself, in Hebrew, a copy of "this law"—whether the book of Deuteronomy or the entire Pentateuch. Then he is to read it every day for the rest of his life (17:18-20). The multiple purposes of this task are explicit: that he may revere the Lord his God, carefully follow all his words, and in consequence not consider himself better than his fellow citizens, and not turn aside from the law. The result will be a long-lasting dynasty.

It is not difficult to imagine how the entire history of Israel would have been radically different if these five criteria had been adopted by each king who came to the throne of David. It would be almost a millennium and a half before there would arise in Israel a king who would be the Lord's chosen servant, someone "made like his brothers in every way" (Heb. 2:17), a mere craftsman without wealth or power, a man not seduced by beauty or power or paganism (despite the devil's most virulent assaults), a man steeped in the Scriptures from his youth and who carefully followed all the words of God. How we need that king!

∽

Deuteronomy 18; Psalm 105; Isaiah 45; Revelation 15

∽

THE PROPHECY OF THE COMING of a prophet like Moses (**Deut. 18:15-18**) must first of all be understood within its own context. Four observations bring this passage to sharp focus.

First, the preceding verses (18:9-13) condemn the religious practices of the nations the Israelites are displacing, especially those religious practices used for guidance: divination, sorcery, interpretation of omens, witchcraft, casting of spells, spiritism, and necromancy. These "detestable practices" (18:12) constitute part of the reason why these nations were driven out—a lesson many in the West have not learned, to our great danger. Such practices implicitly deny God's sovereignty, and encourage people to rely for their safety and well-being on either superstitious nonsense or demonic power. In the transition verse (18:14), Moses contrasts the Israelites: "But as for you, the LORD your God has not permitted you to do so." Far from it: as the Lord gave his word through the prophet Moses, so after Moses' death God will raise up a prophet like Moses. "You must listen to him" (18:15). God's people are to be led by the word of God faithfully delivered by his prophets, not by religious superstition.

Second, that raises the question as to who is a true prophet (18:20-22), a theme Moses had already discussed (Deut. 13; see the June 9 meditation) but which is here briefly reintroduced. For if people will know the Word of God through God's prophets, it is important to reiterate some of the criteria by which one may distinguish true prophets from false.

Third, Moses reminds the Israelites of the essentially mediatorial role of the prophet (18:16-17). Of course, this is true at a fairly trite level: genuine prophets reveal words from God that would otherwise be unknown, and thus mediate between God and people. But Moses refers to something more profound. When God displayed himself at Sinai, the people were so terrified that they knew they dared not approach this holy God: they would be destroyed (Ex. 20:18-19). The people *wanted* Moses to be the mediator of the revelation from God. God praises them for this judgment, this right-minded fear of God (Deut. 18:17). In the same way, God will raise up another prophet who will exercise the same mediating function.

Fourth, at some level this promise was fulfilled in every genuine prophet God sent. But the language of this promise is so generous it is difficult not to see that some special prophet is finally in view: he will not only tell everything that God commands him, but if anyone does not listen to God's words spoken in God's name, God himself will hold him to account. Meditate not only on Acts 3:22-23; 7:37, but on John 5:16-30.

∽

Deuteronomy 19; Psalm 106; Isaiah 46; Revelation 16

∿

THE JUSTICE ENVISAGED IN **Deuteronomy 19** seems to stand a considerable distance from the views that prevail in Western nations today.

With part of this text's emphasis, most of us will find ourselves in substantial sympathy: the courts must not convict a person on meager evidence. In the days before powerful forensic tools, this almost always meant that multiple witnesses should be required (19:15). Today the kind of evidence thought to be sufficient has expanded: fingerprints, blood-typing, and so forth. Most of us recognize that this is a good thing. But enough reports have circulated of evidence that has been tampered with that the concern of our text is scarcely out of date. Procedures and policies must be put in place that make it difficult to corrupt the court or convict an innocent person.

But the rest of the chapter (19:16-21) seems, at first, somewhat alien to us, for three reasons. (1) If careful judges determine that some witness has perjured himself, then the judges are to impose on that person the penalty that would have been imposed on the defendant wrongfully charged: you are to "do to him as he intended to do to his brother" (19:19). (2) The aim is "to purge the evil from among you" (19:20). (3) Once again, the *lex talionis* (the "eye for an eye" statute) is repeated (19:21; cf. Ex. 21:24, and the meditation for March 11).

All three points are looked at very differently in Western courts. (1) Punishment for malicious perjury is usually negligible. But this means there is little official effort to fan the flame of social passion for public justice. You lie if you can get away with it; the shame is only in getting caught. (2) Our penal theorists think incarceration serves to make society a safer place, or provides a venue for reform (therapeutic or otherwise), or ensures that an offender "pays his debt to society." So much effort goes into analyzing the social conditions that play a contributing role in shaping a criminal that everywhere there is widespread reluctance to speak of the *evil* of a person or an act. Perhaps that is why revenge movies have to depict really astoundingly horrendous cruelty in one-dimensional monsters before the revenge can be justified. The Bible's stance is truly radical (i.e., it goes to the *radix*, the root): judicially, the courts must purge out the *evil* among you. (3) We incarcerate; we rarely think about the justice of making a punishment "fit" the crime. But that was one of the functions of the *lex talionis*.

When one focuses on justice and personal accountability, it is our own judicial and penal system that seems increasingly misguided and alien.

∿

Deuteronomy 20; Psalm 107; Isaiah 47; Revelation 17

HISTORICALLY, REVIVAL REFERRED TO a time of God-sent blessing beyond the ordinary. Ministers of the Word went about their work, praying, preaching, catechizing, counseling, whether in times of persecution, or in times of relative quiet and steady growth. But if the Lord God visited his people with *revival,* it was immediately evident in an extraordinary sense of the presence of God, in deep-seated repentance and a renewed passion for holiness, and ultimately in the sound and indisputable conversion of many people. It could be relatively disciplined, or it might be mixed with the spurious.

Although "revival" still has this sense in some circles, in others it refers to a meeting or series of meetings where preachers speak on personal holiness or give evangelistic messages. It is assumed that if the preacher is gifted there will be obvious fruit. In some circles in the southern part of the United States, one hears expressions like "holding a revival" or "preaching a revival." It would aid clarity of thought if instead they spoke of "holding a Bible conference" or "preaching an evangelistic series."

Psalm 107 lists a diverse array of circumstances in which people find themselves in great danger or under horrible oppression, usually because of their own sin. In each case, God comes to the rescue. Those who wandered in desert wastelands cried to the Lord, and were delivered from their thirst and hunger (107:4-9). Others sat in chains, prisoners, "for they had rebelled against the words of God" (107:11), and the Lord freed them (107:13-14). Still others became so corroded by their folly that they loathed life. But when they cried to the Lord, "he sent forth his word and healed them" (107:20). Others found themselves in mortal peril on the seas, and here, too, the Lord responded to their cries and saved them (107:23-32). Indeed, this God humbles the haughty, and for the sake of the needy and afflicted he turns the desert into fertile fields (107:33-42).

Lest we misunderstand the psalmist's point, he makes it clear for us in two ways. First, in most of the sections, when he describes those who have been saved, he prescribes, "Let them give thanks to the LORD *for his unfailing love and his wonderful deeds for men*" (107:8, 15, 21, 31). Second, the opening of the psalm reminds us that God is good, and *his love endures forever* (107:1), while the closing insists, "Whoever is wise, let him heed these things *and consider the great love of the LORD*" (107:43). This, and this alone, is the ultimate source of God's blessings—not the least being revival. And the last verse goes further, and provides the sanction for studying revivals among the blessings of God.

Deuteronomy 21; Psalms 108—109; Isaiah 48; Revelation 18

PSALM 108 IS RATHER DISTINCTIVE in the book of Psalms. Apart from minor changes, it is made up of parts of two other psalms. Psalm 108:1-5 follows 57:7-11; Psalm 108:6-13 follows 60:5-12. Nevertheless the "feel" of the result is startlingly different.

Both Psalms 57 and 60 find David under enormous pressure. In the former, the superscription places David in flight from King Saul, and hiding in a cave; in the latter, David and his troops have been defeated. In both cases, however, the psalm ends in praise and confidence—and the respective sections on praise and confidence from these two psalms are now joined together to make Psalm 108. Although Psalm 108 still hints at a stressful situation that includes some chastening by God (108:11), the tone of the whole slips away from the dark moods of the early parts of the other two psalms, and in comparison is flooded with adoration and confidence.

That simple fact forces us to recognize something very important. The earlier two psalms (57 and 60) will doubtless seem especially appropriate to us when we face peril—individual or corporate—or suffer some kind of humiliating defeat. The present psalm will ring in our ears when we pause to look back on the manifold goodness of God, reminding ourselves of the sweep of his sovereignty and his utter worthiness to receive our praise. It might prove especially useful when we are about to venture on some new initiative for which our faith demands fresh grounding. This perspective of changed application occurs *because the same words are now placed in a new context*. And that is the point.

For although all of Scripture is true and important, deserving study, reflection, and carefully applied thought, the Lord God in his wisdom did not give us a Bible of abstract principles, but highly diverse texts woven into highly diverse situations. Despite the diversity, of course, there is still only one sweeping storyline, and only one Mind ultimately behind it. But the rich tapestry of varied human experience reflected in the different biblical books and passages—not least in the different psalms—enables the Bible to speak to us with peculiar force and power when the "fit" between the experience of the human author and our experience is especially intimate.

For this astonishing wealth, God deserves reverent praise. What mind but his, what compass of understanding but his, what providential oversight over the production of Scripture but his, could produce a work so unified yet so profoundly diverse? Here, too, is reason to join our "Amen" to the words of 108:5: "Be exalted, O God, above the heavens, and let your glory be over all the earth."

Deuteronomy 22; Psalms 110—111; Isaiah 49; Revelation 19

∾

THE OLD TESTAMENT CHAPTER quoted most often in the New Testament is **Psalm 110**. It is an *oracular psalm*: i.e., it does not so much disclose the experience of its writer as set forth words that the writer has received by direct and immediate revelation—as an "oracle" from God. Perhaps there are even parts of it the psalmist himself did not fathom too well (just as Daniel did not understand the meaning of all that he saw in his visions and was required to record for the benefit of a later generation [Dan. 12:4, 8-10]).

In the psalm, the LORD, Yahweh, speaks to someone whom David himself addresses as "my Lord." This element, as much as any other, has convinced countless interpreters, both Jewish and Christian, that this is explicitly a messianic psalm, and that the person whom David addresses is the anticipated Messiah.

I shall focus on verse 4: "The LORD has sworn and will not change his mind: 'You are a priest forever, in the order of Melchizedek.'" Granted that *Yahweh* here addresses the Messiah, what do his words mean? Two elements attract attention:

First, Melchizedek himself—this is only the second mention of him in the Bible. The first is Genesis 14:18-20: after the defeat of the kings, Abraham meets this strange priest-king and pays him a tithe of the spoils. Various things can be inferred from the brief account (see meditation for January 13), but then Melchizedek drops from view until this psalm, written almost a millennium later.

Second, by this time much has taken place in the history of Israel. The people had endured slavery in Egypt, had been rescued at the Exodus, had received the Law of God at Sinai, had entered the Promised Land, and had lived through the period of the judges to reach this point of the beginning of the Davidic dynasty. Above all, Sinai had prescribed a tabernacle and the associated rites, all to be administered by Levites and by high priests drawn from that tribe. The Mosaic Law made it abundantly clear that Levites alone could discharge these priestly functions. Yet here is an oracle from God insisting that God himself will raise up another priest-king with very different links. Yahweh will extend this king's mighty scepter from Zion: i.e., his kingly power is connected with Zion, with Jerusalem, and thus with the fledgling Davidic dynasty. And as priest, he will be aligned, not with the order of Levi, but with the order of Melchizedek.

Small wonder the writer to the Hebrews understands that this is an announcement of the obsolescence of the Mosaic Covenant (Heb. 7:11-12). We needed a better priesthood; and we have one.

∾

Deuteronomy 23; Psalms 112—113; Isaiah 50; Revelation 20

EVERY SO OFTEN IN THE Pentateuch there is a chapter of miscellaneous laws and statutes. One such is **Deuteronomy 23.** It goes beyond these brief meditations to reflect on each topic for which a statute is laid down, or even on the ordering principle of some of these lists. Transparently some of the legislation is based on the historical experience of the Israelites (e.g., 23:3-8). Other parts turn on symbol-laden cleanliness (e.g., 23:9-14). Still others focus on the urgency to keep the covenant people separate from the abominable practices of ancient Canaanite paganism (23:17-18), on progressive steps of social justice (23:15-16), on fiscal principles to enhance both the identity and the well-being of the covenant community (23:19-20), and on keeping one's word, especially in a vow offered to the living God (23:21-23). But today I shall reflect on 23:24-25: "If you enter your neighbor's vineyard, you may eat all the grapes you want, but do not put any in your basket. If you enter your neighbor's grain field, you may pick kernels with your hands, but you must not put a sickle to his standing grain."

There is profound wisdom to these simple statutes. A merely communitarian stance would either let people take what they want, whenever they want, as much as they want; or, alternatively, it would say that since all the produce belongs to the community (or the state), no individual is allowed to take any of it without explicit sanction from the leaders of the community. A merely capitalistic stance (or, more precisely, a stance that put all the emphasis on private property) would view every instance of taking a grape from a neighbor's field as a matter of theft, every instance of chewing on a few kernels of grain as you follow the footpath through your neighbor's field as a punishable offense. But by allowing people to eat what they want while actually in the field of a neighbor, this statute fosters a kind of community-wide interdependence, a vision of a shared heritage. The walls and fences erected by zealous private ownership are softened. Moreover, the really poor could at least find something to eat. This would not be a terrible burden on any one landowner if the statute were observed by all the landowners. On the other hand, the stipulation that no one is allowed to carry any produce away, if observed, serves not only to combat theft and laziness, but preserves private property and the incentives to industry and disciplined labor associated with it.

Many, many statues from the Mosaic Law, rightly probed, reflect a godly balance of complementary interests.

Deuteronomy 24; Psalms 114—115; Isaiah 51; Revelation 21

∾

IT IS STRIKING HOW THE Mosaic Law provides for the poor.

Consider **Deuteronomy 24**. Here God forbids taking a pair of millstones, or "even the upper one" (i.e., the more movable one), as security for a debt (24:6). It would be like taking a mechanic's tools as security, or a software writer's computer. That would take away the means of earning a living, and would therefore not only compound the poverty but would make repayment a practical impossibility.

In 24:10-12, two further stipulations are laid down with respect to security for loans. (1) If you make a loan to a neighbor, do not go into his home to get the pledge. Stay outside; let him bring it out to you. Such restrained conduct allows the neighbor to preserve a little dignity, and curtails the tendency of some rich people to throw their weight around and treat the poor as if they are dirt. (2) Do not keep as security what the poor man needs for basic warmth and shelter.

In 24:14-15, employers are told to pay their workers daily. In a poor and agrarian society where as much as 70% or 80% of income went on food, this was ensuring that the hired hand and his family had enough to eat every day. Withholding wages not only imposed a hardship, but was unjust. Still broader considerations of justice are expressed in 24:17-18: orphans and aliens, i.e., those without protectors or who do not really understand a particular culture's "ropes," are to be treated with justice and never abused or taken advantage of.

Finally, in 24:19-22, farmers are warned not to pick up every scrap of produce from their field in order to get a better return. Far better to leave some "for the alien, the fatherless and the widow." (See also the meditation for August 9.)

Two observations: *First,* these sorts of provisions for the poor will work best in a nontechnological society where labor and land are tied together, and help is provided by locals for locals. There is no massive bureaucratic scheme. On the other hand, without some sort of structured organization it is difficult to imagine how to foster similar help for the poor in, say, the south side of Chicago, where there are few farmers to leave scraps of produce. *Second,* the incentive in every case is to act rightly under the gaze of God, especially remembering the years the people themselves spent in Egypt (24:13-22). These verses demand close reading. Where people live in the fear, love, and knowledge of God, social compassion and practical generosity are entailed; where God fades into the mists of sentimentalism, robust compassion also withers—bringing down the biting denunciation of prophets like Amos.

∾

Deuteronomy 25; Psalm 116; Isaiah 52; Revelation 22

∾

SOMETIMES TRANSLATION DIFFICULTIES prompt Bible translators to include footnotes that preserve alternative possibilities. Sometimes no alternative is included, and something important is lost. One instance of each kind is found in **Psalm 116**, and both deserve thoughtful reflection.

(1) The NIV reads, "I believed; *therefore* I said, 'I am greatly afflicted.' And in my dismay I said, 'All men are liars'" (116:10-11, italics added). The *Revised Standard Version* renders the first line, "I kept my faith, *even when* I said. . . ." The latter is a perfectly possible rendering of the Hebrew, and most modern translations have followed it. Paul quotes from the ancient Greek translation of the Hebrew, commonly called the Septuagint (or LXX), which preserves the meaning found in the NIV of Psalm 116:10-11 (see 2 Cor. 4:13).

But in this case, surprisingly little is at stake. Perhaps the NIV rendering is a trifle stronger: the *reason why* the psalmist said he was greatly afflicted was that he believed ("I believed; *therefore* I said"). In other words, it was nothing other than his faith in God—and the entire relationship with God that such faith presupposes—that enabled him to see that when he faced terrible suffering it was nothing other than the affliction meted out by God. But more importantly, both the NIV and the RSV make a point frequently illustrated in the Psalms, and particularly illustrated in Job: when someone feels crushed (116:10) or utterly disillusioned (116:11), *and says so,* it does not follow that he or she has abandoned faith. Rather, the unguarded accents of pain, offered up to God, give evidence of both life and faith.

(2) The NIV's "precious in the sight of the LORD is the death of his saints" (116:15) is often cited at funerals, and doubtless it expresses an important truth. But there is good reason to think that the word rendered "precious" should be rendered "costly" or the like: hence *Jerusalem Bible*'s "The death of the devout costs Yahweh dear." The psalmist's rescue from the borders of death (116:3, 8) makes that rendering more likely. Certainly Jesus recognizes how costly is the death of one human being (Matt. 10:29-31).

If that is the case, it is vitally important to see that although God in his sovereignty rules over everything, including all deaths, this reign for him is not some cold piece of accounting. He knows better than we do the sheer ugliness and abnormality of death, how it is irrefragably tied to our rebellion and the curse we have attracted. It is immensely comforting to perceive that the death of the devout costs Yahweh dear. Still more wonderful is the price he was willing to pay to supplant death by resurrection.

∾

Deuteronomy 26; Psalms 117—118; Isaiah 53; Matthew 1

WHEN I WAS A BOY, a plaque in our home was inscribed with the words "This is the day which the LORD hath made; we will rejoice and be glad in it." Apart from the change from "hath" to "has," similar words are preserved in the NIV of **Psalm 118:24.**

My father gently applied this text to his children when we whined or complained about little nothings. Was the weather too hot and sticky? "This is the day which the LORD has made; we will rejoice and be glad in it." Were the skies pelting rain, so we could not go out to play? "This is the day the LORD has made; we will rejoice and be glad in it." What a boring day (or place, or holiday, or visit to relatives)! "This is the day the LORD has made; we will rejoice and be glad in it." Sometimes the words were repeated with significant emphasis: "This is the day the LORD has made; we *will* rejoice and be glad in it."

It is not that Dad would not listen to serious complaints; it is not that Scripture does not have other things to say. But every generation of Christians has to learn that whining is an affront against God's sovereignty and goodness.

But the text must first be read in its context. Earlier the psalmist expresses his commitment to trust in God and not in any merely human help (118:8-9), even though he is surrounded by foes (118:10). Now he also discloses that his foes include "the builders" (118:22)—people with power within Israel. These builders were quite capable of rejecting certain "stones" while they built their walls—and in this case the very stone the builders rejected has become the capstone. In the first instance this stone, this capstone, is almost certainly a reference to a Davidic king, perhaps to David himself. The men of power rejected him, but he became the capstone. Moreover, this result was not achieved by brilliant machination or clever manipulation. Far from it: "the LORD has done this, and it is marvelous in our eyes" (118:23). In his own day Isaiah portrays people who make a lie their refuge while rejecting God's cornerstone (Isa. 28:15-16). The ultimate instance of this pattern is found in Jesus Christ, rejected by his own creatures, yet chosen of God, the ultimate building-stone, and precious (Matt. 21:42; Rom. 9:32-33; Eph. 2:20; 1 Peter 2:6-8)—a "stone" disclosed in all his true worth by his resurrection from the dead (Acts 4:10-11). Whether in David's day or in the ultimate fulfillment, this marvelous triumph by God calls forth our praise: *This is the day the LORD has made; let us rejoice and be glad in it* (Ps. 118:24).

Deuteronomy 27:1—28:19; Psalm 119:1-24; Isaiah 54; Matthew 2

∾

HERE THE PAIR OF ITALICIZED passages converge.

The setting envisaged by **Deuteronomy 27—28** is spectacular. When the Israelites enter the Promised Land, they are to perform a solemn act of national commitment. They are to divide themselves into two vast companies, each hundreds of thousands strong. Six tribes are to stand on the slopes of Mount Gerizim. Across the valley, the other six tribes are to stand on the slopes of Mount Ebal. The two vast crowds are to call back and forth in antiphonal responses. For some parts of this ceremony, the Levites, standing with others on Gerizim, are to pronounce prescribed sentences, and the entire host shout its "Amen!" In other parts, the crowd on Gerizim would shout the blessings of obedience, and the crowd on Ebal would shout the curses of disobedience. The sheer dramatic impact of this event, when it was actually carried out (Josh. 8:30-33), must have been astounding. The aim of the entire exercise was to impress on the people the utter seriousness with which the Word of God must be taken if the blessing of God is to be enjoyed, and the terrible tragedy that flows from disobedience, which secures only God's curse.

Psalm 119 is formally very different, but here too there is an extraordinary emphasis on the Word of God. It is almost as if this longest of all biblical chapters is devoted to unpacking what the second verse in the book of Psalms means: "But his delight is in the law of the LORD, and on his law he meditates day and night" (1:2; see also the April 1 meditation). Psalm 119 is an acrostic poem: each of the twenty-two letters of the Hebrew alphabet is given its turn to serve as the opening letter of each of eight verses on the subject of the Word of God. Throughout this poem, eight near synonyms are used to refer to Scripture: *law* (which perhaps might better be rendered "instruction," and has overtones of revelation), *statutes* (which speak of the binding force of Scripture), *precepts* (connected with God's superintending oversight, as of one who cares for the details of his charge), *decrees* (the decisions of the supreme and all-wise Judge), *word* (the most comprehensive term, perhaps, embracing all of God's self-disclosed truth, whether in a promise, story, statute, or command), *commands* (predicated on God's authority to tell his creatures what to do), *promise* (a word derived from the verb *to say,* but often used in contexts that make us think of the English word *promise*), and *testimonies.* (God's bold action of bearing "witness" or "testimony" to the truth and against all that is false; the Hebrew word is sometimes rendered "statute" in NIV, e.g., lit. "I delight in your testimonies.")

∾

Deuteronomy 28:20-68; Psalm 119:25-48; Isaiah 55; Matthew 3

∾

THERE ARE NOT MANY PASSAGES in the Bible more fearsome than **Deuteronomy 28:20-68.** What the text depicts is the judgments that will befall the people of God if they disobey the terms of the covenant and rebel against God, if they "do not carefully follow all the words of this law, which are written in this book, and do not revere this glorious and awesome name—the LORD your God" (28:58).

There are many striking elements about these judgments. Two occupy our attention here.

First, all the judgments depicted could be interpreted by the secular mind as the accidents of changing political and social circumstance, or, within a pagan worldview, as the outworking of various malign gods. On the face of it, the judgments all take place in the "natural" world: wasting disease, drought, famine, military defeat, boils, poverty, vassal status under a superior power, devastating swarms of locusts, economic misfortunes, captivity, slavery, the horrible ravages of prolonged sieges, decrease in numbers, dispersal once again among the nations. In other words, there is no judgment that sounds like some obviously supernatural "Zap!" from heaven. So those who have given up on listening to God's words are in the horrible position of suffering the punishments they do not believe come from him. That is part of the judgment they face: they endure judgment, but so hardened is their unbelief that even such judgment they cannot assess for what it is. The blessings they had enjoyed had been granted by God's gracious pleasure, and they failed to receive them as gifts from God; the curses they now endure are imposed by God's righteous pleasure (28:63), and still they fail to recognize them as judgments from God. The blindness is systemic, consistent, humanly incurable.

Second, God's judgments extend beyond externally imposed tragedies to minds that are unhinged—in part by the sheer scale of the loss, but in any case by God himself. The Lord will give these people "an anxious mind, eyes weary with longing and a despairing heart. You will live in constant suspense, filled with dread both night and day, never sure of your life" (28:65-66). This God not only controls the externals of history, but also the minds and emotions of those who fall under his judgment.

Before such a God, it is unimaginable folly to try to hide or outwit him. What we must do is repent and cast ourselves on his mercy, asking him for the grace to follow in honest obedience, quick to perceive the sheer horror of rebellion, with eyes open to take in both God's providential goodness and his providential judgment. We must see God's hand; we must weigh everything with an unswerving God-centeredness in our interpretive focus.

∾

Deuteronomy 29; Psalm 119:49-72; Isaiah 56; Matthew 4

∽

"THE SECRET THINGS belong to the LORD our God, but the things revealed belong to us and to our children forever, that we may follow all the words of this law" (**Deut. 29:29**). The two principal points bear reflection.

First, the responsibility of the covenant community in this matter is to focus on the things that God has revealed. They not only belong "to us and to our children forever," but were given to us *in order "that we may follow all the words of this law."* That is the fundamental purpose of placing this text at the end of a long chapter on covenant renewal. True, we cannot know many hidden things. But what *has* been revealed to us—in this context, the terms of the Mosaic Covenant, with all their vast potential for blessing and judgment—is what must capture our interest and devoted obedience.

Second, we must frankly admit that some things are hidden from our eyes. We really do not understand, for instance, the relationships between time and eternity, nor do we have much of an idea how the God who inhabits eternity discloses himself to us in our finite, space/time history. It is revealed that he does; we have various words to describe certain elements of this disclosure (e.g., *Incarnation, accommodation*). But we do not know how. We do not know how God can be both personal and sovereign/transcendent; we do not know how the one God can be triune.

Yet in none of these cases is this a subtle appeal to ignorance, or an irresponsible hiding behind the irrational or the mystical. When we admit—indeed, insist—that there are mysteries about these matters, we do not admit they are nonsensical or self-contradictory. Rather, we are saying that we do not know enough, and we admit our ignorance. What God has not disclosed of himself we cannot know. The secret things belong to God.

Indeed, because of the contrast in the text, the implication is that it would be presumptuous to claim we do know, or even to spend too much time trying to find out—lest we should be presuming on God's exclusive terrain. Some things may be temporarily hidden to induce us to search: Proverbs 25:2 tells us it is the glory of God to conceal a matter, and the glory of kings to search a matter out, to get to the bottom of things. But that is not a universal rule: the very first sin involved trying to know some hidden things and thus be like God. In such cases, the path of wisdom is reverent worship of him who knows all things, and careful adherence to what he has graciously disclosed.

∽

Deuteronomy 30; Psalm 119:73-96; Isaiah 57; Matthew 5

∿

IN ITS UNFOLDING REFLECTIONS on God and his revelation, Psalm 119 is unsurpassed. Here I shall focus on three themes that surface in **Psalm 119:89-96.**

(1) God's revelatory word, that word that has been *inscripturated* (i.e., written down to become Scripture) is not something that God made up as he went along, as if he did not understand or could not predict exactly how things were going to pan out. Far from it: "Your word, O LORD, is eternal; it stands firm in the heavens" (119:89). It was always there, eternal, in his mind. That is one of the reasons why he can be trusted absolutely: he is never caught out, never surprised. Because God's word stands firm in the heaven, the psalmist can add, "Your faithfulness continues through all generations" (119:90).

(2) There is a connection between the word of revelation and the word of creation and of providence. Thus the first line of verse 90, "Your faithfulness continues through all generations," is tied both to what precedes (end of v. 89) and to what succeeds (end of v. 90). God's faithfulness through all generations is grounded, as we have seen, in the fact that God's word stands firm in the heavens, but it is also grounded in God's creative and providential work: "you established the earth, and it endures. Your laws endure to this day, for all things serve you" (119:90-91). The same omniscient, ordering, reflective mind stands behind both creation and revelation.

(3) Far from being oppressive and limiting, the instruction of God is freeing and illuminating. "To all perfection I see a limit," the psalmist writes; "but your commands are boundless" (119:96). All human, earthly enterprises face limits. There are limitations on resources, on time, on the expanse of life that we may devote to such enterprises. Only so much time can be devoted to even the most sublime exercise. The limits themselves become frustrating barriers. More than one commentator has noted that this verse is almost a two-line summary of Ecclesiastes. There, every enterprise "under the sun" runs its race and expires, or proves unsatisfying and transient. In our experience there is but one exception: "your commands are boundless" (119:96).

This includes more than the well-known paradox: slavery to God is perfect freedom. For a start, freedom must be defined. If our steps are directed to God's word, there is freedom from sin (cf. 119:133); observance of God's "precepts" is tied to walking about in "freedom" (119:45). Moreover, reflection on and conformity with God's words generates not narrow-minded bigotry, but a largeness of spirit that potentially stretches outward to the farthest dimensions of the mind of God; for "your commands are boundless."

∿

Deuteronomy 31; Psalm 119:97-120; Isaiah 58; Matthew 6

∾

REFLECT FOR A MOMENT on the rich and diverse means that God granted to Israel to help them remember what he had done to deliver them, and the nature of the covenant they had pledged themselves to obey.

There was the tabernacle itself (later the temple), with its carefully prescribed rites and feasts: the covenant was not an abstract philosophical system, but was reflected in regular religious ritual. The nation was constituted in such a way that the Levites were distributed amongst the other tribes, and the Levites had the task of teaching the Law to the rest of the people. The three principal high feasts were designed to gather the people to the central tabernacle or temple, where both the ritual and the actual reading of the Law were to serve as powerful reminders (**Deut. 31:11**). From time to time God sent specially endowed judges and prophets, who called the people back to the covenant. Families were carefully taught how to pass on the inherited history to their children, so that new generations that had never seen the miraculous display of God's power at the time of the Exodus would nevertheless be fully informed of it and own it as theirs. Moreover, blessings from God would attend obedience, and judgment from God would attend disobedience, so that the actual circumstances of the community were supposed to elicit reflection and self-examination. Legislation was passed to foster a sense of separateness in the fledgling nation, erecting certain barriers so that the people would not easily become contaminated by the surrounding paganism. Unique events, like the antiphonal shouting at Mounts Gerizim and Ebal at the time of entering the land (see June 22 meditation), were supposed to foster covenant fidelity in the national memory.

But now God adds one more device. Precisely because God knows that in due course the people will rebel anyway, he instructs Moses to write a song of telling power that will become a national treasure—and a sung testimony against themselves (**31:19-22**). Someone has said, "Let me write the songs of a nation, and I care not who writes its laws." The aphorism is overstated, of course, but insightful nonetheless. That is the purpose of the next chapter, Deuteronomy 32. The Israelites will learn, as it were, a national anthem that will speak against them if they shut down all the other God-given calls to remember and obey.

What devices, in both Scripture and history, has God graciously given to help the heirs of the new covenant remember and obey? Meditate on them. How have you used them? What songs do we sing to put this principle into practice, that *teach* the people of God matters of irrevocable substance beyond mere sentimentalism?

∾

Deuteronomy 32; Psalm 119:121-144; Isaiah 59; Matthew 7

∼

ONE OF THE GREAT THEMES OF SCRIPTURE, and one that surfaces with special frequency in **Psalm 119**, is that the unfolding of God's words gives light; "it gives understanding to the simple" (119:130) in at least two senses.

First, the "simple" can refer to people who are foolish, "simpletons"—those who know nothing of how to live in the light of God's gracious revelation. The unfolding of God's words gives light to such people. It teaches them how to live, and gives them a depth and a grasp of moral and spiritual issues they had never before displayed.

Second, God's words expand entire horizons. A few paragraphs earlier the psalmist wrote, "Oh, how I love your law! I meditate on it all day long. Your commands make me wiser than my enemies, for they are ever with me. I have more insight than all my teachers, for I meditate on your statutes. I have more understanding than the elders, for I obey your precepts" (119:97-100). The psalmist is not saying that he has a higher IQ than that of his teachers, or that he is intrinsically smarter than his enemies or brighter than all the elders. Rather, he is claiming that constant meditation on God's instruction (his "law") and a deep-seated commitment to obey God's precepts provide him with a framework and a depth of insight that are unavailable to merely brilliant scholars and well-trained political leaders.

One of my students may serve as illustration. He barely staggered out of high school. He had never been to church. When he asked his father about God, his dad told him not to talk about subjects like that. He joined the United States Army as a lowly GI, and lived a pretty rough life. At various times he was high on LSD. Eventually he joined the Eighty-second Airborne, and started carrying his Gideon Bible as a good-luck charm to ward off disaster when he was jumping out of airplanes. Eventually he started to read it—slowly at first, for he was not a good reader. He read it right through and was converted. He went to one of the local chaplains and said, "Padre, I've been saved." The padre told him, "Not yet, you're not"—and inducted him into some catechism. Eventually he found a church that taught the Bible. He came off drugs (and six months later many of his army drug pals were busted), eventually left the army, squeaked into a college, grew mightily, and is now in the "A" stream of Greek in the divinity school.

He was absorbing the words of God. It transformed his life, and gave him more insight than many of his teachers. The unfolding of God's words "gives understanding to the simple."

Deuteronomy 33—34; Psalm 119:145-176; Isaiah 60; Matthew 8

∿

HOW DOES THE PENTATEUCH end (**Deut. 34**)?

At a certain level, perhaps one might speak of hope, or at least of anticipation. Even if Moses himself is not permitted to enter the Promised Land, the Israelites are on the verge of going in. The "land flowing with milk and honey" is about to become theirs. Joshua son of Nun, a man "filled with the spirit of wisdom" (34:9), has been appointed. Even the blessing of Moses on the twelve tribes (Deut. 33) might be read as bringing a fitting closure to this chapter of Israel's history.

Nevertheless, such a reading is too optimistic. Converging emphases leave the thoughtful reader with quite a pessimistic expectation of the immediate future. After all, for forty years the people have made promises and broken them, and have repeatedly been called back to covenantal faithfulness by the harsh means of judgment. In Deuteronomy 31, God himself predicts that the people will "soon prostitute themselves to the foreign gods of the land they are entering. They will forsake me and break the covenant I made with them" (31:16). Moses, this incredibly courageous and persevering leader, does not enter the Promised Land because on one occasion he failed to honor God before the people. In this respect, he serves as a negative foil to the great Hebrew at the beginning of this story of Israel: Abraham dies as a pilgrim in a strange land not yet his, but at least he dies with honor and dignity, while Moses dies as a pilgrim forbidden to enter the land promised to him and his people, in lonely isolation and shame. We do not know how much time elapsed after Moses' death before this last chapter of Deuteronomy was penned, but it must have been substantial, for verse 10 reads, "Since then [i.e., since Moses' death], no prophet has risen in Israel like Moses." One can scarcely fail to hear overtones of the prophecy of the coming of a prophet like Moses (18:15-18). By the time of writing, other leaders had arisen, some of them faithful and stalwart. But none like Moses had arisen—and this is what had been promised.

These strands make the reader appreciate certain points, especially if the Pentateuch is placed within the storyline of the whole Bible. (1) The law-covenant simply did not have the power to transform the covenant people of God. (2) We should not be surprised by more instances of catastrophic decline. (3) The major hope lies in the coming of a prophet like Moses. (4) Somehow this is tied to the promises at the front end of the story: we wait for someone of Abraham's seed through whom all the nations of the earth will be blessed.

∿

Joshua 1; Psalms 120—122; Isaiah 61; Matthew 9

∽

THE FIFTEEN SHORT PSALMS (Pss. 120—134) immediately succeeding Psalm 119 are grouped together as *songs of ascent*: that is, each carries this heading. The most likely explanation is that these psalms were sung by pilgrims on their way up to Jerusalem and its temple for the great feasts: people "ascended" to Jerusalem from every point of the compass, just as in England one "goes up" to London from every point of the compass. This is not to say that each of the fifteen psalms was necessarily composed for this purpose. Some may have been written in some other context, and then judged appropriate for inclusion in this collection. Thus **Psalm 120** seems to reflect personal experience, but could easily be sung with great empathy by pilgrims who felt their alienation as they lived in a land surrounded by pagan neighbors—an important theme as the pilgrims approached Jerusalem and felt they were coming "home." Indeed, the series of fifteen psalms more or less moves from a distant land to Jerusalem itself (Ps. 122) and finally, in the last of these psalms, to the ark of the covenant, the priests, and the temple "servants of the LORD who minister by night in the house of the LORD" (134:1).

It is into this matrix that **Psalm 121** falls. The first line, "I lift up my eyes to the hills," is often stripped out of its context to justify some form of nature mysticism, or at very least an interpretation that suggests hills and mountains serve to remind us of God's grandeur and therefore draw us to him and set our hearts at rest. In fact, the hills are enigmatic. Do they function symbolically like the mountain in Psalm 11:1, a place of refuge for those who are threatened and afraid? Are they havens for marauding thugs, so that the first line of verse 1 raises the problem that the rest of the psalm addresses? Or—perhaps more likely, since this is a song of ascents—does the pilgrim lift his eyes upward to the hills of Jerusalem, the hills evoking not nature mysticism but the place of the Davidic king, the place of the temple? If this is the right interpretation, then it is as if the psalmist finds these particular hills a call to meditate on the God who made them ("the Maker of heaven and earth," 121:2), the God who "watches over Israel" (121:4) as the covenant Redeemer.

The last verses of the psalm exult in the sheer comprehensiveness of God's care over "you" (in the singular, as if the individual pilgrim is addressed by other pilgrims). "The LORD watches over *you*" (121:5)—day and night (121:6), your whole life (121:7), in all you do ("your coming and going," 121:8), "both now and forevermore" (121:8).

∽

Joshua 2; Psalms 123—125; Isaiah 62; Matthew 10

❧

I ONCE HEARD A LEARNED SOCIOLOGIST, by confession an evangelical, explain with considerable erudition why even a major revival, should the Lord choose to send one to a country like America, could not possibly speedily transform the nation. The problem is not simply the degree of biblical illiteracy in the controlling echelons of society, or the extent to which secularization has penetrated the media, or the history of the Supreme Court decisions that have affected the curricula and textbooks of our schools, and countless other items, but also how these various developments interlock. Even if, say, a million people became Christians in a very short space of time, none of the interlocking social structures and cultural values would thereby be undone.

To be fair to this scholar, he was trying, in part, to steer us away from shallow thinking that fosters a glib view of religion and revival—as if a good revival would exempt us from the responsibility to think comprehensively and transform the culture.

The element that is most seriously lacking from this analysis, however, is the sheer sweep of God's sovereignty. The analysis of this sociologist colleague is reductionistic. It is as if he thinks in largely naturalistic categories, but leaves a little corner for something fairly weak (though admittedly supernatural) like regeneration. Not for a moment am I suggesting that God does not normally work through means that follow the regularities of the structures God himself has created. But it is vital to insist that God is not ever limited to such regularities. Above all, the Bible repeatedly speaks of times when, on the one hand, he sends confusion or fear on whole nations, or, on the other, he so transforms people by writing his Law on their heart that they long to please him. We are dealing with a God who is not limited by the machinations of the media. He is quite capable of so intruding that in judgment or grace he sovereignly controls what people *think*.

As early as the Song of Moses and Miriam, God is praised for the way he sends fear among the nations along whose borders Israel must pass on the way to the Promised Land (Ex. 15:15-16). Indeed, God promises to do just that (Ex. 23:27), and promises the same for the Canaanites (Deut. 2:25). So it should not be surprising to find the evidence of it as the Israelites approach their first walled town (**Josh. 2:8-11**; cf. 5:1).

God may normally work through ordinary means. But he is not limited by them. That is why all the military muscle in the world cannot itself guarantee victory, and all the secularization, postmodernism, naturalism, and paganism in the world cannot by themselves prevent revival. Let God be God.

❧

Joshua 3; Psalms 126—128; Isaiah 63; Matthew 11

∾

THE FIRST VERSE OF **Psalm 127** is often quoted today: "Unless the LORD builds the house, its builders labor in vain." In an age of overpopulation, we less often cite verse 3: "Sons are a heritage from the LORD, children a reward from him." We may gain some helpful perspective by observing four things.

First, in Hebrew the psalm deploys a couple of word plays that are lost in English, and these plays give pointers as to how to read the psalm. The word *house* (127:1) can refer to a building. By extension, this is then applied to the city in a metaphorical sense (127:1b-3). More importantly, *house* can also refer to a household, built up in this case by the blessing of children (127:3-5). Moreover, *builders* and *sons* sound very similar in Hebrew.

Second, this suggests that the unifying theme through the superficially disparate parts of the psalm is that in every sphere of life only the blessing and provision of God can bring about a successful outcome. At the most mechanical level of building a house, this is true. God gives strength to the workers; he sustains them in life; he restrains himself from sending a catastrophic storm that would tear the structure down; countless surprises may be avoided (unsafe concrete, a quagmire under the topsoil, "accidents" that take out workers, and countless more). The same principle is true in the basic defensive operation of watching over a city wall, or defending a nation with a radar system: if God sustains you, your defense will suffice, and if he does not, then no matter how professional and expensive it is, it will prove inadequate. In the home, procreation is a "natural" function, but in a providentially ordered world, children are an inheritance from the Lord. The lesson to be learned is not passivity, but trust and rest, a godly lowering of frenzied labor (127:2).

Third, Psalm 127 stands among the songs of ascent precisely because the pilgrimage up to Jerusalem in observance of the covenantally prescribed feasts provides an excellent occasion to reflect on God's gracious provision in every area of life (compare also Ps. 128).

Fourth, alone among the songs of ascent this one is ascribed to Solomon. Sadly, Solomon is a figure whose great wisdom was sometimes not followed in his own life: his own building program, both physical and metaphorical, became foolish (1 Kings 9:10-19), his kingdom a ruin (1 Kings 11:11-13; see the October 8 meditation), and his household—not least his multiplied pagan marriages—a systematic denial of the claims of the living God (1 Kings 11:1-9). How important to ask God for the grace to live up to what we understand!

∾

Joshua 4; Psalms 129—131; Isaiah 64; Matthew 12

∾

FROM OUT OF WHAT KIND OF "depths" is the psalmist crying in **Psalm 130:1**? In other psalms the sheer despair of the expression is bound up with treasonous "friends" and overt persecution (Ps. 69), or with illness and homesickness (Pss. 6, 42). In this case, however, what has plunged the psalmist into "the depths" is sin and guilt: "If you, O LORD, kept a record of sins, O LORD, who could stand?" (130:3).

Four reflections:

First, this accent on the misery of guilt and the need for forgiveness from God serves as a welcome foil to some of the psalms that ask for vindication on the grounds that the psalmist is fundamentally just or righteous (see meditations of April 10 and 24). Such claims could scarcely be taken absolutely; genuinely righteous people invariably become *more* aware of their personal guilt and need for forgiveness than those who have become so foul and hard they cannot detect their own shame.

Second, the connection between forgiveness and fear is striking: "But with you there is forgiveness; therefore you are feared" (130:4). Perhaps this pair of lines hints that assurance of sins forgiven was at this stage in redemptive history not as robust as it would become this side of the cross. More importantly, the "fear of the Lord" is portrayed as not only the outcome of forgiveness, but one of its goals. It confirms that "fear of the Lord" has less to do with slavish, servile terror (which surely would be decreased by forgiveness, not increased) than with holy reverence. Even so, this reverence has a component of honest *fear.* When sinners begin to see the magnitude of their sin, and experience the joy of forgiveness, at their best they glimpse what might have been the case had they *not* been forgiven. Forgiveness engenders relief; ironically, it also engenders sober reflection that settles into reverence and godly fear, for sin can never be taken lightly again, and forgiveness never lightly received.

Third, the psalmist understands that what he needs is not forgiveness in the abstract, but forgiveness *from God*—for what he wants and needs is reconciliation with God, restored fellowship with God. He waits for the Lord and trusts his promises (130:5). He waits like a watchman waits for the dawn through the most frightening hours but with the assurance that the dawn's breaking is inevitable (130:6).

Fourth, what is most precious about this psalm is that even though the culmination of redemption's plan is still centuries away, the focus is not on the mechanism but on God. "O Israel, put your hope in the LORD, for with the LORD is unfailing love and with him is full redemption. He himself will redeem Israel from all their sins" (130:7-8).

∾

Joshua 5; Psalms 132—134; Isaiah 65; Matthew 13

∽

THREE ELEMENTS ARE striking in **Joshua 5**.

(1) Circumcision is now carried out on all the males that were born during the years of wilderness wandering. At one level, this is rather surprising: How come they weren't done as the boys were born? In many instances the multitude stayed in one place for long periods of time, doubtless developing community life. What prevented them from obeying this unambiguous covenantal stipulation?

There have been many guesses, but the short answer is that we do not know. More important, in this context, is the fact that the rite is carried out now universally. It thereby stands as a decisive turning point, a symbol-laden community-wide affirmation of the covenant as the people stand on the verge of entering the Promised Land. Egypt is now behind; the promised rest awaits. "Today I have rolled away the reproach of Egypt from you" (5:9).

(2) The manna stops (5:10-12). From now on the people will draw their nourishment from "the produce of Canaan." This, too, was a dramatic signal that the days of wandering were over, and the fulfillment of the promise for a new land was beginning to unfold before their eyes. The change must have been both frightening and exciting, especially to an entire generation that had never known life without the security of manna.

(3) In the opening chapters of this book, Joshua experiences a number of things that mark him out, both in his own mind and in the mind of the people, as the legitimate successor to Moses. This chapter ends with one such marker. Doubtless the most dramatic one before this chapter has been the crossing of the Jordan River—a kind of miraculous reenactment of the crossing of the Red Sea (Josh. 3—4). Quite apart from providing an efficient way to move the multitudes across the river, the personal dimension is made explicit: "That day the LORD exalted Joshua in the sight of all Israel; and they revered him all the days of his life, just as they had revered Moses" (4:14—though the last clause must be judged just a little tongue in cheek).

But now, there is another step: Joshua encounters a "man" who appears to be some sort of angelic apparition. He is a warrior, a "commander of the army of the LORD" (5:14). On the one hand, this serves to strengthen Joshua's faith that the Lord himself is going before him in the military contests that lie ahead. But more: the scene is in some respects reminiscent of Moses at the burning bush (Ex. 3:5): "The place where you are standing is holy ground." However unique these circumstances, we too must have leaders accustomed to standing in the presence of holiness.

∽

Joshua 6; Psalms 135—136; Isaiah 66; Matthew 14

EVERY VERSE IN PSALM 135 quotes or alludes to or is quoted by some other part of Scripture.

Verse 1 reorders the phrasing of Psalm 113:1, putting the emphasis on the "servants of the LORD" who are then further described in verse 2—which in turn adapts a clause from Psalm 116:19. Verse 3 is one of three related verses in the book of Psalms in which we are variously told that the Lord's name is good (52:9), that he himself is good (135:3), and that praising him is good (147:1); and further, that both his name (here) and worship of him (147:1) are "pleasant" (or perhaps "delightful"). If verse 3 emphasizes God's character, verse 4 underscores his elective love in a way that calls us back to Deuteronomy 7:6.

Verses 5-7 emphasize God's unlimited power, calling to mind Exodus 18:11; Psalm 115:3; Jeremiah 10:13. The opening clause "I know that . . ." provides an emphasis on personal confession; this is truth not only to know, but to live by. Much of verses 8-12 reappears scattered throughout the next psalm, often word for word (136:10, 18-22). Which way the borrowing went is of little consequence. The references to the defeat of Sihon and Og call us back to Numbers 21:21-35. As for God's name (135:13-14), the allusion is to Exodus 3:15 and Deuteronomy 32:36. Verses 15-18, on the sheer folly of all idolatry, almost exactly follow 115:4-8; thematically similar convictions find expression in Isaiah. The closing verses of this psalm (135:19-21) apparently pick up on 115:9-11, where three of the four groups are told to glorify God.

The result of this pastiche approach to psalm-writing is a wonderful compendium of praise. It is as if the mind of the writer is not only full of much historical data from Scripture, but filled with texts as well. So as he builds his exuberant hymn of praise, consciously or unconsciously he interweaves phrase after phrase, sometimes whole verses, drawn from other Scriptures.

A similar phenomenon was once not uncommon amongst praying evangelicals. As men and women poured out their hearts to the Lord in prayer meetings, both praise and petition were cast in the language of Scripture. Of course, at its worst this sort of thing was a canned recitation of the same half-dozen texts. But at its best, such praise and prayer roamed through ever wider vistas of Scripture, as the people's knowledge of Scripture was itself growing. There is something mature and biblically evocative about such praise, and as different from today's narrow themes of clichéd sentimentalism as Beethoven's Fifth Symphony is from "Mary Had a Little Lamb."

Joshua 7; Psalms 137—138; Jeremiah 1; Matthew 15

∽

IT DOESN'T ALWAYS WORK LIKE THIS, of course. Sometimes it is not the case that the sin of one man and his family—in this case Achan—brings defeat upon the entire believing community (**Josh. 7**). For example, the sin of Ananias and Sapphira brought death only to themselves (Acts 5), and the punishment they suffered induced a godly fear in the rest of the assembly. On the other hand, the sin of David brought tragic repercussions on the entire nation. Perhaps the most frightening cases are those where countless sins are committed by many, many people, and God does absolutely nothing about it. For the worst judgment occurs when God turns his back on people, and resolutely lets sin take its course. Far better to be pulled up sharply before things get out of hand. That is why so much of the previous forty years of wilderness wanderings was given over to the disciplining hand of God: the purpose was as much educative as reformative.

Whatever is the case elsewhere in Scripture, here the sin of Achan and his family brings embarrassing defeat to the contingent of troops sent to take the little town of Ai. Worse, it brought death to about thirty-six Israelites (7:5). In a sense, Achan was a murderer. When in some consternation Joshua seeks God's face, God rather abruptly says, in effect, "Stop your praying and deal with the sin in the camp" (7:10-12). The point is that God had given explicit and repeated instructions. They had been violated. The covenant between God and the Israelites was essentially communal, and so God is determined to teach the entire community to exercise among its own members the discipline that the covenant mandates.

No doubt there are some substantial differences to bear in mind when one turns to the new covenant. Nevertheless, here too God says some explicit things, and expects the covenant community to exercise discipline (e.g., 1 Cor. 5; cf. 2 Cor. 11:4; 13:2-3). Paul warns us that failure to take disciplinary action in the church, when there has been flagrant violation, endangers the entire community (1 Cor. 5:6). Pastors of churches and leaders of other Christian organizations who ignore this perspective are inviting disaster among all the people they are called to lead. In the name of peace, the real motivation may simply be cowardice, or worse, a failure to take God's words seriously. The point is reinforced in the second reading assigned for this date: "I . . . will praise your name for your love and your faithfulness, for you have exalted above all things *your name and your word*" (**Ps. 138:2-3**).

∽

Joshua 8; Psalm 139; Jeremiah 2; Matthew 16

∿

THERE IS A PERVERSENESS TO human thoughts about God that would be risible if it were not so tragic. We find ways to make him small.

A marvelous antidote is **Psalm 139**. It paints an exalted picture of God, yet does so in stunningly personal ways, as befits a psalm. In particular:

(1) *God sees and knows everything* (139:1-6). The psalmist might have made that point as I just did—in the abstract. Instead, true to his form, he addresses God, acknowledging that this God's knowledge is not passive and is not merely comprehensive: it is active and personal. This God knows the psalmist so thoroughly that he knows every movement his body makes, and every habit of his life, but also every thought he entertains and every word he speaks—even before they are formulated. Hebrews 4:13 says as much.

(2) *God is omnipresent, and therefore inescapable* (139:7-12). Yet again, the thought in the text is not abstract. When David asks, "Where can I go from your Spirit? Where can I flee from your presence?" (139:7), it is pretty obvious that there is a part of him that *wants* to get away from God. It cannot be done. If David were to fly to the heavens or descend to Sheol, if he were to travel as far east or as far west as might be imagined, if he were to hide in the darkness—nothing could hide him from God's searching gaze. By the end of the psalm, it is clear that David does *not* want to escape from this God (cf. Rom. 8:38-39).

(3) *God is the Creator and providential Ruler* (139:13-18). Here David does not hark back to the initial creation, but to his own formation in his mother's womb—which formation is, finally, nothing other than a work of God, for all its terrifying complexity. Nor does this God relinquish control once the creature is made: "All the days ordained for me were written in your book before one of them came to be" (139:16). In Scripture, this truth does not compromise human responsibility, but increases our faith. Perhaps it is the sheer breadth of such knowledge that prompts David to pen the last two verses of this section: God's thoughts cannot be numbered, for they are more numerous than the grains of sand by the sea—which is no exaggeration at all.

(4) *God is utterly holy* (139:19-24). David's response to evil people is merely a function of his loyalty to God (139:19-22). What saves it from mere vindictive self-righteousness is the fact that in the light of this God's holiness, David is no less resolved to deal with any evil in his own life (139:23-24).

∿

Joshua 9; Psalms 140—141; Jeremiah 3; Matthew 17

∾

THE ACCOUNT OF THE GIBEONITE DECEPTION (**Josh. 9**) has its slightly amusing elements, as well as its serious point. There are the Israelites, poking around in moldy bread and holding serious conversations about the distance these emissaries must have traveled. Yet the sad fact is that they were snookered. What lessons should we learn from this?

First, many believers who have the courage to withstand direct assault do not have the sense to withstand deception. That is why in Revelation 13 the dragon has *two* beasts—one whose opposition is overt and cruel, and the other who is identified as the false prophet (see the meditation for December 22). That is also why in Acts 20 Paul warns the Ephesian elders not only of rapacious wolves that will try to ravage the flock of God, but also of the fact that from among their own number men will arise who will "distort the truth" (Acts 20:30). Such people never announce what they are doing: "We are now going to distort the truth!" The danger they represent lies in the fact that they are viewed as "safe," and then from this secure vantage they advocate "progressive" positions that distort the Gospel. The deceptive power may be tied to such overt tricks as flattery—the very device used by the Gibeonites (9:9-10). In our day, deception becomes all the easier to arrange because so many Christians are no longer greatly shaped by Scripture. It is difficult to unmask subtle error when it aligns with the culture, deploys spiritual God-talk, piously cites a passage or two, and "works."

Second, the failure depicted in 9:14 has haunted many believers, and not only the ancient Israelites: "The men of Israel sampled their [the Gibeonites'] provisions but did not inquire of the LORD." Doubtless their inquiring of the Lord would have been direct; perhaps the priests would have resorted to Urim and Thummim (see meditation for March 17). We shall never know, because the people felt they did not need the Lord's guidance. Perhaps the flattery had made them cocksure. The fact that their decision was based on their estimate of how far these Gibeonites had come makes it obvious that they were aware of the danger of treaties with the Canaanites. The failure must therefore not be taken as a mere breach of devotions that day, a hastiness that forgot a magic step. The problem is deeper: there is an unseemly negligence that betrays an overconfidence that does not think it *needs* God in this case. Many a Christian leader has made disastrous mistakes when he or she has not taken time to seek God's perspective, probing Scripture and asking him for the wisdom he has promised to give (James 1:5).

∾

Joshua 10; Psalms 142—143; Jeremiah 4; Matthew 18

∽

PSALM 142 SHOULD BE READ IN TANDEM with Psalm 57; both were the product of David's experience of hiding in a cave while fleeing King Saul. In some ways, however, the two psalms are quite different. Although in both cases David is pushed to the edge, in Psalm 57 he sounds reasonably buoyant, perhaps bold—certainly confident of the outcome. Here in Psalm 142, however, the mood is gloomy, characterized by "desperate need" (142:6), with only three rays of hope. It should not be thought strange that the one crisis should precipitate more than one emotional response. Both Scripture and experience testify that extreme danger and uncertainty can push us to conflicting responses. However we think about such matters, Psalm 142 reflects raw despair—and correspondingly, it speaks tellingly to believers whose circumstances draw them through dark waters no less deep.

The opening lines find the psalmist urgently and frankly begging for help: "I cry aloud"; "I lift up my voice"; "I pour out my complaint"; "I tell my trouble"— these are the words of a frightened and desperate man. The word rendered "my complaint" sounds less petulant and whiny than the English: perhaps "what's wrong" or "my troubled thoughts" might be better.

The first ray of hope comes in verse 3a: "When my spirit grows faint within me, it is you who know [sic] my way." When he has sunk so low that he is ready to give up, the psalmist finds reassurance in the fact that God is never taken by surprise: "It is *you* who knows my way."

The worst hurts, of course, are personal betrayals. When all around there is no one who can be trusted, when experience after experience demonstrates that this conclusion is pathetically sound and not a symptom of paranoia, when the sheer loneliness of the fight adds a thick layer of depression ("I have no refuge; no one cares for my life," 142:4), where does the psalmist turn? Here is the second ray of light: "I cry to you, O LORD; I say, 'You are my refuge, my portion in the land of the living'" (142:5). The move from "my refuge" to "my portion" demonstrates that David is not thinking of God as merely the solution to a problem. There is progression from fear to gratitude.

None of this reduces the stark reality of David's "desperate need" (142:6). This need is not merely emotional: his emotional crisis is grounded in the reality that he is being pursued by soldiers and their bitter king. The final ray of hope serves as contrast: God's goodness and fidelity ensure that David will be rescued. David dares to envision the day when the righteous of the land will not only surround him but applaud his reign.

∽

Joshua 11; Psalm 144; Jeremiah 5; Matthew 19

∿

VERSES 12-14 OF PSALM 144 PICTURE an idyllic situation in the land: sons and daughters multiplying and healthy, barns filled with produce, cattle filling the fields, trade flourishing, military defenses secure, freedom from some regional superpower, basic prosperity and contentment in the streets. What will bring about these conditions?

The answer is summarized in the last verse: "Blessed are the people of whom this is true; blessed are the people whose God is YAHWEH" (144:15). This last line means more than that these people happen to have preferred a certain brand of religion. It means, rather, that if this God—the one true God—owns a people— a people who in confessing him as their God trust him and worship him and obey him—that people is blessed indeed. And because this last verse is a summarizing verse, the unpacking of this notion is found in the rest of the psalm.

The psalm opens in praise to "the LORD *my Rock*"—a symbol that is evocative of absolute stability and security. This God trains the hands of the king for war: that is, his providential rule works through the means of supplying and strengthening those whose responsibility it is to provide the national defense, while they for their part rely on him and do not pretend their military prowess is somehow a sign of innate superiority (144:1-2). Far from it: human beings are fleeting, nothing but passing shadows (144:3-4). What we must have is the presence of the Sovereign of the universe, his powerful intervention: "Part your heavens, O LORD, and come down; touch the mountains, so that they smoke" (144:5). When the Lord takes a hand, David and his people are rescued from danger, oppression, and deceit (144:7-8). What this evokes is fresh praise "to the One who gives victory to kings, who delivers his servant David" (144:10). When God takes a hand, the result is the security and fruitfulness described in verses 10-15.

Here is a balance rarely understood—still more rarely achieved. It applies every bit as much to, say, revival in the church, as it applies to the security and prosperity of the ancient nation of Israel. On the one hand, there is a deep recognition that what is needed is for the Lord to rend the heavens and come down. But on the other hand, this generates no passivity or fatalism, for David is confident that the Lord's strength enables him to fight successfully. What we do not need is an arrogant "can do" mentality that tacks God onto the end, or a clichéd spirituality that confuses passion with passivity. What we do need is the power of the sovereign, transforming, God.

∿

Joshua 12—13; Psalm 145; Jeremiah 6; Matthew 20

WHEN WE REFLECTED ON PARTS of Psalm 119 (see the meditations for June 22, 25, and 27), we noted that the psalm is an acrostic poem. In the first section, all the verses begin with the first letter of the Hebrew alphabet; in the second section, all the verses begin with the second letter of the Hebrew alphabet; and so on for twenty-two sections, corresponding to the twenty-two letters of the Hebrew alphabet. But there are seven other acrostic psalms in the Psalter. In these, however, just one verse is devoted to each letter (Pss. 9-10, 25, 34, 37, 111, 112, 145). Five of the eight, including this last one (**Ps. 145**), are ascribed to David.

In most Hebrew manuscripts of this psalm, there is no verse for the Hebrew letter corresponding to our N. But most of the ancient translations supply the missing verse, and now one Hebrew manuscript with an N-verse has shown up as well, so most modern versions squeeze in the extra lines (verse 13b in the NIV). So what we have in this psalm is the last of David's compositions preserved in the book of Psalms, a veritable alphabet of praise.

There are certain themes that receive special emphasis in this psalm.

(1) Although many of David's psalms focus on his own experiences, or sometimes on the joys and sorrows of the Israelite nation, here the horizon expands to take in God's universal kingdom (145:13a), his universal care for all living creatures in his universe—not least providing them with the food they need (145:15-16). None of this denies that this is still a fallen world, of course. Creatures sometimes starve; they grow old and die. Yet we see teeming life, and this life survives and thrives by God's gracious provision.

(2) There is a wonderful mingling of God's glory with God's compassion. "The LORD is gracious and compassionate, slow to anger and rich in love. The LORD is good to all; he has compassion on all he has made" (145:8-9). That is why the entire created order praises him (145:10). At the same time, God's people are the first to talk about his "mighty acts and the glorious splendor" of his kingdom, the sheer glory of his kingdom (145:11-12).

(3) Not only is God's greatness beyond human fathoming (145:3), the account of God's greatness and goodness is passed on from one generation to another (145:4), as others celebrate God's "abundant goodness" and joyfully sing of his righteousness (145:7). Indeed, as we read his words and utter our own "Amen!" our generation receives this glorious communication from three thousand years ago, jointly committed to speaking of God's mighty acts and to meditating on his wonderful works (145:4-5).

Joshua 14—15; Psalms 146—147; Jeremiah 7; Matthew 21

∾

PSALM 146 HAS BEEN THE inspiration of hymns in many languages. Isaac Watts (1674-1748) wrote a hymn that was largely inspired by this psalm. That hymn is still widely sung in the United Kingdom; regrettably, it is virtually unknown in North America. So it is worth reproducing here as today's meditation:

> *I'll praise my Maker while I've breath;*
> *And when my voice is lost in death,*
> > *Praise shall employ my nobler powers.*
> *My days of praise shall ne'er be past,*
> *While life, and thought, and being last,*
> > *Or immortality endures.*
>
> *Happy the man whose hopes rely*
> *On Israel's God! He made the sky,*
> > *And earth, and sea, with all their train.*
> *His truth forever stands secure;*
> *He saves the oppressed, he feeds the poor,*
> > *And none shall find his promise vain.*
>
> *The Lord gives eyesight to the blind;*
> *The Lord supports the fainting mind;*
> > *He sends the labouring conscience peace;*
> *He helps the stranger in distress,*
> *The widow and the fatherless,*
> > *And grants the prisoner sweet release.*
>
> *I'll praise him while he lends me breath;*
> *And when my voice is lost in death,*
> > *Praise shall employ my nobler powers;*
> *My days of praise shall ne'er be past,*
> *While life, and thought, and being last,*
> > *Or immortality endures.*

∾

Joshua 16—17; Psalm 148; Jeremiah 8; Matthew 22

∾

ALL OF THE FIVE CLOSING PSALMS begin with the single Hebrew word *Hallelujah*—"Praise the Lord." This psalm (**Ps. 148**) is remarkable for its emphasis on the sheer range and comprehensiveness of beings and things in the universe that unite the whole creation in praise. The first six verses begin with angels, sweeping down through unconscious participants in the heavens; the next six verses—mirror-images of the first six—begin with the unconscious participants on the earth, and rise to human beings (148:7-12). The last two verses (148:13-14) draw the people in covenant with him. Some notes:

(1) There have always been people who attach their affections and worship to angels (e.g., Col. 2:18), even though angels are our fellow servants (Rev. 22:8-9). Others foolishly think that their destinies are controlled by the stars, even though stars are nothing more than God's creation. Both angels and stars—the one sentiently, the other not—bear witness to *God's* greatness; in that sense they join together in worship (148:2-3).

(2) The phrase "highest heavens" is literally "heaven of heavens," a way of expressing the superlative (like "holy of holies"). The expression "waters above the skies" is a Hebrew poetic way of referring to rain (148:4). Whether one thinks of "the heavens" as the sphere in which the rain condenses out of the atmosphere, or as the abode of God Almighty, there is nothing that has not been created: "he commanded and they were created" (148:5). So there is nothing that does not bear witness to the Creator-God.

(3) The denizens of the earth's oceans, the varied precipitation that waters the ground, the fury of unleashed storms, the majesty and beauty of mountains and hills, the spectacular diversity and color and beauty of earth's flora and fauna, the scarcely imaginable array of the earth's births—all attest, mutely but powerfully, to the goodness and greatness of God. As part of that creation, human beings, in all the diversity of their ranks and stations in life, join this universal chorus of praise (148:11-12), not simply because he is bigger than we are, but because no matter how highly we envisage his glorious splendor, it is higher yet, higher than anything and everything in all creation (148:13).

(4) This unimaginably great God has not only called out his own people, but has raised up for them a "horn" (a symbol for a king), the praise of all his saints (148:14). Living this side of Jesus' incarnation, death, and resurrection, we know who the ultimate King in the Davidic line really is. And so our praise joins that of the rest of the universe with peculiar intensity and gratitude.

∾

Joshua 18—19; Psalms 149—150; Jeremiah 9; Matthew 23

∾

THIS (JOSH. 18—19) IS A GOOD TIME TO reflect on the many chapters of Joshua that have been devoted to the dividing up of the land.

(1) Focusing on the division of the land, these chapters implicitly focus on the land itself. After all, the land was an irreducible component of the promise to Abraham, of the Sinai covenant, of the release of the Israelites from slavery in Egypt. It is now distributed by God's providential supervision of the "lot."

(2) The inevitable conclusion is that God is faithful to his promises. That point is explicitly drawn for us a bare two chapters on: "So the LORD gave Israel all the land he had sworn to give their forefathers, and they took possession of it and settled there. The LORD gave them rest on every side, just as he had sworn to their forefathers. Not one of their enemies withstood them; the LORD handed all their enemies over to them. Not one of all the LORD's good promises to the house of Israel failed; every one was fulfilled" (21:43-45).

(3) These chapters also explain how entrance into the Promised Land did not proceed in a wave of unbroken triumph. Earlier God had warned that he would not give the Israelites the whole thing at once. Now we are repeatedly told that this tribe or that could not dislodge certain Canaanites, and they continue there "to this day." For instance, "Judah could not dislodge the Jebusites, who were living in Jerusalem; to this day the Jebusites live there with the people of Judah" (15:63; cf. Judg. 1:21). In fact, Jerusalem was taken (Judg. 1:8), but not all the Jebusites were dislodged. Details of this sort help to explain how the tussle between fidelity and syncretism could occupy so much of Israel's history.

(4) Some of the elements in these chapters bring earlier strands of the narrative to closure. For instance, Caleb surfaces again. He was Joshua's colleague among the initial group of twelve spies; they were the only two who at Kadesh Barnea, at the first approach to the Promised Land, urged the people to enter it boldly and trust God. In consequence they are the only two of their generation who are still alive to witness the Promised Land for themselves. And now in Joshua 15, Caleb is still looking for new worlds to conquer and receives his inheritance. Similarly, chapters 20—21 detail the designation of the cities of refuge and of the towns set aside for the Levites—steps mandated by the Mosaic Code.

(5) There is trouble ahead. The ambiguities of the situation, and the memories of the final warnings of Moses, signal the reader that these relative victories, good though they are, cannot possibly be God's final or ultimate provision.

∾

Joshua 20—21; Acts 1; Jeremiah 10; Matthew 24

∾

BETWEEN JESUS' ASCENSION AND Pentecost, the nascent church, about one hundred and twenty strong, met together and prayed. At one such meeting, Peter stood up and initiated the action that appointed Matthias to replace Judas Iscariot (**Acts 1:15-26**).

(1) Peter's use of Scripture (1:16, 20) is apparently what guides him to his conclusion that "it is necessary" (1:21) to choose one of the other men who had been with Jesus from the beginning of his public ministry as a replacement for the traitor Judas. At the surface level of Acts, the reasoning is straightforward. Psalm 69:25 says, "May [his] place be deserted; let there be no one to dwell in [it]"; Peter applies this to Judas. Psalm 109:8 insists, "May another take his place of leadership"; this Peter takes as a divine warrant for securing a replacement.

In the context of Psalms 69 and 109, David is seeking vindication against enemies—once close friends—who had betrayed him. Peter's use of these verses belongs to one of two primary patterns. Either: (a) Peter is indulging in indefensible proof-texting. The verses never did apply to Judas, and can be made to do so only by exegetical sleight-of-hand. Or: (b) Peter is already presupposing a fairly sophisticated David-typology. If this sense of betrayal and plea for vindicating justice play such an important role in the experience of great King David, how much more in great David's greater Son? Why should we flinch at such reasoning? During the previous forty days Jesus had often spoken with his disciples (1:3), explaining in some detail "what was said in all the Scriptures concerning himself" (Luke 24:27). Certainly the David-typology crops up in the Gospels on the lips of Jesus. Why should we not accept that he taught it to his disciples?

(2) On the criteria raised here—the replacement apostle had to be not only a witness of the resurrected Jesus, but someone who had been with the disciples "the whole time the Lord Jesus went in and out among us" (1:21-22)—Paul *could not* have met the conditions. Paul's apostleship was irregular, as he himself acknowledges (1 Cor. 15:8-9). We should not entertain nonsense about Peter and the church making a mistake here because they did not wait for the appointment of Paul.

(3) The choosing of one of two by lot (1:23-26) is not a prescription for local church governance procedures. There is no hint of a similar procedure from then on in the church's life, as reported in the New Testament. This sounds more like the climax of an Old Testament procedure, with God himself selecting and authorizing the twelve men of the apostolic band.

∾

Joshua 22; Acts 2; Jeremiah 11; Matthew 25

～

ACTS 2 IS SOMETIMES CALLED the birthday of the church. This can be misleading. There is a sense in which the old covenant community can rightly be designated *church* (7:38—"assembly" in NIV). Nevertheless there is a new departure that begins on this day, a departure bound up with the universal gift of the Holy Spirit, in fulfillment of Scripture (2:17-18) and in consequence of Jesus' exaltation "to the right hand of God" (2:33). The critical event that has brought this incalculable blessing about is the death, resurrection, and exaltation of Jesus Christ; this event was itself foreseen by earlier Scripture.

One of the things that is striking about Peter's address, quite apart from its comprehensiveness, courage, directness, and passionate fire, is the way the apostle, even at this early stage of his postresurrection public ministry, handles what we call the Old Testament Scriptures. His use of Scripture in this Pentecost sermon is too rich and variegated to unpack in detail. But observe:

(1) Once again there is a David-typology (2:25-28, citing Ps. 16:8-11). But here there is also a small sample of apostolic reasoning in this regard. Although it is possible to read 2:27 ("you will not abandon me to the grave, nor will you let your Holy One see decay") as David's conviction that God will not, at that point, let him die, the language is so extravagant, and David's typological role so common, that Peter insists the words point to something more: a greater than David will quite literally not be abandoned in the grave, and will not be permitted to experience decay. David, after all, was a prophet. Whether in this case, like Caiaphas (John 11:50-52), David spoke better than he knew, at least he knew that God had promised "on oath that he would place one of his descendants on his throne" (2:30).

(2) The prophecy of Joel (Acts 2:17-21; see Joel 2:28-32) is more straightforward, in that it is a case of verbal prediction and does not resort to typology. The obvious meaning is that Peter detects in the events of Pentecost the fulfillment of these words: the "last days" (2:17) have arrived. (Whether the sun turning to darkness and the moon turning to blood were both events bound up with the dark hours when Jesus was on the cross, or an instance of Hebrew nature symbolism, need not detain us here.) This Old Testament passage is one of a handful of texts that predict the coming of the Spirit, or the writing of God's law on our hearts, but in any case covenant-wide personal transformation in the last days (e.g., Jer. 31:31ff.; Ezek. 36:25-27).

～

Joshua 23; Acts 3; Jeremiah 12; Matthew 26

∿

ACTS 3 INCLUDES A BRIEF REPORT of a sermon preached impromptu. (Though like many impromptu sermons, doubtless it was made up of pieces Peter had used before!) There are many points of immense interest.

(1) Peter repeatedly ties the coming of Jesus the Messiah with the God of Abraham, Isaac, and Jacob (3:13), with Moses and the promise that God would eventually raise up a prophet like him (3:22; cf. Deut. 18:15-18; see also meditation for June 13), with the prophetic witness of the Old Testament (3:24), and even with God's promise to Abraham that through his offspring all the peoples of the earth would be blessed (3:25; see meditations for January 14—15). At this point Peter did not have as broad an understanding of these points as he would later have, if we may judge by chapters 10—11. But that his understanding had got so far reflects his trainee period with the Lord Jesus.

(2) Peter does not for a moment let the crowd of onlookers off the hook (3:13-15). Many of his hearers were complicit in the demand to crucify Jesus; but, like an Old Testament prophet, Peter saw the people as a whole bound up in the decision of their leaders. The people may have "acted in ignorance" (3:17)—i.e., they did not say, in effect, "Here is the Messiah. Let us kill him."—but kill him they did, and Peter reminds them of their guilt, not only as an unalterable fact of history, *but also because it is guilt that Jesus came to deal with* (3:19-20). Moreover, although the people are guilty, Peter understands that it was precisely through the evil execution of Jesus that "God fulfilled what he had foretold through all the prophets, saying that his Christ would suffer" (3:18). That is the supreme irony of all history.

(3) There is a string of characteristics that unite this sermon with the sermon in Acts 2 and some others in the book of Acts. These features include: the God of our fathers has sent his servant Jesus; you killed him—disowning the Holy and Righteous One, the author of life—but God raised him from the dead; we are witnesses of these things; by the death and resurrection of Jesus God fulfilled the promises he made through the prophets; repent therefore, and turn to God. There are variations on these themes, of course, but these return again and again.

(4) Although "many wonders and miraculous signs were done by the apostles" (2:43), the apostles themselves are in no doubt that they had neither the power nor the godliness to make a crippled beggar walk (3:12). Their self-effacement is a perpetual lesson. "It is Jesus' name and the faith that comes through him that has given this complete healing" (3:16).

∿

Joshua 24; Acts 4; Jeremiah 13; Matthew 27

◌

WHEN PETER AND JOHN were released from their first whiff of persecution, they "went back to their own people" (**Acts 4:23**). The church gathered for prayer, using the words of Psalm 2 (Acts 4:25-26). They understood that Old Testament text to be God's speech ("You spoke") by the Holy Spirit, through the mouth of David (4:25).

At one level, Psalm 2 is an enthronement psalm. Once again, however, the David-typology is strong. The kings of the earth and the rulers gathered against the Lord and against his Anointed One (the Messiah)—and climactically so when "Herod and Pontius Pilate met together with the Gentiles and the people of Israel in this city to conspire against your holy servant Jesus, whom you anointed" (4:27). These earliest of our brothers and sisters in Christ ask for three things (4:29-30): (a) that the Lord would consider the threats of their opponents; (b) that they themselves might be enabled to speak God's word with boldness; and (c) that God would perform miraculous signs and wonders through the name of Jesus (which may mean, in their expectation, "through the apostles"; cf. 2:4; 3:6ff.; 5:12).

But before making their requests, these prayer warriors, after mentioning the wicked conspiracy of Herod, Pilate, and the rest, calmly address God in a confession of staggering importance: "They did what your power and will had decided beforehand should happen" (4:28). Observe:

First, God's sovereignty over the death of Christ does not mitigate the guilt of the human conspirators. On the other hand, the malice of their conspiracy has not caught God flat-footed, as if he had not foreseen the cross, much less planned it. The text plainly insists that God's sovereignty is not mitigated by human actions, and human guilt is not exculpated by appeal to divine sovereignty. This duality is sometimes called *compatibilism*: God's utter sovereignty and human moral responsibility are *compatible*. Complex issues are involved, but there can be no serious doubt that this stance is either taught or presupposed by the biblical writers (see meditation for February 17).

Second, in this case it is doubly necessary to see how the two points hang together. If Jesus died solely as a result of human conspiracy, and not by the design and purpose of God, it is difficult to see how his death can be the long-planned divine response to our desperate need. If God's sovereignty over Jesus' death means that the human perpetrators are thereby exonerated, should this not also be true wherever God is sovereign? And then where is the sin that needs to be paid for by Jesus' death? The integrity of the Gospel hangs on that element of Christian theism called *compatibilism*.

◌

Judges 1; Acts 5; Jeremiah 14; Matthew 28

∾

THE ACCOUNT OF ANANIAS AND SAPPHIRA, whose names are recorded in the earliest Christian records because of their deceit (**Acts 5:1-11**), is disturbing on several grounds. Certainly the early church thought so (5:5, 11). Four observations focus the issues:

First, revival does not guarantee the absence of sin in a community. When many people are converted and genuinely transformed, when many are renewed and truly learn to hate sin, others find it more attractive to be *thought* holy than to *be* holy. Revival offers many temptations to hypocrisy that would be less potent when the temper of the age is secularistic or pagan.

Second, the issue is not so much the disposition of the money that Ananias and Sapphira obtained when they sold a piece of property as the lie they told. Apparently there were some members who were selling properties and donating all of the proceeds to the church to help in its varied ministries, not least the relief of the needs of brothers and sisters in Christ. Indeed, the man called Barnabas was exemplary in this respect (4:36-37), and serves as a foil to Ananias and Sapphira. But these two sold their property, kept some of the proceeds for themselves, and pretended that they were giving everything. It was this claim to sanctity and self-denial, this pretense of generosity and piety, that was so offensive. Left unchecked, it might well multiply. It would certainly place into positions of honor people whose conduct did not deserve it. But worse, it was a blatant lie against the Holy Spirit—as if the Spirit of God could not know the truth, or would not care. In this sense it was a supremely presumptuous act, betraying a stance so removed from the God-centeredness of genuine faith that it was idolatrous.

Third, another element of the issue was conspiracy. It was not enough that Ananias pulled this wicked stunt himself. He acted "with his wife's full knowledge" (5:2); indeed, her lying was not only passive but active (5:8), betraying a shared commitment to deceive believers and defy God.

Fourth, in times of genuine revival, judgment may be more immediate than in times of decay. When God walks away from the church and lets the multiplying sin take its course, that is the worst judgment of all; it will inevitably end in irretrievable disaster. But when God responds to sin with prompt severity, lessons are learned, and the church is spared a worse drift. In this case, great fear fell not only on the church but also on all who heard of these events (5:5, 11).

It is written: "He whose walk is upright fears the LORD, but he whose ways are devious despises him" (Prov. 14:2).

∾

Judges 2; Acts 6; Jeremiah 15; Mark 1

∾

FROM A READING OF JUDGES 1—2, it appears that after the initial Israelite victories, the pace of conquest varied considerably. In many cases tribes were responsible for bringing their own territories under control. With the passage of time, however, it seems to have become unstated policy, as the Israelites grew stronger, not to chase the Canaanites from the land, nor to exterminate them, but to subjugate them or even enslave them, to make them "drawers of water and hewers of wood," to subject them to forced labor (1:28).

The inevitable result is that a great deal of paganism remained in the land. Human nature being what it is, these false gods inevitably became a "snare" to the covenant community (**Judg. 2:3**). Angry with their refusal to break down the pagan altars, the angel of the Lord declares that if the people will not do what they are told, he will no longer provide them with the decisive help that would have enabled them to complete the task (had they been willing!). The people weep over the lost opportunity, but it is too late (2:1-4). It is certainly not that they had never been warned.

This is the background to the rest of the book of Judges. Some of its main themes are then outlined for us in the rest of chapter 2. Much of the rest of the book is exemplification of the thinking laid out here.

The main thrust, shot through with tragedy, is the cyclical failure of the covenant community, and how God intervenes to rescue them again and again. Initially, the people remained faithful throughout Joshua's lifetime and the lifetime of the elders who outlived him (2:6). But by the time that an entirely new generation had grown up—one that had seen nothing of the wonders God had performed, whether at the Exodus, during the wilderness years, or at the time of the entrance into the Promised Land—fidelity to the Lord dwindled away. Syncretism and paganism abounded; the people forsook the God of their fathers and served the Baals, i.e., the various "lords" of the Canaanites (2:10-12). The Lord responded in wrath; the people were subjected to raids, reversals, and military defeats at the hands of surrounding marauders. When the people cried to the Lord for help, he raised up a *judge*—a regional and often national leader—who freed the people from tyranny and led them in covenantal faithfulness. And then the cycle began again. And again. And again.

Here is a sober lesson. Even after times of spectacular revival, reformation, or covenantal renewal, the people of God are never more than a generation or two from infidelity, unbelief, massive idolatry, disobedience, and wrath. God help us.

∾

Judges 3; Acts 7; Jeremiah 16; Mark 2

∾

THE OLD TESTAMENT historical psalms offer plenty of examples in which writers review the shared history of the Israelites for some special theological or ethical purpose. Something similar occurs when 1 and 2 Chronicles retell 1 and 2 Samuel and 1 and 2 Kings, so as to focus on the southern kingdom and on certain theological perspectives. This form of address continues in certain New Testament sermons. Paul in Pisidian Antioch begins the historical recital with the Exodus, and aligns his storytelling priorities to show that Jesus really is the promised Messiah (Acts 13:16ff; see also the meditation for July 26). Here in **Acts 7**, Stephen, the first Christian martyr, begins with Abraham.

What are the advantages of this approach? And what does Stephen, in particular, set out to prove?

One of the advantages is that historical recital gains the attention of the audience—and in this case the audience was overtly hostile and needed calming. Their personal identity was bound up with their national history; initially, at least, this recital was bound to be soothing, to establish common ground, to show that Stephen was within the pale. A second advantage lay in the fact that the shift that Stephen was trying to establish in the minds of his Jewish audience was big enough that it could only be adopted within the framework of a changed worldview. In other words, not only Jesus' identity, but even more, his death and resurrection, could not finally be accepted by thoughtful Jews unless they perceived that this is what Scripture teaches—and this point could not easily be established unless it was anchored in the very fabric of the Old Testament storyline. So the story had to be told and retold so as to highlight the most important points.

One of the points that Stephen makes as he retells the story emerges slowly at first, then faster and faster, and then explosively. That point is the repeated sin of the people. When Stephen begins the story, at first there is no mention of Israel's evil. Then the wickedness of Joseph's brothers is briefly mentioned (7:9). Corporate wickedness re-surfaces in Moses' day (7:25-27, 35). Now the pace quickens. The people refused to obey Moses "and in their hearts turned back to Egypt" (7:39). The golden calf episode is brought up, and likened to idolatry in the time of Amos (7:42-43). We skip ahead to David and Solomon, and the insistence that God cannot be domesticated by a building. Finally there is the explosive condemnation not only of past generations of Israelites who rejected God and his revelation, but also of all their contemporary Spirit-resisting descendants (7:51-53).

What bearing does this point have on the lessons we should draw from the biblical history?

∾

Judges 4; Acts 8; Jeremiah 17; Mark 3

∾

THE CONVERSION OF THE Ethiopian eunuch (**Acts 8:26-40**) marks an important extension of the Gospel across several barriers.

We need to understand who he was. He was "an important official in charge of all the treasury of Candace, queen of the Ethiopians" (8:27). *Candace* was a family name that had become a title, quite like *Caesar* in Rome. In certain matriarchal governments, it was not uncommon for the highest officials, who would have had ready access to Candace, to be eunuchs (whether they were born that way or castrated), for the obvious protection of the queen. This man was equivalent to U.S. Secretary of the Treasury or the like. But although he was an honored and powerful political figure at home, he would have faced limitations in Jerusalem. Since he had gone up to Jerusalem to worship (8:27), we must assume that he had come across Judaism, had been attracted to it, and had gone up to Jerusalem for one of the feasts. But he could not have become a proper proselyte, since from the Jewish perspective he was mutilated. The Word of God had seized this man, and he had traveled for several weeks to see Jerusalem and its temple

In the sheer providence of God, the passage the eunuch was reading, apparently out loud (8:30—a not uncommon practice in those days) was Isaiah 53. He asks the obvious question (8:34): Who is the Suffering Servant of whom Isaiah speaks? "Then Philip began with that very passage of Scripture and told him the good news about Jesus" (8:35).

That is a wonderful verse. Not only would it be difficult for him to find a better place to begin, Philip expounded both that passage and other Old Testament texts: he "*began* with that very passage of Scripture." So the miles passed, and Philip explained text after text, painting a comprehensive picture of the Gospel, the good news about Jesus (8:35).

Thus the Gospel reaches outward in the book of Acts. All the first converts were Jews, whether reared in the Promised Land or gathered from the dispersion. But the beginning of Acts 8 witnesses the conversion of Samaritans—a curious people of mixed race, only partly Jewish, joined to the mother church in Jerusalem by the hands of the apostles Peter and John. The next conversion is that of the eunuch—an African, not at all Jewish—sufficiently devoted to Judaism to take the pilgrimage to Jerusalem even though he could never be a full-fledged proselyte; a man steeped in the Jewish Scriptures even when he could not understand them.

Small wonder that the next major event in this book is the conversion of the man who would become the apostle *to the Gentiles.*

∾

Judges 5; Acts 9; Jeremiah 18; Mark 4

WHAT WAS PAUL'S PERSPECTIVE before he was converted (**Acts 9**)? Elsewhere (Acts 22:2; 23:6; Phil. 3:4-6) he tells us that he was a strict Pharisee, brought up (apparently) in Jerusalem, taught by one of the most renowned rabbis of the day. For him, the notion of a crucified Messiah was a contradiction in terms. Messiahs rule, they triumph, they win. The Law insists that those who hang on a tree are cursed by God. Surely, therefore, the insistence that Jesus is the Messiah is not only stupid, but verges on the blasphemous. It might lead to political insurrection: the fledgling church was growing, and might become a dangerous block. It had to be stopped; indeed, what was needed was a man of courage like Saul, a man like Phinehas who averted the wrath of God by his decisive action against the perverters of truth and probity (Num. 25; see meditation for May 16), someone who really understood the implications of these wretched delusions and who saw where they would lead.

But now on the Damascus Road Saul meets the resurrected, glorified Jesus. Whether he had seen him before we cannot be sure; that he sees him now, Saul cannot doubt. And a great deal of his theology, worked out and displayed in his letters, stems from that brute fact.

If Jesus were alive and glorified, then somehow his death on the cross did not prove he was damned. Far from it: the claim of believers that God had raised him from the dead, and that they had seen him, must be true—and that could only mean that God had vindicated Jesus. Then what on earth did his death mean?

From that vantage point, everything looked different. If Jesus was under the curse of God when he died, yet was vindicated by God himself, he must have died *for others.* Somehow his death absorbed the righteous curse of God that was due others and canceled it out. In that light, the entire history of the Hebrew Scriptures looked different. Was it not written that a Suffering Servant (see yesterday's meditation) would be wounded for our transgressions and chastised for our iniquities? Does the death of countless lambs and bulls really take away human sin? Or do we need, as it were, a human "lamb of God," a human "Passover Lamb"? If the tabernacle and temple rituals are read as pointing to the final solution, what does that say about the present status of the covenant enacted at Sinai? What about scriptural texts that promise a new covenant, a great outpouring of the Spirit in the last days (Acts 2:17-21; see Joel 2:28-32 and the meditation for July 15)? What place does the promise to Abraham have in the scheme of things, that in Abraham's offspring all the nations of the earth would be blessed (Gen. 12:3; see meditation for January 11)?

Grant that Jesus is alive and vindicated, and everything changes.

Judges 6; Acts 10; Jeremiah 19; Mark 5

∾

THE ACCOUNT OF THE CONVERSION of Cornelius occupies much space in the book of Acts. As the Gospel moves outward from its Jewish confines, each step is carefully charted. First it was the Samaritans, a mixed race with a peculiar view of Scripture. (They accepted only Torah, what we call the Pentateuch.) Then it was the Ethiopian eunuch, who could not be a full proselyte—but (it might be argued) perhaps he would have been one if he had not been mutilated. Then comes the conversion of the man who will be the apostle to the Gentiles (see 9:15). Here in **Acts 10** is the conversion of a God-fearer, a Gentile much attached to the Scriptures and to the Jewish synagogue who had chosen *not* to become circumcised and thus an unqualified proselyte—a convert—to Judaism.

The apostle whom God prepares to go to Caesarea and preach the Gospel to Cornelius and his household is Peter. Peter's repeated vision concerns ritually unclean food. Three times he is told to kill and eat unclean creatures; three times he declines, viewing himself as under the Law's food prohibitions. Many have asked how Peter could be so dense, considering the fact that, according to Mark 7:19, Jesus had already uttered a saying declaring all foods clean. But it is far from clear that his disciples understood the ramifications of Jesus' utterance at the time. Mark is writing later, about A.D. 60, long after the Cornelius episode; and, reflecting on what Jesus said, Mark perceives the implications in Jesus' words that were not grasped at the time. Even the commission to take the Gospel everywhere, or Jesus' insistence that people would come from all over the world and join the patriarchs in the kingdom of heaven (Matt. 8:11), had not brought the pieces together for the apostles. Small wonder, then, that Peter is at this stage still sorting things out.

So he wakes up and ponders what the vision means. Providential timing makes that point clear. Kosher Jews were always nervous in a Gentile home—but here God sends Peter not only to spend time in a nonkosher Gentile home, but to preach the Gospel there. Initially, no one is more surprised than Peter (10:28-29, 34), but it is not long before he swings into a full-orbed presentation of the Gospel *to these Gentiles.* Even while Peter is speaking, the Holy Spirit descends on this Gentile household as he had descended on the Jews at Pentecost, and no one is more surprised than Peter and the Jews traveling with him (10:45-47).

The initial impetus to cross lines of race and heritage with the Gospel of Jesus Christ arose not from a committee planning world evangelization, but from God himself.

∾

Judges 7; Acts 11; Jeremiah 20; Mark 6

～

WHAT IS STRIKING ABOUT **Acts 11:1-18** is the amount of space devoted to retelling the narrative already laid out in some detail in Acts 10, often in the very same words. Isn't this a rather extravagant use of the space on a scroll?

But Luke sees this as a turning point. Peter is called on the carpet by the churches in Judea for going into the house of an uncircumcised person and eating with him (11:3). Peter retells his experience. The vision of the sheet with the unclean animals, its repetition three times, the instruction from the Spirit to go with the Gentile messengers, the fact that six of the (Jewish) brothers accompanied him and therefore could corroborate his story, the descent of the Spirit in a manner that tied this event to Pentecost, the linking of this with the words of the Lord Jesus—all lead to Peter's careful conclusion: "So if God gave them the same gift as he gave us, who believed in the Lord Jesus Christ, who was I to think that I could oppose God?" (11:17).

Now some observations:

(1) Although Peter's argument proves convincing (11:18), this does not mean that all of the theological implications have been worked out. This might be well and good for the Gentiles, and a matter for rejoicing. But many questions have not yet been thought through: Will the Gentiles have to be circumcised? Will they come under the kosher food laws *after* believing in Jesus? If not, are Jews permitted to abandon such laws, or was Peter a one-time exception? Should there be two quite different churches, one Jewish and one Gentile? What *should* the Gentiles obey? What is the relationship between this new covenant and the old one? Many of these questions are precipitated in the following chapters.

(2) The primary significance of this baptism in the Spirit is a little different than in Acts 2. Here, the dramatic expressions serve to authenticate this group of new converts to the mother church in Jerusalem—an irrelevant function at Pentecost.

(3) Next we hear of widespread, if unplanned, promulgation of the Gospel among Jews and Gentiles alike (11:19ff.), generating a further crisis. Now the Jerusalem leaders must deal not with an individual or a household that is Gentile, but with an entire church that is predominantly Gentile. They show great wisdom. The envoy they send, Barnabas, displays no evidence of having great theological acuity. But he can see that this is the work of the Spirit, and promptly encourages the new converts to pursue God faithfully—and soon sends off for the best Bible teacher he knows for a mixed race church like this one (11:25-26). That is how Saul of Tarsus comes to be associated with this great church.

～

Judges 8; Acts 12; Jeremiah 21; Mark 7

IN MANY WAYS, Gideon was a great man. Cautious when the Lord first called him, he took the first steps of obedience at night (Judg. 6). Then, filled with the Spirit of God (6:34), and convinced by two extraordinary signs that God was with him (6:36-40), he led his divinely reduced band of three hundred men in an extraordinary victory over the Midianites (Judg. 7).

Yet for all his greatness, Gideon represents something of what is going wrong with the nation. Deep flaws of character and inconsistency multiply and fester, so that by the end of the book the entire nation is in a very bad way.

In the first incident of **Judges 8**, Gideon comes off well, the Ephraimites pretty badly. No one was willing to fight the Midianites before God raised up Gideon. Now that victory under Gideon has already been so stunning, the Ephraimites abuse him for not inviting them into the fray earlier. He responds diplomatically, praising their efforts in the latter part of the operation, and they are appeased (8:1-3). At the towns of Succoth and Peniel, neither the towns nor Gideon appear in a very good light (8:4-9, 13-17). The townspeople are cowardly, unprincipled, and willing to sit on the fence until they see which way the winds are blowing. For all the justice of Gideon's response, however, he seems more than a little vindictive. When it comes to the execution of the Midianite kings Zebah and Zalmunna (8:18-21), his decision is based less on principles of public justice or on the Lord's commands regarding the cleansing of the land than on personal vengeance: his own brothers had been killed in the war.

On the one hand, Gideon does not seem to be power hungry. He turns down the popular acclamation that would have made him king on the grounds that the Lord alone is to rule over this covenant nation (8:22-23). But then he stumbles badly. He makes his request for gold earrings, and ends up with such a hoard that he constructs an elaborate ephod, an outer vestment adorned with more than forty pounds of gold. The state of religion in Israel is so deplorable that soon this ephod has become an idolatrous object of worship, not only for the nation but even for Gideon's family (8:27). The covenantal allegiance he maintains in the nation is partial.

There is worse trouble brewing. He takes not two or three wives, but many, and has seventy sons. Upon his death, the nation returns to unrestrained paganism and displays ugly ingratitude toward Gideon's family (8:33-35). And one of his sons, Abimelech, turns out to be a cruel, power-hungry butcher (Judg. 9).

Judges 9; Acts 13; Jeremiah 22; Mark 8

TODAY I WANT TO DRAW attention to a couple of points drawn from opposite ends of **Acts 13.**

(1) The church leadership in Antioch must have been extraordinarily diverse (13:1). Barnabas's real name was Joseph. He was a Levite from Cyprus (4:36-37). At a time when the church in Jerusalem was growing so quickly it must have been impossible for the apostles to remember everyone's name, this Joseph was noticed for his remarkable gift of encouragement; as a result he was rewarded with a nickname that reflected his character: Barnabas—*Son of Encouragement.* Then there was Simeon "called Niger"—an expression that almost certainly means "Simeon the Black." In the ancient world, unlike the British and American experience, slavery was tied to the economic system (people who went bankrupt might sell themselves into slavery—see meditation on March 11) and to military might; it was *not* restricted to a particular race. (Thus there could be African slaves, English slaves, Jewish slaves, and so forth.) So there was nothing anomalous about having "Simeon the Black" as one of the leaders. About Lucius of Cyrene we know almost nothing. Apparently, he, like Barnabas, was from a Mediterranean island, and the form of his name shows he belongs to the Hellenistic world. Manean had enough connections with minor nobility that he had been reared with Herod the tetrarch. Then there was Saul himself, by this time a veteran evangelist, church planter, and Bible teacher of fifteen years' experience, with many scars to prove it. In the wake of this call, he progressively moved in Gentile circles, and used the name connected with his Roman citizenship, Paul (13:9). (Roman citizens had three names. We do not know the other two in the case of "Mr. Paul"—for Paul was certainly the family name. Saul was an additional name preserved for the sake of his Jewish heritage.) He, too, was from out of town—from Tarsus. What glorious and cosmopolitan diversity there is in this church in Antioch.

(2) After the detailed account of Paul's sermon in Pisidian Antioch, we are told that many Gentiles "honored the word of the Lord; *and all who were appointed for eternal life believed*" (13:48). An excellent exercise is to discover all the ways Acts, or even the entire New Testament, speaks of conversion and of converts—and then to use *all* of those locutions in our own speech. For our ways of talking about such matters both reflect *and shape* the way we think of such matters. There is no biblical passage that speaks of "accepting Jesus as your personal Savior" (though the notion itself is not entirely wrong). So why do many adopt this expression, and *never* speak in the terms of verse 48?

Judges 10; Acts 14; Jeremiah 23; Mark 9

∾

PAUL HAD BEEN EVANGELIZING for fifteen years or more, probably largely around the Tarsus area, before this "first" trip is recorded. Doubtless he built up extraordinary experience evangelizing Jews and Gentiles alike, so that by the time he emerges on the scene as a church-planting apostle he is not a young man finding his way, but a mature, seasoned worker.

(1) It has often been said that everywhere Paul went he started either a revival or a riot, and sometimes both. That's not quite true, of course. Moreover, a riot is not *necessarily* a mark of authenticity: as much depends on the context and the hearers as on the preacher and his message and style. But there is at least some truth to the observation, and it is tied to the apostle's sheer boldness.

(2) In the early years of the church, the persecution Christians suffered was almost entirely sponsored by Jews. Later, of course, far worse persecution was generated by the Roman Empire, until at the beginning of the fourth century the Emperor Constantine switched sides. But in the beginning it was not so. It is hard to bring this up in our historical context, living as we do this side of the Holocaust. But facts are persistent things. One can understand why it was this way. At the beginning, all of the Christians were Jews; for quite awhile, the majority were Jews. In both cases, synagogue discipline was possible within reasonably closed communities. Moreover, in at least some cities influential Jews were well-placed to influence pagan authorities to exert pressure on people that many Jews saw as debasing the Jewish heritage and culture.

(3) In Lystra (**Acts 14:8-20**) there is a spectacular example of the fickleness of a mob. At first the pagans try to honor Paul and Barnabas as, respectively, Hermes (the god of communication) and Zeus (head of the Greek pantheon), owing to the healing they had performed in Jesus' name. Only with great effort could Paul and Barnabas restrain the crowd—which then shortly turns on them when they are stirred up by Jewish opponents who are beginning to dog their steps. The apostolic response was stunning both ways: they do everything they can to turn aside the acclaim (14:14, 18), and they accept the persecution as something only to be expected by those who enter the kingdom (14:22).

(4) On the swing leg home, not more than a few months later, Paul and Barnabas return through the cities where they have already planted churches and appoint elders in each of them (14:23). Clearly, what is meant by a "mature" elder is entirely relative to the age and maturity of the congregation.

Reflect on the relevance of these points in your own context.

∾

Judges 11; Acts 15; Jeremiah 24; Mark 10

HERE I SHALL SQUEEZE TWO SEPARATE meditations into this space, one on each of the primary passages.

In **Acts 15**, it is critically important to understand what the dispute was about that called into existence what has since been labeled "the Jerusalem Council." Some (Jewish) men traveled from Judea to Antioch and began teaching the believers there that even though they believed in Jesus they could not be saved unless they were circumcised in compliance with the law of Moses (15:1). Later history has attached the name *Judaizers* to these people.

From the perspective of the Judaizers, Jesus was the Jewish Messiah, and one could not really follow this Jewish Messiah without becoming a Jew. Doubtless some Jews felt threatened by this influx of uncircumcised Gentiles into the church: the Jewish self-identity was in terrible danger of being diluted and even lost. If these Gentiles all became Jews, however, as signaled by circumcision, that danger would dissolve.

Yet the issue is deeper than the question of Jewish self-identity. It finally develops into the question of how your whole Bible is put together. The Judaizers elevated the law of Moses above Jesus. Jesus could be accepted as the Messiah, only if the result was a group of people even more devoutly committed to obeying the Mosaic Covenant—food laws, circumcision, temple cultus and all. By contrast, the leaders point in another direction. The law was never well obeyed by the Jews (15:10); why impose it on the Gentiles? More importantly, the revelation reflected in the old covenant *points to* Jesus. He is its goal, not its servant. Peter reminds the assembled crowd that in the Cornelius episode God poured out his Spirit on the Gentiles *without* their being circumcised (15:7-8). At issue, finally, is the freedom of God's grace (15:11).

The reports of Paul and Barnabas prove helpful. James, the half-brother of the Lord Jesus—by this time apparently the chief elder of the Jerusalem church—offers both a telling exposition of an Old Testament text and his own pastoral judgment (15:13-21). The combination wins the day—though the argument flares up repeatedly during the next few decades. Understand these issues aright, and your Bible comes together.

Judges 11:30-31, 34-40 is a stellar example of a promise that should not have been made, and a promise that should not have been kept. Despite strong biblical insistence that one should keep one's vows, a vow to do something evil should not be kept but repented of, lest one commit two sins instead of one. Moreover, here is further evidence of the descending spiral of theological and moral stupidity in Israel at the time of the judges.

Judges 12; Acts 16; Jeremiah 25; Mark 11

∾

THREE OBSERVATIONS ON THESE STEPS in the ministry of Paul and Silas (**Acts 16**):

(1) To understand Paul's "Macedonian call" (16:6-10), one must follow his movements on a map. After traveling through the central part of what is now Turkey, the Spirit forbids Paul and Silas from going into Asia (16:6), i.e., Asia Minor, the Western part of modern Turkey. So they travel north. Now they try to enter Bithynia (16:7). Had they been enabled to do so, they would have been on the major east/west road that joined the Roman Empire with India—and heading east. But the "Spirit of Jesus" forbids them from taking that step (16:7), and so they go in the only direction still open to them along the roads of the day: they head toward the port city of Troas. From there, there is only one obvious place to go: across the water to Europe. During the night Paul has a vision of a man in Macedonia, the nearest landfall of Europe, begging him, "Come over to Macedonia and help us" (16:9). This *confirms* Paul and Silas in their movements; it does *not redirect* them. The result is ministry on the continent of Europe, and ultimately a path to Rome.

(2) Paul's first convert in Europe was a woman, an intercontinental business traveler from Thyatira. Note the description of her conversion, and then the description of the Philippian jailer's: "The Lord opened her heart to respond to Paul's message" (16:14); "The jailer . . . had come to believe in God—he and his whole family" (16:34). Let's use both locutions today.

(3) Worth pondering are the occasions when Paul stands on his Roman citizenship, and when he does not. Sometimes he is beaten without a word of protest. In Philippi, Paul and Silas are "severely flogged" (16:23-24), apparently without protesting. Roman citizens were exempt from flogging until they had been found guilty of the crime for which they were charged. Yet when the jailer is told to release the prisoners, Paul protests that he and Silas, both citizens, have been flogged without a trial, and insists that the city's leaders come and escort them out of jail as a kind of public apology (16:37-39). Why not simply suffer in silence, not least since that is what they sometimes do?

It is difficult to prove, but many have argued, believably, that Paul stands on his rights when by doing so he thinks he can establish legal precedents that may help other Christians. Every case on the books where Christians have been shown *not* to be guilty of public disorder or a threat to the Roman Empire can only be a useful legal precedent. If this is right, it is a mark of strategic thinking—for the sake of others.

∾

Judges 13; Acts 17; Jeremiah 26; Mark 12

◕

MOST OF PAUL'S EVANGELIZING of Gentiles began with the synagogue. His regular procedure when he arrived in a new town was to visit the synagogue and (since it was not uncommon to ask visitors to speak) avail himself of the opportunity to preach the Gospel. This meant that his hearers were a mix of Jews, proselytes (i.e., Gentile converts to Judaism), and God-fearers (i.e., Gentiles who were sympathetic to Jews and Jewish monotheism, but who had not formally converted). The book of Acts shows that in several instances (e.g., 13:13-48; 17:1-9), the synagogue authorities soon tired of Paul and banned him. At this point many of the proselytes and God-fearers went with him, so that although he was now preaching to a largely Gentile crowd, the core of that crowd had received some exposure to the Old Testament Scriptures. In other words, in such cases Paul was able to preach to people who largely shared with him the vocabulary, facts, and movements of the Old Testament storyline.

But what would Paul do if he were preaching to biblical illiterates—that is, to people who had never heard of Moses, never read the Old Testament, never learned a single item of the Old Testament plotline? Such people would not only have to be informed, but would have to *unlearn* a lot of notions they had absorbed from some other cultural and religious heritage. We have a glimpse of such an encounter in 14:8-20, when the citizens of Lystra excitedly conclude that Paul and Barnabas are incarnations of Greek gods (see July 27 meditation). The brief report of Paul's address (14:15-17) provides a glimpse of the apostolic response.

But it is the account of Paul's visit to Athens (**17:16-31**) that is most revealing. Here, too, Paul began in the synagogue (17:17), but he also set about evangelizing in the marketplace with whoever happened to be there (17:17), and this precipitates the invitation to speak at the meeting of the Areopagus. And there, one clearly perceives how the apostle Paul has thought this matter through. In a world of finite gods (often supported by one pantheistic deity), cyclical views of history, sub-biblical understandings of sin, multiplied idolatry, dualism that declares all that is material to be bad and all that is spiritual to be good, tribal deities, and not a little superstition, Paul paints a worldview of the true God, a linear view of history, the nature of sin and idolatry, impending judgment, the unity of the human race and the oneness of God—*all as the necessary framework without which his proclamation of Jesus makes no sense.* What does that mean for evangelism today?

◕

Judges 14; Acts 18; Jeremiah 27; Mark 13

∽

SOME OF US HAVE WONDERED why God has occasionally used in powerful ministry people blatantly flawed. This is not to say that God should only use perfect people, for that would mean he would be using no people. Nor am I referring to the fact that we all have weaknesses and faults of various kinds. George Whitefield, for instance, despite his enormous stature as a preacher and evangelist, did not fare very well on the marriage front, or in his (misguided) conviction that his son would be healed of his mortal illness. Virtually *any* Christian leader, whether from biblical times or more recent history, could not stand up under the onslaught of that sort of criticism. No, what I have in mind is the flaw that is so public and awful that one ponders two questions: (a) If this person is so powerful and godly, why the ugly fault? (b) If this person is so filled with the Spirit, why doesn't that same Spirit enable him to clean up his act?

There are no easy answers. Sometimes it is simply a matter of time. Judas Iscariot, after all, engaged in public ministry with the other eleven apostles—even miraculous ministry—yet with time proved apostate. The passage of time would show him up. But sometimes the flaws are there from the beginning to the end.

That is true, it appears, in the life of Samson. The Spirit of God came upon him mightily; the Lord used him to curb the Philistines. But what is he doing marrying a Philistine woman, when the Law strictly forbade marriage to anyone outside the covenant community (**Judg. 14:2**)? When his parents warn him of the consequences, he simply overrides them, and they acquiesce (14:3). True, they did not know that "this was from the LORD" (14:4), in the same way that the selling of Joseph into slavery in Egypt was of the Lord; but that did not make the human actions right. Samson's risky bet (14:12-13) is more cocksure and greedy than it is wise and honorable. Of course, the Philistines are really cruel in the matter (14:15-18, 20), but Samson's murder of thirty men to fulfill the terms of the wager is motivated less by a desire to cleanse the land and restore the covenant people to strength than it is by personal vengeance. Similar things must be said about his tactics in the next chapter, and about his steamy living in the chapter after that.

It appears, then, that Spirit-given power in one dimension of life does not by itself guarantee Spirit-impelled discipline and maturity in every dimension of life. It follows that the presence of spiritual gifts is never an excuse for personal sin.

∽

Judges 15; Acts 19; Jeremiah 28; Mark 14

∾

ONE OF THE STRANGEST ACCOUNTS in the book of Acts concerns the seven sons of Sceva (**Acts 19:11-20**). Paul's ministry in Ephesus lasted some considerable time, perhaps two and a half years, and during that time "God did extraordinary miracles through Paul" (19:11). The result is that various "competitors" tried to keep up with him. By itself, this was not surprising. It has always been so. When God especially empowered Moses to perform miracles before Pharaoh, the magicians of Egypt could reproduce most (though not all) of what he did.

So in Paul's day some Jews steeped in syncretism traveled around, engaging in some kind of deliverance ministry. They had little idea what they were engaged in. When they saw what Paul was doing in the name of Jesus, they started to refer to that name too, as if it were nothing more than some magic talisman: "They would say, 'In the name of Jesus, whom Paul preaches, I command you to come out'" (19:13).

The seven sons of Sceva, a Jewish priest, were particularly engaged in this operation. One day the evil spirit they were trying to exorcise talked back to them: "Jesus I know, and I know about Paul, but who are you?" (19:15). Then the man possessed by this spirit leaped on them and beat up all seven of them. Note:

First, the result of this encounter was entirely beneficial. When the story circulated, many were seized with a healthy fear and an enlarged respect for the name of the Lord Jesus. This was a name so powerful that it could not be treated as a magic formula. This name could not be domesticated. The result was that infatuation with occult practices was curbed. Many confessed their evil deeds, and others brought their occult books and burned them, totaling an enormous value (19:17-19). "In this way the word of the Lord spread widely and grew in power" (19:20).

Second, the really striking element is the utterance of the evil spirit: "Jesus I know, and I know about Paul, but who are you?" One can understand why Jesus would be known among demonic powers. There is no surprise there. *But Paul is known too!* His ministry had been assaulting the powers of darkness. He was known to be protected and defended by the living Christ—there is no way the demon could have used the possessed man to beat him up. These other characters were another matter; as far as the demon was concerned, they were a bit of a joke, easily ignored, easily subdued and shamed. But Paul was known!

Christians engaging the Enemy will be known not only in the courts of heaven but in the courts of hell.

∾

Judges 16; Acts 20; Jeremiah 29; Mark 15

∿

PAUL'S ADDRESS TO THE EPHESIAN ELDERS (**Acts 20:18-35**) can be broken down into three parts. In the first (20:18-24), Paul talks about his own ministry in Ephesus and his own future. In the second (20:25-31), he uses his example of ministry as an encouragement to the elders in Ephesus to "keep watch" over themselves and over "all the flock" of God (20:28) of which the Holy Spirit has made them overseers, with special emphasis on the challenges ahead when people within the church will prove eager to gain disciples and be prepared to distort the truth. In the third (20:32-35), Paul not only commits these elders "to God and to the word of his grace" (20:32), but quietly testifies again to the exacting standards of personal probity in his own life when he served among them.

More commonly than not, when this passage is preached we lay the emphasis on the central section. But here I would like to draw attention to some of the features that characterized Paul's ministry.

(1) The most obvious is the fact that Paul perceived how he lived and served to be a role model. Elsewhere he openly tells the Corinthians to imitate him, as he imitates Christ (1 Cor. 11). In Paul there is no trace of a double standard: Do what I teach but not what I do.

(2) Paul "served the Lord with great humility and with tears," even though he was "severely tested" by the machinations of "the Jews" (20:19). In other words, opposition neither defeated him nor whipped him into a frenzy of retaliation. By contrast, how easy it is to get discouraged and quit, or get angry and destroy what is being built.

(3) Paul's ministry was edifying, and conveyed in a mixture of public meeting and faithful visitation (20:20). One gets the impression that above all it was the ministry of the Word, communicated through a man set on fire by that Word.

(4) Paul did not flinch from dealing with the immutables of the Gospel, no matter how uncomfortable or unpopular they might be. As a result he boldly declared, to Jews and Gentiles alike, "that they *must* turn to God in repentance and have faith in our Lord Jesus" (20:21, emphasis added).

(5) On occasion, Paul felt himself "compelled by the Spirit" to adopt a certain course without knowing exactly where that course would lead (20:22-24). Having enough illumination to decide on an action does not guarantee enough information to know how things will turn out. In this case he knows only that he is promised "prison and hardships"—and all he wants for himself is to complete the task the Lord Jesus has given him, "the task of testifying to the gospel of God's grace."

∿

Judges 17; Acts 21; Jeremiah 30—31; Mark 16

∾

THE SIGNS OF MORAL, SPIRITUAL, and intellectual declension in Israel during the time of the judges now multiply, some of them obvious, some of them subtle. Although **Judges 17** is a brief chapter, it is charged with an abundance of them.

(1) A grown man named Micah has apparently stolen eleven hundred shekels of silver from his mother. That doesn't say much for family relationships—though it is of course only one incident. He confesses the crime to his mother (17:2). Judging by his remarks, he is prompted less by love for his mother or consciousness of sin than by superstitious fear because his mother has pronounced a curse on the thief who was, to her, unknown until that point.

(2) Micah's mother rewards him with a pious word: "The LORD [i.e., Yahweh] bless you, my son!" (17:2)—which shows that there is still a strong awareness of the covenantal God who brought them out of Egypt, or at least a retention of his name. But very quickly the reader perceives that only the shell of covenantal loyalty persists. Syncretism has taken over. Grateful for the return of her money, she gives it back to her son, solemnly consecrating it "to the LORD [Yahweh]" for the purpose of making "a carved image and a cast idol" (17:3), which of course was repeatedly forbidden by the covenant at Sinai.

(3) He promptly hands back the silver to his mother for this purpose. She gives two hundred shekels (which leaves her with nine hundred, despite what she had "consecrated") to a silversmith to make an idol with it. Greed triumphs even over idolatry. The little idol is then placed in Micah's house, both a talisman and a reminder of restored family relationships after a theft, perhaps even something to ward off the curse the mother had pronounced (17:4).

(4) Micah's religious syncretism runs deeper. He has his own shrine, and installs one of his sons as his private priest for offering prayers and sacrifices, and prepares priestly apparel for him (the ephod, 17:5). The breaches are multiplying. Under the covenant, there was supposed to be only one "shrine"—at this point the tabernacle—and only Levites could be priests.

(5) Enough of these stipulations are recalled that when Micah finds a young Levite traveling through, he hires him as his private priest (!). Micah is convinced that this will ensure that the Lord will be good to him (17:13). Covenantal religion has lost much of its structure and all of its discipline and obedience. It is a sad mess of pagan superstition.

For the first time, we read the words, "In those days Israel had no king; everyone did as he saw fit" (17:6).

∾

Judges 18; Acts 22; Jeremiah 32; Psalms 1—2

∾

PERHAPS AN INNOCENT READER might have hoped that yesterday's reading (Judg. 17) reflected a minor aberration among the people of God. Today's (**Judg. 18**) makes that hope less sanguine: one entire tribe of Israel is off the rails, and doubtless others as well.

The historical setting is still early enough that not all the tribes have captured all the land that is to be theirs. That is certainly true of Dan (18:1). So the Danites send out five soldiers to spy out the terrain, and eventually stumble across the house of Micah. There they find the young Levite, and either recognize him from some previous encounter, or else recognize him for what he is, perhaps by overhearing his praying or study (which was often done out loud). They inquire of him whether their trip will be successful. Perhaps the "ephod" Micah has made (Judg. 17:5) includes something like the Urim and Thummim for discerning, ostensibly, the will of the Lord. In any case, he reassures them and they go on their way.

The soldiers spy out the town of Laish, which was not part of the land that had been assigned to them. But it looks like a soft and attractive target, and they report accordingly. When six hundred armed Danites return, they interrupt their military raid to walk off with all of Micah's household gods, not to mention the young Levite priest and the ephod, for clearly they think of this as a way of bringing "luck" or at least direction to their enterprise. The Levite himself is delighted: to him, this feels like a promotion (18:20). But can "bought" clergy ever exercise a prophetic witness?

When he and his men catch up with this warrior band, Micah frankly sounds pathetic: "You took the gods I made, and my priest, and went away. What else do I have? How can you ask, 'What's the matter with you?'" (18:24). He detects no irony in his own utterance, the sheer futility of attaching so much to gods you have *made*.

The Danites threaten to annihilate Micah and his household, and that settles the matter. Might, not justice or integrity, rules the land. The Danites capture Laish, attacking "a peaceful and unsuspecting people" (18:27), and rename the place Dan. There they set up their idols, and the young Levite, *now identified as a direct descendant of Moses* (18:30), functions as their tribal priest, and passes on this legacy to his sons, even while the tabernacle still remains in its rightful place in Shiloh (18:30-31).

The levels of covenantal faithlessness in the religious realm are multiplied by increased violence, tribal selfishness, personal aspirations of power, ingratitude, crude threats, and massive superstition. It is not uncommon for these sins to grow together.

∾

Judges 19; Acts 23; Jeremiah 33; Psalms 3—4

∿

BY THE TIME WE REACH **Judges 19**, the law of the jungle has triumphed in the fledging nation of Israel.

The Levite introduced to us at this point takes on a concubine. (Levites were supposed to marry only virgins; see Lev. 21:7, 13-15.) She sleeps around and moves out, returning to her father's home. In due course the Levite wants her back, so he travels to Bethlehem and finds her. Owing to a late start on the return trip, they can't make the journey home in one day. Preferring not to stop in one of the Canaanite towns, they press on to Gibeah, a Benjamite settlement. A local homeowner warns the Levite and his concubine not to stay in the town square overnight—it is far too dangerous. And he takes them in.

During the night, a mob of lusty hooligans want the homeowner to send out the Levite so they can sodomize him. That is stunning. In the first place, by the social standards of the ancient Near East, it was unthinkable not to show hospitality—and they want to gang rape a visitor. And as the account progresses, it is very clear that they will happily rape males or females—they don't really care.

But perhaps the ugliest moment in the narrative occurs when the homeowner, remembering the rules of hospitality and doubtless frightened for himself as well, offers them his daughter and the Levite's concubine. The account is crisp and brief, but it does not take much imagination to conjure up their terror—two women not defended by their men but abandoned and betrayed by them and offered to a howling mob of gang rapists so that the men can save their own skins. The mob insists that even that isn't enough, so the Levite shoves his concubine out the door, alone. So began her last night on earth in a small town belonging to the people of God.

The morning dawns to find the Levite ordering this woman to get up; it's time to go. Only then does he discover she is dead. He hauls her corpse back home, cuts her up into twelve pieces, and sends one piece to each part of Israel, saying, in effect: When does the violence stop? At what point do we put our collective foot down and reverse these horrible trends?

"In those days Israel had no king" (19:1).

Yet what about his own profound complicity and cowardice? The sheer horror of the dismembered body parts was bound to stir up a reaction, but by this time it could not be the righteous reaction of biblically thoughtful and restrained people. Only the naive could imagine that the outcome would be anything other than a descent into a maelstrom of evil and violence.

∿

Judges 20; Acts 24; Jeremiah 34; Psalms 5—6

ONE MIGHT HAVE EXPECTED that only the guilty would be hunted down and executed (**Judg. 20**). But the Levite is stirring up the nation (without, of course, disclosing his own disgraceful behavior). So far as our records go, Gibeah does not offer to hand over the offenders. If they had, that would have been the end of the matter. Nor do the tribal leaders of Benjamin offer to intervene and ensure that justice is done. Instead, they close ranks and offer to take on all comers, doubtless expecting that the rest of the nation will be unwilling to pay too high a price to capture a few rapists at a time when the entire nation has slid into violence.

For their part, the rest of the tribes foam at the mouth but act stupidly. Instead of embarking on a massed assault, initially they decide to send the troops of only one tribe at a time. When we are told that the Israelites inquired of God which tribe should go first, probably this means that they went through the Urim and Thummim procedure with a priest of the sanctuary. The Israelites lose twenty-two thousand men the first day (20:21), and eighteen thousand the next (20:25). Finally the Lord does truly promise that he will give Gibeah and the Benjamites into the hands of the rest of the Israelites (20:28). The third day, the Israelites set up an ambush, and at last they are victorious. Vast numbers of Benjamites die.

That is the sort of thing that happens when the rule of law dissolves, when people start acting out of tribal loyalty and not principle, when vengeance overtakes justice, when superstitious vendettas displace courts, when brothers no longer share a common heritage of worship and values, when government is by fear and not by the consent of the governed. There is no logical stopping place. It can start a regional conflict, it can ignite a Bosnia, it can start a world war. It is the stuff of dictators and war lords, the lubricant of gangs and violence.

The sad reality is that every culture is capable of this. The ancient Israelites sink into this quagmire not because they are worse than all others, but because they are typical of all others. A society that no longer hangs together, whether on the ground of religion, shared worldview, or at least agreed and respected procedurals, is heading for violence and anarchy, which, sooner or later, becomes the best possible breeding ground for the ordered response of tyrants—power authorized by sword and gun.

That is how secular historians see it. We see all this, too, and discern behind the blood and evil the just hand of God, who intones, "So far will you go, and no further."

Judges 21; Acts 25; Jeremiah 35; Psalms 7—8

∽

THE LAST WRETCHED STEP in the violence precipitated by the rape and murder of the Levite's concubine now plays out (Judg. 21). In a fury of vengeance, the Israelites have swept through the tribal territory of Benjamin, annihilating men, women, children, and cattle (20:48). The only Benjamites left are 600 armed men who have holed up in a stronghold at Rimmon (20:47). But now the rest of the nation is entertaining second thoughts. As part of their sanctions against Benjamin, they had vowed not to give any of their daughters to a Benjamite. If they keep their vow, Benjamites will die off: only male Benjamites are left.

Their solution is as nauseating, cruel, and barbaric as anything they have done. They discover that one large town in Israel, Jabesh Gilead, never responded to the initial call to arms. Partly as punishment, partly as a way of finding Israelite women, the Israelite forces destroy Jabesh Gilead, killing all the men and all the women who are not virgins (21:10-14). This tactic provides 400 wives for the 600 surviving Benjamites. The ruse for finding a further 200 is scarcely less evil. The remaining 200 Benjamites are given sanction to kidnap suitable women at a festival time in Shiloh, their fathers and brothers being warned off (21:20-23). So the tribe of Benjamin, greatly reduced in numbers, survives. One can scarcely imagine the multiplied levels of bitterness, grief, fear, resentment, loneliness, retaliation, furious rage, and billowing bereavement that attended these "solutions."

By now it is clear that the Israelites face two kinds of problems in the book of Judges. The presenting problem, as often as not, is enslavement or repression from one or other of the Canaanite tribes that share much of the land or that live not far away. When the people cry to him, God repeatedly raises up a hero to rescue them. But the other problem is far deeper. It is the rebellion itself, the chronic and persistent abandonment of the God who rescued them from Egypt and who entered into a solemn covenant with them. This issues not only in more cycles of oppression from without, but in spiraling decadence and disorientation within.

For the fifth and final time, the writer of Judges offers his analysis: "In those days Israel had no king; everyone did as he saw fit" (21:25). How this nation needs a king—to order it, stabilize it, defend it, maintain justice, lead it, pull it together. But will he be a king who solves the problems, or whose dynasty becomes part of the problem? Thus a new chapter in Israel's history opens. A new, royal institution soon becomes no less problematic—until he comes who is King of kings and Lord of lords (Rev. 19:16).

∽

Ruth 1; Acts 26; Jeremiah 36, 45; Psalm 9

∽

THERE IS SCARCELY A MORE ATTRACTIVE figure in all of Scripture than Ruth.

She is a Moabitess (**Ruth 1:4**). She lives in troubled times, and faces her own terrible grief. She and another Moabitess, Orpah, marry two recent immigrants called Mahlon and Kilion. These two men and their parents had arrived in Moabite territory to escape famine back home in Bethlehem. Some years pass, and the men's father—Elimelech—dies. Then both Mahlon and Kilion die. That leaves the three women: the Moabitesses' mother-in-law Naomi, and the two Moabitesses themselves, Orpah and Ruth.

When Naomi hears that the famine back home is over, which was the original reason for their migration to Moab, she decides to go home. Families often worked in extended clan relationships. She would be looked after, and the pain of her loneliness would be mitigated. Wisely, she encourages her two daughters-in-law to stay in their own land, with their own people, language, and culture. Who knows? In time they might even find new mates. Certainly they cannot reasonably expect Naomi to produce them!

So Orpah accepts the counsel, stays home in Moab, and nothing more is heard of her again. But Ruth clings to Naomi: "Don't urge me to leave you or to turn back from you. Where you go I will go, and where you stay I will stay. Your people will be my people and your God my God. Where you die I will die, and there I will be buried" (1:16-17). She even puts herself under the threat of a curse: "May the LORD deal with me, be it ever so severely, if anything but death separates you and me" (1:17).

Ruth does not mean this to sound heroic. She is simply speaking out of her heart. Had she come to a genuine and consistent faith in the Lord God during her ten-year marriage? What kind of solid and subtle links had been forged between Ruth and the Israelite members of this extended family, and in particular between Ruth and Naomi?

Our culture makes all kinds of snide remarks about mothers-in-law. But many a mother-in-law is remarkably unselfish, and establishes relationships with her daughters-in-law that are as godly and as deep as the best of those between mothers and daughters. So, apparently, here. Ruth is prepared to abandon her own people, culture, land, and even religion, provided she can stay with Naomi and help her.

She could not have known that in making that choice she would soon find herself married again. She could not have known that that marriage would make her an ancestor not only of the imposing Davidic dynasty, but of the supreme King who centuries later would spring from it.

∽

Ruth 2; Acts 27; Jeremiah 37; Psalm 10

THE NARRATOR HAS ALREADY TOLD US that when Naomi and Ruth arrive back in Bethlehem it was the time of barley harvest (Ruth 1:22). Now (**Ruth 2**) the significance of that bit of information is played out.

It was long-standing tradition, stemming from Mosaic Law, that landowners would not be too scrupulous about picking up every bit of produce from their land. That left something for the poor to forage (cf. Deut. 24:19-22; see meditation for June 19). So Ruth goes out and works behind the proper reapers in a field not too far from Jerusalem. She could not know that this field belonged to a wealthy landowner called Boaz—a distant relative of Naomi's and Ruth's future husband.

The story is touching, with decent people acting decently on all fronts. On the one hand, Ruth proves to be a hard worker, barely stopping for rest (2:7). She is painfully aware of her alien status (2:10), but treats the locals with respect and courtesy. When she brings her hoard back to Naomi and relates all that has happened, another small aside reminds us that for a single woman to engage in such work at this point in Israel's history was almost to invite molestation (2:22)—which attests her courage and stamina.

Naomi sees the hand of God. From a merely pragmatic perspective of gaining enough to eat, she is grateful, but when she hears the name of the man who owns the field, she not only recognizes the safety that this will provide for Ruth, but she realizes that Boaz is one of their "kinsman-redeemers" (2:20)—that is, one of those who under so-called *levirate* law could marry Ruth, with the result that their first son would carry on the legitimate rights and property entitlements of her original husband.

But it is Boaz who is, perhaps, seen in the best light. Without a trace of romance at this stage, he shows himself to be not only concerned for the poor, but a man who is touched by the calamities of others, and who quietly wants to help. He has heard of Naomi's return and of the persistent faithfulness of this young Moabitess. He instructs his own workers to provide for her needs, to ensure her safety, and even leave behind some extra bits of grain so that Ruth's labor will be well rewarded. Above all, he is a man of faith as well as of integrity, a point we hear in his first conversation with the woman who would one day be his bride: "May the LORD repay you for what you have done. May you be richly rewarded by the LORD, the God of Israel, under whose wings you have come to take refuge" (2:12). Well said—for the Lord is no one's debtor.

Ruth 3—4; Acts 28; Jeremiah 38; Psalms 11—12

∾

SCHOLARS DISAGREE SOMEWHAT over the social significance of each action taken in **Ruth 3—4**, but the general line is clear enough. Almost certainly the levirate laws, which allowed or mandated men to marry widowed in-laws under certain circumstances to keep the family name alive, were not followed very consistently. Following Naomi's instruction, Ruth takes a little initiative: she lies down at Boaz's feet in a "men only" sleeping area. When he wakes up, she says, "Spread the corner of your garment over me, since you are a kinsman-redeemer" (3:9). This was an invitation, but not a cheap one. It signaled her willingness to become his wife, if Boaz will discharge his duties as a kinsman-redeemer. Boaz takes this as a compliment: apparently there is enough difference between their ages (3:10, plus his habit of referring to Ruth as "my daughter") that he is touched by her willingness to marry him instead of one of the young men.

The story plays out with romantic integrity. Hollywood would hate it: there is no blistering sex, certainly not of the premarital variety. But there is a seductive charm to the account, allied with a wholesome respect for tradition and procedure, and a knowing grasp of human nature. Hence, Naomi confidently predicts that Boaz "will not rest until the matter is settled today" (3:18).

She is right, of course. The town gate is the place for public agreements, and there Boaz marshals ten elders as witnesses and gently demands that the one person who is a closer relative to Naomi (and therefore with the right of "first refusal") discharge the obligations of kinsman-redeemer or legally abandon the claim (4:1-4). Apparently at this point the marriage rights are tied to ownership of the land of the deceased husband. This particular kinsman-redeemer would love to obtain the land, but does not want to marry Ruth. Her firstborn son in such a union would maintain the property and family heritage of the deceased husband; later sons would inherit from the natural father. But the situation is messy. Suppose Ruth bore only one son?

So Boaz marries Ruth, and in due course she gives birth to a son, whom they call Obed. Naomi is provided not only with a grandson, but with a family eager and able to look after her.

At one level, this is a simple story of God's faithfulness in the little things of life, at a time of social malaise, religious declension, political confusion, and frequent anarchy. God still has his people—working hard, acting honorably, marrying, bearing children, looking after the elderly. They could not know that Obed's was the line that would sire King David—and, according to the flesh, King Jesus.

∾

1 Samuel 1; Romans 1; Jeremiah 39; Psalms 13—14

~

HOW DOES THE WRATH OF GOD manifest itself, according to the Scriptures?

There is no short answer to that question, because the answers are many, depending on an enormous array of circumstances. God's wrath wiped out almost the entire human race at the Flood. Sometimes God's punishment of his own covenant people is remedial. Sometimes it is immediate, not the least because it then tends to be instructive (like the defeat of the people at Ai after Achan stole some silver and fine Babylonian clothes); at other times, God forbears, which at one level is gracious, but granted the perversity of God's image-bearers, is likely to let things get out of hand. The final display of God's wrath is hell itself (see, for instance, Rev. 14:6ff.).

Romans 1:18ff. pictures the revelation of God's wrath in a slightly different way. What Paul presents here is not the only thing to say about God's wrath—even in Paul—but it contributes something very important. Not only is God's wrath being revealed *against* "all the godlessness and wickedness of men who suppress the truth by their wickedness" (1:18), but it manifests itself *in* such sins—that is, in God's giving people over to do what they want to do (1:24-28). In other words, instead of rebuking them in remedial judgment or curtailing their wickedness, God "gave them over": to "shameful lusts" (1:26) and a "depraved mind" (1:28). The result is multiplying "wickedness, evil, greed and depravity" (1:29). The picture painted in the rest of the verses of Romans 1 is not a pretty one.

We must reflect a little further as to what this means. In our shortsightedness we sometimes think God is a little abrupt when in certain passages, not least in the Old Testament, he instantly chastens his people for their sins. But what is the alternative? Quite simply, it is *not* instantly chastening them. If chastening were merely a matter of remedial education to morally neutral people, the timing and severity would not matter very much; we would learn. But the Bible insists that this side of the Fall we are by nature and persistent choice rebels against God. If we are chastened, we whine at God's severity. If we are not chastened, we descend into debauchery until the very foundations of society are threatened. We may then cry to God for mercy. Well and good, but at least we should see that it would have been a mercy if we had not been permitted to descend so far down into the abyss.

Granted the shape and trends in Western culture, does this not argue that we are already under the severe wrath of God? Have mercy, Lord!

~

1 Samuel 2; Romans 2; Jeremiah 40; Psalms 15—16

∽

IF ROMANS 1 CONDEMNS the entire human race, Romans 2 focuses especially on Jews. They have enormous advantages in that they were the recipients of the Law—the revelation from God mediated through Moses at Sinai. But here too, Paul argues, all are condemned; possession of the law does not itself save. By 3:19-20, the apostle explicitly insists that those "under the law" are silenced along with those without the law: all are under sin. This prepares the way for the glorious gospel solution (3:21-31).

Here in Romans 2, however, there is one paragraph that has generated considerable discussion (**Rom. 2:12-16**). In verse 12 Paul makes the general point that God judges people by what they know, not by what they do not know. Hence: "All who sin apart from the law will also perish apart from the law, and all who sin under the law will be judged by the law" (2:12). Jesus had similarly tied human responsibility to human privilege: the more we know, the more severely we are held accountable (Matt. 11:20-24). Mere possession of the law isn't worth anything. Those (Jews) are righteous who *obey* the law. Then Paul adds, "Indeed, when Gentiles, who do not have the law, do by nature things required by the law, they are a law for themselves, even though they do not have the law, since they show that the requirements of the law are written on their hearts, their consciences also bearing witness, and their thoughts now accusing, now even defending them" (2:14-15).

Many writers take this to mean that some Gentiles may be truly saved without ever having heard of Jesus, since after all, Paul says that some Gentiles "do by nature things required by the law," and insists their consciences are "even defending them." Others try to avoid this implication by arguing that the positive option is for Paul purely hypothetical. But Paul is not arguing that there is a subset of Gentiles who are so good that their consciences are always clean, and therefore they will be saved. Rather, he is arguing that Gentiles everywhere have some knowledge of right and wrong, even though they do not have the law, and that this is demonstrated in the fact that they sometimes do things in line with the law, and have consciences that sometimes accuse them and sometimes defend them. His argument is not that some are good enough to be saved, but that all display, by their intuitive grasp of right and wrong, an awareness of such moral standards, doubtless grounded in the *imago Dei*, that they too have enough knowledge to be held accountable. For Paul is concerned to show that "Jews and Gentiles alike are all under sin" (3:9).

∽

1 Samuel 3; Romans 3; Jeremiah 41; Psalm 17

THE LORD DOES NOT CALL all his prophets in the same way, or at the same time of life. Amos was called when he was a shepherd in Tekoa. Elisha was called by Elijah to serve an apprenticeship. But Samuel was called even from before conception.

Samuel's conscious experience of the call of God (**1 Sam. 3**) occurred when he was still quite a young lad—not, surely, a tiny tot, as some of our more romantic pictures have portrayed it, for he knew enough to be able to understand what the Lord said to him, to be troubled by it and to hesitate before repeating it to Eli. But he was not very old, still a "boy" (3:1).

The story is so well known it scarcely needs repeating. But some observations may focus matters a little:

(1) The voice that comes to Samuel is a real voice, speaking Hebrew, a real language. This is not some merely subjective "feel" of being called. Real calls, real visions, real revelations take place in the Bible; but in the days of Samuel they were "rare" (3:1). Certainly up to this point Samuel had never had such an experience; he "did not yet know the LORD: The word of the LORD had not yet been revealed to him" (3:7).

(2) Eli is a sad figure. In his own life, he is a person of integrity—even though he is a disaster with his family. His long experience enables him, on the Lord's third calling of Samuel, to guess what is going on, and to guide young Samuel in an appropriate response: "Speak, LORD, for your servant is listening" (3:9).

(3) The substance of the revelation given to Samuel on this occasion concerns a coming setback so startling that it "will make the ears of everyone who hears of it tingle" (3:11). Included in this tragedy will be the destruction of Eli's family, in line with what the Lord had previously told Eli: God would judge Eli's family forever "because of the sin he [Eli] knew about; his sons made themselves contemptible, and he failed to restrain them" (3:13). Such neglect is always wicked, of course, but it is especially wicked in religious leaders who promote their sons to positions where they use their power to abuse people and treat God himself with contempt (2:12-25).

(4) When Eli manages to get Samuel to tell him all the Lord said, his own response, while preserving a show of trust, betrays his irresponsibility: "He is the LORD; let him do what is good in his eyes" (3:18). Why does he not immediately repent, take decisive action against his sons, exercise the discipline that was within his priestly right, and ask the Lord for mercy?

1 Samuel 4; Romans 4; Jeremiah 42; Psalm 18

∿

WHEN PEOPLE KNOW LITTLE about the God who has actually disclosed himself, it is terribly easy for them to sink into some perverted view of this God, until the image held of him has very little to do with the reality.

One can understand the Philistines' ignorance (**1 Sam. 4**). In their polytheistic world, full of idols providing concrete representations of their gods, the arrival of the ark of the covenant in the Israelite camp is understood to be the arrival of the Israelite god (4:6-7). But this god, even if he proved so powerful that he could at one point take on the Egyptians, is merely one more god, finite, limited, local. So the Philistines, having to choose between buckling under and courageous defiance, opt for the latter, and win. Implicit in their win are an *assumption* and a *result*: the *assumption* is that God is no longer laying on the hearts of the Canaanites the mortal dread of the Israelites that had accompanied the early Israelite victories (and this spells judgment for the Israelites); the *result* is that the Philistines will now have an even more diminished view of God. Knowing the God of the Bible, we can be certain that this is a situation that will not last long; God will take action to defend his own glory.

The Israelites' ignorance of God is wholly without excuse, but is of a piece with the horrible declension toward the end of the period of the judges. They are getting trounced by the Philistines. Their theological reasoning is so bad that they think they can reverse the fortunes of war by bringing the ark of the covenant into the military camp like an oversized good-luck charm. The writer hints at the sheer preposterousness of the notion: they bring "the ark of the covenant of the LORD Almighty, who is enthroned between the cherubim" (4:4). Sadly, Eli's sons, the priests Hophni and Phinehas, are complicit in these arrangements. Is God's favor so easily manipulated? Does he care as much about the location of a box as he does about the conduct and (in)fidelity of his image-bearers and covenant community? What kind of pared-down and domesticated image of God did the leaders of Israel hold at this juncture that they should utter such nonsense?

Yesterday I received in the mail a letter from one of America's premier television preachers, inviting me to send money and offering me in return a Christmas tree ornament of an "angel" with a trumpet, to remind me that God had commanded the angel looking after me to blow a trumpet to celebrate me. What kind of pared-down and domesticated image of God do such leaders hold that they should utter such nonsense?

1 Samuel 5—6; Romans 5; Jeremiah 43; Psalm 19

∾

GOD IS NEVER AMUSED at being treated with contempt, nor by having his explicit instructions ignored or defied. For then he would not be *God*.

God is well able to defend himself. In **1 Samuel 5—6**, the unfolding account can be as restrained as it is precisely because it is as obvious to the reader as it was to the Philistines that God himself is behind the tragic illnesses and deaths they were suffering. The surprises began with the capsizing of their fish god, Dagon. It soon spread to a plague of rats, an epidemic of tumors, multiplying deaths—and not only in the city of Ashdod, to which the ark of the covenant was first taken, but in other cities to which it was transported—Gath and Ekron. Panic ensued.

But at the end of the day, all the phenomena the Philistines were experiencing *could* have been natural. That's not what they thought, of course; but still, it was difficult to be sure. So the Philistine priests concoct a test so much against nature that should the test succeed, the people will be convinced that what they are suffering comes from the hand of "Israel's god" (6:5, 7-9). The cows are separated from their calves and draw along the cart to Beth Shemesh, on the Israelite side: God himself plays along with their superstitions and their fears.

While the Israelites rejoice at the return of the ark of the covenant, "God struck down some of the men of Beth Shemesh, putting seventy of them to death because they had looked into the ark of the LORD" (6:19). There is no reason to think this happened instantaneously. If one had peeked into it and been struck down immediately, others would have been pretty quickly discouraged from doing so. There is no hint that a blinding and consuming light swept out of the opened box and melted the flesh off people, like some sort of ancient Harrison Ford film. Rather, seventy men from Beth Shemesh looked into the ark (which of course was strictly forbidden under pain of death), and doubtless saw what was there: the tablets of stone (apparently the pot of old manna and Aaron's rod that budded had disappeared, perhaps removed by the Philistines). Then the deaths started, all premature, by whatever means—and the only commonality was that they were occurring among men who had looked into the ark. "Who can stand in the presence of the LORD, this holy God?" the people ask (6:20)—not intending to learn the ways of holiness, but to get rid of the ark—precisely the same pattern as in the pagan cities.

God will not be treated with contempt, nor forever permit his covenant people to ignore his words.

∾

1 Samuel 7—8; Romans 6; Jeremiah 44; Psalms 20—21

∾

WHY PEOPLE ASK FOR SOMETHING is at least as important as *what* they ask for.

This is true in many domains of life. I know an executive in a midsize corporation who successfully talked his bosses into setting up a new committee. The reason he gave was that it was needed to oversee some new development. What he did not tell his bosses was his real reason: he could in time use this committee to sidestep another established committee that was questioning some of his projects and holding them up. He saw the new committee as a managerial trick to avoid being controlled, and thus to shin up the ladder a little faster. What *might* have been construed as a shrewd device for peacefully circumventing an unnecessary roadblock in the company's structure (had he explained what he was doing to the bosses) was in fact presented in quite different terms, because he could not honestly tell them what he was doing—he knew they thought the established committee was doing a good job. Hence the deceit.

We need not look so far. How many of our own requests—in the home, in church, at work, in our prayers—mask motives that are decidedly self-serving?

That was the problem with Israel's request for a king (**1 Sam. 8**). The problem was not the request itself. After all, God would eventually give them the Davidic dynasty. Moses had anticipated the time when there would be a king (Deut. 17). The problem was the motive. They looked at their recent ups and downs with the local Canaanites and perceived few of their own faults, their own infidelities. They did not want to rely on the word of God mediated through prophets and judges and truly learn to obey that word. They figured that there would be political stability if only they could have a king. They wanted to be like the other nations (!), with a king to lead them in their military skirmishes (8:19-20).

God not only understands their requests, but he perceives and evaluates their motives. In this instance he knows that the people are not simply loosening their ties to a prophet like Samuel, they are turning away from God himself (8:7-8). The result is horrific: they get what they want, along with a desperate range of new evils they had not foreseen.

That is the fatal flaw in Machiavellian schemes, of course. They may win short-term advantages. But God is on his throne. Not only will the truth eventually come out, whether in this life or the next, but we may pay a horrible price, within our families and in our culture, in unforeseen correlatives, administered by a God who loves integrity of motive.

∾

1 Samuel 9; Romans 7; Jeremiah 46; Psalm 22

∾

OCCASIONALLY SOMEONE COMES ALONG who shows exceptional promise from his or her youth, and then lives up to that promise. But that does not seem to be the common way of things. Who would have thought that a minor painter from Vienna could become the monstrous colossus the world knows as Adolf Hitler? Who would have thought that a failed haberdasher from Missouri, a chap with a high-school education, would succeed Roosevelt, drop the atom bomb on Hiroshima and Nagasaki, sack General Douglas MacArthur, and order the racial integration of the armed forces?

Consider Saul (**1 Sam. 9**). He was a Benjamite, and thus from the little tribe reduced in numbers and prestige by the horrible events recorded in Judges 19—21 (see meditations for August 5-7). He was not even from a major clan within that tribe (9:21). Physically he was a strapping young man, getting on with the farming chores his father assigned him, with no pretensions—so far as we know—of glory or power. Indeed, in the next chapter he has to be cajoled from his hiding place in the luggage to come out and accept the acclaim the people wanted to give him.

It is not yet the time to trace all the things that went wrong—some of them will be mentioned in later meditations. But people with even a cursory knowledge of Scripture know what a mixed character Saul turned out to be, and how tragic his end. What should we learn?

(1) If we ourselves are on an upward curve of great promise, we must resolve to persevere in the small marks of fidelity and humility. A good beginning does not guarantee a good end.

(2) If we are responsible for hiring people, whether pastors and other Christian leaders or executives for a corporation, although some of us prove more insightful and farsighted than others, all of us make mistakes—for the simple reason that, quite apart from the bad choices we make, a good choice can turn into a bad choice (and vice-versa) because people change.

(3) It follows that every organization, not least the local church, needs some sort of mechanism for godly removal of leaders who turn out to be evil or woefully inadequate. That wasn't possible in ancient Israel, so far as the king went. It is not only possible but mandated so far as New Testament leadership is concerned.

(4) Only God knows the end from the beginning. After we have exercised our best judgment, nothing is more important than that we should cast ourselves on God, seeking to please him, trying to conform our judgments to what he has disclosed of himself in his Word, trusting absolutely in the only One who knows the end from the beginning.

∾

1 Samuel 10; Romans 8; Jeremiah 47; Psalms 23—24

❧

WHAT DOES IT MEAN FOR Christians to be "more than conquerors" (**Rom. 8:37**)? A considerable body of thought pictures a special group of illustrious Christians who "live above it all," powerful in confronting temptation, victorious in their prayer lives, fruitful in their witness, mature and faithful in their relationships. And none of that is what the text says.

First, the "us" to whom the apostle refers includes *all* Christians. *All* Christians are the ones whom God has foreknown, "predestined to be conformed to the likeness of his Son," called, justified, glorified (8:29-30). The people referred to are not the elite of the elect; they are ordinary Christians, all genuine Christians.

Second, the actual evidence that they are "more than conquerors" is that they persevere regardless of all opposition. That opposition may take the form of horrible persecution, of the kind that Scripture describes (8:35-38). It may be some other hardship, all the way to famine. The glories of life will not finally seduce them; the terrors of death will not finally sway them; neither the pressures of the present nor the frustrations of the future will destroy them (8:38). Neither human powers nor anything else in all creation, not even all the powers of hell unleashed, can "separate us from the love of God that is in Christ Jesus our Lord" (8:39).

Third, as the last sentence already makes clear, that from which Christians cannot be finally separated is the "love of Christ" (8:35) or the love of God in Christ (8:39). At one level, of course, that is simply saying that no power can stop Christians from being Christians. That is why we are "more than conquerors." But that point could have been made a lot of different ways. To make it *this* way, with an emphasis on the love of Christ as that from which we cannot be separated, reminds us of the sheer glory and pleasure that is ours, both now and in eternity, to be in such a relationship. We are not simply acquitted; we are loved. We are loved not simply by a peer, but by God himself. Nor is this a reference to the general love that God has for his entire creation. What is at stake here is that special love that attaches to "all who have been called according to his purpose" (8:28).

Fourth, the guarantee that we shall prevail and persevere, and prove to be "more than conquerors" in this sense, is nothing other than the sovereign purposes of God (8:29-30), manifest in the death of his Son on our behalf (8:31-35). "If God is for us, who can be against us?" (8:32). No greater security is imaginable.

❧

1 Samuel 11; Romans 9; Jeremiah 48; Psalm 25

ONE OF THE IMPORTANT QUESTIONS that the first Christians had to answer, as they bore witness to Jesus the Messiah, went something like this: "If Jesus really is the promised Messiah, how come so many Jews reject the claim?" Inevitably, there were variations: e.g., "If you Christians are right, doesn't this mean that God didn't keep his promises to the Jews?" or: "Why do apostles like Paul spend so much time evangelizing Gentiles, as if they've walked away from their own group?"

Many complementary answers are provided in the pages of the New Testament to respond to these and similar questions. Here we note components of Paul's answer (**Rom. 9**).

First, whatever the focus on Gentiles within Paul's ministry, he has never written off those of his own race. Far from it: he could wish himself damned if by so doing he could save them (9:3). It would be easy to dismiss such language as hyperbole grounded in a merely hypothetical possibility. But the fact that Paul can write in such terms discloses, not an apostle who is merely a cool and analytic expert in apologetics, but a man with passion and extraordinary love for his own people. The church today urgently needs evangelists with the same kind of heart.

Second, Paul insists that even if many Jews do not believe, it is *not* because God's word has failed (9:6). Far from it: it has *never* been the case that all of Abraham's children would be included in the covenant. God insisted that the line would be through Isaac, not Ishmael or the children of Keturah (9:7). To put the matter differently, only the "children of the promise" are regarded as Abraham's offspring, not all the natural children (9:8). Moreover, Paul had already reminded his readers of the promise to Abraham that in his seed all the nations of the earth would be blessed (Rom. 4:16-17), not Jews only.

Third, the defense of these propositions takes a dramatic turn. God arranged a *selection* among the children of Abraham—and not only in Abraham's generation but also with respect to the children of Isaac (9:8-13)—"in order that God's purpose in election might stand: not by works but by him who calls" (9:11-12). Nothing makes clearer the ultimacy of grace than the doctrine of election. God did not have to save any. If he saved one, it would be a great act of grace. Here he saves a vast number of guilty people, out of his grace alone, having compassion on whom he will (9:15), as is his right (9:16-24).

Fourth, Old Testament Scripture had foreseen that one day the people of God would not be restricted to the Jewish race (9:25-26).

1 Samuel 12; Romans 10; Jeremiah 49; Psalms 26—27

∾

HERE I WISH TO REFLECT on one small part of **Romans 10.**

As part of his insistence that Jews and Gentiles alike must be saved by faith or not at all, the apostle Paul reviews the fundamental Christian "word of faith": "That if you confess with your mouth, 'Jesus is Lord,' and believe in your heart that God raised him from the dead, you will be saved" (10:9). This is then slightly expanded: "For it is with your heart that you believe and are justified, and it is with your mouth that you confess and are saved" (10:10). The additional verse does not lay out salvation in two discrete steps: step one, believe in your heart and be justified; step two, confess with your mouth and be saved. This would almost imply that justification can take place apart from salvation, and that faith is an inadequate means that must be supplemented by confession. It would be closer to the apostle's thought to say that the two lines are parallel—not because each says exactly the same thing as the other (they don't), but because each throws light on the other, clarifying the other, expounding a little what the other means. Faith in the heart without confession with the mouth thus becomes unbelievable; conversely, confession with the mouth that is merely formal and not generated by faith in the heart is not what the apostle has in mind either. He propounds the faith that generates confession; this confession is borne along by faith. Out of this faith/confession comes justification/salvation—again, overlapping categories, such that in Paul you can't have one without the other.

So Paul drives the point home: in this respect there is no difference between Jew and Gentile, for the same Lord is Lord of all, and blesses all who call on him, as Scripture says: "*Everyone* who calls on the name of the Lord will be saved" (10:13; Joel 2:32). That means that Christians need to send people with the good news, for otherwise how shall people call on him of whom they have not heard (10:14-15)?

The point to observe is that the same Paul who insists so strongly in Romans 8 and 9 that God is unconditionally sovereign insists no less strongly in Romans 10 that people must believe in their hearts and confess gospel truth with their mouths if they are to be saved, and lays on the conscience of believers the imperative to bring this good news to those who have not heard. Any theology that attempts to diminish God's sovereignty by appealing to human freedom is as profoundly un-Pauline as any theology that somehow diminishes human responsibility and accountability by appealing to some crude, divine fatalism.

∾

1 Samuel 13; Romans 11; Jeremiah 50; Psalms 28—29

❧

ROMANS 11 HAS BEEN UNDERSTOOD in mutually contradictory ways. There is not space here to list them, let alone evaluate them. I shall simply lay out the flow of Paul's argument as I see it.

(1) Does Paul's argument in Romans 9—10 mean that God has utterly abandoned "his people," that is, the Israelites? Paul pens a hearty "No way!"—"By no means!" (11:1). The first bit of counter-evidence (11:1-6) is that Paul himself is a Jew, a Benjamite at that (one of the two tribes that did not break away from the Davidic dynasty after the death of Solomon). In other words, one cannot say that God has cast away the Israelites if Israelites are still being saved. Moreover, it never was the case that *all* Israelites demonstrated transforming grace. For instance, when Elijah, in a desperate depression, thought he was the only one left, the Lord informed him that he had reserved seven thousand loyal Israelites who had never succumbed to Baal worship (1 Kings 19:4, 10, 18; see also the October 16 meditation). So likewise in Paul's time and in ours: God has preserved a "remnant" of Jews who have proved faithful to God's ongoing self-disclosure. From God's perspective, it is a remnant "chosen by grace," and therefore not grounded in something as feeble as works (11:5-6).

(2) But if the nation as a whole, in line with scriptural prophecies, stumbled so badly (11:7-10), does this mean there is no hope for them, that they are "beyond recovery? Not at all!" (11:11). For in the sweep of God's redeeming purposes, the substantial hardening of the Jews has been the trigger that has spread the Gospel to the Gentiles—and "if their transgression means riches for the world, and their loss means riches for the Gentiles," and "if their rejection is the reconciliation of the world," then "how much greater riches will their fullness bring," and "what will their acceptance be but life from the dead?" (11:12, 15). This sounds very much as if Paul envisages a major swing still future to his own day. In the providence of God, the "rejection" of much of Israel has meant much grace for the Gentiles; the "acceptance" of much of Israel will mean even more grace for the world. Paul envisages a major turning to Jesus on the part of his fellow Jews, a turning that will issue in still greater gospel outreach worldwide.

(3) Paul draws some practical lessons for his Gentile Christian readers, using an analogy of a tree with branches broken off and grafted on (11:17-25). But the culminating high point of his argument is his acclamation of the unfathomable wisdom and knowledge of God in bringing about this spectacular result (11:33-36).

❧

1 Samuel 14; Romans 12; Jeremiah 51; Psalm 30

∾

AMONG THE MAJOR POINTS that Paul has been making in his letter to the Romans is the sheer gratuity of grace, the amazing measure of mercy that has won Jews and Gentiles alike. Alike we are guilty; alike we are justified, forgiven, renewed, owing to the measureless mercy of God.

In view of such mercy, Paul urges his readers "to offer [their] bodies as living sacrifices, holy and pleasing to God" (**Rom. 12:1**). We are so familiar with this verse that its strangeness no longer strikes us. In the ancient world, a sacrifice must be living to begin with, of course, but what makes it a sacrifice is that it is put to death. But Paul wants us to offer our bodies as *living* sacrifices, that is, as ongoing "sacrifices" that respond to God's mercy by devoting ourselves, not least our bodies, to him. Such sacrifices are "holy and pleasing to him." The idea is that in the light of the matchless mercy we have received, the least we will want to do is to be pleasing to him.

Such sacrifices constitute our "spiritual worship." The adjective rendered "spiritual" embraces both "spiritual" and "reasonable" or perhaps "rational." These are not sacrifices offered in a temple, begun with a bloodletting, continued with a burning of the body, and completed in selective eating of the meat. New covenant worship is no longer bound up with the temple and the ritual demands of the Sinai covenant. The way we live, in response to the mercy of God, lies at the heart of Christian worship.

If we want to know what this looks like, the second verse spells out the practicalities in principle, and the ensuing verses give them concrete form. To offer up our bodies in living sacrifice to God means conforming no longer to the pattern of this world, but being transformed by the renewing of our minds (12:2). In other words, what is at issue is not merely external behavior, while inwardly we remain in the grip of carefully masked hate, lust, deceit, envy, greed, fear, bitterness, and arrogance. What is at issue is the transformation of the way we think, bringing our minds in line with the ways and Word of God. That will produce all the change in behavior that is necessary and wise—and that change will be radical. By this fundamental transformation, we shall be enabled to test and approve in our own experience what God's will is—and find it "good, pleasing and perfect" (12:2). In the light of Romans 8:9, doubtless the motivating power for this transformation is the Spirit of God. But that magnificent truth does not absolve us of resolve; it empowers it.

∾

1 Samuel 15; Romans 13; Jeremiah 52; Psalm 31

SAUL ALREADY HAS A CHECKERED RECORD. On the one hand, he courageously res-cued the city of Jabesh from the Ammonites and displayed an admirable restraint in the early use of his royal power (1 Sam. 11). Nevertheless it was not long before he starts treating the Lord God as a talisman, and his word as the equivalent of a magical or astrological hint of what he should do, rather than something that is first of all to be reverenced and obeyed (1 Sam. 13). By chapter 14, only the inter-vention of his own men keeps him from killing his son Jonathan over a promise that should never have been made and should certainly not have been kept (com-pare the meditation for July 28). Here in **1 Samuel 15**, several traits of character ensure that Saul will not head a dynasty. He will be replaced by another king.

(1) Despite explicit instructions from the Lord regarding the Amalekites, Saul and his army spare the best sheep and cattle, and even the Amalekite King Agag, perhaps as a kind of trophy. Worse, Saul then lies about this to Samuel—as if God could be deceived. The lie betrays the fact that by this time Saul is thinking with-out reference to an all-knowing God; he is thinking like a mere politician, like a pagan or a secularist.

(2) Samuel understands the heart of the problem to lie in Saul's changed per-ceptions of himself (15:17): at one time he was small in his own eyes, and could scarcely imagine being king. Now he is ready to lie to God's prophet and never, never, truly repent.

(3) Saul changes his tactics, and insists that the reason he kept the best sheep and cattle was to offer a great sacrifice to the Lord. There is nothing like a little religious patter to pull the wool over some people's eyes. But not Samuel's. "Does the LORD delight in burnt offerings and sacrifices as much as in obeying the voice of the LORD?" he asks. "To obey is better than sacrifice, and to heed is better than the fat of rams. For rebellion is like the sin of divination, and arrogance like the evil of idolatry" (15:22-23). Such reminders need to be enshrined in contempo-rary evangelicalism.

(4) So Saul offers formal repentance—but makes the excuse that he was afraid of the people. He simply will not face his own responsibility—and Samuel sees this clearly (15:24-26).

(5) Saul tries formal repentance once more; but once again he betrays his own heart when he shows that he finds it more important to be honored before the elders of Israel than by the God of Israel (15:30-31). We are lost when human opinion means more to us than God's.

1 *Samuel 16; Romans 14;* Lamentations 1; Psalm 32

∿

THE ANOINTING OF DAVID as King over Israel (**1 Sam. 16:1-13**), even though his enthronement is years away, is full of interest.

(1) Sometimes prophets and preachers are slower to let go of a bad leader than God Almighty (16:1). This is not because we are more compassionate than God, but because inertia or nostalgia or personal bonds of affection blind us to the sheer damage the leader is doing. For all his compassion, God is never blinded.

(2) Saul was elevated to the throne by God's sanction. Is he so foolish as to think that he can outwit God in order to keep it? It is terribly sad to find Samuel afraid to anoint the next king, because Saul will kill anyone, even a prophet of God, who threatens a dynasty that God himself has declared will never be established.

(3) Saul had looked very promising when he was first elevated to the throne. Now Samuel thinks he can detect kingly material in the sons of Jesse—Eliab, for instance, the firstborn. But God says, "Do not consider his appearance or his height, for I have rejected him. The LORD does not look at the things man looks at. Man looks at the outward appearance, but the LORD looks at the heart" (16:7).

This is a lesson that must be learned afresh, especially in our day, for our day loves images more than reality. Even some preachers devote more thought to how "to dress for success" and how to develop a compelling and authoritative voice than they do to maintaining a pure heart.

(4) The most important factor in the life and service of David is that the Spirit of the Lord comes upon him "in power" (16:13). This is the regular experience of those prophets, priests, kings, and a few other leaders, who were given special roles under the terms of the old covenant. However difficult it is to be discerning in such matters, one cannot say too often or too loudly that what the church needs are leaders with *unction*—a word favored by the Puritans. It simply means "anointing," i.e., an anointing by the Spirit. Is that too much to ask, in an age when under the terms of the new covenant all of the covenant people of God receive the Spirit poured out at Pentecost?

(5) Those who know their Bibles cannot help but feel a thrill of excitement at the simple words of verse 12. There the Lord tells Samuel with respect to David, "Rise and anoint him; he is the one." Indeed, David was the one. Here are the inauspicious beginnings of a major new step in the history of redemption, one that leads directly to David's most eminent descendant—and his Lord.

∿

1 Samuel 17; Romans 15; Lamentations 2; Psalm 33

∽

THE NAMES OF DAVID and Goliath (**1 Sam. 17**) conjure up a story many have known from their youth. Sometimes David is made into a very little boy, though in reality he is at least a young man who has bested both a lion and a bear. But today the pair of names becomes evocative of little people and organizations taking on the "Goliaths." Doubtless there are lessons to be learned about courage and boldness, but the most important lessons lie on slightly different lines.

(1) Perhaps one should first reflect on the slightly obscure chronology. At the end of 1 Samuel 16, David already appears in Saul's court to play soothing music; yet after David's fight with Goliath, Saul must still find out who the young man is (17:55-58). Skeptical scholarship insists the problem cannot be resolved, and therefore infers that there is plenty of nonhistorical material here. Yet: (a) There is no particular reason why Saul should have made special inquiries into the background of just one more musician in the royal court, no matter how soothing he was. Saul may not have been motivated to find out until after the events in chapter 17. (b) More probably, the events in chapter 17 may have taken place *before* 15:14-23. Hebrew verbs do not convey time distinctions the way English verbs do, and it has been shown that there is no reason why we could not translate 17:1, "Now the Philistines *had* gathered . . ." etc., establishing important background for the relationship between Saul and David that occupies the attention of the succeeding chapters.

(2) Although David's words to army personnel (17:26) could be taken as the impetuous arrogance of untested youth (and certainly David's brother Eliab took them that way, 17:28), behind the brashness is a transparent concern for the glory of God, a concern that drives him to answer Goliath without a hint of personal bravado but with an abundance of faith (17:45-47). Of course, manipulators sometimes hide behind God-talk. But David is not of that ilk. At this stage of life he might be faulted for lacking the polish of self-restraint, but at least his heart is in the right place.

(3) Above all, one must not read this chapter without remembering Samuel's anointing of David: "from that day on the Spirit of the LORD came upon David in power" (16:13). There lies the source of the God-centeredness, the source of the courage, of the unerring aim, the great victory, and the elevation of the name and glory of God.

The text calls us not to admire David the man and no more, but to ponder what the Spirit of God may do with one person.

∽

1 Samuel 18; Romans 16; Lamentations 3; Psalm 34

❧

THE KIND OF JEALOUSY described in **1 Samuel 18** is a terrible thing.

(1) It is grounded in an ugly self-focus, a self-focus without restraint. In his world, Saul must be number one. This means that peers must not best him or he becomes jealous. Not for an instant does he look at anything from the perspective of others—David's perspective, for instance, or Jonathan's. Ultimately, he cannot look at anything from God's perspective either. His self-focus belongs to the genus of self-centeredness that lies at the heart of all human sinfulness, but in its degree and intensity it is so unrestrained that it simultaneously loses touch with reality and adopts the most elemental idolatry.

(2) It is triggered by endless comparisons, endless assessments of who's up and who's down. Thus if David's successes redound well on Saul, Saul is pleased; but if someone starts making comparisons between Saul and David that are in any way invidious to Saul, he is jealous (18:7-8). Insofar as David's successes are an index of the fact that "the LORD was with David" (18:12-28), Saul is jealous because he knows that the Lord is not with him. The tragedy is that this recognition does not breed repentance, but jealousy. Even the love Saul's daughter Michal has for David exacerbates Saul's jealousy (18:28-29). Inevitably, this kind and degree of jealousy is very much bound up with fear; again and again we are told that Saul *feared* David (18:12, 15, 29). David has become an unbearable threat. Jealousy of this order cannot tolerate competence in others.

It has to be said that many leaders, not least Christian leaders, even when they do not succumb to this degree of malevolence, fill the positions around them with less competent people, thinking that they thereby preserve their own image or authority. They don't, of course; they simply become masters of incompetent administrations. On the long haul, their own reputations are diminished. But jealousy is such a blinding sin that such obvious realities cannot be admitted.

(3) In the worst cases, this sort of jealousy is progressively devouring. It nags at Saul's mind and multiplies like a cancer. It erupts in uncontrolled violence (18:10-11); it slips into twisted schemes enmeshing Saul's own family (18:20-27). In the chapters ahead it settles into something beyond rage—implacable hatred that deploys the armed forces against one innocent man who makes Saul feel insecure.

A believer who above all wants the name of the Lord to be exalted, who genuinely desires the good of the people of God, and who is entirely content to entrust his or her reputation to God, will never succumb to the sin of jealousy.

❧

1 Samuel 19; 1 Corinthians 1; Lamentations 4; Psalm 35

∾

EVANGELICALS REGULARLY DRAW a line between justification and sanctification. Justification is God's declaration that an individual sinner is just—a declaration grounded not in the fact that he or she is just, but in God's accepting Christ's death instead of the sinner's, in God's reckoning Christ's righteousness to the sinner. It marks the beginning of the believer's pilgrimage. From the believer's vantage point, to be justified is a once-for-all experience bound up with God's good purposes in Christ's once-for-all death.

By contrast, sanctification in the Protestant tradition has normally been understood to refer to the process by which believers progressively become more holy. (Holy and sanctified/sanctification have the same root in Greek.) This is not a once-for-all experience; it reflects a lifelong pilgrimage, a process that will not be finally complete until the onset of the new heaven and the new earth. It is not what God reckons to us; it is what he empowers us to become.

Failure to distinguish between justification and sanctification frequently ends up with a blurring of justification. If justification takes on a shading of personal growth in righteousness, pretty soon the forensic, declarative nature of justification is lost to view, and we start reimporting some kind of works-righteousness through the back door.

Historically, of course, the warning is well merited. One must always be vigilant to preserve Paul's emphasis on justification. But the SANCTIFICATION word-group has not always been well-served by this analysis. Those who study Paul have long noted that sometimes people are said to be "sanctified" in a POSITIONAL or DEFINITIONAL sense—that is, they are set apart for God (POSITIONAL), and therefore they already are sanctified (DEFINITIONAL). In such passages the process of progressively becoming more holy is not in view.

Most of the places where Paul talks about being "holy" or "sanctified" fall into this POSITIONAL or DEFINITIONAL camp. That is certainly the case in 1 Corinthians 1:2: Paul writes to "the church of God in Corinth, to those sanctified in Christ Jesus and called to be holy." The Corinthians already are sanctified; they have been set apart for God. Therefore, they have been called to be holy— that is, to live life in line with their calling (which, by and large, they have been failing to do, quite spectacularly, judging by the rest of the book).

Of course, there are many passages that speak of growth and improvement that do not use SANCTIFICATION; for a start, meditate on Philippians 3:12-16. If we choose to use SANCTIFICATION as a term drawn from systematic theology to describe such growth, we do no wrong. But then we should not read this meaning back into Paul's use where his focus is elsewhere.

∾

1 Samuel 20; 1 Corinthians 2; Lamentations 5; Psalm 36

∽

THERE ARE NOT MANY CHAPTERS in the Bible that devote much space to the theme of friendship, but **1 Samuel 20** is one of them.

Strictly speaking, of course, 1 Samuel 20 is not about friendship per se, in the way that friendship is a theme to be explored by a gifted novelist. The account fits into the larger narrative of the decline of Saul and the rise of David, a major turning point in redemptive history. Yet the way that account unfolds turns in important ways on the relationship between Jonathan and David.

Jonathan turns out to be a wholly admirable young man. Earlier he had shown considerable physical courage when he and his armor-bearer routed a contingent of Philistines (1 Sam. 14). When David became part of the royal court, one might have expected Jonathan to display many malevolent emotions: jealousy at David's rising popularity, competitiveness in the military arena, even fear that David would one day usurp his right to the throne. But "Jonathan became one in spirit with David, and he loved him as himself" (18:1). He entered into a "covenant" with David that made David, in effect, his own brother (18:3-4)—an astonishing step for a royal to take with a commoner. By the time we arrive at chapter 20, Jonathan is aware that David will one day be king. How he acquired this knowledge we cannot be sure. Given their friendship, David may have confided in Jonathan the account of his anointing at the hands of Samuel.

Not only does Jonathan not share his father's malevolence, but, having once before effected a reconciliation between his father Saul and David (19:4-7), he finds it hard to believe that his father is as implacably determined to kill David as David believes (20:1-3). So the elaborate plan of this chapter is put into effect. Jonathan discovers that his own father is resolved on Jonathan's best friend's death. Indeed, his father is so enraged that Jonathan himself is in mortal danger (20:33).

David and Jonathan meet. They renew their covenant, as they will do once more (23:17-18). David, for his part, vows to look after Jonathan's family if and when Jonathan is no longer around—a harbinger of things to come, and rather different from the normal bloodletting that customarily took place when a new king sought to wipe out the potential heirs of a previous dynasty.

But perhaps the most striking thing is that Jonathan stays in town with his father. For the fact of the matter is that we choose our friends, but we do not choose our family; yet our responsibilities to our families take a prior claim. Otherwise friendship itself becomes an excuse for a new form of selfishness.

∽

1 Samuel 21—22; 1 Corinthians 3; Ezekiel 1; Psalm 37

ᴙ

THE TWO EXTENDED METAPHORS that Paul deploys in **1 Corinthians 3:5-15** make roughly the same point, although each carries a special shading not found in the other.

In the agricultural metaphor (3:5-9), the Lord is the farmer, Paul prepares the ground and plants the seed, Apollos waters the fledgling plants, and the Corinthians are "God's field" (5:9). In the context, which is designed to combat the Corinthians' penchant for division based on attaching themselves to particular "heroes" (3:3-4), Paul is concerned to show that he and Apollos are not competitors, but "fellow workers" (5:9)—indeed, "God's fellow workers" (i.e., they are fellow workers who belong to God, not fellow workers along with God, as if God makes up a threesome). Not only so, but neither Paul nor Apollos can guarantee fruit: God alone makes the seed grow (3:6-7). So why adopt a reverential stance toward either Paul or Apollos?

The architectural metaphor initially makes the same point: the various builders all contribute to one building, and therefore none should be idolized. Now the Corinthians are not the field, but the building itself (3:9-10). Paul laid the foundation of this building; otherwise put, he planted the church in Corinth. The foundation that Paul laid is Jesus Christ himself (3:11). Since his departure from this building project, others have come and built on this foundation. Thus, so far the architectural metaphor implicitly makes the same point that the agricultural metaphor made explicitly.

But now the architectural metaphor turns in a slightly different direction. Paul insists that later builders are responsible to choose with care the material they put into this building (3:12-15). A "Day" is coming (3:13), the day of judgment, when all that is not precious in God's sight will be consumed. It is possible that a builder could use such shoddy materials that in the end, all that he has built is devoured, even if he himself escapes the flames.

Two observations: (1) The person Paul describes as being "saved, but only as one escaping through the flames" (3:15), is not some purely nominal Christian whose conduct is indifferentiable from that of any pagan. Such do not enter the kingdom (6:9-10). This is a "builder," not the mass of Christians who constitute the "building" (3:10). The question is whether these evangelists and pastors are using proper materials. (2) In 3:16-17, the building, the church of God, becomes a temple. Later on, God's temple is the individual Christian's body (6:19-20), but here it is the local church. God loves this building so much that he openly threatens to destroy those who destroy God's temple. Damage the church, and you desecrate God's temple—and God will destroy you.

ᴙ

1 Samuel 23; 1 Corinthians 4; Ezekiel 2; Psalm 38

∾

PAUL IN 1 CORINTHIANS 3 HAS BEEN telling the Corinthians how *not* to view servants of Christ. They are *not* to view any particular servant of Christ as a group guru, for that means other servants of Christ are implicitly inferior. When each different group within the church has its own Christian guru, there are therefore two evils: unnecessary division within the church, and a censorious condescension that pronounces judgment on who is worthy to be a guru and who is not. Paul insists that *all* that God has for the church in a Paul or an Apollos or a Cephas rightly belongs to the *whole* church (3:21-22).

At the beginning of **1 Corinthians 4**, Paul goes on to tell the Corinthians how they *are* to view servants of Christ: "as those entrusted with the secret things of God" (4:1). The word rendered "secret things" does not mean "mysterious things" or "things that only the elite of the elect may learn." The word is often rendered "mysteries" in our older versions. In the New Testament, it most commonly refers to something that God has in some measure kept veiled, hidden, or secret in the past, but which he is now making abundantly clear in Christ Jesus. In short, these "servants of Christ" are entrusted with the Gospel—all that God has made clear in the coming of Jesus Christ.

Those given a trust must prove faithful to the one to whom they are accountable (4:2). For that reason, Paul knows that how the Corinthians view him is of little importance; indeed, how he assesses himself has no great significance either (4:3). Paul knows that it is important to keep a clear conscience before the Lord. But it is possible to have a clear conscience and still be guilty of many things, because conscience is not a perfect instrument. Conscience may be misinformed or hardened. The only person whose judgment is absolutely right, and of ultimate importance, is the Lord himself (4:4). It follows that the Corinthians should not appoint themselves judges over all the "servants of Christ" whom Christ sends. When the Lord returns, the final accounting will become clear. At that point, Paul says, "each will receive his praise from God" (4:5)—a wonderful thought, for it appears that the final Judge will prove more encouraging and positive than many human judges.

Some place remains in the church for discernment and judgment: see tomorrow's meditation! But there are always batteries of critics who go way "beyond what is written" (4:6) with legalistic tests of their own disgruntled devising, attaching themselves to their gurus and abominating the rest. They often think they are prophetic, whereas in fact their pretensions come close to usurping God's place.

∾

1 Samuel 24; 1 Corinthians 5; Ezekiel 3; Psalm 39

༄

IN CASE ANYONE WERE TO READ 1 Corinthians 4 and conclude that no standards whatsoever are to be maintained in the church—after all, maintenance of standards requires judging, doesn't it?—the next chapter, **1 Corinthians 5**, provides a case where Paul berates the church in Corinth for *not* exercising judgment and discipline. We must reflect a little on this case itself, and then on the way it is linked to the previous chapter.

Paul insists that, with respect to the man he describes in 5:1, two evils are in view. The first is sexual. A member of the church "has his father's wife." The peculiar language suggests he is sleeping with his stepmother. In any case the sin is so gross that it would be shocking even among the pagans. The second is the limp response of the church. Despite this wickedness among them, their penchant for arrogant strutting, which surfaces in many chapters of 1 and 2 Corinthians, never falters. They should have been consumed with grief; they should have excommunicated the man who did this (5:2).

We cannot reflect on all the elements of this judgment, but observe the following:

(1) The judgment Paul wants meted out is to be communal. The entire church, "assembled in the name of our Lord Jesus" (5:4), in the consciousness of his powerful presence, is to take action. Thus the failure to do so is a church-wide failure.

(2) One of the reasons for taking this action is because "a little yeast works through the whole batch of dough" (5:6); evil in the church that no one deals with soon affects the entire church.

(3) This has nothing to do with disciplining the outside world. Paul assumes that the world outside the church will allow sin to fester. What he has in mind is discipline within the church of God (5:9-10).

(4) Paul's understanding of what conduct should be subject to church discipline is not restricted to the sexual arena, or this particular form of sexual sin. He means to include major moral defection and gives an exemplary list: greed, idolatry, slander, drunkenness, swindling. Elsewhere, he adds to major moral defection two other arenas: major doctrinal deviation, and persistent drive for schism.

Now all of this he openly calls "judging" (5:12-13). Christians *are* to judge "those inside," while God judges "those outside." At the very least, chapters 4 and 5 must be kept in creative tension. More importantly, the Corinthians in chapter 4 were imposing judgments "beyond what is written" (4:6), i.e., deploying standards and criteria with no basis in God's revelation, and out of mere party interest. They were *not* imposing judgments in chapter 5 *despite* what Scripture, properly understood, says. *Both* are breaches of God's revelation.

༄

1 Samuel 25; 1 Corinthians 6; Ezekiel 4; Psalms 40—41

∿

DESPITE ITS GREAT INTEREST and deft characterizations, one must ask why the story found in **1 Samuel 25** is included. How does it advance the storyline of 1 and 2 Samuel?

Once some of the social conventions of the day are understood, the account itself is clear. Apparently at this point David is not actively being pursued by Saul (see 1 Sam. 24), but relations are still so tender that David and his men keep right out of Saul's way. Much of this culture was bound up with two values that many in the West rarely experience: (1) Every good deed must necessarily be repaid with another. The forms of courtesy extend to reciprocal gift-giving. Failure in this respect calls down shame on the person who defaults, and treats the other person with contempt. (2) The demands of hospitality mean it is unconscionable to turn another away. That would signal rudeness and greed. Mere courtesy demands that one offer one's best to guests. This is especially true when one is wealthy.

So when David's men arrive at Nabal's door, they are not asking for protection money. When Nabal sends them on their way, he is not an upright man who refuses to be bullied by a brigand, but an ungrateful wretch who will take and take from everyone, never give anything in return, thumb his nose at the courtesies and conventions of the culture, bring down shame on himself without caring what people think, and treat the man who has contributed to the wealth and well-being of his operation with insufferable contempt.

Abigail cuts the best figure in the narrative. With grace and tact, she assuages David's wrath and preserves the lives of her husband and the men he employs. David is a mixed figure. By the light of day, doubtless he had some warrant for the vengeance he was planning, but it could only presage more bloodshed and a style of leadership that would sully the throne he would one day occupy. All this Abigail sees—and winningly convinces him she is right.

So why is the account included? Superficially, of course, there are little hints that David is coming closer to the throne. Samuel, the prophet who anointed him, is dead (25:1). David now heads an armed band of six hundred. Abigail represents the rising number of Israelites who recognize that sooner or later David will be their king (25:28, 30). But above all, David is now heading in a different *moral* direction from Saul. As Saul's power has increased, so also has his passion for vengeance. David is heading in the same wretched direction, until Abigail checks him, as he himself recognizes (25:32-34). There are important lessons here for many powerful Christian leaders.

∿

1 Samuel 26; 1 Corinthians 7; Ezekiel 5; Psalms 42—43

∾

IN THE COURSE OF HIS treatment of "virgins" (**1 Cor. 7:25-38**—the word refers to the sexually inexperienced, whether male of female), Paul writes, "Because of the present crisis, I think that it is good for you to remain as you are" (7:26). Thus it is good for the celibate to remain celibate, for the married not to seek a divorce, and so forth. This does *not* mean, Paul adds, that if a virgin marries, she is sinning. But he does insist that "the time is short" (7:29). What does this mean?

(1) Some have argued that in common with everyone else in the early church, Paul believed that Jesus was going to return very soon, certainly within their lifetime. With so limited a horizon, Paul says that on the whole it is better for those who are celibate to remain unmarried. This reading of the passage means, of course, that Paul and the rest of the early church were just plain wrong: Jesus did *not* come back that quickly. But there are so many passages in the New Testament that envisage the possibility of long delay that we cannot go along with the notion that early Christians suffered under this particular delusion.

(2) Some have argued that "the present crisis" (7:26) refers to some specially troubling period of persecution. If the authorities are out to get Christians, especially their leaders, it might be an advantage to be celibate: you are more mobile, can hide more easily, and the authorities cannot exert pressure on you by leaning on your family. But this interpretation has two insuperable problems. (a) It may fit the celibates, but it doesn't fit all the other people to whom Paul makes application: e.g., those who mourn should live as if they did not mourn, those who are happy as if they were not, those who buy something as if it were not theirs to keep (7:29-30). (b) Above all, there is no good evidence that the Corinthians were being threatened with persecution. The entire tone of this letter suggests they were finding life a bit of a lark.

(3) The word rendered "crisis" simply means "necessity" or "compulsion." What Paul is referring to is neither the return of Christ nor persecution, but the present "necessity," the present "compulsion," of living with the End in view. Unlike pagans and secularists, we cannot make our chief joy turn on marriage, prosperity, or any other temporal thing. They all fall under the formula "as if not": live "*as if not* engrossed in them. For this world in its present form is passing away" (7:31, emphasis added). There are responsible ways for Christians to enjoy these things, or mourn, or be happy—but *never* as if these things are ultimate.

∾

1 Samuel 27; 1 Corinthians 8; Ezekiel 6; Psalm 44

APPARENTLY SOME CHRISTIANS in Corinth, secure in their knowledge that idols are nothing at all, and that all meat has been created by the one true God so that it is good to eat even if it had been offered to an idol, feel wonderful liberty to eat whatever they like. Others, converted perhaps from a life bound up with pagan superstition, detect the demonic in the idol, and think it unsafe to eat food that has been offered to them (**1 Cor. 8**). The thrust of Paul's argument is plain enough. Those with a robust conscience on these matters should be willing to forgo their rights so that they do not damage other brothers and sisters in Christ.

It may nevertheless crystallize the application if we underline several elements:

(1) The issue concerns something that is not *intrinsically* wrong. One could not imagine the apostle suggesting that some Christians think adultery is all right, while others have qualms about it, and the former should perhaps forgo their freedom so as not to offend the latter. In such a case, there is *never* any excuse for the action; the action is prohibited. So Paul's principles here apply only to actions that are *in themselves* morally indifferent.

(2) Paul assumes that it is wrong to go against conscience, for then conscience may be damaged (8:12). A conscience hardened in one area, over an indifferent matter, may become hard in another area—something more crucial. Ideally, of course, the conscience should become more perfectly aligned with what God says in Scripture, so that in indifferent matters it would leave the individual free. Conscience may be instructed and shaped by truth. But until conscience has been reformed by Scripture, it is best not to contravene it.

(3) The "weak" brother in this chapter (8:7-13) is one with a "weak" conscience; that is, one who thinks some action is wrong even though there is nothing intrinsically wrong in it. Thus the "weak" brother is more bound by rules than the "strong" brother. Both will adopt the rules that touch things truly wrong, while the weak brother adds rules for things that are not truly wrong but that are at that point wrong for him, since he thinks them wrong.

(4) Paul places primary onus of responsibility on the "strong" to restrict their own freedoms for the sake of others. In other words, it is never a sufficient question for the Christian to ask, "What am I allowed to do? What are my rights?" Christians serve a Lord who certainly did not stand on his rights when he went to the cross. Following the self-denial of Jesus, they will also ask, "What rights should I give up for the sake of others?"

1 Samuel 28; 1 Corinthians 9; Ezekiel 7; Psalm 45

∾

THERE ARE SEVERAL QUESTIONS about the witch of Endor (**1 Sam. 28**) that we cannot answer. Was the prophet Samuel actually called up by her mediumistic activity, or was this some sort of demonic deception? If Samuel was called up, was this an exception of what God normally allows or sanctions? And if it really is Samuel, why does he bother answering Saul at all, thereby satisfying Saul's lust for knowledge of the future, *by whatever means,* even means that were specifically condemned in Israel?

While it is difficult to provide confident answers to some of these questions, certain points stand out.

(1) What is evil in spiritism is not that it never works (some of it may be manipulative hocus-pocus; some of it may actually provide answers), but that it plays into the hands of the demonic. Above all, it turns people away from God, who alone controls both the present and the future. To find guidance for one's life by such means will not only lead one astray sooner or later, it is already a badge of rebellion—a terrible thumbing of the nose at God.

(2) Saul is playing the part of the hypocrite. On the one hand, he has banished mediums and spiritists from the land (28:3); on the other, he desperately wants one himself. Had Saul lived longer, there is no way this two-facedness would have long remained hidden from the people. The very foundations of order and justice in a society are unraveling when the powers that be indulge not only in the personal hypocrisies that afflict a fallen race, but in public breaches of the law they are sworn to uphold.

(3) When God does not answer by any of the means he has himself designated (28:6, 15), this does not constitute warrant for defiance of God, but for repentance, perseverance, and patience. There is something dismally pathetic about seeking God's counsel while happily taking action that God himself has prohibited.

(4) The heart of Saul's sin is what it has been for a long time. He wants a domesticated god, a god like the genie in Aladdin's lamp, one pledged to do wonderful things for him as long as he holds the lamp. He somehow feels that David now holds the lamp and wishes he could get the power back, but does not perceive that the real God is to be worshiped, reverenced, obeyed, feared, and loved—unconditionally. Here is a man who thinks of himself as at the center of the universe; whatever gods exist must serve him. If the covenant God of Israel does not help him as he wishes, then Saul is prepared to find other gods. This is the black heart of all idolatry.

∾

1 Samuel 29—30; 1 Corinthians 10; Ezekiel 8; Psalms 46—47

∾

FIRST CORINTHIANS 10 INCLUDES several passages worthy of prolonged meditation. But today we reflect on a passage which, superficially speaking, is one of the easiest of them.

Paul tells the Corinthians that the things that happened to "our forefathers" (10:1) that are recorded in Scripture "occurred as examples to keep us from setting our hearts on evil things as they did" (10:6). After giving some examples, the apostle again says, "These things happened to them as examples and were written down as warnings for us, on whom the fulfillment of the ages has come" (10:11).

(1) It is important to observe the diversity of purposes the Scriptures have. Elsewhere we learn, for instance, that the Old Testament Scriptures, or parts of them, were given to make sin appear as the awful thing it is, nothing less than trangression; to prepare the way for Christ, not only by prophetic words but also by models, patterns, and "types" that anticipated what Christ would be like; to announce the time when God would take definitive action on behalf of his people; to warn against sin and judgment; and much more. But here, the Bible provides us with examples to keep us from pursuing evil things. That means that although the Old Testament narratives doubtless offer *more* than "mere" moral lessons, they do not offer *less*. While we seek out the complex layers of inner-canonical connection, we must not overlook the moral instruction that lies on the very surface of the text.

(2) The gross sins that Paul lists by way of example—idolatry, sexual immorality, "testing" the Lord (i.e., by doubting his goodness or ability, as in Ex. 17:2), and grumbling (10:7-10)—are not unknown among contemporary believers.

(3) According to Paul, God's *intention* was that the writing down of these materials in Scripture was so that *we* should benefit from it—the "we" referring to those "on whom the fulfillment of the ages has come" (10:11). Doubtless this should not be taken as an exhaustive statement of God's intention, but it is certainly meant to be a foundational one. Thus from God's perspective, the Old Testament books were not meant simply for those who read them when they were first written, but for "us" who live at this formidable moment in world history when the first installment of the promises of the ages is being experienced.

(4) Implicitly, it is all the more shocking if we who have received so much instruction and warning from ages past ignore the wealth of privilege that is ours. In our blindness we sometimes marvel at how some Old Testament figures or groups could so quickly abandon the godly heritage and covenant they received. How much worse if we do so!

∾

1 Samuel 31; 1 Corinthians 11; Ezekiel 9; Psalm 48

∾

THREE OBSERVATIONS ABOUT the Lord's Supper, from the many that could be drawn from Paul's treatment of it (**1 Cor. 11:17-34**):

First, it is a temporary ordinance. It is to be observed only "until he comes" (11:26). In part this is because of its "memorial" function ("do this in remembrance of me," 11:24). In the new heaven and the new earth, transformed believers will not need a rite like this one to "remember" Jesus, for he will perpetually be the center of their focus and adoration. Knowing this, each time we participate in the Lord's Supper we are not only helped to look backward to Jesus' broken body, but forward to the consummation.

Second, properly observed, the Lord's Supper is to have a *kerygmatic function*. The word *kerygmatic* comes from the verb *kerysso,* "to proclaim": Paul says that by this Supper we *proclaim* the Lord's death until he comes (11:26)—though he uses a different verb here. Normally the verb used is found in an evangelistic context: we *proclaim* or *announce* the Gospel to people still unconverted. If that is what Paul means, then one of the functions of the Lord's Supper—its kerygmatic function—is evangelism. Certainly I have been in churches where that is the case. Unbelievers are part of the service. They are warned not to partake, but are encouraged to observe and reflect on what they see and hear. Something of the significance of the rite is explained, perhaps its function as witness to Jesus the bread of life who gives his life for the life of the world (John 6:51). The ordinance and the word together proclaim the Lord's death.

Third, the approach of the Lord's Supper provides an opportunity for each Christian to examine himself or herself *before* eating the bread and drinking the cup (11:27-28). Interpreters disagree as to what the failure to recognize the body of the Lord means (11:29). To evaluate the options is not possible in this context. I may simply record my conclusion: Paul warns that "anyone who eats and drinks without recognizing the body of the Lord," which was offered up on the cross and to which witness is borne in this rite, "eats and drinks judgment on himself." How could it be otherwise? To say, by participating, "We remember," and "We proclaim," while cherishing sin, is to approach this table in an unworthy manner; it is to sin "against the body and blood of the Lord" (11:27). But regardless of whether this particular interpretation is correct, the warning itself must be taken with utmost seriousness. It is not a question of being good enough, for no one is. The only "worthy manner" by which to approach this Supper is contrition and faith.

∾

2 Samuel 1; 1 Corinthians 12; Ezekiel 10; Psalm 49

∾

WHEN DAVID HEARS OF the deaths of Saul and Jonathan (**2 Sam. 1**), his grief is not merely formal. He could not help but know that the way to the throne was now open to him. Nevertheless, his sorrow is so genuine that he composes a lengthy lament (1:19-27), sets it to music, and teaches it to the men of his tribe (1:18) so that it will be sung for a long time as one of the folk ballads of the land.

Many elements of this lament deserve long reflection. Today I shall reflect on just one verse: "Tell it not in Gath, proclaim it not in the streets of Ashkelon, lest the daughters of the Philistines be glad, lest the daughters of the uncircumcised rejoice" (1:20). Formally, the text is plain enough. Gath and Ashkelon were the two leading Philistine cities. David is saying, in effect, not to let the Philistines know of the deaths of Saul and Jonathan, lest they be glad and rejoice.

Of course, the Philistines could not help but find out, and David, of all people, knew that. But his purpose in penning these words is not literally to keep the Philistines in the dark a little while longer. How could that be? They had already hoisted the body of Saul onto the wall of Beth Shan (1 Sam. 31:10) and sent messengers with the news throughout Philistia (31:9). But if these lines from David's pen do not function as literal advice, what is their function?

In part, it is simply a lament. It is a powerful way of saying that the opponents of the Israelites would be delighted with the news, and therefore their pleasure is a measure of the tragedy. But I suspect there is another overtone. When one of our leaders falls, conduct yourself in such a way as not to give strength to the opposition.

That is a lesson that must be learned again and again by the church. When a minister of the Gospel is caught embezzling funds or having an affair, then certainly the biblical principle for discipline must be brought to bear immediately. If the law has been broken, the civil authorities must be contacted. If families have been damaged, there may be a great deal of pastoral work to be done. But understand well that many unbelievers will be gleefully rubbing their hands and saying, "See? What can you expect? All this religious stuff is so hypocritical and phony." Thus Christ is despised and the credibility of Christian witnesses diminished. Christians must restrain their tongues, watch what they say, and be especially careful about saying anything unnecessary to unbelievers. This is a time for mourning, not gossip. "Tell it not in Gath. . . ."

∾

2 Samuel 2; 1 Corinthians 13; Ezekiel 11; Psalm 50

∾

ALTHOUGH 1 CORINTHIANS 13 FORMS part of a sustained argument that runs through chapters 12—14, the passage constitutes such a lovely unit with so many wonderfully evocative lines that it has called forth countless extended treatments. Today I shall reflect a little on the first three verses.

This text does *not* say that love is everything and that the other things mentioned—speaking in tongues, the gift of prophecy, an ability to fathom mysteries and all knowledge, a faith that can move mountains, self-denying surrender of all possessions for the sake of the poor, and suffering a martyr's death—are nothing. Rather, it insists that those things are utterly insignificant unless they are accompanied by love. Love does not displace them; its absence renders them pointless and ultimately valueless.

This paragraph is calculated to abase the arrogant. History offers sad examples of people who have become proud of their gift of tongues, of their prophetic gift, even of their philanthropy and self-sacrifice. But it is a contradiction in terms to be proud of one's love, in any Christian sense of love. Perhaps that is one of the reasons why these other virtues are destroyed if unaccompanied by love.

One of the most striking features of this statement about love is how it rules out of bounds one of the definitions of love that still persists in some Christian circles. They say that Christian love does not belong to the emotional realm, but is nothing other than an unswerving resolve to seek the other's good. That is why, they say, love can be commanded: one may thoroughly dislike the other person, but if one conscientiously resolves upon his or her good, and acts accordingly, it is still love. Quite frankly, that sort of casuistry is reductionistic rubbish. What has just been dubbed "love" is nothing other than resolute altruism. But in these verses Paul firmly distinguishes between altruism and love: "If I give all I possess to the poor and surrender my body to the flames" (13:3): here are both altruism and self-sacrifice, but Paul can imagine both without love. So love must be something other than, or more than, mere altruism and self-sacrifice.

It may be difficult to provide a perfect definition for Christian love. But it is not difficult to find its supreme example. Christ's love for us is not grounded in our loveliness, but in his own character. His love is not merely sentimental, yet it is charged with incalculable affection and warmth. It is resolute in its self-sacrifice, but never merely mechanical self-discipline. If we wish to come to terms with the apostolic depiction of Christian love as "the most excellent way" (12:31b; see also the meditation for October 11) that all believers must follow, we need only imitate Jesus Christ.

∾

2 Samuel 3; 1 Corinthians 14; Ezekiel 12; Psalm 51

EVEN AFTER THE DEATH OF King Saul, David did not immediately become king of Israel. At first David is anointed king over Judah (2 Sam. 2:1-7), and *only* Judah: even Benjamin, which remained with Judah following the division between "Israel" and "Judah" after the death of Solomon, at this point was allied with the other tribes (2:9).

Abner, the commander of what was left of Saul's army, installed Ish-Bosheth, Saul's surviving son, as king of Israel (2:8-9). Skirmishes multiplied between David's troops and those of Ish-Bosheth. Many battles in those days brought the opposing troops together in a fierce clash, followed by a running fight: one side ran away, and the other chased it. In one such clash, one of the three sons of Zeruiah—Asahel, from David's forces—is killed by Abner (2:17-23). The killing was "clean," i.e., within the rules of warfare and not a murder. Nevertheless, this death precipitates some of the most important actions in **2 Samuel 3**.

Bringing the different parts of the country together into united allegiance under David was a messy and sometimes ignoble business—a reminder that God sometimes uses the folly and evil of people to bring about his good purposes. Abner sleeps with one of Saul's former concubines (3:6-7). This was not only a breach of moral law, but in the symbolism of the time Abner was claiming the right of royalty for himself. It was a major insult and reproach to Ish-Bosheth. Thus Abner's reasons for taking the eleven tribes over to David seem to have less to do with integrity and a desire to recognize God's calling than out of frustration with Ish-Bosheth and some lust for power himself. Then Abner is murdered by Joab and his men (3:22-27), Joab being one of Asahel's brothers. But this really is murder, and a defiance of David's safe-conduct.

How David handles this crisis reflects both his great strengths and one of his greatest weaknesses—strengths and weaknesses that will show up again. Politically, David is very astute. He distances himself utterly from Joab's action, and insists that Joab and other leaders become part of the official mourning party of the slain Abner. "All the people took note and were pleased; indeed, everything the king did pleased them" (3:36). On the other hand, David does not bring Joab to account, fobbing off his responsibility by protesting that "these sons of Zeruiah are too strong for me" (3:39). In other words, he shirked his responsibility—as he would do later with his son Amnon (2 Sam. 13), the consequences of which triggered Absalom's revolt and almost cost David his throne. It is *never* God's way to abdicate biblically mandated responsibility.

2 Samuel 4—5; 1 Corinthians 15; Ezekiel 13; Psalms 52—54

CLEARLY THE WRITER OF 2 Samuel (whose identity we do not know) thinks it important to record the various steps by which David came to rule over all Israel. Canonically, this is important because it is the beginning of the Davidic dynasty that leads directly to "great David's greater Son" (see the May 17 meditation). Within this framework, I wish to reflect on several features in these two chapters (**2 Sam. 4—5**).

(1) It is quite stunning to observe how David was prepared to wait for the throne, without taking the kind of action that would have secured it for him more quickly. Not least impressive is his stance toward Ish-Bosheth. Ish-Bosheth's murderers, Baanah and Recab, who think they will curry favor with the rising star by their vicious assassination (in line with the common standards of the day), learn that David's commitment to justice ensures their execution. The only slightly sour overtone is the double standard: these murderers pay a just penalty for their crime (2 Sam. 4), while in the preceding chapter the murderer Joab, because of his power, is publicly shamed but does not face the capital sentence.

(2) This book carefully chronicles how "all the tribes of Israel" (5:1) approach David at Hebron and invite him to become their king. In God's providence the evil assassination by Baanah and Recab brings about the fulfillment of God's promise to David.

(3) David's capture of Jerusalem (5:6-12) has to be recorded, for this not only becomes David's capital city but in due course becomes the resting place for the tabernacle. During the reign of his son Solomon it will become the site for the temple. Enormously important theological issues revolve around Jerusalem and the temple. These are taken up in turn by the prophets (before and after the Exile), by Jesus himself, and by the New Testament writers. Reflect, for instance, on John 2:13-22; Galatians 4:21-31; Hebrews 9; 12:22-23; Revelation 21—22.

(4) Above all, when the Israelites invite David to become their king, they say, "And the LORD said to you, 'You will shepherd my people Israel, and you will become their ruler'" (5:2). The "shepherd" theme is more comprehensive than the "ruler" theme, and is developed in various ways. At the outset of the Exile, God excoriates the false "shepherds" who are more interested in fleecing the sheep than in securing and nurturing the flock (Ezek. 34)—a phenomenon not unknown today. So God repeatedly promises that he himself will be the shepherd of his people; indeed, he will send forth this servant "David" (three-and-a-half centuries after David's death!) to be their shepherd (Ezek. 34:23-24; see the meditation for March 20). In the fullness of time, the rightful heir of David's line declares, "I am the good shepherd" (John 10:11).

2 Samuel 6; 1 Corinthians 16; Ezekiel 14; Psalm 55

∾

DAVID WOULD DOUBTLESS make many of us uncomfortable if he lived today. He was such an intense man—exuberant in his pleasures, crushed in his discouragement, powerful in his leadership, unrestrained in his worship.

(1) One occasion that displays much of the man displays no less of God, viz. bringing the ark of the covenant, and presumably the entire tabernacle, up to Jerusalem (**2 Sam. 6**). David does not send down a few clerics—the designated Levites—and no more. He gathers thirty thousand crack troops and representatives from the whole house of Israel, to say nothing of musicians and choirs.

(2) When Uzzah stretches forth his hand to stabilize the ark because the oxen pulling the cart have stumbled, the "LORD's anger burned against Uzzah because of his irreverent act; therefore God struck him down and he died there beside the ark of God" (6:7). That certainly put a damper on the festivities. David is both angry with God (6:8) and afraid of him (6:9). For the time being he resolves not to bring the ark of the Lord up to Jerusalem. Certainly there is something in most of us that silently thinks David is right.

Yet all along God has been profoundly concerned to eradicate any hint that he is nothing more than a talisman, a controllable god, some godlet akin to other neighborhood godlets. One of his strongest prohibitions was not to touch the ark, or look inside it. Indeed, on the latter point seventy men of Beth Shemesh had paid with their lives a bare generation earlier (1 Sam. 6:19-20; see the meditation for August 15), when they had ignored the edict. Our text calls Uzzah's act "irreverent" (2 Sam. 6:7). What made it "irreverent" or "profane" was not that Uzzah was malicious, but that there was no reverent fear before his eyes, no careful distinction between all that God says is holy and what is merely common. The horror of profanity is identical: people say they do not mean anything by it when they take the Lord's name in vain. That is precisely the point: they do not mean anything by it. God will not be treated that way.

(3) The ark remains with Obed-Edom for three months, and he experiences so much blessing that David becomes interested again (6:11-12). Blessing and reverence go hand in hand, and David—and we—had better realize it.

(4) Michal turns out to be her father's daughter: she is more interested in pomp, form, royal robes, and personal dignity than in exuberant worship (6:16). She despises David precisely because he is so God-centered he cares very little about his persona. People constantly fretting about what others think of them cannot be absorbed by the sheer God-awareness and God-centeredness that characterize all true worship.

∾

2 Samuel 7; 2 Corinthians 1; Ezekiel 15; Psalms 56—57

AFTER HIS PALACE IS BUILT, David recognizes that he is living in splendor in comparison with the small and unostentatious tabernacle. He desires to build a temple, a "house" in which to place the ark of the covenant (**2 Sam. 7**).

Through Nathan the prophet, however, God puts the shoe on the other foot. David wants to build a "house" for God, but God declares that he himself will build a "house" for David. The word *house* can refer to a building, but it can extend to household and even to a dynasty (e.g., the house of Windsor). David hopes to build a "house" for God in the first sense; God tells David he is building a "house" for him in the third sense. Although David's son Solomon will build a "house" for God, in the last analysis God himself is the ultimate Giver, and the "house" he proposes to build will prove more enduring.

In this context, then, God makes some remarkable promises to David. "The LORD declares to you that the LORD himself will establish a house for you" (7:11), God says. To continue David's line after his death, God adds, "I will raise up your offspring to succeed you, who will come from your own body, and I will establish his kingdom. He is the one who will build a house for my Name, and I will establish the throne of his kingdom forever" (7:12-13). The referent goes no farther than Solomon. In the storyline of 1 and 2 Samuel, Saul serves as the prime example of a king who reigned and whose throne was not secured, whose "house" was not built. But it will not be so with David. His offspring will reign. When Saul sinned, in due course God rejected him. But when David's son does wrong, God says, "I will punish him with the rod of men, with floggings inflicted by men. [So this "son" is certainly not Jesus.] But my love will never be taken away from him, as I took it away from Saul" (7:14-15). So far, then, Solomon occupies the horizon.

But then once again God takes the long view: "Your house and your kingdom will endure forever before me; your throne will be established forever" (7:16). This either means that there will always be someone on the throne in the line of David, or something more powerful. In the course of time, the prophecies about the coming "David" or "son of David" become freighted with much greater promise. Isaiah foresees someone who "will reign on David's throne and over his kingdom," but who is also called "Mighty God" and "Everlasting Father" (Isa. 9:6-7). Here is an heir to David who maintains the Davidic dynasty not by passing it on, but by his own eternal reign.

2 Samuel 8—9; 2 Corinthians 2; Ezekiel 16; Psalms 58—59

∾

IT IS BEYOND THESE BRIEF REFLECTIONS to provide a history of the difficult visits and painful letters that generated deep emotion in the apostle's relations with the Corinthians. Relations between Corinth and Paul are apparently improving in the opening chapters of 2 Corinthians, but remain a trifle raw.

In this context Paul devotes quite a bit of attention to explaining the nature of his ministry, whether its grand design or discrete decisions he has made. For example, in 2 Corinthians 1, it is fairly obvious that the Corinthians had charged Paul with being fickle. He had said he would come, and then he had changed plans and not arrived. Paul acknowledges that he had indeed changed plans, but insists this does *not* indicate fickleness (1:15-17). In his conduct he tries to imitate God's steadfast faithfulness (1:18-22). And then he gives the real reason why he did not show up: he was trying to spare the Corinthians, for he knew that if he had shown up at that point he would have had to take action that would have caused even more distress (1:23—2:2).

In **2 Corinthians 2**, Paul is still unpacking various elements of his ministry. Here we note two.

First, Paul understands his ministry to be akin to a device that distributes the fragrance of the knowledge of God (2:14). Otherwise put, before God Paul himself is an aroma, "the aroma of Christ among both those who are being saved and those who are perishing" (2:15). "To the one we are the smell of death; to the other, the fragrance of life" (2:16). In other words, Paul insists that he does not himself change, depending on his audience. He is the same aroma; he proclaims the same Gospel, the same discipleship, the same Christ, the same way to live. Whether he is perceived to be a sweet fragrance or a foul stench does not depend on some change in him, but on the people who must deal with him. Implicitly, the Corinthians must recognize that some animus against the apostle is the animus of the unregenerate heart. "And who is equal to such a task?" (2:16).

Second, many Corinthians (as becomes clear later in this letter) thought that teachers should command substantial salaries, and if they didn't, they weren't worth much. In that kind of atmosphere, it would be easy to despise even a gifted apostolic teacher who refused your money. But because he was teaching a gospel of grace, Paul evangelized for free. (He accepted support money from elsewhere.) On the long haul, he did not want to gain a reputation for peddling the word of God for profit; rather, he wanted to be known as a man sent from God (2:17).

∾

2 Samuel 10; 2 Corinthians 3; Ezekiel 17; Psalms 60—61

IN SOME WAYS, Paul finds himself in an embarrassing position. If he fails to answer some of the concerns that the Corinthians entertained about him and his ministry, he could lose them—not lose them personally (that wouldn't have bothered Paul), but lose their loyalty to him *and therefore to the message that he preached.* On the other hand, if he goes on at length about himself, at least some of his detractors will say that he is stuck on himself, or that he is insecure, or that a real apostle would not have to defend himself, or something else of the same sort.

Precisely what their charge was, we cannot be sure. That Paul is sensitive to the danger is pretty obvious from several places in the Corinthian correspondence, not least **2 Corinthians 3:1-3.** At the end of chapter 2, Paul had insisted that "we [either an editorial 'we' or a self-conscious reference to the apostles] speak before God with sincerity, like men sent from God" (2:17)—not at all like peddlers working for profit. Now he rhetorically asks, "Are we beginning to commend ourselves again?" (3:1). The "again" is what betrays the fact that Paul has had to face this problem before with the Corinthians. More specifically, he asks, "Or do we need, like some people, letters of recommendation to you or from you?" (3:1). It sounds as if "some people" have attempted to establish their credentials by bringing letters of introduction with them. They or the Corinthians then become dismissive of Paul because he neither fits into the cultural pattern of proving his credentials by asking for a high fee (chap. 2), nor does he bring along papers—from Jerusalem or some other authoritative center—to establish his bona fides.

But Paul does not reply by defending his apostolic status in terms of the resurrected Christ's direct revelation to him. (Elsewhere, however, that is exactly what he does, and even in this chapter he insists that his competence is from God himself, 3:5). Here he wisely adopts a stance that simultaneously points to the peculiar nature of his own ministry, and gently encourages the Corinthians to acknowledge that they are in no place to think differently. What he tells them, in effect, is that their existence as Christians constitutes, for them, adequate credentialing of Paul. Paul preached the Gospel to them. They *are* his "letter of recommendation"—the result of his ministry (3:1, 3). And since genuine conversion is the work of the Spirit of God, they, as Paul's letter of recommendation, should see themselves as having been "written" not with ink but "with the Spirit of the living God," and not on a papyrus sheet or a stone tablet, but on the human heart (3:3).

2 Samuel 11; 2 Corinthians 4; Ezekiel 18; Psalms 62—63

∾

HERE IS DAVID AT HIS WORST (**2 Sam. 11**). In the flow of the narrative through 1 and 2 Samuel, it is almost as if adversity brought out the best in David, while his chain of recent unbroken military and political successes finds him restless, foolish, and not careful.

The sins are multiple. Besides the obvious transgressions of lust, adultery, and murder, there are deep sins scarcely less grievous. His attempt to cover his guilt by bringing Uriah home fails because Uriah proves to be that most exceptional of men: an idealist—an idealist who sees even his military responsibilities in terms of his covenantal faith (11:11). And all this from a converted Hittite! Worse, David's extraordinary manipulation of the military and political levers of power shows that this king has become intoxicated by power. He thinks he can arrange anything; he thinks he has the right to use the state to advance and then cover up his own sin. The name of that game is corruption.

There are other remarkable elements in the narrative.

First, almost nothing is said of Bathsheba, except that she was beautiful, was seduced, and eventually married David. Of course, at one level she was no less guilty than he. But of this the text does not say a word. Elsewhere the Bible can record the exploits of good women (Ruth) and evil women (Jezebel); indeed, toward the end of David's life Bathsheba herself plays a significant role. Perhaps in part the text does not cast blame on her here because she has been manipulated by a figure far more powerful. More likely the silence signals not relative degrees of blame but primary focus: the account is of David, and ultimately of David's line.

Second, it is astonishing that David thought he could get away with this. Even politically, too many people had to know what he had done; the story could not be kept quiet. And how could David imagine, even for a moment, that God himself would not know? Was he at this point badly alienated from God? At the very least, this chapter provides a dramatic witness to the blinding effects of sin.

Third, the chapter ends—somberly and powerfully—with the simple sentence, "But the thing David had done displeased the LORD" (11:27). Doubtless David was quietly congratulating himself for his clever cover-up. He had sinned and gotten away with it. Some of his more servile lackeys may even have congratulated their master. But God knew, and was not pleased. Believers who are walking with their Creator and Redeemer never forget that God sees and knows, and that what pleases him is the only thing that really matters; what displeases him will sooner or later catch up with us.

∾

2 Samuel 12; 2 Corinthians 5; Ezekiel 19; Psalms 64—65

IN NATHAN'S DRAMATIC CONFRONTATION with King David (**2 Sam. 12**), the prophet's courage was mingled with a formidable sagacity. How else could a prophet grab the attention of an autocratic king and denounce his sin to his face, apart from this oblique approach?

Certain features of this chapter must be reflected on.

First, the fundamental difference between David and Saul is now obvious. Both men abused power in high office. What makes them different is the way they respond to a rebuke. When Samuel accused Saul of sin, the latter dissembled; when Jonathan questioned Saul's policy, a spear was thrown at him. By contrast, although Nathan approaches his subject obliquely, the sin is soon out in the open: "You are the man!" (12:7). Yet David's response is radically different: "I have sinned against the LORD" (12:13).

That, surely, is one of the ultimate tests of the direction of a person's life. We are a race of sinners. Even good people, people of strong faith, even someone like David—who is "a man after God's own heart" (cf. 1 Samuel 13:14)—may slip and sin. There is never an excuse for it, but when it happens it should never surprise us. But those who are serious about the knowledge of God will in due course return with genuine contrition. Spurious converts and apostates will string out a plethora of lame excuses, but will not admit personal guilt except in the most superficial ways.

Second, only God can forgive sin. When he does so, sin's proper punishment, death itself, is not applied (12:13).

Third, even when sin's ultimate sanction is not applied, there may be other consequences that cannot be avoided in this fallen and broken world. David now faces three of them: (1) that the child Bathsheba is carrying will die; (2) that throughout his lifetime there will be skirmishing and warfare as he establishes his kingdom; (3) that at some point in his life he will see what it is like to be betrayed: someone from his own household will temporarily seize the throne, exemplified by sleeping with the royal harem (12:12-13). Each is piquant. The first is bound up with the adultery itself; the second is perhaps a hint that the reason David was tempted in the first place was because he had not gone forth to war along with Joab, but had stayed home (11:1), clearly longing for peace; and the third treats David to the betrayal that he himself has practiced.

Fourth, David's response to the most pressing of the judgments is altogether salutary. God is not the equivalent of impersonal Fate. He is a person, and a person may be petitioned and pursued. Despite his massive failure, David is still a man who knows God better than his numerous critics.

2 Samuel 13; 2 Corinthians 6; Ezekiel 20; Psalms 66—67

THE THREAT TO DAVID'S REIGN predicted by the prophet Nathan begins with a sordid side-tale that nevertheless betrays exactly what is wrong with David's rule (**2 Sam. 13**).

The multiplicity of royal wives meant that there were many half brothers and half sisters. This sets up the wretched rape of Tamar. The profiles of the people involved, with the exception of Tamar, betray what today we would label a dysfunctional family. Of course, only two of the brothers, Amnon and Absalom, are seen close up. But David's handling of them—or better, his utter failure to handle them—is of a piece with the way he had earlier failed to handle Joab (see meditation on September 9).

Amnon is lustful, immature, irresponsible, deceptive, and brutal. One of the most revealing statements about him is what is said immediately after he has raped Tamar: "Then Amnon hated her with intense hatred. In fact, he hated her more than he had loved her" (13:15). We are dealing with a spoiled child who has become an evil man.

If at this point David had exercised the justice he should have displayed in his role as head of state, the history of the next few years would have been entirely different. He shares the sin of Eli (see 1 Samuel 3 and the August 13 meditation): he sees his sons doing evil, and does nothing to restrain them. If he had required Amnon to face the full force of the law, not only would he have fired a shot across the bows of any other potentially wayward son, he would have proved he cared for what had happened to his daughter, and he would have drawn the horrible bitterness and vengefulness that Tamar's full brother Absalom now brings to a boil.

At this point Absalom is a tragic figure. He rightly holds Amnon accountable. Unable to find redress in the legal system that his own father has short-circuited, he opts for vengeance, then has to flee his father's wrath. Doubtless he should not have slain Amnon, but up to this point he is presented as a more attractive and principled character than the man he assassinates. Yet he knows that even David cannot ignore this particular murder, so he flees, leaving his father to look foolish and indecisive.

Relationships between fathers and sons are rarely both rich and straightforward. But the pattern of David's life, juxtaposed with Eli's but a few short chapters earlier, illustrates the kinds of disasters that befall families where the father, however loving, indulgent, godly, and heroic he may be, never holds his children to account, never disciplining them when they go astray. David's failure with Amnon and Absalom was not a first: it was the continuation of a moral and familial failure begun when the boys were in diapers.

2 Samuel 14; 2 Corinthians 7; Ezekiel 21; Psalm 68

∾

WHAT A TWISTED THING SIN IS. Its motives and machinations are convoluted and perverse.

At one level the account of **2 Samuel 14** is pretty straightforward. At another, it is full of thought-provoking ironies.

David adopts the worst of all possible courses. At first he cannot simply forgive Absalom, for that would in effect be admitting that he, David himself, should have taken decisive action against Amnon. On the other hand, David cannot bring himself to ban Absalom decisively, so he secretly mourns him. After Joab's ruse with the "wise woman" (14:2), he resolves to bring Absalom back. Even here, however, he is indecisive. If he is going to allow Absalom back in the country and the capital, why does he exclude him from seeing David—and thus intrinsically from family gatherings and the like? By the end of the chapter there is a reconciliation. But at what cost? The issues have not been resolved, merely swept under the table. On the other hand, if David is determined to forgive his son, why does he leave him in limbo for a few years? How much does this treatment by his own father foment the rebellion described in the next chapter?

There is no small irony in the fact that the man who convinces David, via this "wise woman," to bring Absalom back, is the very man whom David should have disciplined years before (see September 9 meditation). If David had disciplined Joab, where would he have been at this point? Probably not manipulating the king's counselors and petitioners.

On the face of it, Absalom is willing to go to some extraordinary lengths to get an audience with Joab and eventually be restored to the good graces of the king. Burning down a man's standing grain is a pretty big step (14:29-32). Yet despite all of his sincere passion to be readmitted to the king's court and presence, it will not be long before Absalom attempts to usurp the throne (chap. 15). That is the supreme irony. After so much effort, Absalom is finally admitted to David's presence: "he came in and bowed down with his face to the ground before the king. And the king kissed Absalom" (14:33). He had gained what he wanted. So what kind of power-hungry resentment is it that mounts the vicious insurrection of the next chapter?

People who have been following the story right along will not only perceive all the proximate causes of the rebellion, the understandable connections among all the personal failures that brought about the terrible conclusion. They will also recall that God himself had predicted, as a matter of judicial punishment on David over the matter of Bathsheba and Uriah, that he would bring calamity on him from someone in his household.

∾

2 Samuel 15; 2 Corinthians 8; Ezekiel 22; Psalm 69

THE LONGEST SUSTAINED ENCOURAGEMENT in the New Testament to give money is found in 2 Corinthians 8—9. Today I shall reflect on some of the emphases in **2 Corinthians 8.**

(1) Paul encourages the Corinthians to give by referring to the generosity of the Macedonians, who lived in the province to the north and were often viewed by those in Achaia, including the Corinthians, as a slightly inferior breed. Relaying evidence of the grace of God in the lives of some brothers and sisters in Christ can become an incentive to others to conform more closely to Christ.

(2) Paul stresses that the Macedonians were not only generous in the context of their own "severe trial" (8:1-3), but that their financial giving was a function of the fact that "they gave themselves first to the Lord and then to us in keeping with God's will" (8:5). The apostle does not think nearly so much of the kind of gift that is a substitute for giving oneself in principle to the Lord Jesus, and, derivatively, to his servant-leaders.

(3) There is considerable stress on perseverance and consistency in this matter of giving. Apparently the Corinthians had pledged the year before to give a certain amount. Now Paul sends Titus to encourage them to bring to completion what they began so well. So today: planned, regular, generous giving is better than the big binge that is wrung out of you by one emotional appeal, in part because the former is a better index of a heart consistently devoted to Christ and his work.

(4) Paul judges that Christian generosity is one of the things in which Christians as a whole should excel—along with such virtues as pure speech, knowledge, complete earnestness, and love for godly leaders (8:7).

(5) Paul does not want Christian generosity to be the result of a new legal demand: "I am not commanding you," he writes (8:8). The highest possible incentive to be generous, in a self-denying way, is found in the Lord Jesus Christ himself, who "though he was rich, yet for your sakes he became poor, so that you through his poverty might become rich" (8:9). For Paul, it is unthinkable that anyone who really delights in knowing this Christ could be stingy.

(6) Paul wants the Corinthians to know that although this money is going to help other believers (8:13-14—presumably the poor believers in Judea), this is not to make them rich as Croesus, but to relieve their poverty.

(7) Paul takes extraordinary pains, even by his choice of the emissaries he sends to transport the money, not only to do what is right in financial matters, but to be seen to be doing what is right (8:16-24).

2 Samuel 16; 2 Corinthians 9; Ezekiel 23; Psalms 70—71

∿

SECOND CORINTHIANS 9 IS THE second of two consecutive chapters that Paul devotes to the subject of giving.

(1) He resumes with a lovely delicacy (9:1-5). On the one hand, he assures the Corinthians that they do not really need reminders; on the other, he gently reminds them, so that neither he nor they will be embarrassed. After all, just as he used the Macedonians' example of giving even in the midst of severe trial as an example to the Corinthians (8:1-3), so he has been using the Corinthians' generosity and enthusiasm as an example to the Macedonians! He does not want them to be caught short.

(2) A principle that every farmer knows has a bearing on this matter of giving: "Whoever sows sparingly will also reap sparingly, and whoever sows generously will also reap generously" (9:6). Some argue that this promises a tit-for-tat reciprocity between financial giving and material prosperity. You give three hundred dollars to my ministry, and God will give you at least five hundred (or a thousand, or whatever). Of course, the preachers who say this sort of thing either do not believe it, or do not believe it applies to them, for otherwise they would be rapidly giving away all of their money. But the focus in Paul's presentation turns on two other points:

(a) The amount we give is measured less in absolute terms of currency than in the cheerfulness and heart-generosity with which we give (9:7).

(b) The return is more comprehensive than mere material prosperity, and far more beneficial: God is able to make us abound in every good work (9:8), and he will supply and increase our store of seed (continuing the agricultural metaphor) and will enlarge "the harvest of [our] righteousness" (9:10). God will make us "rich in every way" so that we can be all the more "generous on every occasion" (9:11). One should reflect on the fact that the "you" to whom such promises are given are the people of God collectively. It does not *necessarily* follow that each individual in the church is thereby promised to become "rich in every way" and not, say, die early of cancer.

(3) Paul's focus, finally, is not on the givers at all. Paul sees in the gifts not only a service that supplies the needs of God's people but one that overflows "in many expressions of thanks to God" (9:12), as believers praise him for the obedience of the Corinthians and intercede for them because they recognize in them the "surpassing grace" of God (9:13-14). For in the final analysis, we are all debtors to God's "indescribable gift" (9:15).

∿

2 Samuel 17; 2 Corinthians 10; Ezekiel 24; Psalm 72

∿

THERE IS A GREAT DEAL OF BOASTING in Western evangelicalism. Some of it is so flagrant that it is repulsive to all serious-minded people. Much of it, however, is subtle and potentially subversive. Probably most of us are guilty of it sometimes.

On first reading, it sounds as if Paul in **2 Corinthians 10** is also caught up in *boasting,* a word that recurs in the final four chapters of this book. In fact, the issues raised by this chapter are extraordinarily complex. I can here mention only a few of them.

(1) The tone of 2 Corinthians 10—13 sets this section off from the rest of the book. It may be that more information about the situation in Corinth has reached Paul. Whatever the case, critics in Corinth are demeaning the apostle on several grounds. They say he is weak and timid in person, while putting on airs of power and authority when he is absent and wielding his pen (10:1, 10). In an age when "persona" and rhetoric meant a great deal, they say, "His letters are weighty and forceful, but in person he is unimpressive and his speaking amounts to nothing" (10:10). They spend time patting each other on the back in a system of mutual approbation and letters of reference (10:12). The next chapters reflect even more elements of this barrage of criticism that Paul must endure.

(2) At the heart of it is a stance toward boasting that is antithetical to all that Paul holds dear. A certain style of self-promotion, of confidence in one's knowledge and rhetoric, of belonging to the "in" group, conspires to construct a clique of egos. Doubtless some of them were threatened by Paul, but whatever their motives, they made a habit of running him down. This put him in an impossible position. If he said nothing, he was in danger of losing the confidence of the entire church; but if he set forth his credentials as a way of responding to these attacks, he would be falling into exactly the same moral failure that beset his opponents.

(3) In the initial response to this dilemma, Paul does three things. (a) He carefully distinguishes his standards from "the standards of the world," his weapons from "the weapons of the world" (10:2, 4), and warns that on his next trip to Corinth, despite their caricature of his presence, he will be prepared to administer punishment (10:6). (b) He insists that his exercise of authority has been for their good, not for his own gain or advancement (10:7-11). (c) He subtly reminds the Corinthians that they are believers because of his ministry (10:12-16), while insisting that proper Christian boasting is boasting in the Lord (10:17-18).

∿

2 Samuel 18; 2 Corinthians 11; Ezekiel 25; Psalm 73

∾

IN THE CONTINUING PRESSURE he felt to respond to those who were undermining his authority in Corinth, Paul finds he must "boast" while not "boasting" (see yesterday's meditation). In 2 Corinthians 10 Paul climaxes his argument by insisting that the Christian's only proper boasting is in Christ Jesus: "Let him who boasts boast in the Lord" (10:17). In **2 Corinthians 11:16-33**, he adopts a slightly different slant to get at the same truth.

What Paul does is take a kind of "time out": he says he will boast, not as Paul the apostle, not even as Paul the Christian, but rather as Paul the "fool" (11:16-21). He is frightfully embarrassed to do even this (11:21b, 23), but he cannot see another way forward. True, he says, he was steeped in Hebrew culture and language from his youth, and he is a "servant of Christ" no less than others—but to talk like this is so painful that he explodes parenthetically, "I am out of my mind to talk like this" (11:23). *And then he inverts all the categories.* He "worked much harder": he means he worked physically, with his hands—something no first-class, self-respecting Hellenistic teacher would do. Further, he says, he has a longer prison record than they do. He has been flogged more often. Five times he has endured the synagogue sanction, the thirty-nine lashes. He has been shipwrecked three times in his voyages for the Gospel (11:25)—and this was written before the one recorded in Acts 27. Constant danger has bedeviled him in his travels, and he has often been forced to go without food. Worse, he has been betrayed by "false brothers" (11:26) while facing the perpetual stress of his concern for all the churches (11:27-28).

We must not read this with Western Christian eyes as an exciting saga of endurance under pressure. We read Paul's sufferings and admire his faithfulness and steadfastness, his conformity to the Christ who went to the cross. But his opponents would see all these "boasts" as signs of weakness and even stupidity: he does not even have enough sense to keep himself out of trouble. But Paul is determined to invert human boasting; he will boast about the things that display his weakness (11:30). Even his last shot runs along these lines (11:31-33). We tend to see Paul's escape from Damascus through Luke's eyes (Acts 9). Paul himself saw his flight as an embarrassing defeat. At a time when the highest Roman military honor went to the soldier of centurion rank or higher who was first over the wall at the end of a siege, Paul avers he was the first down.

In what ways do you boast of your weaknesses?

∾

2 Samuel 19; 2 Corinthians 12; Ezekiel 26; Psalm 74

"I MUST GO ON BOASTING," Paul writes (**2 Cor. 12:1**), though of course he has been doing so only in the most ironic way (see yesterday's meditation and the one for September 21). But now he faces a new dilemma. Apparently his opponents have been boasting about their spiritual experiences. They may even have been saying something like, "Well, of course, Paul had that Damascus Road experience, but that was a long time ago. What has he known of God since then? Yesterday's grace grows stale." In this case, of course, Paul cannot simply deploy irony and boast about the opposite of all that his opponents judge important, as he did in chapter 11. For the opposite of having various spiritual experiences is *not* having them—and in Paul's case, to deny that he has enjoyed such experiences would not be true. So reluctantly he goes on "to visions and revelations from the Lord" (12:1). But he cannot bear to talk about himself in this regard, so he retreats to a literary device: he speaks about himself in the third person: "I know a man in Christ," he writes (12:2), though clearly he is talking about himself (12:5-6).

Even in this case, Paul offers three emphases to turn the focus away from himself and strip any virtue from the habit of boasting.

First, in his case, he says, the spectacular experiences of heaven he enjoyed fourteen years earlier he was "not permitted to tell" (12:4). The "third heaven" (12:2) is the abode of God; "paradise" is where God dwells. Some of what he saw was "inexpressible": people who have not enjoyed such visions do not have the categories to grasp them. More importantly, these visions were meant to strengthen Paul; he was not permitted to talk about them. Hence his silence.

Second, Paul is afraid people will think too much of him (the opposite of our fears), so as a matter of principle he dislikes talking about inaccessible matters. If he must be judged, he wants to be judged by what he does and says (12:6), not by claims of visions and revelations that are inaccessible to public scrutiny.

Third, Paul recognizes that along with the great advantages he has received, God has imposed, through the agency of Satan, a "thorn in [the] flesh" that is not going to be removed, despite his most fervent intercessory prayer (12:7-10). It was given to keep him from becoming conceited, to keep him "weak," so that he would learn that God's strength is perfected in our weakness, and he would therefore never rely on or be puffed up by the extraordinary grace he had received. In this fallen world, it is a mercy that great grace is accompanied by great weakness, as well as the other way around.

2 Samuel 20; 2 Corinthians 13; Ezekiel 27; Psalms 75—76

∾

IN MANY CHURCHES AROUND THE WORLD, though comparatively less frequently in North America, the minister at the end of the service will quietly utter the two words, "The grace." Those gathered know that this is a signal for the entire congregation to pray together, reciting the verse from which these two words are drawn: "May the grace of the Lord Jesus Christ, and the love of God, and the fellowship of the Holy Spirit be with you all" (**2 Cor. 13:14**).

The text is short and simple, and we are in danger of flying by without reflecting on it.

(1) The triune God is the source of these blessings. That in itself is noteworthy: there was no long delay before Christians like Paul saw the implications of who Jesus is, and the implications of the gift of the Spirit, for their understanding of God himself. The entire Godhead is engaged in this vastly generous salvage operation that takes God's fallen image-bearers and restores them to fellowship with their Maker.

(2) In the first two parts, the "grace" is undoubtedly the grace that the Lord Jesus Christ gives or provides, and the "love" is the love that God himself pours out. That makes it overwhelmingly likely that the third clause, "the fellowship of the Holy Spirit" does not refer to our fellowship with the Spirit, but to the fellowship that the Holy Spirit bestows, enables, or gives. The Holy Spirit is finally the author of Christian fellowship. We enjoy Christian fellowship with one another because of the Spirit's work in each of us individually and in all of us corporately, turning our hearts and minds from self-focus and sin to adoration of God and a love of holiness and a delight in Jesus and his Gospel and teachings. Without such transformation, our "fellowship," our partnership in the Gospel, would be impossible.

(3) Not for a moment should we imagine that grace comes exclusively from Jesus, love exclusively from God the Father, and fellowship exclusively from the Spirit—as if Jesus could not love or generate fellowship, the Father could not display grace, and so forth. There is a sense in which grace, love, and fellowship come from the triune God. Yet one may usefully connect grace with the Lord Jesus, because his sacrificial, substitutionary death on the cross was offered up out of sheer grace; we may usefully connect love with God, because the entire plan of redemption springs from the wise and loving heart of God, of whom it is said, "God is love" (see 1 John 4:8 and the October 11 meditation); we may usefully connect fellowship with the Holy Spirit, since his is the work of transformation that unites us together in the partnership of the Gospel.

Praise God from whom all blessings flow; praise Father, Son, and Holy Ghost.

∾

2 Samuel 21; Galatians 1; Ezekiel 28; Psalm 77

∾

THE OPENING LINES OF Paul's letters are usually crafted with great care. The simplest form of letters in the ancient Greek world was: "From me, to you, Greetings"—often followed by some statement of thanks, and then the body of the letter. But Paul's customary practice is to "tweak" every component to anticipate what is coming in the rest of his letter. Thus a study of his letter as a whole enriches our understanding of his opening lines—and vice versa (**Gal. 1:1-5**).

(1) Paul does not always introduce himself as "an apostle." Sometimes he uses no designation (e.g., 1 and 2 Thess.); sometimes he refers to himself as a "servant" (Rom. 1:1). Here he is "Paul, an apostle" because some people were troubling the Galatian Christians with a "different gospel" that was "really no gospel at all" (1:6-7), and to do so they had to undermine Paul's authority and dismiss him as, at best, a derivative apostle.

(2) Not so, Paul says: not only is he an apostle, but he was "sent not from men nor by man, but by Jesus Christ and God the Father" (1:1). His apostleship was not mediated, as if he had been commissioned by the Jerusalem church, or by some individual first-class apostle there. Rather, he was sent "by Jesus Christ," based on his Damascus Road experience of seeing the risen and exalted Jesus himself, and by God the Father.

(3) Paul further designates God the Father as the one who raised Jesus from the dead. Paul had seen the *raised* Jesus, the *resurrected* Jesus. In his years as a devout Pharisee, he had dismissed Jesus as an evil pretender, a malefactor, cursed by God as was clear from the manner of his death. Seeing the resurrected Jesus for himself made Paul rethink everything. Jesus was vindicated by God himself, and the good news of which Paul was an apostle is grounded in Jesus' crucifixion and resurrection.

(4) However much he insists on his apostolic status and authority, Paul wisely associates himself and his teaching with "all the brothers" with him (1:2). If the Galatians angle off toward this "different gospel," they must know that they are not only turning away from Paul, but from the countless believers who agree with Paul.

(5) Instead of the traditional greeting *Chairein*, Paul uses the Christian word *grace* (*charis*) and the Jewish greeting *peace* (*shalom* in Hebrew) and grounds these blessings in the substitutionary death of the Lord Jesus (1:3-5)—not on any particular relationship to the Law of Moses.

(6) Astonishingly, Paul leaves out the "thanks" section, and immediately drives toward his astonished rebuke of the impending defection of his readers (1:6-10). However rare, there are times when a rebuke will not wait.

∾

2 Samuel 22; Galatians 2; Ezekiel 29; Psalm 78:1-39

SOME COMMENTATORS UNDERSTAND Paul in **Galatians 2:1ff.** to be saying that after some years he returned to Jerusalem to set before the Jerusalem apostles and other leaders the Gospel he had been preaching among the Gentiles, because he wanted to have himself checked out. He did this privately, of course; yet the fact of the matter is that Paul was afraid he was running or had run his race in vain (2:2). This proves that Paul was not as secure in his own mind as he pretends to be in the previous chapter. There is a sense in which he *was* a derivative apostle.

This reading will not stand up. What Paul means is something quite different. The Galatians have been invaded by agitators from the outside, men who have presented themselves as being authorized by Jerusalem, as somehow supported by the "regular" apostles. The book of Acts supplies evidence that Paul was sometimes dogged by such people. So he goes to Jerusalem, not to have his gospel validated or recast (at this point, Paul is not going to change his mind or direction), but to ensure there are no misrepresentations among the Jerusalem leaders as to what he is preaching, and to encourage those leaders to disassociate themselves entirely from the "false brothers" who are unfairly appealing to Jerusalem to damage Paul and his ministry among the Gentiles. In short, Paul takes steps to ensure that he is not running his race in vain; these agitators are trying to undo his work. He wants to take all proper steps to undermine their pretensions and destroy their influence. Acts 15 shows that that is precisely what the Jerusalem Council achieved. Indeed, Galatians 2:11-14 suggests that Paul achieved gospel consistency more quickly than some of the other apostles. Far from submitting to their judgment on the *content* of what he was preaching, he was prepared to administer his own rebukes if he saw them behaving inconsistently.

Although there are many piercingly important theological issues that emerge from these confrontations, at this juncture we may fasten on a practical one. While the Gospel is something worth contending for, there are right ways and wrong ways to go about this business. When Peter's inconsistency is public and doing public damage, Paul's rebuke is public (2:11-21). When Paul is trying to clear the air, find out what is going on, and present the tenor of his own work, he approaches the others "privately" (2:2). His concern, after all, is the advance of the undiluted Gospel, not his own public vindication. When we find ourselves in the place where we must tenaciously contend for the Gospel, we must think through how to do so most winsomely and strategically.

2 Samuel 23; Galatians 3; Ezekiel 30; Psalm 78:40-72

∾

GALATIANS 3 COULD USEFULLY occupy us for an entire book as long as this one. But here I shall restrict myself to two observations.

First, in the first five verses Paul appeals to experience. He asks the Galatians whether their conversion and all their experience of the grace of God and the power of the Spirit came to them as a function of their observance of the Law of Moses, or as a function of their faith. After all, Christ had been placarded before their eyes as the crucified Savior (3:1). They believed what they heard (3:2), and they received the Spirit. This stance had cost them: they had suffered persecution (3:4). Moreover, they had witnessed miraculous, transforming works of the Spirit, all in function of their God-given faith (3:5). Why, then, should they think that, having begun with the Spirit, having begun by faith, they should now try to attain their "goal"—presumably further steps of maturation and knowledge of God—by carefully observing the law? That approach, Paul implies, is in contradiction to their conversion, a slur on the suffering they have endured, and in antithesis to their own experience of the power of the Spirit of God.

What this means is that the path to the Christian's "goal" is faith and the life and power of the Spirit, not observance of multiplied law. To think otherwise is to be "foolish," to listen to those who have "bewitched" us with false notions of spirituality that tear us away from Jesus crucified (see 3:1).

Second, the argument in the rest of the chapter focuses not on the individual Christian's experience, but on the history of God's redemptive purpose. In other words, Paul is not saying that the law of God must operate in each unbeliever's conscience if that person is to come to Christ. That may or may not be true, but it is not what Paul is addressing. Rather, Paul seeks to establish the priority of faith for our justification as far back *in history* as Abraham (3:6-9). That immediately raises the question as to why the Law of Moses was "added" at all. Paul does not here offer a complete analysis of the various purposes served by the Law, but emphasizes certain points: it was not added to overturn the principles already established at the time of Abraham, nor to offer an alternative path to salvation. Rather, it made human sin clear and undeniable as it exposed it as transgression; thus it drove people, across the redemptive-historical time line, to Jesus Christ. One of the ways in which Paul's understanding of the Old Testament differs from that of his Jewish colleagues is that he insists on reading it along its temporal axis: Paul is explaining how the Bible fits together.

∾

2 Samuel 24; Galatians 4; Ezekiel 31; Psalm 79

GALATIANS 4 INCLUDES a couple of sections that have long prompted Christians to ponder exactly how Paul understands the history of Israel—especially the so-called "allegory" of 4:21-31. They attract a great deal of attention. Tucked into the middle of the chapter, however, are two short paragraphs that disclose a great deal of the apostle's heart (4:12-20), even though they are easily overlooked.

(1) The first (4:12-16) finds the apostle pleading with the Galatians. He insists that his strong language with them has nothing to do with personal hurt: "You have done me no wrong" (4:12). Indeed, he reminds them, the earliest stage of their relationship established a link Paul could never break. He first went among them, he says, "because of an illness" (4:13). We cannot be sure what it was. Perhaps the best guess (though it is no more than a guess) is that Paul arrived by boat on the southern coast of what is now Turkey, and while ministering there contracted malaria or some other subtropical disease. The best solution in those days was to travel into the highlands—into the regions of the Galatians. There Paul found a people remarkably helpful and welcoming. As he preached the Gospel to them, they treated him as if he were "an angel of God" (4:14). How could Paul possibly resent them or write them off? But tragically, their joy has dissipated. They have become so enamored with the alien outlook of the agitators that they view Paul as an enemy because he tells them the truth (4:16).

Here, then, is an apostle intimately involved in the lives of the people to whom he preaches, ready and eager to engage with them out of the complex history of their relationships, yet unwilling to compromise the truth in order to smooth out those relationships. In Paul, integrity of doctrine must stand with integrity in relationships; they are not to be pitted against each other.

(2) Paul perceives and gently exposes a deep character flaw in the Galatians: they love zealous people, not the least those who are zealously pursuing them, without carefully evaluating the direction of the zeal (4:17-20). Paul warns: "It is fine to be zealous, provided the purpose is good" (4:18). Unable to communicate by telephone or e-mail and thus have an instant update, the apostle is uncertain how best to proceed. Should he continue his rebuke? Should he now change his tone and woo them? He feels like a mother who has to go through the agony of labor a second time to bring to birth all over again the child she has already borne.

Should contemporary pastors and leaders care less for those in their charge who stray?

1 Kings 1; Galatians 5; Ezekiel 32; Psalm 80

∽

THE TRANSFER OF REGAL AUTHORITY from David to Solomon (**1 Kings 1**) is messy. One of David's sons, Adonijah, confers with Joab, the head of the military, and tries to take over. Bathsheba, Solomon's mother, reminds her ailing husband of his promise that Solomon would be the heir, and the complicated account plays out.

Once again the chronic family failure of David stands out. The author of 1 Kings draws it to our attention in the parenthetical comment of 1:6. Referring to Adonijah, who was attempting the coup, he remarks, "His father had never interfered with him by asking, 'Why do you behave as you do?' He was also very handsome and was born next after Absalom"—as if good looks bred a kind of easy arrogance that thought everything, including the crown itself, was his by right.

Of the many important lessons, we may highlight two:

First, even gifted and morally upright believers commonly manifest tragic flaws. Occasionally a Daniel arises, of whom no failure is recorded. But most of the best in Scripture betray flaws of one sort or another—Abraham, Moses, Peter, Thomas, and (not least) David. The reality must be faced, for it is no less potent today. God raises up strategically placed and influential leaders. The odd one is so consistent that it is very difficult to detect any notable fault line. But usually that is not the case. Even the finest of our Christian leaders commonly display faults that their closest peers and friends can spot (whether or not the leaders themselves can see them!). This should not surprise us. In this fallen world, it is the way things are, the way things were when the Bible was written. We should therefore not be disillusioned when leaders prove flawed. We should support them wherever we can, seek to correct the faults where possible, and leave the rest to God—all the while recognizing the terrible potential for failures and faults in our own lives.

Second, once again the sovereignty of God works *through* the complicated efforts of his people. When David is informed of the problem, he does not throw his hands into the air and pray about the situation: he immediately orders that decisive, symbol-laden, and complex steps be taken to ensure that Solomon ascends the throne. Trust in God's sovereign goodness is never an excuse for inactivity or indolence. Long years of walking by faith have taught David that whatever else "walking by faith" means, it does not warrant passivity. If we are to avoid acting in defiance of God, or in vain efforts to be independent of God, we must also avoid the pietism that is perennially in danger of collapsing trust into fatalism.

∽

1 Kings 2; Galatians 6; Ezekiel 33; Psalms 81—82

∾

THE END OF **GALATIANS** 6 brings several themes together.

(1) Paul's practice was to dictate his letters. Nevertheless, in order to authenticate them, he commonly wrote the last little bit in his own distinctive hand (compare 2 Thess. 3:17). So here (Gal. 6:11). Some have suggested that his "large letters" betray failing eyesight. That is possible but not certain. The important issue is that Paul wants his readers to recognize the real voice behind this epistle.

(2) The agitators are trying to get the Galatian Gentile believers to accept circumcision (6:12). That would make them (they thought) good Jews—a necessary condition for them to become genuine Christians. Yet Paul detects that at least part of their motivation is to maintain acceptability in Jewish synagogue circles. At this stage in the church's history, most persecution came from synagogue councils exerting discipline. Paul himself had suffered his share: the thirty-nine lashes, endured five times (2 Cor. 11), was a synagogue punishment. Paul holds that some Jews who call themselves Christians and who insist that Gentile Christians become Jews are simply unwilling to face the opprobrium they will have to suffer from some fellow Jews if their closest "brothers" and "sisters" are unkosher Gentiles.

(3) Not only so, but circumcision was a mark of professed covenant fidelity. Here, Paul insists, lies the real problem: those who have been circumcised find it impossible to "obey the law," so why should they try to compel others to go down that track (6:13)? Some of them want to count converts to Judaism like scalps on a spear. But Paul insists that the Christian boasts in nothing but the cross of the Lord Jesus (6:14). That is the sole basis of our acceptance before God, nothing else—not circumcision, not law-keeping, not kosher tables, not belonging to the right community. The sole ground is the cross, so that is our sole "boast." If you believe that, what the world thinks will matter little: it is as if the world has been crucified so far as you are concerned, and you are crucified so far as it is concerned.

(4) Out of this cross-work of Jesus Christ rises the "new creation" (6:15). That is what counts—men and women so transformed, because of faith in Jesus, that they belong to the new creation still to be consummated. This is invariably true, even for "the Israel of God"—which might refer to the church as the true Israel, or may be saying that racial Israel must face this truth the same as everyone else.

(5) At the personal level, Paul quietly reminds his Galatian readers that he has paid for his beliefs in suffering. Can the agitators claim the same? So why should any true Christian now be adding to Paul's sufferings?

∾

1 Kings 3; Ephesians 1; Ezekiel 34; Psalms 83—84

CHRISTIANS SOMETIMES ASK WHY, if Solomon was so wise, he married many wives, ended his reign rather badly, and eventually compromised his loyalty to God.

The answer partly lies in the difference between what we mean by *wisdom* and the various things the Bible means by *wisdom.* We usually mean something pretty generic, like "knowing how to live well and make wise choices." But whereas wisdom in the Bible can refer to something broad—such as knowing how to live in the fear of God—very often it refers to a particular skill. This may be the skill of knowing how to survive in a dangerous world (Prov. 30:24), or some technical know-how (Ex. 28:3). But one of the skills to which *wisdom* can refer is the skill of administration, not least the administration of justice. And transparently, that is what Solomon asks for in **1 Kings 3.**

When he responds to God's gracious offer to give him anything he asks for, Solomon acknowledges that he is only a little child and does not know how to carry out his duties (3:7). What he wants therefore is a discerning heart to govern the people well, not least in distinguishing between right and wrong (3:9). God praises Solomon because he has not asked for something for himself, nor even something vindictive (such as the death of his enemies), but "for discernment in administering justice" (3:11). God promises to give Solomon exactly what he asked for, along with riches and honor (3:12-13). The account of the two prostitutes each claiming the same live baby and denying that the dead one is hers, and Solomon's resolution of their case (3:16-27), proves that God answered the king's request. The entire nation perceives that Solomon has "wisdom from God to administer justice" (3:28). Certainly most Western nations today could do with a few more people similarly endowed.

As much as God praises him for his choice, this does not mean that such wisdom is all that Solomon needs to walk in fidelity to the covenant. Indeed, quite apart from the wisdom, wealth, and honor that he will bestow, God tells him that "if you walk in my ways and obey my statutes and commands as David your father did, I will give you a long life" (3:14). But already clouds threaten: to secure his southern border, Solomon marries an Egyptian princess (3:1). Because they are popular, he does not abolish the proscribed "high places," but participates in worship there (3:2-4).

God sometimes bestows wonderful gifts of wisdom—technical, social, administrative, and judicial skills—but unless we also receive from him a heart attuned to loving him truly and obeying him wholly, our paths may end disastrously.

1 Kings 4—5; Ephesians 2; Ezekiel 35; Psalm 85

∾

CHRISTIANS ARE OFTEN TAUGHT to memorize **Ephesians 2:8-9**: "For it is by grace you have been saved, through faith—and this not from yourselves, it is the gift of God—not by works, so that no one can boast." Certainly wonderful truths are expressed in these lines. But I shall focus on some of the things Paul says in the surrounding verses.

(1) Before our conversion, we, like the Ephesians, were dead in our "transgressions and sins" (2:1). Because of our addiction to transgression and sin, because of our habit of following the ways of the world (2:2), because we were simultaneously deceived by the Devil (2:2) and committed to gratifying the desires and thoughts of our sinful natures (2:3), there was simply no way we could respond positively to the Gospel. Worse, our tragic inability was a moral inability: "Like the rest, we were by nature objects of wrath" (2:3). There was no hope for us unless God himself intervened and brought life where there was only death, and showed mercy where his own justice demanded wrath.

(2) That is what God did: while we were still dead, out of his great love for us, "God, who is rich in mercy, made us alive with Christ" (2:4-5). This was out of his sheer grace: we certainly could not help ourselves, for "we were dead" (2:5).

(3) Indeed, God so unites us to Christ that in his eyes we are already raised with him and seated "in the heavenly realms in Christ Jesus" (2:6). God has taken these steps "in order that in the coming ages he might show the incomparable riches of his grace, expressed in his kindness to us in Christ Jesus" (2:7). So our ultimate hope and expectation is what still awaits us. No Christian is stable who does not see and value this futurist perspective.

(4) At this point Paul stresses the sheer graciousness of the gift of salvation, a gift received by faith that is itself the gift of God, and is quite apart from any works that we could perform. For if we could, we would boast of them.

(5) But none of this means that we continue to live as we did before—dead in transgressions, following our own desires and thoughts. Far from it: we who have received God's grace, and the faith to apprehend it, are "God's workmanship, created in Christ Jesus to do good works, which God prepared in advance for us to do" (2:10). One can no more enjoy saving grace without performing good works, than one can experience saving grace without ever knowing the incomparable riches that await us in the age to come. This great salvation is one superb package!

∾

1 Kings 6; Ephesians 3; Ezekiel 36; Psalm 86

∼

A MYSTERY IN PAUL'S WRITINGS is not normally something "mysterious," still less a whodunit. It is a truth or a doctrine which in some measure has been kept hidden in previous generations, and now with the coming of the Gospel has been disclosed and made public. Sometimes the Gospel itself is treated as a *mystery*; more commonly, some element of the Gospel is labeled a *mystery*.

In **Ephesians 3:2-13**, Paul insists that, along with other "apostles and prophets" (3:5), he enjoys deep insight into "the mystery of Christ, which was not made known to men in other generations as it has now been revealed by the Spirit" (3:4-5). Then he tells us the content of this mystery: "that through the gospel the Gentiles are heirs together with Israel, members together of one body, and sharers together in the promise in Christ Jesus" (3:6).

We should reflect on the ways in which this *mystery* was hidden. Certainly the Old Testament Scriptures sometimes anticipate the extension of the grace of God to men and women of all races. The Abrahamic covenant foresaw that in Abraham's seed all the nations of the earth would be blessed (Gen. 12:3; see meditation for January 11). What is hidden about that? Yet the fact remains that the space devoted in the Bible to the Law of Moses, coupled more importantly with the rising body of interpretation that made Mosaic Law the interpretive grid that controlled the reading of much of the Old Testament, ensured that this broader emphasis was often lost to view. So on the one hand, this hiddenness can be viewed as a careful plan of God to hide the glory of "his eternal purpose" (3:11) until the time was ripe for it to be unfolded; on the other, this hiddenness owes something to human perversity, reading the Old Testament Scriptures in a way that domesticates and dwarfs the true dimensions of Old Testament promises.

With the coming of Christ Jesus, the ways in which the Old Testament books pointed forward were made incalculably clearer. Jesus' Great Commission stamped the mission of his disciples with an internationalism that shames all parochialism. Above all, Jesus' understanding of the Old Testament established some new paradigms. Read properly, in its linear, historical sequence, the Old Testament storyline does not lay as much emphasis on the Law of Moses as some thought. Indeed, the Mosaic Covenant turns out to be a failure, in terms of how well it changed people. Its brightest success is in providing the models that predict what the ultimate Savior, the ultimate priest, the ultimate temple, the ultimate sacrifice, would look like. And Paul is the apostle who not only preaches this *mystery*, but does so to the Gentiles, the people most affected by its content.

∼

1 Kings 7; Ephesians 4; Ezekiel 37; Psalms 87—88

∾

ONE OF THE REMARKABLE FEATURES of Paul's letters is that much space is devoted to teaching people how to live. Indeed, the Bible as a whole is interested in teaching us what to believe (because these things are true), and it is no less interested in teaching us faithful conduct. Nowhere is such balance more evident than in Paul's letters.

The reason for this comprehensiveness lies in the nature of God. The God of the Bible, the God who is there (as Francis Schaeffer taught us to say), is God of everything. He is not the God of thoughts only, or of some spiritual or religious realm exclusively. He is *God*. As our Maker and providential Ruler, his interests and writ extend to every aspect of our being, beliefs, utterances, and conduct. Thus to preserve some horrible tension between our belief systems and our conduct is not only an invitation to schizophrenia, it is also an insult against God, a horrible rebellion no less ugly for being selective.

This means that our teaching and preaching must include not only truths to be believed, but also instruction on how to live. Entirely exemplary in this respect is the example of Paul in **Ephesians 4:17-32**. No one seriously doubts that this epistle contains rich doctrine. Here, however, we find Paul insisting that his readers "no longer live as the Gentiles do, in the futility of their thinking" (4:17). He ties this "futility" to their ignorance of God on the one hand, and to their disgusting conduct on the other. "You, however, did not come to know Christ that way" (4:20). You were "created to be like God in true righteousness and holiness" (4:24). That means "put[ting] off" the old self, and being "made new in the attitude of your minds" and "put[ting] on" the new self (4:22-24).

All of this could remain a little ethereal. Paul will not allow such an escape. The rest of the chapter is frank and practical. The conduct Paul expects includes truthful speech—"for we are all members of one body" (4:25), and a practical commitment to let no day end in anger, lest the devil be given a foothold (4:26-27). Converted thieves must steal no more. They must work, doing something useful, learning to be generous with what they earn (4:28). Our talk must not only eliminate what is blasphemous, vulgar, or "unwholesome," but must learn to utter "what is helpful for building others up according to their needs" (4:29). Comprehensively: "Get rid of all bitterness, rage and anger, brawling and slander, along with every form of malice. Be kind and compassionate to one another, forgiving each other, just as in Christ God forgave you" (4:31-32).

∾

1 Kings 8; *Ephesians 5*; Ezekiel 38; Psalm 89

∿

THE DEDICATION OF THE TEMPLE in Jerusalem and Solomon's prayer on that occasion (**1 Kings 8**) overflow with links that reach both backward and forward along the line of redemptive history.

(1) The structure of the temple is a proportionate reproduction of the tabernacle. Thus the rites prescribed by the Mosaic Covenant, and the symbol-laden value all that God prescribed through Moses, continue: the altar, the table for the bread of consecration, the Most Holy Place, the two cherubim over the ark of the covenant, and so forth.

(2) Most spectacularly, after the ark of the covenant has been transported to its new resting place and the priests withdraw, the glory of the Lord, manifested in the same sort of cloud that signaled the Lord's presence in the tabernacle, fills the temple. Not only does God approve the temple, but a new step has been taken in God's unfolding purposes. While the symbolism of the tabernacle is retained in the temple, no longer is this edifice something mobile. The wandering years, and even the uncertain years of the judges, are over. Now God's presence, manifested in this solid building, is tied to one location: Jerusalem. A new set of symbol-laden historical experiences adds rich new dimensions to the accumulating wealth pointing to the coming of Jesus. Here is a stable kingdom—and the kingdom of God; Jerusalem, and the new Jerusalem; the glorious temple, and the city that needs no temple because "the Lord God Almighty and the Lamb are its temple" (Rev. 21:22). Here are tens of thousands of animals slaughtered—and the Lamb of God, who takes away the sin of the world.

(3) At his best, Solomon is thoroughly aware that no structure, not even this one, can contain or domesticate God. "The heavens, even the highest heaven, cannot contain you. How much less this temple I have built!" (8:27).

(4) But that does not stop him from asking God to manifest himself here. Above all, Solomon knows that what the people will need most is forgiveness. So in wide-ranging and prescient descriptions of experiences the people will pass through, Solomon repeats some variation of the refrain: "Hear from heaven, your dwelling place, and when you hear, forgive" (8:30ff). That is exactly right: hear *from heaven*, even if the eyes of the people are toward this temple, and forgive.

(5) Solomon's forward glance includes the dreadful possibility of exile (8:46-51), followed by rescue and release. Further, while Solomon urges fidelity on the people (8:56-61), he also echoes a prominent point in the Abrahamic covenant (Gen. 12:3): Israel must be faithful "so that all the peoples of the earth may know that the LORD is God and that there is no other" (8:60).

∿

1 Kings 9; Ephesians 6; Ezekiel 39; Psalm 90

JUST BEFORE THE CLOSING LINES of Paul's letter to the Ephesians, he invites his readers to pray for him (**Eph. 6:19-20**): "Pray also for me, that whenever I open my mouth, words may be given me so that I will fearlessly make known the mystery of the gospel, for which I am an ambassador in chains. Pray that I may declare it fearlessly, as I should."

(1) Elsewhere when Paul provides models for how his converts should pray (e.g., Eph. 3:14-21; Phil. 1:9-11), the theme of mission does not arise as powerfully as here. True, Paul elsewhere asks others to pray for him (1 Thess. 5:25), but here he specifies what he wants them to ask for (compare Col. 4:4; 2 Thess. 3:1). He wants to be able to speak the "mystery" of the Gospel fearlessly.

(2) Surely it is encouraging that Paul should feel the need for such prayer. We sometimes place the apostle on such a high pedestal that we forget he was an ordinary mortal faced with the same temptations that confront us. He was very well aware of how easy it is to skew the Gospel, to trim it a little, to get around the bits we think our hearers will find awkward or offensive. So he knew that to preach the Gospel *faithfully,* he would have to preach it *fearlessly.* This does not reflect an "in your face" style. It means, rather, that Paul wanted to speak without fearing what his hearers would think or say about him, or what they might do to him, lest he compromise the Gospel he came to announce.

It does not take much imagination to detect ways in which today's preachers in the Western world stand in need of much prayer in this regard. Suppose you are preaching to university undergraduates at a pagan university, or to bright businesspeople in their 20s and 30s in, say, New York. When you expound Romans, exactly how will you handle homosexuality in chapter 1 and election in chapter 9? How will you talk about hell in the many passages where Jesus himself deploys the most horrific images? How might you be tempted to flinch when you must deal with the sheer exclusiveness of the Gospel or when you talk about money to rich people?

(3) We should not miss the fact that Paul is willing to ask for prayer. Some leaders think they must never admit a weakness, a fear, or a need. They act as if they are above the fray. Not Paul. His request for prayer is not *pro forma*: he asks for prayer to preach the Gospel fearlessly because he has been preaching long enough, and knows himself well enough, to know the power and danger of preaching for merely popular acclaim. By asking for prayer, he admits his fears, and secures their divine remedy.

1 Kings 10; Philippians 1; Ezekiel 40; Psalm 91

∾

THE VISIT OF THE QUEEN OF SHEBA (**1 Kings 10**) has often been spiced up in books and films until it has become a royal love story. Not a hint of love interest or sex scandal peeps out of the biblical text. The function of the queen of Sheba is to demonstrate by a concrete example that Solomon's reputation had extended far and wide, and that that reputation was grounded in reality. Some observations on the encounter:

First, at a rather superficial level, this account provides an opportunity to say something about the nature of *truth* in the Old Testament. Some have argued that the Hebrew word for "truth," *'emet,* really means "faithfulness" or "reliability," and that it has to do with relationships and not propositions. Indeed, some argue, Old Testament writers simply do not have a category for *true propositions.* Like most errors, this one has a modicum of truth (if I may use the word) to it. Certainly *'emet* has a broader range of meaning than the English word *truth,* and can refer to faithfulness. But words can display faithfulness, too. The queen of Sheba tells Solomon that the report she heard in her own country about his achievements and wisdom was *'emet:* it was "true" (10:6, NIV); more literally, because the report was faithful, i.e., because the propositions conformed to the reality, the report was the *truth.* Away, then, with a reductionistic analysis of what ancient Hebrews could or could not have known.

Second, much of the chapter provides succinct descriptions of Solomon's wealth, military muscle, successful trading expeditions in seagoing vessels, musical instruments, and more. Yet space is reserved for several explicitly theological themes. Royalty visited Solomon to listen to his wisdom—and this wisdom God himself had put in his heart (10:24). Indeed, Solomon enjoyed an extraordinary reputation for maintaining justice and righteousness in his kingdom, so much so that the queen of Sheba thought his achievements in this regard demonstrated "the LORD's eternal love for Israel" (10:9).

But *third,* all of this is in some ways a setup for the next chapter. Despite all the blessings, wisdom, power, wealth, prestige, and honor that Solomon enjoyed, all received from the hand of God, the sad fact of the matter is that his own conduct was paving the way for judgment and the undoing of the Davidic dynasty. These convoluted developments await tomorrow's meditation. Here it is enough to reflect on the fact that extraordinary blessings do not necessarily signal faithfulness. Because God is so slow to anger (surely a good thing!), the judgments that our corruptions deserve are often long delayed. Do not be hasty to assume that present blessings signal present fidelity: the terrible fruit of faithlessness may take a long time in coming.

∾

1 Kings 11; Philippians 2; Ezekiel 41; Psalms 92—93

∾

IN FEW PLACES DOES THE WORD *however* have more potent force than in **1 Kings 11:1**: "King Solomon, *however*, loved many foreign women." In those days, the size of a king's harem was widely considered a reflection of his wealth and power. Solomon married princesses from everywhere, not least, the writer painfully explains, "from nations about which the LORD had told the Israelites, 'You must not intermarry with them, because they will surely turn your hearts after their gods'" (11:2).

That is exactly what happened, especially as Solomon grew old (11:3-4). He participated in the worship of foreign gods. To please his wives, he provided shrines, altars, and temples for their deities. Doubtless many Israelites began to participate in this pagan worship. At the very least, many would have their sense of outrage dulled, not least because Solomon was known to be such a wise, resourceful, and successful king. Eventually his pagan idolatry extended to the detestable gods to whom one sacrifices children. Thus Solomon "did evil in the eyes of the LORD; he did not follow the LORD completely, as David his father had done" (11:6). Of course, David himself failed on occasion. But he lapsed from a life of principled devotion to the Lord God, and he repented and returned to the Lord; he did not live in a stream of growing religious compromise like his son and heir to the throne.

The sentence is delivered (11:9-13): after his death, Solomon's kingdom will be divided, with ten tribes withdrawing, leaving only two for the Davidic dynasty—and even this paltry remainder is conceded only for David's sake. Had Solomon been another sort of man, he would have repented, sought the Lord's favor, destroyed all the high places, promoted covenant fidelity. But the sad truth is that Solomon preferred his wives and their opinions to his covenant Lord and his opinion. During the closing years of his reign, Solomon had plenty of signs that God's protective favor was being withdrawn (11:14-40). Nothing is sadder than Solomon's futile effort to have Jeroboam killed—evocative of Saul's attempt to have David killed. But there is no movement, no repentance, no hunger for God.

There are plenty of lessons. Be careful what, and whom, you love. Good beginnings do not guarantee good endings. Heed the warnings of God while there is time; if you don't, you will eventually become so hardened that even his most dire threats will leave you unmoved. At the canonical level, even the most blessed, protected, and endowed dynasty, chosen from within the Lord's chosen people, is announcing its end: it will fall apart. Oh, how we need a Savior, a king from heaven!

∾

1 Kings 12; Philippians 3; Ezekiel 42; Psalm 94

☙

THE DIVISION OF THE unified kingdom into two unequal parts—the kingdom of Israel with its ten tribes in the north and the kingdom of Judah with two tribes in the south (**1 Kings 12**)—once again presents us with a remarkable dynamic between God's sovereignty and human responsibility.

God had already predicted, through Ahijah the prophet, that Jeroboam would take away the ten northern tribes from Solomon's successor (11:26-40). Jeroboam was explicitly told that if he then remained faithful to the Lord, the Lord would establish a dynasty for him. Yet the first thing that Jeroboam does, once he secures the northern tribes, is erect golden calves at Bethel and Dan, and consecrate non-Levitical priests, because he does not want his people making the trek to the temple in Jerusalem (12:25-33). Doesn't he realize that if God has the power to give him the ten tribes, and the concern to warn him about disloyalty, he certainly has the power to preserve the integrity of the northern kingdom even if the people go up to Jerusalem for the high festivals? But Jeroboam makes his political judgments, refuses to obey God, and shows himself ungrateful for what has come his way. His only enduring legacy is that throughout the rest of the Old Testament he is designated as "Jeroboam the son of Nebat, who caused Israel to sin" (e.g., 2 Kings 14:24).

More inexplicable yet is Rehoboam, Solomon's son. Solomon may have been a skilled administrator of justice, but by the end of his life his enormously expensive projects were wearing down his people. Their representatives assure Rehoboam that they will be loyal to him if only he will lighten their load a little. The elders assure Rehoboam that their request is reasonable: he should adopt the stance of being "a servant to these people and serve them," for then he will discover that "they will always be your servants" (12:7). With massive insensitivity and piercing stupidity, Rehoboam adopts instead the wretched advice of "young men" full of themselves and their opinions, with no understanding of people generally and of this nation in particular (12:8). So Rehoboam responds harshly, not only rejecting the people's request but promising more demands and increased brutality. And suddenly the rebellion is underway.

Yet the writer comments, "So the king did not listen to the people, for this turn of events was from the LORD, to fulfill the word the LORD had spoken to Jeroboam son of Nebat through Ahijah the Shilonite" (12:15). God's sovereignty (see, for example, the meditation for June 3) does not excuse or mitigate Rehoboam's stupidity and Jeroboam's rebellion; their stupidity and sin do not mean that God has lost control. Such mysteries of providence make it difficult to "read" history; they also prove immensely comforting and make it possible for us to rest in Romans 8:28.

☙

1 Kings 13; Philippians 4; Ezekiel 43; Psalms 95—96

SOME PRACTICAL ADVICE FOR Christians (**Phil. 4:4-9**):

(1) Always rejoice in the Lord (4:4). This command is so important that Paul repeats it. Our responsibility to obey it is independent of circumstances, for regardless of how utterly miserable our situation is, the Christian always has the most profound reasons for rejoicing in Christ Jesus: sins forgiven and the prospect of resurrection life in the new heaven and the new earth—not to mention the consolation of the Spirit even now, and much more. Practically speaking, Paul well knows that the believer who is truly rejoicing in the Lord cannot possibly be a back-biter, a cheat, a whiner, a thief, or lazy, bitter, and filled with hate.

(2) Be known for gentleness (4:5). That is almost a delicious oxymoron. So much in our culture wants us to be known for aggressiveness, or for some intrinsic strength or superiority. The gentle person does not usually think in terms of being known. But Paul wants us so to focus on gentleness that eventually we become known for gentleness. The ground Paul offers is that the Lord is "near." In this context, probably Paul does not mean that the Lord's coming is near, but that the Lord himself is never far from his people: he is near, and is watching us, as he watches over us, all the time. That becomes our motivation for acting as he wishes us to act.

(3) Stop worrying (4:6-7). Paul is not advocating irresponsible escapism, still less a Pollyanna-like optimism. Moreover, strictly speaking he is not telling us to *stop* worrying and nothing more, but rather he tells us *how* to stop worrying—by replacing this constant fretting with something else: "in everything, by prayer and petition, with thanksgiving [there's the praise theme again], present your requests to God" (4:6). Paul does not deny the agony and sorrow of many human experiences. How could he? His letters show that he suffered his share of the worst. But he knows the solution. Either worrying drives out prayer, or prayer drives out worrying. Moreover, Paul insists, this disciplined, thankful, intercessory prayer brings with it "the peace of God, which transcends all understanding" (4:7).

(4) Think holy thoughts (4:8-9). Garbage in, garbage out. We are renewed by the transforming of our minds (Rom. 12:1-2). So watch what you feed your mind; watch what you think; determine to drive your mind into good and healthy channels, not those characterized by bitterness, resentments, lust, hate, or jealousy. Reflect on all the kinds of things Paul includes in his diverse list of verse 8. Moreover, here too Paul serves as an important example (4:9): he is not telling us to do anything he does not practice himself.

1 Kings 14; Colossians 1;Ezekiel 44; Psalms 97—98

∽

FAITH, HOPE, AND LOVE are together sometimes referred to as the *Pauline triad.* They occur in Paul's letters in various combinations. Sometimes only two of the three show up; sometimes all three.

Probably the best known verse with the Pauline triad is 1 Corinthians 13:13: "And now these three remain: faith, hope and love. But the greatest of these is love." Here no relationship is expressed among the three. Paul tells us that these three virtues—faith, hope, and love (and this last one he calls "the most excellent way" (12:31b; see the September 8 meditation) rather than a "gift")—all "remain": what he means, I think, is that these all remain into eternity, and therefore should be nurtured and pursued even now. But the greatest of these three, Paul insists, is love. Why this is so, Paul does not tell us. Based on what the New Testament says elsewhere, we might reasonably hold that the reason why love is the greatest is that it is an attribute of God. God does not exercise faith; he does not "hope" in the sense of looking forward to the fulfillment of something that some other brings about. But he does love: indeed, 1 John 4:8 tells us that God is love; no text says he is faith or hope. So the greatest of the three is love.

Here in **Colossians 1:3-6**, however, the relationship among the three elements of the Pauline triad is quite different. Paul thanks God when he prays for the Colossians, he says, "because we have heard of your *faith* in Christ Jesus and of the *love* you have for all the saints—the faith and love that spring from the *hope* that is stored up for you in heaven and that you have already heard about in the word of truth, the gospel that has come to you" (1:4-6). This NIV rendering is slightly paraphrastic, but it catches the sense very well. Note:

(1) Paul did not plant the Colossian church. But now that he has come to hear of these believers, he prays for them constantly, with thanksgiving.

(2) What Paul has heard of these Colossian believers is their faith and love, both demonstrable virtues. If you have faith in Jesus, and if you love the saints, neither virtue can be hidden. These virtues were so evident among the Colossians that reports of their faith and love circulated to Paul. Do reports of the faith and love of our churches circulate widely?

(3) Paul says this faith and love "spring from the hope" that is stored up for them (1:5). Living with eternity in view vitalizes faith and calls forth love.

(4) This hope that has grounded their faith and love has itself been grounded in the Gospel, the word of truth that was preached to them (1:5-6).

∽

1 Kings 15; Colossians 2; Ezekiel 45; Psalms 99—101

∼

THE SETTING WAS A Bible study led by a lady in the church where I was serving as pastor. A woman from one of the more popular cults had infiltrated this group, and the lady from our church soon discovered she was a little out of her depth. I was invited along, and soon found myself in a public confrontation with the intruder's cult "pastor" (though he did not call himself that). One of the things he wanted to deny in strong terms was the deity of Jesus Christ. As we started looking together at biblical references which, on the face of it, say something about the deity of Christ, eventually we came to **Colossians 2:9.** He wanted to render the verse, rather loosely, something like "in Christ all the attributes of the Deity live in bodily form."

I asked him which of the attributes of God Jesus does not have. He immediately saw the problem. If he said, "eternality" (which is what he believed), he would be trapped, for his own rendering would contradict him. If he said, "none" (in defiance of his own beliefs), then how can Jesus and God be as sharply distinguished as he proposed?

In any case, Colossians 2:9 is even stronger than his translation allowed: "in Christ all the fullness of the Deity lives in bodily form." Observe:

(1) In this context, the Colossians are exhorted to continue to live in Christ, just as they "received Christ Jesus as Lord" (2:6)—which as usual bears an overtone of Jesus' divine identity, since "Lord" was commonly the way one addressed God in the Greek versions of the Old Testament.

(2) Both then and now, there are people who try to ensnare you through a "hollow and deceptive philosophy, which depends on human tradition" (2:8). In virtually every case, the aim of such deceptive philosophies is to reduce or relativize Christ, to redirect attention and allegiance away from him. Not only these verses but much of the letter to the Colossians show that, whoever these heretics are, their attack is against Christ. Paul will not budge: "all the fullness of the Deity" lives in him in bodily form—and you are complete in him, in him you enjoy all the fullness you can possibly know (2:10). To turn from him for extras is disastrous, for he alone is "the head over every power and authority" (2:10).

(3) Apparently at least one branch of the Colossian heretics was trying to get the believers to add to Christ a bevy of Jewish rituals. Paul does not budge: he understands that the rites and rituals mandated by the Old Testament constitute "a shadow of the things that were to come; the reality, however, is found in Christ" (2:17).

∼

1 Kings 16; Colossians 3; Ezekiel 46; Psalm 102

FIRST AND 2 KINGS narrate the declining fortunes of both the northern and southern kingdoms. Occasionally there is a reforming king in one realm or the other. But on the whole the direction is downward. Some orientation (**1 Kings 16**):

(1) Although 1 and 2 Kings treat both the northern and the southern kingdoms, the emphasis is on the former. By contrast, 1 and 2 Chronicles, which cover roughly the same material, tilt strongly in favor of the kingdom of Judah.

(2) In the south, the Davidic dynasty continues. During its history, there are, humanly speaking, some very close calls. Nevertheless God preserves the line; his entire redemptive purposes are bound up with continuity of that Davidic line. The stance throughout is well expressed in 1 Kings 15:4. Abijah king of Judah, who reigned only three years, was doubtless an evil king. "Nevertheless, for David's sake the LORD his God gave him a lamp in Jerusalem by raising up a son to succeed him and by making Jerusalem strong." In the north, however, no dynasty survives very long. The dynasty of Jeroboam lasted two generations and was then butchered (15:25-30), replaced by Baasha (15:33-34). His dynasty likewise produced two kings, and then the males in his family were wiped out by Zimri (16:8-13), whose reign lasted all of seven days (16:15-19). And so it goes. If the Davidic line continues in the south, it is all of grace.

(3) These successions in the north are brutal and bloody. For instance, after Zimri the citizens of Israel face a brief civil war, divided as they are between Omri and Tibni. The followers of the former win. The text wryly comments, "So Tibni died and Omri became king" (16:22). In short, there is perennial lust for power, few systems for orderly hand over of government, no hearty submission to the living God.

(4) From God's perspective, however, the severity of the sin is measured first and foremost not in terms of the bloody violence, but in terms of the idolatry (for example, 16:30-33). Omri was a strong ruler who strengthened the nation enormously, but little of that is recorded: from God's perspective he "did evil in the eyes of the LORD and sinned more than all those before him" (16:25). Building programs and a rising GDP do not make up for idolatry.

(5) Details in these accounts often tie the narrative to events much earlier and later. Thus the rebuilding of Jericho (16:34) calls to mind the curse on the city when it was destroyed centuries earlier (Josh. 6:26). The founding of the city of Samaria (16:24) anticipates countless narratives of what takes place in that city—including Jesus and the woman at the well (John 4; see March 14 meditation).

1 Kings 17; Colossians 4; Ezekiel 47; Psalm 103

∾

HERE AND THERE IN THE New Testament we are suddenly given brief glimpses of arrays of Christian people. Romans 16 provides such a snapshot, and **Colossians 4:7-18** provides us with another. The men and women briefly introduced lived entire, complex, interlocked lives, of which we know almost nothing. But they are our brothers and sisters in Christ; they faced temptations, overcame challenges, discharged very different tasks, and played out their roles in diverse strata of society. The brief glimpses afforded here fire our imaginations; our fuller curiosity will be satisfied only in heaven.

A few comments may hint at some of the things that may be learned from the information Paul's letter provides.

(1) Paul kept a team of people working with him. One of their roles was to travel back and forth between wherever Paul was and the churches for which he felt himself responsible. Combining Paul's letters with Acts, it is often possible to plot some of their constant travels. Here, Paul sends Tychicus to the Colossians with explicit pastoral purposes (4:7-8).

(2) The "Mark" of 4:10 is almost certainly John Mark, and the author of the second Gospel. Here he is identified as a relative of Barnabas. This may account, in part, for the dispute between Barnabas and Paul as to whether Mark should be given a second chance after he withdrew from the first missionary expedition (Acts 13:5, 13; 15:37-40). Certainly by the end of Paul's ministry, Mark had been restored in the apostle's eyes (2 Tim. 4:11).

(3) Paul's co-workers often included both Jews and Gentiles (4:11). It does not take much imagination to recognize the challenges and stresses, as well as the blessings and richness, that this arrangement entailed.

(4) Epaphras emerges as a formidable model. He is "always wrestling in prayer" for the Colossian believers. What he prays, above all, is that they "may stand firm in all the will of God, mature and fully assured" (4:12). How the church of Christ needs prayer warriors with similar focus today!

(5) The "Luke" mentioned in 4:14 is almost certainly the author of Luke and Acts, and a Gentile (since he is in the Gentile part of this list, 4:11ff.). This makes him the only Gentile writer of a New Testament document. Demas is mentioned in the same breath, but he is probably the same one who ultimately deserts the mission and the Gospel (2 Tim. 4:10). Good beginnings do not guarantee good endings.

(6) Churches in the first century did not have their own buildings. Believers regularly met in the homes of their wealthier members. Nympha of Laodicea is one of the wealthy women of a wealthy city, and the church there met in her home (4:15).

∾

1 Kings 18; 1 Thessalonians 1; Ezekiel 48; Psalm 104

∿

IT IS TEMPTING TO COMMENT further on the Pauline triad found in **1 Thessalonians 1:3** (see meditation on October 11), but the confrontation on Mount Carmel (**1 Kings 18**) beckons.

The most shocking thing about that confrontation is that it was needed. These are the covenant people of God. It is not as if God has never disclosed himself to them. The corporate mind of the ten tribes of the northern kingdom has all but abandoned its heritage. When Elijah challenges the people with the words, "How long will you waver between two opinions? If the LORD is God, follow him; but if Baal is God, follow him" (18:21), the people say nothing.

Yet before we indulge in too many self-righteous musings, we need to reflect on how often the church has moved away from her moorings. The Great Awakening was a powerful movement of the Spirit of God, yet a century later many of the churches that had been filled with fresh converts, robust theology, and godly living had degenerated into Unitarianism. Who would have guessed that the land of Luther and the Reformation would have given us Hitler and the Holocaust? Why is it that twentieth-century evangelicalism, as it mushroomed between, say, 1930 and 1960, soon bred varieties of self-designated evangelicals whom no evangelical leader of the earlier period would have recognized as such? The sad reality is that human memory is short, selective, and self-serving. Moreover, each new generation begins with a slightly different baseline. Since all its members need conversion, the church is never more than a generation or two from extinction. If we forget this simple point, it becomes all too easy to rest on our laurels when we are comfortable, and somehow lose sight of our mission, not to say of our Maker and Redeemer.

The setup on Mount Carmel was spectacular: one prophet against 850, Yahweh against Baal—and Baal was often thought of as the god of fire. It is as if Elijah has set up the contest on Baal's turf. His mocking words whip up the false prophets into an orgy of self-flagellation (18:28). By God's instruction (18:36), Elijah increases the odds by soaking the sacrifice he is preparing. Then, in the evening, his own brief prayer brings down explosive fire from heaven, and the people cry, "The LORD—he is God! The LORD—he is God!" (18:39). And in response to Elijah's intercessory prayer, the rain comes again to the parched land.

Something deep in the hearts of many Christians cries, "Do it again!"—not, of course, exactly the same thing, but a focused confrontation that elicits decisive and massive confession of the living God.

But did even this change Israel? Why or why not?

∿

1 Kings 19; 1 Thessalonians 2; Daniel 1; Psalm 105

∼

DOUBTLESS ELIJAH EXPECTED THAT, after the triumphant confrontation on Mount Carmel, Israel would turn back to the living God (**1 Kings 19**). As he had executed the false prophets, so Queen Jezebel herself would be eliminated—by the popular demand of an outraged populace determined to be faithful and loyal to the covenant. Perhaps even King Ahab would repent and come on board.

It doesn't work out that way. King Ahab reports everything that has happened to Jezebel, and Jezebel lets Elijah know that he is as good as dead (19:2). The people are nowhere to be seen. "Elijah was afraid and ran for his life" (19:3), we are told. In fact, a textual variant (which may be original) reads "Elijah saw, and ran for his life"—i.e., he now saw the dimensions of the whole problem, and ran. He heads south to Beersheba on the southern edge of the kingdom of Judah, drops off his servant, and keeps on going. Eventually he arrives at Mount Horeb, the site of the giving of the Law. He is so deeply depressed he wants to die (19:4). Worse, he succumbs to not a little self-pity: everybody else has rejected God, all the Israelites have broken the covenant, all the prophets except Elijah have been put to death—"I am the only one left, and now they are trying to kill me too" (19:10).

One can sympathize with Elijah's despair. In part, it is grounded in unfulfilled expectations. He thought that all that had taken place would trigger massive renewal. Now he feels not only isolated, but betrayed. And yet:

(1) He has his facts wrong. He knows that at least a hundred of the Lord's prophets are still alive, even if they are in hiding (18:13).

(2) He is not in a fit state to judge the hearts of all the Israelites. Some may be loyal to Yahweh, but terrified of Jezebel, and therefore keeping their heads down. After all, isn't that what he himself is doing?

(3) God himself assures Elijah that he has "reserved" for himself seven thousand people who have never bowed to Baal and never kissed him (19:18). Here is the beginning of a major biblical theme—the doctrine of the remnant. The covenant community as a whole may become apostate, but God Almighty still "reserves" for himself a faithful remnant—which in the fullness of time will become the nucleus of the fledgling New Testament church.

(4) God sometimes works and speaks in quiet ways, not in massive confrontation (19:11-13).

(5) Sooner or later even the strongest leaders, *especially* the strongest leaders, need a younger apprentice and helper to come alongside, shoulder part of the burden, and finally take over the work (19:19-21).

∼

1 Kings 20; 1 Thessalonians 3; Daniel 2; Psalm 106

∾

THE INTENSITY OF THE RELATIONSHIP between Paul and his converts surfaces again and again. There is never a trace of mere professionalism in Paul. For all that he is prepared on occasion to stand on his apostolic authority, his stance toward churches he has founded is never one of distant superiority. When Paul found himself unable to visit the Thessalonian believers to find out how they were getting on—and in this case he was especially concerned since his entire ministry in Thessalonica lasted only about a month, so that these believers were not as well grounded as most converts—Paul determined to send Timothy to find out (**1 Thess. 3:1-2**). Now that Timothy has rejoined Paul in Athens, bringing with him wonderful reports of the Thessalonians' faith and love (3:6—two elements in the Pauline triad; see October 11 meditation), not to mention their loyalty to Paul and to the apostolic gospel, Paul's joy knows no bounds: "Therefore, brothers, in all our distress and persecution we were encouraged about you because of your faith. For now we really live, since you are standing firm in the Lord" (3:7-8). Even that is not enough. Paul exclaims, "How can we thank God enough for you in return for all the joy we have in the presence of our God because of you?" (3:9).

This in turn triggers Paul's disclosure of how he prays for the Thessalonians.

(1) Paul constantly prays ("Night and day," he says), "most earnestly," that somehow he will be able to return to Thessalonica "and supply what is lacking in your faith" (3:10-11). This fledgling church has enjoyed little grounding. Paul feels an enormous weight of responsibility to supply it, to outline the whole counsel of God, articulate the Gospel comprehensively, teach these brothers and sisters how the Bible is put together, and provide a clear vision of the proper object of their faith so that their (subjective) faith will be well grounded.

(2) Meanwhile, he prays that the love of the Thessalonians for each other will "increase and overflow" (3:12). Paul knows that a Christian community that loves well not only reflects the Gospel in life, but provides the nurturing framework in which biblical teaching is taken on board. A squabbling community drives people away. Moreover, in this culture many relationships were established on the basis of obligation. A "benefactor" provided something, and the recipient owed the benefactor certain obeisance or service. By contrast, Paul wants Christians to transcend such cultural limitations, and so live that *every* Christian constantly discharges the "obligation" to love one another, vastly outstripping mere tit-for-tat niggardliness.

(3) Paul prays that God himself will strengthen the Thessalonian believers so to live that they will be ready for the return of Jesus (3:13).

∾

1 Kings 21; 1 Thessalonians 4; Daniel 3; Psalm 107

∾

IN 1 THESSALONIANS 4, Paul once again provides explicit instruction to his converts on how to live (see meditation for October 4). Although his time with the Thessalonians was brief, Paul can look back on those few weeks and comment, "Finally, brothers, we instructed you *how to live in order to please God,* as in fact you are living" (4:1). In what follows in this chapter, there are four areas of such instruction (and still more in the next chapter, though we shall not pursue them here). The first three of these "how to live" paragraphs are laced with theological terminology and motivations; the fourth is primarily theological in its argumentation, but the reason for writing is entirely practical.

(1) Paul insists that God's will for the Thessalonians is that they be "sanctified" (4:3). Although for Paul sanctification is often *definitional* or *positional* (i.e., he is thinking of the way believers have been sanctified in Christ at the moment of their conversion, in other words, set aside for God and his use; see meditation for August 27), here he is thinking of the entailments of conversion in the way believers live. In particular, he is concerned with the sexual arena. The Greek text of verse 4 could mean "learn to control his own body" (in the sexual arena), or "learn to live with his own wife" (in honorable sexual harmony, not sexual exploitation or manipulation), or even "learn to acquire a wife" (in an honorable way, not in a relationship based on nothing more than lust). The fact that "God did not call us to be impure, but to live a holy life" (4:7) has immediate bearing on our sexual conduct.

(2) Love in the Christian community is a mark that a church has been "taught by God." However excellent the reputation of the Thessalonians in this respect, Paul urges improvement (4:9-10).

(3) Christian ambition should aim at quiet faithfulness, minding one's business, and working hard so as not to be a burden to others. Judging by the frequency with which Paul returns to this theme, one suspects that more than a few idle people filled the church's ranks in Thessalonica (5:14; 2 Thess. 3:11-13).

(4) The last paragraph (4:13-18) concerns "those who fall asleep," whom the context shows to be Christians who have died. What befalls them? Apparently Paul had not had the time to flesh out much on such matters while he was still with them. Not wanting them to be ignorant (4:13), he sketches what happens. But the point to observe is that this doctrine is shaped to assuage any grief that befalls bereaved believers: we sorrow, but not "like the rest of men, who have no hope" (4:13). Instruction on how to live even extends to how to grieve.

∾

1 Kings 22; 1 Thessalonians 5; Daniel 4; Psalms 108—109

∾

THE LAST CHAPTER OF 1 KINGS, **1 Kings 22**, many believers find troubling. For here God himself is presented as sending out "a lying spirit" (22:22) who will deceive King Ahab and lead him to his destruction. Does God approve of liars?

The setting is instructive. For once, the kingdom of Judah and the kingdom of Israel are pulling together against the king of Aram, instead of tearing at each other's throats. Jehoshaphat, king of Judah, comes across as a good man who is largely desirous of adhering to the covenant and being loyal to God, yet is a bit of a wimp. He treats the prospective military expedition as if it were an adventure, but he does want Ahab, king of Israel, to "seek the counsel of the LORD" (22:5). After the false prophets have finished, Jehoshaphat has sufficient smarts to ask if there is some other prophet of the Lord, and Micaiah surfaces. Yet despite Micaiah's warnings, he goes off with Ahab, and even agrees to retain his royal robes while Ahab's identity is masked.

But the heart of the issue turns on Micaiah. Observe:

(1) Implicitly, Ahab has surrounded himself with religious yes-men who will tell him what he wants to hear. The reason he hates Micaiah is because what Micaiah says about him is bad. Like all leaders who surround themselves with yes-men, Ahab sets himself up to be deceived.

(2) When Micaiah begins with a sarcastic positive prognostication (22:15), Ahab instantly recognizes that Micaiah is not telling the truth (22:16). This hints at a conscience more than a little troubled. After all, God had previously told Ahab that because of his guilt in the matter of Naboth, dogs would one day lick up his blood (21:19). He thus *expected* bad news someday, and at a deep level of his being could not really trust the happy forecasts of his domesticated "prophets."

(3) When Micaiah tells him of impending disaster, he also provides a dramatic reason for the coherence and unanimity of the false prophets: God himself had sanctioned a deceitful spirit. Ahab's time has come: he will be destroyed. God's sovereignty extends even over the means to send Ahab's tame prophets a "strong delusion" (compare 2 Thess. 2:11-12). Yet the fact that Ahab is *told* all this demonstrates that God is still graciously providing him with access to the truth. But Ahab is so far gone that he cannot stomach the truth. In a ridiculous response, he believes enough of the truth to hide his own identity in the hordes of common soldiers, but not enough to stay away from Ramoth Gilead. So he dies: God's sovereign judgment is enacted, not least because Ahab, hearing both the truth and the lie, preferred the lie.

∾

2 Kings 1; 2 Thessalonians 1; Daniel 5; Psalms 110—111

∾

I ONCE HEARD A PASTOR PREACH THROUGH **2 Thessalonians 1** under the following outline:

1. A good church going through a rough time (1:3-4)
2. A good God waiting for the right time (1:5-10)
3. A good man praying in the meantime (1:11-12)

Today I wish to reflect a little on the second point.

(1) Paul can speak of the Thessalonians being "worthy" of the kingdom of God that will come in consummated power when Jesus returns (1:5, 11). The context shows that Paul is not supposing that somehow they become worthy enough to be accepted by God in the first place. The idea, rather, is that, having become Christians, they are manifesting Christian faith and love (1:3-4), and are persevering in the Christian way despite suffering and trials (1:4-5). This continued display of grace under fire, this perseverance, is evidence of what is going on in their lives, and "as a result you will be counted worthy of the kingdom." In other words, genuine Christians, by God's grace, persevere in the Gospel, and this marks out their fitness for the consummation. In this sense they prove "worthy."

(2) "God is just" (1:6). Therefore there will be payback time for those who have cruelly opposed his people (1:7) and ignored his Word (1:8). When Christ returns he "will punish those who do not know God and do not obey the gospel of our Lord Jesus" (1:8). What is presupposed is that the perfections of God's justice are not manifest until Jesus returns. Some outworking of his justice is displayed in this broken world, but let's face it: in this world, many evil people seem to get away with a lot, and many people of extraordinary goodness suffer a lot. Wise parents often tell their children, "Life isn't fair. Don't expect it to be." Yet at the same time, God is "fair"; he is perfectly just. But do not expect his justice to be manifested in instantaneous rewards and retribution. His time scale is not ours. Life isn't fair on our time scale. When Jesus returns, however, not only will justice be done, it will be seen to be done.

(3) At that time, Christ himself, and not any of us individuals, is the center of everything. Because of Christ's centrality, punishment is almost *defined* in terms of being "shut out from the presence of the Lord and from the majesty of his power," thereby being "punished with everlasting destruction" (1:9). Conversely, among his saints, his "holy people," that same Lord Jesus will be "glorified" and "marveled at among all those who have believed" (1:10). If Christ were not there, heaven would be hell.

∾

2 Kings 2; 2 Thessalonians 2; Daniel 6; Psalms 112—113

∾

IT HAS ALWAYS BEEN EASY to get things wrong about the return of Jesus. Sometimes this springs from ignorance, sometimes from a distorted emphasis. Judging from **2 Thessalonians 2:1-12**, such dangers have been present since the early church.

We maintain plenty of our own skewed interpretations about these matters today. For example, because in 1 Thessalonians 4:17 Paul writes, "After that, we who are still alive and are left will be caught up together with them in the clouds to meet the Lord in the air," many contemporary scholars hold that Paul thought the Lord's return would take place during his own lifetime, and of course he was wrong. In reality, 1 Thessalonians 4:17 no more proves Paul believed Christ would return during his lifetime than 1 Corinthians 6:14 proves he thought Christ would *not* return in his lifetime. There Paul writes, "By his power God raised the Lord from the dead, *and he will raise us also.*" Although he uses the first person in both places, Paul is simply identifying himself with the Christians who will enjoy these experiences—whether meeting the Lord and thus escaping death, or dying and ultimately rising from the dead. Yet the contemporary misconception on this point is widespread.

The misconception behind 2 Thessalonians 2:1-12 is not entirely clear, but apparently the Thessalonians had received a letter falsely purporting to be from Paul but lacking his well-known handwriting and signature at the end (which is why Paul draws the attention of his readers to these features in 3:17). That deceptive letter somehow convinced some Thessalonians that "the day of the Lord" had already come (2:1-2); either they had in some way been abandoned, or else they were being taught some sort of "over-realized" eschatology that tried to reserve all the blessings of salvation for the present. Perhaps there is immortality beyond death, but under this vision there is no need for a personal return of Jesus Christ, or a crisis of judgment and triumphant reign.

So Paul gives some reasons for saying that the day of the Lord has *not* come. In this he is following the example of the Lord Jesus, who also gave some instruction about those who would falsely identify someone as the Christ (Matt. 24:23-27). Certain things must take place before the Lord Jesus returns, and then he will decisively and unambiguously destroy the opposition "with the breath of his mouth" and "by the splendor of his coming" (2:8). The lies may even be surrounded and supported by "counterfeit miracles, signs and wonders" (2:9); at heart, however, people perish because they refuse to love the truth (2:10). Sooner or later God pronounces judgment by sending the delusion they much prefer.

∾

2 Kings 3; 2 Thessalonians 3; Daniel 7; Psalms 114—115

THE PASSAGE IN **2 Thessalonians 3:6-13** is unique in the New Testament. Nowhere else do we find so many lines devoted to the sin of idleness.

Certainly it is possible to transform work itself, or the rewards that stem from work, into an idol. That is often what people have in mind when they speak disparagingly of the "Protestant work ethic." Still, one must insist that the proper response to the sin of making work an idol is not leisure: that may simply make leisure and hedonism an idol. The proper response is repentance, and faith in and obedience toward God. Then work must find its proper place in a world framed by God and his Word.

Readers of the Bible cannot help but notice that God says a great deal more about work than about leisure. The much-maligned "Protestant work ethic" began rather simply: devout Christians thought they should offer all their work to God. That guaranteed that, on the whole, they worked somewhat harder and a great deal more honestly than many others. The inevitable happened: many of them prospered. Of course, two or three generations on, many began focusing on the work itself, either as the essential mark of piety, or as a means to win prosperity, or both—and sometimes God was squeezed to the periphery. But while we rightly seek to condemn work as idolatry, we should be very careful about swinging the pendulum the other way, and seeing work as something that merely has to be done, so that we can get on with the really important thing: having fun and serving self. Biblically speaking, it is difficult to see how this stance is an improvement in any sense.

We do not know exactly what prompted a number of the Thessalonian believers to be lazy. Perhaps some were simply sponging off the generosity of Christians. Certainly some were less interested in being busy than in being "busybodies" (3:11). But Paul will not have it. This is not a case of Christians needing to show compassion to those genuinely in need. Rather, this is a case of Christians needing to crack the whip against those who claim they are Christians but who disobey the apostle's explicit injunctions (3:12) and ignore his remarkable personal conduct (3:7-9). He worked (i.e., at his trade), precisely to teach the point: "If a man will not work, he shall not eat" (3:10). Now Paul goes a step farther: responsible Christians are to shun these shysters, to keep away from them entirely (3:6). That way they cannot corrupt the church. More importantly, outsiders will not confuse the conduct of such people with the conduct of Christians who happily take on apostolic instruction.

2 Kings 4; 1 Timothy 1; Daniel 8; Psalm 116

SOME YEARS AGO I RECEIVED a letter from someone who told me that he had read one of my books and was upset that I had often referred to the Lord Jesus Christ as "Jesus." He quoted several passages about confessing Jesus as Lord (e.g., Rom. 10:9), and how such confession is the mark of having the Spirit (1 Cor. 12:3). I wrote back, explaining that when I refer to the Lord Jesus Christ as Jesus, I am not thereby *denying* his lordship. Rather, I am not *at that point* affirming it. Further, the book he had read dealt with one of the synoptic Gospels. In the Gospels, the Lord Jesus is most commonly referred to simply as "Jesus." So since I was commenting on one of the Gospels, I tended to refer to Jesus in the same way that Scripture does. When expounding some passage from, say, Paul, I tend to use, predominantly, the forms for addressing or referring to Jesus that the apostle uses.

I received back from him a multi-page document giving most of the passages that refer to Jesus as Lord, offering many reasons for the importance of such a confession, and much more of the same. He did not respond to a single point in my letter: I was merely fodder for his tirade.

It was not worth answering. From his vantage point, he was upholding the Gospel. To me, he was more than a little like people to whom Paul refers: "They want to be teachers of the law, but they do not know what they are talking about or what they so confidently affirm" (**1 Tim. 1:7**).

Of course, Paul has particular opponents in mind, and their profile does not exactly match that of my letter writer. Nevertheless, in every generation there are people circulating in and around the church who teach "false doctrines" (1:3) and devote themselves to peripheral matters. One chap I taught in an evening school became convinced he had the key to the Scriptures by some elaborate typology of circumcision. Another has written me from Australia, offering a massive synthesis that is remarkably silly, and condemning all the publishers because they are so narrow-minded and heterodox they won't give his views the airing he thinks they deserve. Yet another has written voluminous and repeated letters insisting I should publish his manuscript because the entire world needs to read it.

What these people have in common is false doctrine, a focus on peripheral matters (even if not genealogies, 1:4) that distort what is central, and an arrogance that discloses itself in endless "meaningless talk" (1:6). What they lack is the goal of the gospel command, which is love, and sincere faith promoting God's work (1:4-5).

2 Kings 5; 1 Timothy 2; Daniel 9; Psalms 117—118

❧

CURRENT AGENDAS MEAN THAT WHEN 1 Timothy 2 is referred to in contemporary discussions, usually the focus is on 2:11-15. So we shall reflect on **1 Timothy 2:1-7**.

(1) Transparently, Paul urges that Christians pray for all who are in authority (2:1-2). The primary end of such praying is "that we may live peaceful and quiet lives in all godliness and holiness" (2:2). God's sovereignty extends beyond the church to all the affairs of humankind. Paul knows well that an ordered and secure society is conducive to regular, disciplined living, and therefore to "godliness and holiness."

(2) When Paul says "This is good," it is not immediately clear whether *this* refers to the godly living he wants displayed among believers, or to the prayers that they are supposed to raise to Almighty God on behalf of those who are in authority. If the former, then the connection with what follows must be along these lines: if we live godly lives, our very living will bear evangelistic witness to the people all around us whom God wants "to come to a knowledge of the truth" (2:4). If the reference is to our praying, then the connection with what follows is a little different: Paul is saying that we should pray for those in authority, not only to the end that society may be stable, but to the end that they may be saved—since God wants all people to come to a knowledge of the truth.

(3) Either way, the assumption is that God is vitally interested in the conversion of people everywhere. This is not at all at odds with what the Bible elsewhere says about election. Doubtless God exercises a special love toward his elect. Nevertheless, the Bible constantly portrays God as crying out, in effect, "Turn! Turn! For the Lord has no pleasure in the death of the wicked." His stance toward his fallen image-bearers, however much characterized by righteousness and judgment, includes this element of yearning for their salvation.

(4) In this context 1 Timothy 2:5 says, in effect, that the doctrine of monotheism has an entailment: if there is but one God, then he must be the God of all, whether recognized as such or not. If there is but one mediator between God and fallen human beings, then the only hope for any human being is that one mediator.

(5) Potentially, then, he is the ransom for all men and women everywhere (2:6). There is no other mediator. He is not the mediator of the Jews only. In "its proper time" (2:6) this truth has been made clear—and it lies at the heart of the apostolic gospel that Paul has been appointed to preach, not least among the Gentiles.

❧

2 Kings 6; 1 Timothy 3; Daniel 10; Psalm 119:1-24

∾

IN THE NEW TESTAMENT, there are two explicit church offices. On the one hand, there are *pastors* (the word comes from the Latin expression for "shepherds"), who are also called *elders* or *overseers* (the word rendered "bishops" in older translations). On the other hand, there are *deacons*. It was not until the second century that *bishops* became a kind of third rank of ecclesiastical authority, supervising several pastors/elders under them.

So when Paul briefly outlines the criteria for becoming an "overseer" (**1 Tim. 3:1-7**), he is in fact providing the criteria of the pastoral office. Brief reflection on some of his points may be of help:

(1) At one level, the standards Paul provides are not particularly elevated or difficult. There is nothing about an elite education, a certain kind of personality, belonging to the aristocratic sectors of society, or displaying a certain kind of leadership capability. The list includes things like not getting drunk, not being quarrelsome, and the like.

(2) With the exception of only two qualifications, everything else in this list is elsewhere mandated of *all* Christians. For instance, if the overseer is to be "hospitable" (3:2), the same thing is laid on all Christians in Hebrews 13:2. If Christian pastors are not to be "given to drunkenness" (3:3), neither should any other Christian be. In other words, what must characterize the Christian pastor, in the first instance, is that he display the kinds of graces and signs of maturity that are being imposed on all believers without exception. So the Christian elder is to be a model of what Christian living should look like. In that sense the standards *as a whole* are high indeed.

(3) The two that are distinctive are as follows: (a) The Christian pastor must be "able to teach" (3:2). That presupposes both knowledge and the ability to communicate it. That is the *distinctive* function of this office. (b) Christian pastors must not be recent converts (3:6). Obviously that excludes some Christians. What "recent convert" means will doubtless vary according to the age and maturity of the church, as the criterion is necessarily relative to how recently others have been converted.

(4) The tight connection between the home and the church (3:4-5) is quite startling. Not every Christian father is eligible to be an elder in the church; every Christian father is nevertheless presupposed to have elderlike functions to discharge in his own home.

(5) Several of the qualifications are bound up with the distinctive responsibility of this office. If he is to teach, the elder must be hospitable, maintain a good reputation with outsiders, not prove quarrelsome, and be untouched by money's attractions. A merely bookish theologian with no love for people will not do.

∾

2 Kings 7; 1 Timothy 4; Daniel 11; Psalm 119:25-48

WHEN I WAS STILL A VERY YOUNG MAN, I became pastor of a smallish church in Canada. The people were very kind toward me, and were far more patient of my faults and errors than I deserved.

There was one woman in that church whom I sometimes found to be particularly exasperating. Almost every Sunday morning, she would thank me profusely for the sermon, and then add, "But you're so young." This went on for many weeks, until it was little more than a formula. Eventually my zeal exceeded my sense. After listening yet again to her formulaic outburst "You're so young," I smiled sweetly and remarked (citing the King James Version in those days), "Yes, but Scripture says, 'Let no man despise thy youth'—no man." However intemperate my outburst, it seemed to do the trick, for she never said anything like that to me again.

On reflection, however, I came to realize I had cited the first part of **1 Timothy 4:12**, but not the last part. The first part reads, "Don't let anyone look down on you because you are young." I suppose if that line of text stood all by itself, then one of the ways to stop others from looking down on you when you are young is to clobber them with this text. But Paul writes, "Don't let anyone look down on you because you are young, *but set an example for the believers in speech, in life, in love, in faith and in purity.*" In other words, if you are a young believer, not least a young believer in a position of leadership like Timothy, the way to stop others from looking down on you is to set such an example—"in speech, in life, in love, in faith and in purity"—that your transparent godliness silences them.

If you are diligent in the gifts and graces that God has given you, Paul adds, everyone will see your progress (4:15). Your diligence must be comprehensive, and the places where others detect your progress will also be encompassing: "Watch your life and doctrine closely" (4:16). The result will include not only your own perseverance issuing in the salvation of the consummation, but the salvation of many of those to whom you minister (4:16).

Embedded in this counsel to a young man is an array of Christian moral teaching. Actions often speak louder than words. Christian leaders are to lead not only by words but by action in conformity with those words. The authority that accrues to a Christian leader is gained not so much from the office itself, as earned over time by the quality of the Christian living. Small wonder then that much of the next chapter is given over to specific instruction on how to treat brothers and sisters in Christ in varied stations of life. *How to treat people* is always near the center of Christian discipleship.

2 Kings 8; 1 Timothy 5; Daniel 12; Psalm 119:49-72

∾

ALTHOUGH I DID NOT KNOW IT, while I was in my last year of high school my parents made a quiet vow before the Lord. For reasons too complicated to go into here, they decided that unless certain things happened, at the end of the year Dad would resign from the pastoral charge he had maintained for fifteen years.

I finished school, left home, and went off to university. Within a month or so I received a letter from my parents: Dad had resigned as pastor of that church.

My parents had very little money. There was no other French-speaking church that was open to him. At this juncture Dad felt too old to start another church in another locale. He refused to consider pastorates in English Canada: both his call and his heart were tied up with Quebec. So I found out what my parents had decided: they were moving to Hull, on the French side of the river across from Ottawa, the nation's capital, where Dad would support his family as a federal translator, and give as much time as he could to the French-speaking church in Hull.

I did not get "home" until Christmas. Somewhere along the line I probed my father to try to understand his reasoning. Granted his conviction that he should stay in a French-speaking part of Canada, the question soon arose as to how he would support his family. "For Scripture says," Dad explained, "that if a man does not support his own family, he is worse than an infidel": he was using the King James Version form of words of **1 Timothy 5:8**: "If anyone does not provide for his relatives, and especially for his immediate family, he has denied the faith and is worse than an unbeliever."

Obviously this text has some exceptions. If a man is too ill to work, for example, he is exempt—and judging by the tone of the entire chapter, the church itself should pick up whatever support is necessary, if the family cannot manage. But what strikes the reader about many of the instructions in this chapter is the way the church's provision for the social needs of her people is prescribed with extraordinary sensitivity to the dangers. At the risk of oversimplification, the pattern Paul lays out can be summarized like this: those in genuine need are looked after by the church, but those with the capacity to find their way and support themselves must do so—both so as not to be a burden on the church, and for their own good—or be charged with abandoning the faith. Laziness is not next to godliness.

I cannot think of many times when I had greater respect for Dad's obedient faith.

∾

2 Kings 9; 1 Timothy 6; Hosea 1; Psalm 119:73-96

∾

IT IS WORTH COMPARING the anointing of David (1 Sam. 16) with the anointing of Jehu (**2 Kings 9**)—or, more precisely, it is worth comparing not only the two anointings, but what follows from the two anointings.

The story of David is the better known (1 Sam.). When Samuel anointed him to be king, David was still a young man, a youthful shepherd. The anointing changed nothing of his immediate situation. In due course he gained heroic dimensions by defeating Goliath and then maturing into an efficient and loyal officer of King Saul. When Saul became embittered and paranoid, forcing David to hide in the hill country of Judea, David seemed a long way from the throne. Providence gave him two startling opportunities to kill Saul, but David restrained himself; indeed, he even restrained some of his own men who were quite prepared to do the deed that David would not touch. His reasoning was simple. Though he knew he would be king, he also knew that at the moment Saul was king. The same God who had anointed David had first installed Saul. To kill Saul was therefore to kill the Lord's anointed. He was unwilling to grasp the inheritance that the Lord himself had promised him, if the price to be paid was an immoral act. God had promised him the throne; God would first have to vacate it of its current incumbent, for David would not stoop to intrigue and murder. This was one of David's finest hours.

How different is Jehu! When he is anointed, he is assigned the task of punishing and destroying the wicked household of Ahab. But he waits for no providential sign: as far as he is concerned, his anointing is incentive enough to embark immediately on a bloody insurrection. Moreover, for all his pious talk about wiping out the idolatry of the wretched household of Ahab (e.g., 9:22), his own heart is betrayed by two evil realities. *First,* he not only assassinates the current incumbent of the throne of Israel, but when he has the opportunity he kills Ahaziah, the king of Judah as well (9:27-29), not sanctioned by the prophet, however. Did Jehu perhaps entertain visions of a restored, united kingdom, brought together by assassination and military power? *Second,* although Jehu reduced the power of Baal worship, he promoted other forms of idolatry no less repugnant to God (10:28-31). Unlike David, he was not "a man after God's own heart" (cf. 1 Sam. 13:14). Far from it: "He did not turn away from the sins of Jeroboam, which he had caused Israel to commit" (10:31).

The lesson is important. Not even divine prophecy frees a person from the obligations of morality, integrity, and loyal and obedient faith in God. The end does not justify the means.

∾

2 Kings 10—11; 2 Timothy 1; Hosea 2; Psalm 119:97-120

∾

IN THE TWO DESIGNATED PASSAGES for this day we find a study of two grand-mothers.

The first is Athaliah (**2 Kings 11**). She is the utterly vile mother of Ahaziah, the king of Judah who was killed by Jehu (as we saw yesterday) in the mayhem pre-cipitated by the insurrection in the northern kingdom of Israel. One could imag-ine a lot of different actions that a queen mother might take on learning of the assassination of her son. Athaliah's reaction is to kill her entire family. She so com-mands the palace guard that her dead son's children and grandchildren are wiped out, save for her infant grandson Joash, who is saved by an aunt (who herself may have been killed) who hides him with his wet nurse. Thus Athaliah secures power for herself.

A few years later, when Joash is still but a lad of seven, Jehoiada the priest arranges to bring the child out and have him declared the rightful king, protected by military units loyal to Jehoiada and his determination to preserve the Davidic line. When Athaliah discovers the plot, her cries of "Treason!" (11:14) ring a lit-tle hollow. For the sake of power, this evil woman was willing not only to com-mit murder (not a rare thing), but to murder her children and grandchildren—a much rarer thing, immeasurably more callous—and now she charges with trea-son those who call her to account.

Contrast the mother and grandmother briefly mentioned in **2 Timothy 1:5**. Timothy's grandmother Lois and his mother Eunice are women of "sincere faith," according to Paul, and they have passed this heritage on to their son and grand-son, Timothy. How they did this is not detailed. But judging by patterns laid out elsewhere in Scripture, the least they did was display personal example and pro-vide concrete instruction. They passed on both the teaching of Scripture and the pattern of their own "sincere faith"—not only the pattern of their own walk with God, but the integrity that characterized their lives as a result. Indeed, hidden in this passage lies hope for men or women in mixed marriages. According to Acts 16:1, Timothy's mother Eunice was both a Jewess and a Christian believer; his father was a Greek, apparently a pagan. The Christian influence prevailed.

Not all women are as evil as Athaliah; not all are as faithful as Lois and Eunice. Among both men and women, however, are not a few who, in home, at work, even in church, are much more interested in power than in anything else. They may not stoop to murder, but they will lie, cheat, and slander to gain more authority. They will face God's judgment. But blessed are those whose sincere faith stamps the next generation.

∾

2 Kings 12; 2 Timothy 2; Hosea 3—4; Psalm 119:121-144

∾

ONE OF THE MANY PRACTICAL DECISIONS a busy pastor has to face is whether to engage some particular error that rears its head.

The factors that go into that sort of decision are many. How many people are actually being affected by it? Is it threatening to split the church, or is it the fixation of only one or two people? Is it about some relatively peripheral matter, or does it go to the heart of the Gospel? Is it something about which the Bible is really quite clear, or does it concern something on which the Bible does not pronounce anything very substantial? Moreover, even when the issue is clearly important, one must make sober decisions about how much time and energy you should devote to it. Too little, and many of your flock may be adversely affected; too much, and you are being drawn away from what should be the primary focus of your ministry; you will gradually get sucked into a sea so vast you will never again see the shore.

Over the years I have been invited to address any number of "problems" or "interpretations" that have lasted no more than a few months or a few years. It may be expedient to do the studying necessary to engage a few of them; anything more is a waste of time. Just a month or so before the "Heaven's Gate" mass suicide, this cult sent me (and doubtless many others) one of their videos and a great deal of literature. I spent all of ten minutes scanning the literature to see where it was going. It was such unadulterated rubbish I filed it away, hoping I would never have to respond to this particular brand of nonsense. A few weeks later, most of the adherents were dead.

Two years ago a pastor phoned me and berated me because I had not yet responded with anything substantive to Michael Drosnin's book, *The Bible Code*. Out of interest I had accumulated a fairly substantial file, but that was not enough for this pastor: he felt that the people in his church were terribly vulnerable, and he insisted that I spend some time working on it. I refused. Two months later I discovered that the person in his church most fixated by this problem was the pastor himself, who could not leave the subject alone.

What a welcome contrast, then, to hear Paul telling Timothy what to say to new generations of pastors: "Warn them before God against quarreling about words; it is of no value, and only ruins those who listen" (**2 Tim. 2:14**). Or again: "Don't have anything to do with foolish and stupid arguments, because you know they produce quarrels" (2:23). Answer when you must; never fixate on the peripheral; do not lose the focus on what is primary; do not be enticed into stupid arguments. The real issues are simply too important.

∾

2 Kings 13; 2 Timothy 3; Hosea 5—6; Psalm 119:145-176

∿

LIFE IN "THE LAST DAYS" (**2 Tim. 3**) does not sound very appealing: "People will be lovers of themselves, lovers of money, boastful, proud, abusive, disobedient to their parents, ungrateful, unholy, without love, unforgiving, slanderous, without self-control, brutal, not lovers of the good, treacherous, rash, conceited, lovers of pleasure rather than lovers of God—having a form of godliness but denying its power" (3:2-5). Endless sins of sensuality combine with multiplying information so wedded to a corrupt epistemology that people cannot acknowledge the truth (3:6-7). That is what life is like in "the last days." The immediacy of the warning for Paul's readers is one of several signals that Paul thinks these "last days" range from Christ's ascension to his return.

So what must we do about it?

First, we must resolve to follow the best mentors (3:10-11). These are the people whose lives reflect the Gospel, and who have been tested by hardship and protected by God. In a world of many pop idols, not least in the field of religion, we must become intentional about choosing the best mentors, or by default we shall probably choose poor ones.

Second, we must be realistic about the world (3:12-13). We should expect opposition. If we do, we shall not be surprised by it. When Paul says that "evil men and impostors will go from bad to worse, deceiving and being deceived" (3:13), he is probably not saying that each generation will be worse than the previous one, but that in every generation evil people spiral downward into hopeless corruptions. We should not be surprised by this. Apart from the intervention of the grace of God, this is what sin does to people.

Third, we must rely on the Bible (3:14-17). Not only do the Scriptures shape the Christian's mind into a worldview profoundly alien to the secularist and the endlessly selfish person, and not only do the Scriptures make us "wise for salvation through faith in Christ Jesus" (3:15), but precisely because they are "God-breathed," the Scriptures are "useful for teaching, rebuking, correcting, and training in righteousness" (3:16). The danger in contemporary evangelicalism is not formal rejection of Scripture, but an unrealistic assumption that we know the Bible while in fact we press "on" (in reality, slouch backwards) toward endless conferences on leadership, techniques, tools, gimmicks, agendas. Some of these might even be useful if the Bible itself were not so commonly sidelined.

Fourth—though this takes us into the next chapter—we must proclaim the Bible (4:1-5). Nothing else has transforming power. Verse 2 prescribes the content, the constancy, the scope, and the manner of such preaching in the last days.

∿

2 Kings 14; 2 Timothy 4; Hosea 7; Psalms 120—122

ONE OF THE ATTRACTIVE AND DISTURBING things about the Bible is its realism. Simplistic idealism would very much like the "good" people to be more or less consistently rewarded, and to be fruitful and blessed in their work; similarly, it would like the "bad" people to turn out to be failures. Doubtless on the longest haul, before God's tribunal, justice will be done and will be seen to be done. Doubtless, too, there are enough temporal rewards and blessings to remind us that God is in control. But in the mystery of providence, there are also enough anomalies to remind us that ultimate justice is not found in this world. And this, of course, is true to life, the ultimate realism.

The point is well illustrated in the two kings of **2 Kings 14.** Amaziah, son of Joash, reaches the throne of Judah at the age of twenty-five. "He did what was right in the eyes of the LORD, but not as his father David had done" (14:3). Though he was not as consistent as David, he was on many fronts a good man. Even in the matter of capturing and executing the assassins of his father King Joash, Amaziah refrained from wiping out their families—a not uncommon practice at the time—for he was following the law of God (Deut. 24:16; 2 Kings 14:6). And then, after enjoying moderate military success (14:7), which apparently went to his head, he taunted the northern tribes for no good reason into a war he lost disastrously. The stupidity was gargantuan. Eventually Amaziah was himself assassinated after a twenty-nine-year reign.

By contrast, on gaining the throne of the northern kingdom Jeroboam II "did evil in the eyes of the LORD and did not turn away from any of the sins of Jeroboam son of Nebat, which he had caused Israel to commit" (14:24). Nevertheless he proved to be an able administrator and military leader. Because the Lord was sensitive to the cries of his people as they faced the crushing power of Syria to the north, he used Jeroboam II to restore the boundaries of Israel against Syrian encroachment, eventually recovering for Israel both Damascus and Hamath, which had belonged to Israel in the days of the united monarchy. Jeroboam II reigned for forty-one years and died in peace.

Observe: (1) A good king may do bad and stupid things. (2) A bad king may do good and important things. (3) It follows that one should never evaluate the morality of a leader simply on the basis of select good things or bad things they do. Even Hitler restored German confidence and created jobs. Presidents have been known to win wars and keep the economy going while living, sexually speaking, in the gutter.

2 Kings 15; Titus 1; Hosea 8; Psalms 123—125

IN SOME DENOMINATIONS, it is held that the Bible prescribes three church officers: bishops, who preside over several congregations; elders/pastors, who serve at the level of the local church, especially with respect to the ministry of the word and prayer (some would add "sacrament"), and deacons, who help in the administration of funds, especially with respect to caring for the physical needs of the flock (see the October 25 meditation).

It is widely recognized, however, that in reality the New Testament recognizes only two officers: the bishop/elder/pastor and the deacon. One of the most convincing treatments of the matter was written in the last century by J. B. Lightfoot, himself an Anglican. The breakdown into *three* divisions, he rightly contends, takes place after the New Testament documents have been written.

This means, of course, that one of the two offices enjoys three labels, partly because the work has many facets. The word *pastor* comes from a Latin root for "shepherd" (1 Peter 5:2). Shepherds feed, defend, guide, and discipline the flock. *Elder* terminology derives both from the rule of ancient villages and from synagogues: the leaders are to be mature and respected. Because *bishop* nowadays has so many ecclesiastical overtones, the NIV adopts the not uncommon practice of rendering the word "overseer" (e.g., 1 Tim. 3:1) to capture the elements of oversight, godly management, and spiritual accountability bound up with the task.

One of the reasons why so many have come to the conclusion that *bishop, elder,* and *pastor* are all words applicable to one office is that the lists of qualifications for these tasks are so similar. Thus, compare **Titus 1:6-9** regarding an elder with 1 Timothy 3:1-7 regarding an overseer (bishop).

One point of apparent divergence in the NIV calls forth pangs of conscience among some pastors. First Timothy 3:4 stipulates that the overseer "must manage his own family well and see that his children obey him with proper respect." By contrast, Titus 1:6 stipulates that the elder must be "a man *whose children believe* and are not open to the charge of being wild and disobedient." This sounds like more stringent requirements for the elder. But in fact, the NIV rendering is both mistaken and unworkable. The Greek is justifiably rendered "whose children are faithful"—in the sense that they are not "wild and disobedient." As long as the children are under their father's roof, the bishop/elder must so order his household as to demonstrate he is capable of ordering the church. If Titus 1:6 were understood as in the NIV to stipulate that his children be believers, one might well ask, "From what age?" In short, the mistranslation is also unworkable. What the text actually says aligns it well with 1 Timothy 3.

2 Kings 16; Titus 2; Hosea 9; Psalms 126—128

∿

THE BOOKS OF 1 AND 2 KINGS, though they follow the fortunes of both Judah and Israel (the southern and northern kingdoms, respectively, after the division that followed Solomon's death), lay more emphasis on Israel, the northern ten tribes. More space is devoted to Israel's kings than to Judah's. Eventually, of course, the northern kingdom collapses (see tomorrow's meditation), and then all the attention is focused on the south. By comparison, 1 and 2 Chronicles recount more or less the same history, but turn the spotlight primarily on the southern kingdom of Judah.

Even in 2 Kings, however, substantial attention is sometimes focused on one of the kings of Judah. So it is in **2 Kings 16**. By and large, the northern kings degenerated more quickly than in the south. In the south, many kings are described as following the Lord, but not as David had done; in the north, many are described as following in the footsteps of Jeroboam the son of Nebat, who caused Israel to sin. But every once in a while a really evil or stupid king arises in the south. And such is Ahaz.

Religiously and theologically, Ahaz was a disaster. "Unlike David his father, he did not do what was right in the eyes of the LORD his God. He walked in the ways of the kings of Israel and even sacrificed his son in the fire, following the detestable ways of the nations the LORD had driven out before the Israelites" (16:2-3). Politically he fared no better. Harried by Israel and Syria to his north, King Ahaz of Judah decided to strip the temple of its wealth and send it to King Tiglath-Pileser of Assyria. Assyria was the rising superpower. Sending money to him as a kind of tribute, with a plea to get him to lean on Syria and Israel so as to reduce pressure on Judah, was a bit like throwing a hunk of meat to a crocodile: you could be sure that this crocodile would want more. Worse, King Ahaz became so enamored of Assyria that he introduced some of its pagan ways into the temple service. Fear turned Ahaz toward pagan power, and "deference to the king of Assyria" (16:18) fostered fresh compromises.

Contrast Hezekiah, two chapters later, who, while facing a far more serious threat from the Assyrians, brought on in no small part because of the stupidity and faithlessness of Ahaz, brooks no compromise but diligently seeks the face of God. There he discovers, in line with the experience of Moses and the fathers of Israel, that God is able to defend his people against few or many—it is all the same with him.

∿

2 Kings 17; Titus 3; Hosea 10; Psalms 129—131

∾

SECOND KINGS 17 IS A DEFINING moment in Old Testament history. The northern kingdom of Israel comes to an end as a political entity. The trigger for this last step in the destruction of the nation is a piece of deceit perpetrated by her last king, Hoshea. While nominally maintaining her allegiance to Assyria (the regional super-power), Hoshea opened negotiations with Egypt, still an impressive political and military power, in the hope that Israel could come under her umbrella under better terms. Shalmaneser, king of Assyria, could only interpret this as treason and destroyed Samaria, the capital of Israel (17:1-6). He transported the leading Israelites to Assyria and then, as the end of the chapter makes clear, imported pagans from elsewhere in the empire, who intermingled with the poor Israelites left behind.

The rest of the chapter provides us with two explicit explanations, and a subtler, implicit one.

First, the ultimate reason for the destruction of the nation was not political or military, but religious and theological (17:7-17). The nation of Israel succumbed to idolatry. While maintaining superficial allegiance to the living God, they "secretly" built up pagan high places—as if the all-seeing God could be deceived! Asherah poles and Baal worship multiplied. The people ignored the prophets God sent them. "They followed worthless idols and themselves became worthless" (17:15; cf. Jer. 2:5). Rejecting the temple in Jerusalem, they constructed two calf idols. They worshiped astrological deities, messed around in the occult, and finally sank into the abominable practice of child sacrifice to Molech. "So the LORD was very angry with Israel and removed them from his presence" (17:18).

Second, this chapter explains the origins of the syncretistic religion of Samaria (17:24-41). The immigrant pagans mingled with the remaining Jews of the land. Racially and theologically, the results were mixed. Despite warnings from God (in the form of rampaging lions—no longer found in that part of the world, but at one time plentiful), the best this breed can muster is pathetic: they "worshiped the LORD, but they also served their own gods" (17:33). This is the background to the "Samaritans" we come across in Jesus' day.

The *third* explanation is only implicit. It is obvious only when this chapter is read in the flow of canonical development. Fallen humanity is judged at the Flood; only a few survive. The patriarchs of the nascent Jewish nation end up in slavery. When God delivers them, their unbelief delays their entry into the Promised Land. The period of the judges ends in debauchery, corruption, decay. And now the period of the monarchy is winding up in similar shame.

God help us: we need a more radical answer than these.

∾

2 Kings 18; Philemon; Hosea 11; Psalms 132—134

◯

IN THE FIRST CENTURY, a slave who ran away could legally be executed. A master might not enforce that punishment, but at the very least the runaway slave who was caught would face very brutal treatment.

Onesimus is a slave who has run away from **Philemon**. Somewhere along the line, Onesimus has been converted. Whether he sought out Paul before his conversion or after, Onesimus is now with Paul, probably in Rome. The apostle is in prison awaiting trial, and Onesimus, now a believer, is running errands for him and otherwise helping him out.

But Paul knows this cannot continue. The apostle himself could be charged with aiding and abetting a fugitive. Legally, even morally, Onesimus must go back to Philemon and square things. But where is the morality in Roman slavery itself?

So Paul writes to Philemon and Apphia, knowing they are Christians, presumably well-to-do, with a home big enough to house the church where they live. The letter is a masterpiece of firm, godly diplomacy.

Paul commends Philemon for his love and encouragement (v. 7). He mentions that he could simply order him to take certain actions (v. 8), yet he prefers to appeal to him "as Paul—an old man and now also a prisoner of Christ Jesus" (v. 9) so that Philemon will act out of love. Only then does he mention Onesimus, and state what the appeal consists in. Paul wants Philemon to take back Onesimus, whom Paul characterizes as his "son," now a "useful" person (which is what the name *Onesimus* means), and so loved by the apostle that he is Paul's "very heart" (vv. 10-12). Paul would have been happy to keep him, but would not do anything without Philemon's "consent" (v. 14). Of course, Onesimus had run away, but regardless of how reprehensible that act had been, in the larger scheme of things "perhaps the reason he was separated from you for a little while [a convenient passive!] was that you might have him back for good—no longer as a slave, but better than a slave, as a dear brother" (vv. 15-16). Surely he will therefore be dear to Philemon, "both as a man and as a brother in the Lord" (v. 16).

So Philemon is to welcome back Onesimus as he would welcome the apostle himself (v. 17), who hopes to come soon on a visit that will check up on things (v. 22). Apparently Onesimus stole from Philemon when he left: Paul says he will gladly repay the full amount—though Paul gently reminds Philemon of the supreme debt he owes to the man who brought him the Gospel.

Nothing can destroy brutal relationships faster than the Gospel rightly applied.

◯

2 Kings 19; Hebrews 1; Hosea 12; Psalms 135—136

∽

THE CONTRASTS IN THE OPENING VERSES OF **Hebrews 1** all tend in the same direction. "In the past" contrasts with "in these last days." God spoke "to our forefathers" stands over against the fact that in these last days he has spoken "to us." In the past God spoke to the forefathers "through the prophets at many times and in various ways." But in these last days God has spoken to us "by his Son" (1:1-2).

Indeed, the form of that expression, "by his Son," in the original, suggests pretty strongly that the author of Hebrews does not think of the Son as one more prophet, or even as the supreme prophet. The idea is not that while in the past the word of God was mediated by prophets, in these last days the word has been mediated by the Son, who thus becomes the last of the prophets. Something more fundamental is at issue. The Greek expression, over-translated, means "in Son." The absence of the article "the" is significant. Moreover, "in Son" contrasts not only with "through the prophets" but with "through the prophets at many times and in various ways."

The point is that in these last days God has disclosed himself in the Son revelation. In the past, when God used the prophets he sometimes gave them words directly (in oracles or visions), sometimes providentially led them through experiences they recorded, sometimes "spoke" through extraordinary events such as the burning bush: there were "many times" and "various ways" (1:1). But now, God has spoken "in Son"—we might paraphrase, "in the Son revelation." It is not that Jesus simply mediates the revelation; he is the revelation. It is not that Jesus simply brings the word; he is himself, so to speak, the Word of God, the climactic Word. The idea is very similar to what one reads in the Prologue of John's Gospel. The Son is capable of this because he is "the radiance of God's glory and the exact representation of his being" (1:3).

Strictly speaking, then, Christians are not to think of the New Testament books as just like the Old Testament books, bringing the next phase of God's redemptive plan to us. Mormons argue that that is all they are—and then say that Joseph Smith brought a still later revelation to us, since he was yet another accredited prophet. But the author of Hebrews sees that the climax of all the Old Testament revelation, mediated through prophets and stored in books, is not, strictly speaking, more books—but Christ Jesus himself. The New Testament books congregate around Jesus and bear witness to him who is the climax of revelation. Later books that cannot bear witness to this climactic revelation are automatically disqualified.

∽

2 Kings 20; Hebrews 2; Hosea 13; Psalms 137—138

∾

2 KINGS 20 IS ONE OF the sadder chapters of Scripture. It pictures a man who has been faithful in the past, now withering away in the complacency of selfishness.

King Hezekiah ruled over Judah, the southern kingdom, in the waning days of the northern kingdom of Israel. Once the Assyrians had defeated Israel and transported its leading citizens, leaving behind only a shattered wreck of a nation, there was plenty of reason for discouragement in the south. But in truly heroic fashion, Hezekiah, guided in part by the prophet Isaiah, withstands the withering siege of King Sennacherib of Assyria, simply relying on the mercy of the Lord God. Sent by God himself, plague sweeps through the Assyrian camp, killing almost two hundred thousand people. Jerusalem and Judah are spared (2 Kings 18—19; Isa. 36—37). Moreover, Hezekiah's commitment to God in the early years of his reign was not characterized by the typical compromise, which maintained some sort of allegiance to Yahweh while not touching the high places and other sites of pagan worship. Far from it: he cleaned things up, earning the judgment, "He did what was right in the eyes of the LORD, just as his father David had done" (18:3-4). He even recognized that the bronze serpent Moses had made (Num. 21:4-9) had now become a superstitious snare, and destroyed it.

Then he fell ill and wept bitterly. Somehow he got himself into the position where he thought his righteous deeds meant that God *owed* him a long and prosperous life (20:2-3). In his mercy, God assigned him fifteen more years, and gave him a miraculous sign to confirm the promise (20:1-11). During that fifteen-year span, however, Hezekiah failed an important test: when emissaries came from Babylon, instead of seeking the Lord's face and walking humbly, Hezekiah played the role of a proud potentate, showing off the kingdom's rising wealth. Everything was duly recorded in the books of Babylon, in preparation for the day, more than a century later, when Babylon would be the superpower and crush Jerusalem and send her people into exile (20:12-18).

But this is not Hezekiah's most grievous lapse. When Isaiah the prophet tells him what will happen, the king does not repent of his arrogance, or seek forgiveness, or intercede with God. The threatened judgment is slated for the future: Hezekiah refuses to accept any deeply felt responsibility. He piously comments, "The word of the LORD you have spoken is good"—while the writer comments, "For he thought, 'Will there not be peace and security in my lifetime?'" (20:19). Hezekiah has become a moral and strategic pygmy.

Far better to die young after genuine, godly, achievements, than to die old and embittered, poisoning your own heritage.

∾

2 Kings 21; Hebrews 3; Hosea 14; Psalm 139

∽

MANY PEOPLE HAVE SUGGESTED that a suitable summary of the theme of Hebrews is "Jesus is better." In chapters 1—2 he is better than the angels; in chapter 3 he is better than Moses. In Hebrews 4, the rest he offers is better than the rest provided by the Promised Land. In chapters 5 and 7 his high priesthood is better than the Levitical priesthood; in chapter 8, the new covenant over which he presides is better than the old covenant. In chapters 9—10, he officiates over a better sanctuary than the tabernacle, exercises a better ministry, and offers a better sacrifice. In short, "Jesus is better." The message is designed to strengthen the hearts and minds of Jewish Christians who, though they have willingly suffered for Christ in the past, at this point are tempted to return to the Jewish rites and practices they inherited. The writer of Hebrews is afraid that they are abandoning exclusive confidence in Christ, somehow succumbing to the temptation to think that, although Jesus Christ is all right, one may gain a bit more substance, or spirituality, or historical depth, or acceptance among the kinfolk—whatever—thereby sliding toward an implicit denial that "Jesus is better."

None of this means the old covenant was bad; it simply means it was not ultimate. Thus in the brief comparison of Moses and Jesus in **Hebrews 3:1-6**, Moses, we are told, "was faithful in all God's house" (3:2); he "was faithful as a servant in all God's house, testifying to what would be said in the future" (3:5). There is not a word of reproach.

But Jesus is better. It helps to understand that in both Hebrew and Greek *house* can mean "household." Like Moses, the author of Hebrews avers, Jesus "was faithful to the one who appointed him" (3:2). Nevertheless, "Jesus has been found worthy of greater honor than Moses." Why? Because "the builder of a house has greater honor than the house itself" (3:3). That seems to suggest that Jesus' role with respect to God's "house" or "household" is radically different from that of Moses. Moses was faithful as a servant within the household, and his most important role was testifying to what was to come. Jesus is faithful as "a son over God's house" (3:6)—and that household is the community of believers (3:6). Moses appears as one servant within the household, looking to the future; Jesus appears as God's Son over the household, building that household (3:3) and proving to be the very substance of that to which Moses was pointing in the future.

However important the comparisons between the two men, the differences are the more striking.

∽

2 Kings 22; Hebrews 4; Joel 1; Psalms 140—141

∾

THE LAST SERIOUS ATTEMPT at moral and theological reformation in the kingdom of Judah is reported in **2 Kings 22**. After that, there is only the final slide into exile.

King Hezekiah, the effect of whose reign was so largely good, was succeeded by his son Manasseh. He reigned a long time, fifty-five years, but his reign was notorious for its "evil in the eyes of the LORD, following the detestable practices of the nations the LORD had driven out before the Israelites" (21:2). There was no form of current idolatry he did not adopt. According to 2 Chronicles 33, Manasseh repented toward the end of his life, but the religious and institutional damage could not easily be undone. He was succeeded by his wicked son Amon, who lasted only two years before he was assassinated (21:19-26).

Then came Josiah, a boy of eight when he came to the throne (22:1). He reigned thirty-one years—which means, of course, he died a premature death at the age of thirty-nine. Initially he would have been under the guidance and control of others. But in the eighteenth year of his reign, Josiah, then in his mid-twenties, initiated temple cleanup and repair—and the "Book of the Law" was rediscovered. Probably this refers to the book of Deuteronomy. (Nineteenth- and twentieth-century scholars of skeptical bent contend that this was in fact when Deuteronomy and other parts of the Pentateuch were actually written, so that this story of "rediscovering" the law was made up to justify these new developments. This theory is increasingly being dismissed; its foundation is little more than raw speculation.)

The reforms instituted by Josiah were sweeping. On every front, wherever he could effect change, Josiah brought the nation into line with the Law of God. He fully recognized the terrible threat of wrath that hung over the covenant people, and he resolved to do what was right, leaving the outcome with God. If the day of reckoning could not finally be removed, at least it could be delayed.

Of the important lessons to be learned here, I shall focus on one. Some people find it difficult to believe that the nation could descend into complete biblical ignorance so quickly. After all, Hezekiah was Josiah's great-grandfather: the reformation he led was not that long ago. True—but long enough. The intervening three-quarters of a century had begun with the long and wicked reign of Manasseh. The history of the twentieth century testifies to how quickly a people can become ignorant of Scripture—and we live this side of the printing press, not to mention the Internet. The church is never more than a generation or two from apostasy and oblivion. Only grace is a sufficient hedge.

∾

2 Kings 23; Hebrews 5; Joel 2; Psalm 142

THE WORDS FROM PSALM 2:7, "You are my Son; today I have become your Father," are quoted three times in the New Testament: (a) in Acts 13:33, where it serves as a kind of proof-text to justify the resurrection of Jesus; (b) in Hebrews 1:5, where the author infers that because Jesus alone is the Son of God, he is superior to the angels; and (c) in **Hebrews 5:5**, where it is cited to prove that just as Aaron did not take on the high priesthood by himself, but was called by God to the task, so also Jesus was appointed by God to his high priesthood.

So Psalm 2:7 is variously taken to support the resurrection of Jesus, to provide evidence of Jesus' superiority over the angels, and to demonstrate that when Jesus became high priest he did not take on the job himself, but was appointed by God. On the face of it, none of these applications of Psalm 2:7 is very obvious.

It helps to remember two things. *First*, Psalm 2:7 is an enthronement psalm. It celebrates the appointment to office of the next Davidic king. At that point the man becomes "God's son." In the ancient world, sons usually ended up doing what their fathers did. God rules with justice and equity; the king, functioning as God's "son," was to do what God does: among other things, rule with justice and equity. And this Davidic line finally ends in one who is the "Son" *par excellence*.

Second, at the risk of oversimplification, New Testament christology falls into one of two patterns. In the first, the account of Christ begins in eternity past, descends in humiliation to this world and to the ignominy and shame of the cross, and rises through the resurrection and exaltation of Christ to triumph. We might think of it as the "up-down-up" model. Philippians 2:6-11 and John 17:5 are memorable examples. In the second, there is no mention of Jesus' origin in eternity past: it is a "down-up" model. The entire focus is on his triumph through death, resurrection, ascension, exaltation. This great, redemptive event is the critical thing, the time when Jesus is appointed king, the time when his priestly role commences, the moment when he is "declared with power to be the Son of God by his resurrection from the dead" (Rom. 1:4). This is not to say that there is no sense in which Jesus is the Son, or the king, or exercises priestly functions, *before* the cross and resurrection. But this model of christology has no doubt where the greatest turning point of history lies.

These are the presuppositions that lie behind all three uses of Psalm 2:7. It is a useful exercise to reflect on them again, with these structures in mind.

2 Kings 24; Hebrew 6; Joel 3; Psalm 143

THE FINAL UNRAVELING OF THE Davidic dynasty was not pretty. The last reforming king, Josiah, made a major mistake when he unnecessarily confronted Pharaoh Neco of Egypt. In 609 B.C., Josiah not only lost, but lost his life (1 Kings 23:29) while still a relatively young man. His son Jehoahaz became king at the age of twenty-three, but his reign lasted a mere three months, until Pharaoh Neco arrested him and ultimately transported him to Egypt, where he died. Pharaoh Neco installed another son of Josiah on the throne, viz. Jehoiakim. He lasted eleven years. **Second Kings 24** picks up the account from there.

Jehoiakim's Judah was squeezed between Egypt in the south and west, and Babylon in the north and east. The latter got the upper hand. Jehoiakim himself was corrupt, religiously perverse, and had grandiose visions of himself. He reintroduced pagan cults; violence abounded. In the fourth year of his reign, in 605 B.C., Pharaoh Neco of Egypt was crushed by the Babylonians at the battle of Carchemish on the northern Syrian border; Egyptian power did not manage to reassert itself for almost three hundred years. Jehoiakim and the tiny country of Judah became a vassal tributary of the Babylonian empire.

But in 601 B.C., Jehoiakim rebelled. Nebuchadnezzar sent contingents of his armed forces to harry Judah. Then in December 598 B.C., he moved his powerful army to besiege Jerusalem. Jehoiakim died. His eighteen-year-old son Jehoiachin reigned for three months. Faced with an impossibly difficult decision, on March 16, 597 B.C., he abandoned resistance and surrendered. King Jehoiachin, the queen mother, the palace retinue, the nobility, the men of valor, the leading craftsmen, and the priestly aristocracy (including Ezekiel) were transported seven hundred miles away to Babylon—at a time when seven hundred miles was a long, long way. Jehoiachin remained in prison and house arrest for thirty-seven years before he was released; but even then he never returned home, never saw Jerusalem again. The Babylonians still regarded him as the rightful king (as did the exiles), but meanwhile they installed a caretaker king back in Judah—his uncle Zedekiah, still only twenty-one years of age (24:18). His end belongs to the next chapter.

"Surely these things happened to Judah according to the LORD's command, in order to remove them from his presence because of the sins of Manasseh and all he had done, including the shedding of innocent blood. For he had filled Jerusalem with innocent blood, and the LORD was not willing to forgive. . . . It was because of the LORD's anger that all this happened to Jerusalem and Judah, and in the end he thrust them from his presence" (24:3-4, 20).

2 Kings 25; Hebrews 7; Amos 1; Psalm 144

∾

IN THIS LAST CHAPTER OF 2 Kings (**2 Kings 25**), Jerusalem slouches off into shame and defeat. But there is a twist in the tale.

The narrative itself is grubby. Zedekiah, the caretaker king, was weak and corrupt. Jeremiah was preaching submission: God had decreed that Judah be punished in this way, and therefore the nation must not rebel against Babylon. Seven hundred miles away, Ezekiel was preaching much the same thing to the exiles: Judah and Jerusalem, he insisted, were much worse than most people thought, and God had decreed judgment upon her. Several years before the final destruction, he predicted that the glory of God would abandon Jerusalem, and the city would be destroyed (Ezek. 8—11)—a devastating message to the exiles, for to them it meant there would be no home to which to return, and an abandonment by God so total they scarcely had categories to comprehend it.

But Zedekiah rebelled anyway. Babylonian retaliation was as brutal as it was inevitable. By 588 B.C., the mighty Babylonian army was back at Jerusalem's gates. The city was taken in 587 B.C. Zedekiah tried to escape, but was captured near Jericho and taken to Nebuchadnezzar's headquarters at Riblah. There his sons were killed before his eyes—and then his eyes were gouged out. Most of the city was burned, and the walls were taken down stone by stone. Anyone of any substance was transported to Babylon. Over the poor who remained in the land to tend the vines, Nebuchadnezzar appointed Gedaliah as governor, who set up his administrative center at Mizpah, since Jerusalem was so thoroughly destroyed. A mere seven months later, Gedaliah was assassinated by stupid toughs of royal blood: apparently they were affronted that a governor had been appointed from outside the Davidic line. Realization of what they had done finally dawned. Fearing retaliation from the Babylonians, the remaining people fled to Egypt.

If that is the way 2 Kings ended, the themes of justice and judgment would be served, but the reader would be left wondering if there was any hope for the Davidic line and the sweeping messianic promises bound up with it. But in fact, the book ends with a twist in the tale. The last few verses (25:27-30) quietly report that in the thirty-seventh year of his exile, King Jehoiachin was released from his imprisonment. For the rest of his life, he was supported by the Babylonian state: He "put aside his prison clothes and for the rest of his life ate regularly at the king's table," receiving "a regular allowance as long as he lived." The story of redemption is not yet done, the Davidic line not yet extinct. In the midst of crushing sin and slashing judgment, hope still beckons.

1 Chronicles 1—2; Hebrews 8; Amos 2; Psalm 145

∽

THERE IS A THEMATIC LINK between today's two primary readings.

First Chronicles 1—2 begins long chapters of annotated genealogical information. This is not the sort of material to which we are instantly drawn. Yet biblical genealogies accomplish many things besides the obvious one of recording genealogical descent. If one were reading the Bible through, at this point the lists of names would serve, in part, as a review: the beginnings up to David, with 1 and 2 Chronicles taking the reader to the end of the active Davidic dynasty. The genealogy also sets out in brief compass some of the branches that can easily be lost to view in the tangle of reading the narratives themselves. How are Abraham's descendants tied to Noah? Abraham himself had children by three women: Hagar, Keturah, and Sarah. Where did they end up?

Of course, the genealogy does not aim to be comprehensive. It is heading toward Judah, toward the Davidic dynasty. And this is the point: There is movement and change, there are developments and fresh covenants, but from the beginning the Bible's storyline has been a unified account heading toward the Davidic line, and ultimately toward "great David's greater Son" (see the meditations for May 17 and September 10).

In genre and emphasis, **Hebrews 8** is very different from the genealogies of the opening chapters of 1 Chronicles. Yet part of the argument in this chapter overlaps with lessons from 1 Chronicles. At this point in Hebrews, the author is arguing that the tabernacle (and, in principle, the temple) established by the covenant at Sinai must not be taken as the final expression of God's will for the worship of his people. That is to misunderstand its purpose in the sweep of redemptive history. The author has already argued at length for the superiority of Jesus' priesthood over the Levitical priesthood (Heb. 5—7)—indeed, that this superior priesthood was announced by the Old Testament Scriptures themselves. Now he draws attention to the fact that the "sanctuary" constructed in the desert followed exactly the "pattern" shown Moses on the mountain (8:5). The reason for this, the author argues, is that it was only a shadow of the reality. To make it the ultimate reality is to misconstrue it. Moreover, readers of the Hebrew canon should know this. That tabernacle was tied to the Mosaic Covenant. But centuries later, at the time of Jeremiah, God promised the coming of a *new* covenant (8:7-12). "By calling this covenant 'new,' he has made the first one obsolete; and what is obsolete and aging will soon disappear" (8:13). The dawning of the new covenant not only relegates the old covenant's tabernacle to the past, but displays the unity of the Bible's storyline, however diverse the streams—for the varied streams converge in Jesus.

∽

1 Chronicles 3—4; Hebrews 9; Amos 3; Psalms 146—147

∽

THE RICH ARGUMENT OF HEBREWS 9 would take us beyond the limits of this meditation. Here I shall make clear some of the contrasts the author draws between the countless deaths of sacrificial animals in the Old Testament, and the death of Jesus that lies at the heart of the new covenant.

First, part of his argument depends on what he has said so far. If the tabernacle and the Levitical priesthood were from the beginning meant to be only temporary institutions that taught the covenant people some important lessons and pointed forward to the reality that would come with Christ, then the same thing applies to the sacrifices. So the author sums up his position to this point: the entire system was "an illustration for the present time, indicating that the gifts and sacrifices being offered were not able to clear the conscience of the worshiper. They are only a matter of food and drink and various ceremonial washings—external regulations applying until the time of the new order" (9:9-10).

Second, the very repetition of the sacrifices—for example, those offered on the Day of Atonement—demonstrates that none of these sacrifices provides a final accounting for sin. There will always be more sin, demanding yet more sacrifice, with the priest still standing to kill one more animal and offer yet more blood. Contrast Christ's sacrifice, offered once (9:6, 9, 25-26; 10:1ff).

But the *third* and most important point is the nature of the sacrifice. How could the blood of bulls and goats really deal with sin? The animals themselves were not volunteering for this slaughter; they were dragged to the altar by their owners. The animals lost their lives, but they were scarcely willing victims. So far as "willingness" went, it was the people who owned the sacrificed animals who were losing something. Of course, this sacrificial system was appointed by God himself. He taught thereby that sin demands death—and in the sweep of the Bible's storyline, that a better "lamb" would be needed. The sins of the people were thus covered over until such a sacrifice should appear. But the blood and ashes of animals provided no final answer.

How different the sacrifice of Jesus Christ! He "through the eternal Spirit offered himself unblemished to God"—that is, not "by the Holy Spirit," but "through [his own] eternal Spirit," an act of will, a supreme act of *voluntary* sacrifice, the Son acquiescing to the Father's plan. There indeed was a sacrifice of untold merit, of incalculable significance. That is why his blood, his life violently and sacrificially offered up, is able to "cleanse our consciences from acts that lead to death, so that we may serve the living God!" (9:14).

∽

1 Chronicles 5—6; Hebrews 10; Amos 4; Psalms 148—150

HEBREWS 10 BRINGS TOGETHER many of the earlier arguments of this book, while advancing some new ones. It also marks a transition: from 10:19 on, the balance of explanation and exhortation changes. Now there is more of the latter and less of the former.

The summary of the antecedent instruction is found at the beginning of the chapter: "The law [by which the author means the entire law-covenant, not least its tabernacle, priestly system, and sacrifices] is only a shadow of the good things that are coming—not the realities themselves. For this reason it can never, by the same sacrifices repeated endlessly year after year, make perfect those who would draw near to worship" (10:1).

By contrast, "we have confidence to enter the Most Holy Place [not the Most Holy Place of the old tabernacle or temple, but the very presence of the living God] by the blood of Jesus, by a new and living way opened for us through the curtain" (10:19-20). That generates a sequence of five "let us" statements.

(1) *Let us draw near to God* (10:22). Because so full and final a sacrifice has been offered for us, let us make use of it, approaching this holy God "with a sincere heart in full assurance of faith," precisely because our consciences have been purged.

(2) *Let us hold unswervingly to the hope we profess* (10:23). What Christ has accomplished on the cross is the fulfillment of the Old Testament models and predictions, but the climax of what it inaugurates is still future. Our ultimate vindication and transformation lie ahead. But this hope is as certain as the triumph of Christ was effective, "for he who promised is faithful" (10:23).

(3) *Let us consider how we may spur one another on toward love and good deeds* (10:24). We do not seek the consummation as spiritual lone rangers; Christians live now in the community of the church and will live then in the community of the heavenly city.

(4) Negatively, *let us not give up meeting together* (10:25). Just because some fall into withdrawal patterns is no reason why we should, if we truly grasp the greatness of the salvation in which we are participating and the glory yet to be revealed.

(5) Comprehensively, *let us encourage one another*—indeed, more and more "as you see the Day approaching" (10:25). Everyone will grow weary from time to time, or lapse into unrest or self-focus. If all believers pledge themselves to encourage one another *in the gospel and all it grants and promises*, there will be far fewer individual failures, against which the author warns in the remaining verses of the chapter.

1 Chronicles 7—8; Hebrews 11; Amos 5; Luke 1:1-38

∾

FAITH HAS MANY FACETS. Some of them emerge in **Hebrews 11**—and also what faith isn't.

(1) Not once does "faith" take on the modern sense of "religious preference" or "belief without grounding in fact or truth." So much has scientism brainwashed our world in this respect that we easily think of "faith" in this purely subjective sense. If you tell others what you believe, they do not ask you what your reasons are to determine whether or not your belief is well grounded. It is automatically assumed that such faith *cannot* be more than religious preference, for which there are, by definition, no useful criteria.

(2) By contrast, faith in this chapter is a faculty to perceive what is objectively true. The author is not calling in doubt the proposition that "the universe was formed at God's command" (11:3). Rather, he implies that we have no ready way to demonstrate it; we can acknowledge the truthfulness of this proposition only if the one Person who was there discloses what happened—and we *believe* him. Similarly, the author entertains no doubt that the Christian consummation, "what we hope for" (11:1), is coming. But we cannot measure it or bottle it or prove it. For very good reasons, we believe the promises of God regarding what is to come. Our "faith" is thus a glorious God-given facility that enables us to be "sure of what we hope for and certain of what we do not see" (11:1).

(3) In certain respects, then, this faith is like the faith of "the ancients" (11:2). For many of them were promised things that they did not see in their lifetimes. Because they believed the promises of God and acted upon them, they were commended for their faith. Thus Abraham acted on the promise that his descendants would multiply abundantly and inherit the land of Canaan. He did not live to see it, but he acted on it. The twelve patriarchs believed the promise, Joseph so strongly that he gave instructions to the Israelites about taking his body with them when they left Egypt, though that departure was centuries away. Many of those promises have *already* come to pass; by analogy, ought we not to await with glad faith the fulfillment of the promises of God yet outstanding?

(4) Such faith works out not only in those readily seen as victors (e.g., 11:32-35a) but in those seen as victims (11:35b-38). Whether we belong to those called to conquer kingdoms, administer justice, escape the edge of the sword, and receive the dead back to life, or to those who are tortured, who face jeers and floggings, imprisonment, destitution, and ignominious death, is entirely secondary. The critical question is whether or not we take God at his word.

∾

1 Chronicles 9—10; Hebrews 12; Amos 6; Luke 1:39-80

THE EFFORTS OF THE AUTHOR of the epistle to the Hebrews to help his readers grasp the transcendent importance of Jesus and the new covenant, over against the old covenant given by God at Sinai, precipitate a new and interesting contrast in **Hebrews 12:18-24.**

On the one hand, Christians "have not come to a mountain that can be touched and that is burning with fire" (12:18)—the reference is clearly to Mount Sinai when God came down upon it and met with Moses. The terror of that theophany is spelled out in graphic terms. God himself declared, "If even an animal touches the mountain, it must be stoned" (12:20). Even Moses experienced deep fear (Deut. 9:19; Heb. 12:21). Christians have not drawn near to that particular mountain.

On the other hand, Christians have come to another mountain. But here the author throws us a curve. At first it sounds as if he is saying that the mountain we approach is not Sinai, connected with the desert and the giving of the law, but Mount Zion, the place where the temple was built in Jerusalem, the seat of the Davidic dynasty. And then suddenly it becomes clear that the text is not focusing on the geographical and historical Zion, but on its antitype: "the heavenly Jerusalem, the city of the living God" (12:22).

There is a great deal that could be said about this typology, but I shall restrict myself to two observations.

First, it extends to other biblical books. The typology itself is grounded in the return from exile. The hope of the exiles was that they return to Jerusalem. Jerusalem became the symbol of all that was restorative. Already in the literature of second-temple Judaism, Jews sometimes speak of "the new Jerusalem" or the like, which is heavenly, perfect. Similarly in the New Testament. Paul can speak of "the Jerusalem that is above" (Gal. 4:26). The last book of the Bible envisages the New Jerusalem coming down out of heaven (Rev. 21).

Second, if Christians have "come" to this "heavenly Jerusalem," what does this in fact mean? It means that by becoming Christians we have joined the assembly of those "gathered" before the presence of the living God. Our citizenship is in heaven; our names are inscribed in heaven. We join the joyful assembly of countless thousands of angels around the throne. In short, we have "come to God, the judge of all men"; we have joined "the spirits of righteous men made perfect" (Heb. 12:23). Above all, we have come "to Jesus the mediator of a new covenant" (12:24). Here is the ultimate vision of what it means to be the gathered "church of the firstborn" (Heb. 12:23).

1 Chronicles 11—12; Hebrews 13; Amos 7; Luke 2

THE BENEDICTION OF HEBREWS 13:20-21 invites prolonged reflection. Some observations:

(1) The thrust of the prayer is twofold: first, that God would equip "*you*" (the Christian readers) "with everything good for doing his will"; and second, that he would work "in *us* what is pleasing to him" (13:21, italics added). In other words, there is a tremendous emphasis on doing God's will, on living in ways that are pleasing to him. Although the prayer is *for* Christians, the entire focus is on God and what pleases him. The most important prayer *for* Christians is that they do God's will, that God will work in them what is pleasing to him.

(2) The change in person from *you* to *us* does not mean that the first petition is only for the readers and the second is only for the author. The *us* is almost certainly inclusive, i.e., embracing both the author and his readers, and thus, implicitly, Christians everywhere. The switch from *you* to *us* may well be motivated, at least in part, by a desire to avoid giving the impression that the author is praying for *others* to do the will of God without praying the same thing for himself.

(3) God is referred to as "the God of peace" (13:20). The reference is not primarily to psychological peace. The fundamental peace at issue (as chaps. 9—10 presuppose) is peace with God—the reconciliation of guilty rebels to their Maker and Redeemer. The author petitions the God who reconciles sinners to equip them to be conformed to his will.

(4) This God "brought back from the dead our Lord Jesus" (13:20). At one level this is a fairly constant New Testament theme: God raised up Jesus from the dead. But this passage stipulates that God did so "through the blood of the eternal covenant" (13:20). The reference is to Jesus' blood, to Jesus' death, which inaugurates the new covenant (as chaps. 8—10 make clear)—and this new covenant is not some temporary expedient but "eternal" in its binding authority. At first it seems strange to think of God raising up Jesus through Jesus' blood, through Jesus' death. But the point is probably that the eternal covenant inaugurated by Jesus' *successful* death, his *completed* sacrifice, his *perfect* atonement, expressed in his triumphant cry "It is finished!", is the covenantal bedrock that means it is *right* for God to raise up Jesus and vindicate him.

(5) Jesus himself is "that great Shepherd of the sheep." Many images flood to mind. God himself promised to shepherd his people; indeed, he would send the Davidic king to exercise this role (Ezek. 34). Above all, the Good Shepherd gives his life for the sheep (John 10; see the meditation for March 20). Small wonder the prayer is offered "through Jesus Christ, to whom be glory for ever and ever" (13:21).

1 Chronicles 13—14; James 1; Amos 8; Luke 3

ACCORDING TO JAMES 1:2-4, 12, there are two reasons why Christians should rejoice when they face trials of various kinds. Other reasons are articulated elsewhere, but these two are remarkably comprehensive.

First, we should rejoice because we know that when our faith is tested, the result is perseverance (1:2-3). As an athlete endures in order to build up endurance, so a Christian perseveres under trial in order to build up perseverance. Perseverance contributes something important to our character. It "must finish its work so that [we] may be mature and complete, not lacking anything" (1:4). The alternative is a personality that may love the Lord when things are going well, a character that is bold and happy on bright days in the Spring, but knows little of steadfastness under duress, of contentment when physical comforts are withdrawn, of quiet confidence in the living God when faced with persecution, of stability in the midst of a frenetic pace or a massive disappointment. In other words, in a fallen world perseverance contributes maturity and stability to our character—and trials build perseverance. So James is very bold: we should, he says, "consider it pure joy" whenever we face trials of various kinds. This is not a perverse form of Christian masochism, but an entirely appropriate response *if we remember the Christian's goals.* If our highest goals are creature comforts, this passage is incomprehensible; if our highest goals include growth in Christian character, James's evaluation makes eminent sense.

Second, the Christian who perseveres under trial is blessed "because when he has stood the test, he will receive the crown of life that God has promised to those who love him" (1:12). In other words, perseverance is a necessary ingredient to genuine Christianity. A real Christian, on the long haul, sticks: he or she perseveres. There may be ups and downs, there may be special victories or temporary defeats, but precisely because the One who has begun a good work in us completes it (Phil. 1:6), real Christians stick (cf. Heb. 3:14). They continue to be "those who love him." Thus Christians facing a trial must perceive not only the threat or the unpleasantness or the disappointment, but also the challenge for which God's grace equips us: to press on—always to press on—knowing full well that the ultimate reward, meted out by grace, is "the crown of life"—the crown that is life, life in its consummated splendor, the life of the new heaven and the new earth, the heritage of all Christians. Thus, once again James is entirely realistic to perceive that the person who perseveres under trial is "blessed." It is an easy calculation, provided *we remember the Christian's goals.*

1 Chronicles 15; James 2; Amos 9; Luke 4

⌘

IN 1 CHRONICLES 15 WE FIND ELEMENTS of David's reasoning not found in the parallel passage in 2 Samuel 6.

After capturing Jerusalem, David eventually determined to bring the ark of the covenant up to the new capital city. On the way, Uzzah reached out his hand to steady the ark as the cart on which it was riding jolted its way along the rutted roads—and he was instantly slain. David was both angry with God and afraid of him (1 Chron. 13:11-12), and abandoned his mission. The ark was parked in the home of Obed-Edom the Gittite. During the three months of the ark's temporary residence there, the household of Obed-Edom was so abundantly blessed that everyone took notice. So in due course David made another attempt to transport the ark to Jerusalem.

This much could have been gleaned from either 2 Samuel or 1 Chronicles. What 1 Chronicles 15:1-24 adds is something of David's reasoning and arrangements. I shall focus on one point.

Apparently cooling down after the shocking loss of Uzzah, David returns to the Scriptures. True, Uzzah should not have touched the ark. But were David and his people transgressing any other legal prescriptions in the way they were handling it? David's Bible reading reminds him that only Levites are permitted to transport it, and how they are to do it. So he tells the Levites to prepare themselves for the task, and explains his reasoning: "It was because you, the Levites, did not bring it up the first time that the LORD our God broke out in anger against us. We did not inquire of him about how to do it in the prescribed way" (15:13). In other words, David concludes that God's wrath in the matter of Uzzah's thoughtlessness was the outcropping of God's deeper displeasure. Transporting the ark was not to be a willy-nilly matter. God expected to be obeyed, and the symbol of his presence was to be handled in line with the covenantal stipulations.

So that is what the Levites did: "The Levites carried the ark of God with the poles on their shoulders, as Moses had commanded, *in accordance with the word of the LORD*" (15:15).

Here is a profound lesson. At one level, doubtless God approves childlike praise and enthusiastic zeal. But he expects those with authority among his people to know what his Word says and obey it. No amount of enthusiasm and zeal can ever hope to make up for this lack. Zeal that is heading in the wrong direction never reaches the goal. It must either be redirected in the direction staked out in God's Word, or however enthusiastic, it is still wrong-headed and misdirected. There is no substitute for faith working itself out in informed obedience.

⌘

1 Chronicles 16; James 3; Obadiah; Luke 5

∽

PROBABLY JAMES 3 IS ONE OF THE BEST-KNOWN passages in all of literature dealing with the tongue.

(1) The burden of 3:3-6 is that although the tongue is a very small organ, in many respects it controls and, in the worst case, inflames the rest of the human being. Each of the analogies James draws casts a fresh hue on the subject. The bit is tiny compared with the rest of the horse, yet it steers the horse. Something similar can be said of the rudder with respect to the ship, only now it is part of the ship rather than separate from it. The spark is tiny compared with the conflagration it causes—but in this case the focus is not only on relative size but on the horrible damage the tongue can achieve.

(2) The next section (3:7-8) adapts the last of these three analogies, and purposely distances itself from the first. The notion of a bit in a horse's mouth might conjure up mental expectations of control and discipline. The reality, James insists, is closer to conflagration. We manage to tame "all kinds of animals, birds, reptiles, and creatures of the sea" (3:7), but no one can tame the tongue. "It is a restless evil, full of deadly poison" (3:8).

(3) In particular, it is the tongue's wild inconsistency that is so offensive (3:9-12). The analogies James draws suggest that if with the one tongue we praise God and abuse God's image-bearers, the praise we offer to God cannot possibly be more than religious cant. One stream cannot provide both fresh water and bitter.

(4) All of this is in danger of being misunderstood. The focus on the tongue is rhetorically powerful, of course, but we all know that the tongue is not independent of the person. Perhaps that is one of the reasons why James goes on to contrast two kinds of wisdom (3:13-18). At issue is who we are as persons. If our hearts "harbor bitter envy and selfish ambition" (3:14), that will surface in our speech. *We* control our own tongues—and what we need is "the wisdom that comes from heaven" (3:17), so graphically described in the last two verses of the chapter.

(5) Similarly, the opening two verses of the chapter cannot be abstracted from what James says about the tongue. These two verses are frightening to any thoughtful teacher of Scripture: "We who teach will be judged more strictly" (3:1) That is part of a biblical axiom: responsibility is assessed as a function of knowledge. But teachers know that their performance is tied to what they *say* (3:2). We have returned to the tongue—or, by only the slightest extension, to the printed page and the CD-ROM.

∽

1 Chronicles 17; James 4; Jonah 1; Luke 6

FIRST CHRONICLES 17 FAIRLY CLOSELY parallels 2 Samuel 7. In both passages, David expresses his desire to build a "house" for God. The prophet Nathan initially approves the project, and then, after receiving explicit revelation from God, presents David with a very different picture. Far from David building a "house" for God, God will build a "house" for David—that is, a "household" (as the original word is ambiguous, the play on the meaning intentional). The "house" or "household" that God will build for David is nothing other than the Davidic dynasty. David's line will never suffer the fate of Saul and his line. When David's line sins, God's judgments will be temporal (17:12-14); the line will not be destroyed.

David responds in a moving prayer (17:16-27) pulsating with gratitude. The prayer is wonderfully God-centered; David is fully aware that if his line is treated so differently from that of Saul, the ultimate difference is grace. So the closing words of the prayer are frankly touching and revealing: "You, my God, have revealed to your servant that you will build a house for him. So your servant has found courage to pray to you. O LORD, you are God! You have promised these good things to your servant. Now you have been pleased to bless the house of your servant, that it may continue forever in your sight; for you, O LORD, have blessed it, and it will be blessed forever" (17:26-27).

One must not forget, however, that these words must be read as part of a two-volume work—1 and 2 Chronicles—whose storyline ends in unmitigated disaster for the Davidic line—apart from the last two verses of 2 Chronicles, which offers a sliver of hope. Today we automatically place them within the larger framework of the Bible's storyline, and see where they fit into the pattern that brings forth Jesus, the ultimate Davidic king. But the first readers did not enjoy our perspective; the unknown compiler who put together the court records and other sources, covering about five hundred years of history, into the form of our "1 and 2 Chronicles," did not enjoy our perspective.

Mere cynicism, or the brutality of their experience under the Exile, might have led them to downplay the words we find here in 1 Chronicles 17:27: "Now you have been pleased to bless the house of your servant, that it may continue forever in your sight; *for you, O LORD, have blessed it, and it will be blessed forever.*" Instead, the words function for them as a stabilizing promise when all of their recent experience seemed to controvert them. In short, they show us what it means to walk by faith in the promises of God, and not by sight.

1 Chronicles 18; James 5; Jonah 2; Luke 7

❧

IT IS ONE THING TO WAIT for the Lord's coming; it is another to wait well.

One may honestly and self-consciously wait for the Lord's coming, not only acknowledging that the Second Advent is a necessary part of our creed but even after a fashion looking forward to the Parousia, and hoping it will occur in our lifetime—only to find, on reflection, that the way we live has been affected very little by this perspective. In fact, this waiting for the return of the Lord may be nothing more than a hobbyhorse in our reading or teaching, a well-handled map of the future that divides us from other believers, rather than a fixed point in our worldview that decisively shapes how we conduct ourselves.

Of course, there is an element in waiting for the Lord's return that is just that—waiting. Just as "the farmer waits for the land to yield its valuable crop" (**James 5:7**), so we too must "be patient and stand firm" (5:8).

But like all analogies, this one isn't perfect (it isn't meant to be), and James himself quickly leaves it behind. After all, the farmer is patient because he knows more or less when the harvest will take place; we do *not* know when Jesus' return will take place.

There are other differences. The farmer is waiting for crops; we are waiting for the Judge who "is standing at the door" (5:9). That means that what we are waiting for has an immediate bearing on how we live: "Don't grumble against each other, brothers, or you will be judged" (5:9) by that very Judge himself.

Moreover, although farmers may have to work hard as they wait for the harvest, in the normal course of events their waiting is not characterized by suffering and persecution. Christians waiting for the End encounter both of those things, James insists—and with that in mind, our waiting might more properly be likened to the perseverance of the prophets (5:10) than to the placidity of the farmer. They "spoke in the name of the Lord," and more often than not were reviled for it. That suffering did not tame their faithful proclamation. But we need not restrict the models we look for to the prophets. Consider Job, a righteous man, who faced catastrophic reversals yet nevertheless persevered—and you "have seen what the Lord finally brought about. The Lord is full of compassion and mercy" (5:11). That perspective is important: in the end, not only God's justice but his compassion and mercy prevail. The focus on Jesus' return and on the End not only shapes our current living, but will bring with it perfect vindication in the unqualified goodness of the consummation.

❧

1 Chronicles 19—20; 1 Peter 1; Jonah 3; Luke 8

∾

ONE OF THE GREAT PRETENSIONS OF human existence is that this mortal life lasts forever. Though young people theoretically know there is an end to each human life, they act as if death will never catch them. Decades later, they know better, but even then most act as if their families will inevitably continue, or at least their culture or their nation will survive.

The most farsighted know it is not so. Individuals die; so do family connections. For all but those most committed to genealogical archaeology, we do not know much about our past families beyond three or four generations back—and we ourselves will not be remembered a few generations hence. Mighty empires fall. They are partitioned, sink into vassal status as third-rate or fourth-rate powers, or dissolve into oblivion. We may have an immortal destiny, but nothing restrictively bound up with this life is secure, nothing is changeless, nothing endures. "All men are like grass, and all their glory is like the flowers of the field; the grass withers and the flowers fall" (**1 Peter 1:24**).

Yet there is one more line in this quotation from Isaiah 40:6-8: *"but the word of the Lord stands forever"* (1 Peter 1:25). It follows, then, that human beings who hunger for the transcendent cannot do better than align themselves with God's unchanging and enduring word. And there are several hints in this chapter as to what that means in practical terms.

(1) "And this is the word that was preached to you" (1:25): the very Gospel that was declared to Peter's readers is the word of the Lord that stands forever. Adherence to the Gospel is adherence to that which endures forever. The same cannot be said of adherence to a political system or an economic theory or professional advancement.

(2) More precisely, Christians have been "born again, not of perishable seed, but of imperishable, through the living and enduring word of God" (1:23). That which has transformed us and granted us new life from God himself has not been physical impregnation, but spiritual new birth, brought about by the enduring word of God.

(3) The word mediated through prophets before Jesus looked forward to the revelation that came exclusively with him (1:10-12). That means it was all one: this was always the plan, however much those Old Testament prophets had or had not grasped of it.

(4) The "new birth" (1:3) that we have experienced by the action of the enduring word of God introduces us to "an inheritance that can never perish, spoil or fade—kept in heaven for you, who through faith are shielded by God's power" (1:4-5).

∾

1 Chronicles 21; 1 Peter 2; Jonah 4; Luke 9

SECOND SAMUEL 24, which roughly parallels **1 Chronicles 21**, says that *the anger of the LORD* burned against Israel, so *he* incited David to number the people, which act was strictly forbidden—and then that act brought down the wrath of God on the nation (24:1). The passage before us says that "*Satan* rose up against Israel and incited David to take a census of Israel" (**1 Chron. 21:1**).

The two stances are not mutually exclusive, of course, nor even particularly antithetical. In God's universe, it is impossible to escape the outermost bounds of God's sovereignty. Whether his providential will over the Devil is portrayed as permissive (as in the case of Job), or something more directive, God is in charge. As for the moral dimensions of the matter, it is important to recall that even within the framework of 2 Samuel 24, God is not arbitrarily and whimsically tempting David to do evil, and then rather viciously clobbering him for it. Whatever God sanctions is portrayed as God's response to antecedent sin: God's anger burned against Israel, we are told, so that certain things took place. In the same way, the mark of God's anger on the nation of Israel during the waning years of the reign of the Davidic dynasty was more and more callous corruption on the throne and among the ruling elite, with the result, of course, that there was more sin in the nation, and more immediacy to God's threats of judgment.

Nevertheless, having said this, the *feel* of these two chapters, 2 Samuel 24 and 1 Chronicles 21, is quite different. In both cases David is held responsible to follow the Scriptures of the covenant, regardless of the temptation or the complexities of its provenance. But the explicit mention of Satan in 1 Chronicles 21 underlines the dimension of the cosmic fight between good and evil. Three other perspectives are also highlighted:

(1) Joab is always portrayed as a considerable military leader, but not as a particularly spiritual or even moral man. Here he stands up to the king with godly advice, and he is not listened to (21:3-4). Godly counsel may come from a variety of sources. Doubtless one must listen to all of them—but at the end of the day all counsel must be tested by the Word of God.

(2) Some actions have immense repercussions on others. This was especially true under the old covenant, where kings, prophets, and priests stood in a representative relationship with the people. Though the new covenant is configured differently, it is still true, for instance, that the sins of the fathers are visited on the children for three and four generations.

(3) God is more merciful than people. It is better to fall into his hand, unmediated by human agents, than into any other hand.

1 Chronicles 22; 1 Peter 3; Micah 1; Luke 10

❧

THE TRANSITION BETWEEN THE account of David's numbering of the people (1 Chron. 21) and the account of David's formidable preparations for the construction of the temple that his son Solomon would build (**1 Chron. 22**) is one verse, the first verse of chapter 22, with no parallel in 2 Samuel: "Then David said, 'The house of the LORD God is to be here, and also the altar of burnt offering for Israel'" (22:1).

So the place where the temple was built is the place where David built an altar to the Lord, calling on him with sacrificial offerings (21:25-27), and where the angel of death sheathed his sword.

So David laid in formidable supplies of building materials and prepared the people to help his son Solomon build the promised temple. "Now devote your heart and soul to seeking the LORD your God. Begin to build the sanctuary of the LORD God, so that you may bring the ark of the covenant of the LORD and the sacred articles belonging to God into the temple that will be built for the Name of the LORD" (22:19).

There are some lessons to be learned from this siting of the temple.

(1) The place chosen for the temple is the place where a sacrifice was offered and the wrath of God against sin was averted. Of course, the very design of tabernacle and temple was meant to remind people that sin had to be atoned for, that one could not simply saunter into the presence of the holy God, that the sacrifices God himself had prescribed had to be offered by the designated high priest once a year, first for his own sins and then for the sins of the people. But the siting of the temple on this location reinforces the point. Worship and religion are not primarily about offering to God something called praise, something God prefers not to be without. Worship and religion are first of all about God-centeredness—and because we are rebels, that means that worship and religion are in the first instance about being reconciled to this God, our Creator and Redeemer, from whom we have willfully become alienated. The heart of the temple is not its choirs, its incense, its ceremonies. The heart of the temple is about averting the wrath of God, by the means he himself has provided.

(2) The siting of the temple is also a mingling of priestly and kingly lines of authority. Originally, the priests and Levites alone were responsible for the tabernacle; the pillar of cloud determined when it would move. But here the king establishes the site—anticipating the offices of king and priest in one man: Jesus Christ.

❧

1 Chronicles 23; 1 Peter 4; Micah 2; Luke 11

❧

IN CERTAIN RESPECTS THE structure of Israelite life, including some facets of its religious life, changed when the people entered the Promised Land and were no longer nomadic. The first changes were obvious. The Lord stopped the daily supply of manna: the people had to gather food for themselves and grow things. Urbanization began. The Sabbath laws were increasingly applied to trade and commerce as well as to agrarian life.

Now with the establishment of the monarchy and the impending construction of the temple, much more organization and centralization must take place. In particular, David concerns himself not only with providing Solomon with the wherewithal to construct the temple, but with laying the foundations for the new organizational structures that would be necessary to keep it operating. Such matters are of central interest in 1 Chronicles 23—26.

Already in **1 Chronicles 23** David himself reflects on the changes that are coming. One of the duties of the Levites in the past, begun during the wilderness years, was to pack up and transport the tabernacle in the prescribed way, whenever the Lord indicated it was time to move. David reflects on the fact the Lord has now granted his people "rest": they are in the Promised Land. Moreover, he has chosen "to dwell in Jerusalem forever" (23:25), so some of the duties of the Levites must change: "the Levites no longer need to carry the tabernacle or any of the articles used in its service" (23:26). Meanwhile, new functions are introduced: more thought is given to temple choirs, and thus to schools of music and training.

So the Levites are reorganized. They are divided into major families, minor clans, and so forth. Moreover, the temple and its needs will not be allowed to take over. True, the following chapters focus on the kinds of tasks that those who serve the temple will have to discharge—not only the immediately priestly duties and the obviously menial tasks surrounding the temple, but the major responsibilities of upkeep, maintenance, finance, and administration. But from the beginning the priests were also to teach the people the law, and serve as "officials and judges." David allots six thousand Levites for the latter tasks (23:4).

From all of this we derive significant lessons. Most importantly, this is a lesson in contextualization within the canon—that is, how to take the old "givens" of revelation and adapt them to a new context without sacrificing the givens. As the church has expanded outward into new cultural contexts, those sorts of questions have had to be addressed again and again. One party will latch onto mere traditionalism *from another culture*; another party will start to abandon *what Scripture actually says*. What we really need is faithfulness and flexibility.

❧

1 Chronicles 24—25; 1 Peter 5; Micah 3; Luke 12

∾

FIRST PETER 5:1-4 PROVIDES as compelling a glimpse of Christian ministry as any passage in the New Testament.

The apostle Peter addresses elders, whom he also calls "overseers" and "shepherds," i.e., pastors (see meditation for November 2). Indeed, he addresses them as *fellow* elders, rather than speaking to them as an apostle to elders. This does not prevent him from alluding to one of the factors that separates him from most other elders: unlike them, he was "a witness of Christ's sufferings" (5:1). But even here where he distinguishes his own experience from theirs, he does so in a way that points not to himself but to Christ and his sufferings.

These elders are exhorted to "be shepherds of God's flock that is under [their] care" (5:2). Shepherds lead, nurture, heal, protect, discipline, feed, and care for their flocks. The task involves oversight: "serving as overseers," Peter adds. Then Peter adds three clauses with the form "not this . . . but that," all of which sum up Christian ministry in telling ways:

(1) "Not because you must, but because you are willing, as God wants you to be" (5:2): Mere duty will never suffice. Sad to say, ministers of the Gospel can feel trapped, "serving" simply because they feel they must, for they cannot let the side down, nor are they trained for anything else. At that point it is time either to change your heart, or get out of the ministry. There must be a heart willingness to serve this way, even in the midst of disappointment and suffering—even as our Master made his Father's will his own.

(2) "Not greedy for money, but eager to serve" (5:2): This is not a job that earns money by the hour or by the piece; nor is it a profession associated with a high tax bracket. Unfortunately, TV evangelists and some others have distorted the image. While churches sometimes treat their ministers with surly miserliness ("Lord, you keep them humble and we'll keep them poor"), ministers can respond with a crass materialism that is no less unbecoming. In the best cases, the church is constantly generous, and the ministers care little for material possessions. Pastors ought to be motivated primarily by a desire to serve.

(3) "Not lording it over those entrusted to you, but being examples to the flock" (5:3): Here there is a style of leadership that should eliminate the power hungry from the ministry (though, sadly, some such people do slip into positions from which they should be excluded). Pastors should be more concerned about being examples than about standing on their authority.

No minister is more than an under-shepherd. All must give an account to "the Chief Shepherd"—and he alone rewards his staff (5:4).

∾

1 Chronicles 26—27; 2 Peter 1; Micah 4; Luke 13

∾

SECOND PETER 1:5-9 PROVIDES us with a remarkable sequence of steps. Peter knows his readers are believers. Now he exhorts them to add some things to their faith.

(1) Add goodness to faith (1:5): Probably the kind of faith Peter does *not* want to see is the kind of faith that James 2 dismisses: faith that is merely intellectual, merely affirming, but devoid of transparent trust and ready obedience. Genuine faith issues in obedience—but as usual, believers are responsible to go down that track and are discouraged from mere passivity. So add goodness to faith.

(2) Add knowledge to goodness (1:5): Some knowledge is necessary for faith, but Peter has moved beyond that point. Elsewhere Timothy is encouraged to persevere in his "doctrine" (1 Tim. 4:16); here Christians are similarly exhorted to add knowledge to goodness. Nothing is as stabilizing and as motivating as a growing grasp of the mind of God.

(3) Add self-control to knowledge (1:6): Mere knowledge may simply puff one up (1 Cor. 8:1-3) and fail to transform anyone. But if self-control, that blessed element in the fruit of the Spirit (Gal. 5:22-23), is present in abundance, the potential for good is incalculable.

(4) Add perseverance to self-control (1:6): It is one thing to be self-controlled in a crisis, or for a short period of time, or when things are going well. It takes long-term perseverance to bring self-control to a shining polish.

(5) Add godliness to perseverance (1:6): Otherwise, perseverance may turn out to be little more than a supreme effort of merely human will. God-centeredness, a genuine religious element in every virtue, transforms mere stoic resolve into transparent godliness.

(6) Add brotherly kindness to godliness (1:7): Everyone hates the self-righteous. Self-control and perseverance, even godliness, have been known to generate rigid and unforgiving Pharisees. Add brotherly kindness.

(7) Add love to brotherly kindness (1:7): That is better yet. For then we are mirroring, however falteringly or poorly, the character of the Master himself.

Note carefully what brackets these seven steps. *First*, at the front end, Peter tells us we are to "make every effort" to pursue this list, "for this very reason" (1:5). "This very reason" is spelled out in the previous verses (1:3-4). God's glory and goodness have provided great and precious promises, so that through them we may participate in the divine nature and escape the corruption of the world. *For this reason* we are to make every effort to pursue these seven steps. *Second*, at the back end Peter assures us that these qualities will prevent us from being ineffective and unproductive in our knowledge of our Lord Jesus Christ (1:8-9).

∾

1 Chronicles 28; 2 Peter 2; Micah 5; Luke 14

∾

WE HAVE ALREADY OBSERVED that 1 and 2 Chronicles differ from the books of Samuel and Kings (though the Chronicles cover roughly the same period of history as Samuel and Kings) in placing much more emphasis on the southern kingdom of Judah, after the monarchy divides. Even at this juncture, however, during the period of the united monarchy, 1 and 2 Chronicles greatly expand on anything to do with the temple.

In this framework, **1 Chronicles 28** discloses a little more detail not only of the transfer of power from David to Solomon, but of the origin of the temple's plans. On the former point, David charges the people with serving Solomon well; he charges Solomon with serving the Lord God with his whole heart: "For the LORD searches every heart and understands every motive behind the thoughts. If you seek him, he will be found by you; but if you forsake him, he will reject you forever" (28:9). In particular, David charges Solomon with the building of the temple for which he, David, has made such large provision (29:10, 20-21). Nothing is reported of the attempt by David's son Adonijah to usurp the throne before Solomon could be crowned, or of Bathsheba's strategic protection of her son Solomon (1 Kings 1); nothing is mentioned of the substantial array of other charges David gave to Solomon (1 Kings 2). All the focus here is on the transfer of power *as it affects the construction of the temple.*

There is a new element of stellar importance. We are told that David gave Solomon "the plans of all that the Spirit had put in his mind for the courts of the temple of the LORD and all the surrounding rooms, for the treasuries of the temple of God and for the treasuries for the dedicated things" (28:12)—as well as for the divisions of the priests and Levites, the amount of gold or silver to be used in the various instruments, and so forth (28:13-17). Above all, "he also gave him the plan for the chariot, that is, the cherubim of gold that spread their wings and shelter the ark of the covenant of the LORD" (28:18) in the Most Holy Place. "'All this,' David said, 'I have in writing from the hand of the LORD upon me, and he gave me understanding in all the details of the plan'" (28:19).

Here is the counterpart to the constant emphasis in Exodus on the fact that Moses and his peers built the tabernacle in exact accordance with the plan shown Moses on the mountain. That is then picked up in Hebrews 8:5: this proved the tabernacle was only a copy of a greater original (see the meditation for March 14). Implicitly, the same care is taken with the construction of the temple, with David, not Moses, now serving as the mediator.

∾

1 Chronicles 29; 2 Peter 3; Micah 6; Luke 15

THE CHRONICLER'S ACCOUNT OF David's death is preceded by the story of the wealthy gifts that would finance temple construction after David's demise and the prayer David offered in this connection (**1 Chron. 29**). It is not so much the quantity of money given by David and the others that is striking, as the theology of David's prayer. The highlights include the following points:

(1) In the opening doxology (29:10-13), David acknowledges that everything is God's (29:11). If we human beings "own" anything, we must frankly confess, "Wealth and honor come from you; you are the ruler of all things" (29:12). Hence in the body of the prayer, David says, "Everything comes from you, and we have given you only what comes from your hand" (29:14); again, as for all this wealth that is being collected, "it comes from your hand, and all of it belongs to you" (29:16). Such a stance utterly destroys any notion of us "giving" something to God in any absolute terms. It becomes a pleasure to give to God, not only because we love him, but because we happily recognize that all we "own" is his anyway.

(2) Small wonder, then, that the prayer begins with exuberant expressions of praise (29:10).

(3) David recognizes that all human existence is transient. God himself is to be praised "from everlasting to everlasting" (29:10), but as for us, "we are aliens and strangers in your sight, as were all our forefathers. Our days on earth are like a shadow, without hope" (29:15). This passage is extraordinary. The Israelites are in the Promised Land, at "rest"; yet, as in Psalm 95 and Hebrews 3:6—4:11; 11:13, this cannot be the ultimate rest, for they are still "aliens and strangers." David is king, the head of a powerful and enduring dynasty. Individually, however, monarch and peasant alike must confess that their "days on earth are like a shadow" (29:15). Here is a man of faith who knows he must be grounded in the One who inhabits eternity, or else he amounts to nothing.

(4) David lays formidable stress on integrity: "I know, my God, that you test the heart and are pleased with integrity. . . . And now I have seen with joy how willingly your people who are here have given to you" (29:17). The success of this fundraising is not measured in monetary value, but in the integrity with which the wealth was given.

(5) In the final analysis, David frankly recognizes that continued devotion and integrity of life are impossible apart from the intervening grace of God (29:18). Thus any possibility of personal hubris based on the amount of money donated is dissolved in grateful recognition of God's gracious sovereignty.

2 Chronicles 1; 1 John 1; Micah 7; Luke 16

∾

THE OPENING PARAGRAPH OF **1 John 1** boasts many treasures. I want to focus on verse 3, with a sidelong glance at verse 4.

Assuming that the author is the apostle John, the "we" that is doing the proclaiming is most likely an editorial *we*, or a *we* that is self-consciously speaking from the circle of apostolic witnesses. Thus in this context it is distinguished from the "we" of all Christians; it is distinguished, in particular, from the "you" who constitute the readers: "*We* proclaim to *you* what *we* have seen and heard" (1:3). The previous two verses specify *what* John and the other witnesses have seen and heard. It is nothing less than the Incarnation: "That which was from the beginning" (1:1) one with God was nothing other than what appeared in real history and was repeatedly heard, seen, and touched. The eternal Word became a man (1:14 in John's gospel); here, the "life appeared; we have seen it and testify to it, and we proclaim to you the eternal life, which was with the Father and has appeared to us" (1:2). So John reiterates, "We proclaim to you what we have seen and heard" (1:3).

There is no Christianity without the Incarnation. Moreover, the Incarnation is not some vague notion of the divine identifying with the human. It is relentlessly concrete: the Word that was with God and that was God became flesh (as John writes elsewhere, 1:1, 14 in the gospel of John). That is fundamental in John's day, when he is combating those who presuppose that what is truly spiritual might *don* human flesh but could not *become* a human being; it is fundamental today, when we might be combating a philosophical naturalist who insists that the only reality is what occupies the continuum of space and time.

John tells his readers that he proclaims this truth to them, "so that you also may have fellowship with us. And our fellowship is with the Father and with his Son, Jesus Christ" (1:3). *Fellowship* in the New Testament is more than warm fuzzies. It is committed partnership, in which personal interests are subsumed under the common mission. The first witnesses entered into fellowship "with the Father and with his Son, Jesus Christ." John's readers may enter that fellowship by entering into the fellowship of the apostles. That is why John proclaims what he has seen and heard. The apostles mediate the Gospel to others. We cannot enter into fellowship with God and with his Son Jesus Christ without entering into fellowship with the apostles who were the first witnesses of the Incarnation.

None of this fosters stuffy religion. John writes to make "our" or "your" joy complete (1:4): whichever variant is original, it tells the truth on this point.

∾

2 Chronicles 2; 1 John 2; Nahum 1; Luke 17

ONE MIGHT WELL WONDER WHY God should be praised for loving the world (John 3:16) when Christians are forbidden to love it (**1 John 2:15-17**).

The *world,* as is habitually the case in John and 1 John, is the moral order in rebellion against God. When we are told that God loves the world, his love is to be admired because the world is so bad. God's love is the origin of his redemptive work. While his holiness entails his wrath (John 3:36), his character as love (1 John 4:8, 16) calls into being his redemptive mission.

What God forbids in 1 John 2:15-17, however, is something quite different. God loves the world with the holy love of redemption; he forbids us to love the world with the squalid love of participation. God loves the world with the self-sacrificing love that costs the Son his life; we are not to love the world with the self-seeking love that wants to taste all the world's sin. God loves the world with the redemptive power that so transforms individuals they no longer belong to the world; we are forbidden to love the world with the moral weakness that wishes to augment the number of worldlings by becoming full-fledged participants ourselves. God's love for the world is to be admired for its unique combination of purity and self-sacrifice; ours incites horror and disgust for its impurity and rapacious evil.

The *world* that John envisages in these verses is not pretty. It is characterized by all the lusts of our sinful natures ("the cravings of sinful man," 2:16), all the things from without that assault us and tempt us away from the living God ("the lust of the eyes," 2:16), all the arrogance of ownership, dominance, and control ("the boasting of what he has and does," 2:16). None of this comes from the Father but from the world.

But Christians make their evaluations in the light of eternity. "The world and its desires pass away, but the man who does the will of God lives forever" (2:17). Pity the person whose self-identity and hope rest on transient things. Ten billion years into eternity, it will seem a little daft to puff yourself up over the car you now drive, the amount of money or education you have received, the number of books you owned, the number of times you had your name in the headlines. Whether or not you have won an Academy Award will then prove less important than whether or not you have been true to your spouse. Whether or not you were a basketball star will be less significant than how much of your wealth you generously gave away. The one "who does the will of God lives forever" (2:17).

2 Chronicles 3—4; 1 John 3; Nahum 2; Luke 18

∽

"HOW GREAT IS THE LOVE the Father has lavished on us, that we should be called children of God! And that is what we are!" (**1 John 3:1**). All of us at one time belonged to the world; to use the language of Paul, we were all "by nature objects of wrath" (Eph. 2:3). The love of the Father that has accomplished the transformation is lavish precisely because it is undeserved. Moreover:

(1) "And that is what we are!" This emphatic exclamation was probably called forth in the first instance because those who had left the church (2:19) were adept at manipulating the believers. They insisted that they alone had an inside track with God, that they alone really understood the true knowledge (*gnosis*), that they alone enjoyed the true anointing. This had the effect of undermining the believers. John insists that his readers have received the real anointing (2:27), that their right conduct demonstrates that they have been born of God (2:29), that they have had the love of God lavished on them and thus become children of God— "And that is what we are!" The same point must be made for the sake of believers in every generation who feel threatened by the extravagant but misguided claims of the "super-spiritual" crowd who exercise their pitiful manipulation by a kind of spiritual one-upmanship. "We are the children of God," Christians quietly affirm—and that is enough. If others do not recognize the fact, it may only attest that they themselves do not know God (3:1b).

(2) Although we are now already the children of God, "what we will be has not yet been made known" (3:2). On the one hand, we must not denigrate or minimize all that we have received: "*now* we are children of God." On the other, we await the consummation and our own ultimate transformation (3:2).

(3) In fact, every child of God who lives with this prospect ahead, "who has this hope *in him* [which probably means 'in Christ' or 'in God,' specifying the object of the hope, rather than 'in himself,' merely specifying the one who entertains the hope] purifies himself, just as he is pure" (3:3). The Christian looks to what he or she will become in the consummation and is already interested in becoming like that. We receive the Father's love; we know that one day we shall be pure; so already we strive to become pure now. That is in perfect conformity with the way chapter 2 ends: "If you know that he is righteous, you know that everyone who does what is right has been born of him" (2:29).

∽

2 Chronicles 5:1—6:11; 1 John 4; Nahum 3; Luke 19

ONCE THE TEMPLE HAS BEEN BUILT, the final step before the dedication of the temple is bringing up the ark of the covenant from the old tabernacle, now resting in Zion, the City of David (part of Jerusalem), to its new resting place in the Most Holy Place of the temple. **Second Chronicles 5:1—6:11** not only records this transition, but Solomon's opening remarks to the people before his prayer of dedication (see tomorrow's meditation). Both the moving of the ark and Solomon's opening remarks prove important.

The move itself follows the prescriptions of the Law: the Levites alone are permitted to handle the ark. But the move is nevertheless a national event. The elders of Israel and the heads of clans come together from all over Israel for this great celebration. The move is accompanied by such lavish sacrifices that the number of animals killed could not be recorded (5:6). Finally the ark is lodged beneath the wings of the cherubim in the Most Holy Place. As an aside, the chronicler mentions that at this point only the tablets of the Law still rest in the ark of the covenant. Presumably the pot with manna and Aaron's rod that had budded were removed when the ark was held by the Philistines. In any case, the orchestras and choirs cut loose, including a 120-piece trumpet section. The singers praise God in the well-known couplet, "He is good; his love endures forever" (5:13).

Two details deserve special comment.

(1) In the past, the evidence of God's presence in the tabernacle was a cloud. Now the same cloud fills the temple; indeed, the glory of the Lord so fills the temple that the priests are driven out and find themselves unable to enter and perform their duties (5:13-14). This demonstrates that God is pleased with the temple; that he himself has sanctioned the move from tabernacle to temple; and above all that if the temple is *his* temple, it is not to be domesticated by mere rites, no matter how lavish. The glory of his presence is the important thing.

(2) Solomon's opening remarks also contribute to the sense of continuity. Perhaps some purists were tempted to say that it would have been better to stick with the tabernacle: after all, that is what God ordained on Mount Sinai. So Solomon reviews the steps that have brought the narrative to this point: *God's* promises to David, *God's* choice of Jerusalem and of this temple site, *God's* selection of Solomon over David to do the actual building, and so forth. Thus the temple, far from being a questionable innovation, is the next step in redemptive history and the fulfillment of *God's* good promises (6:10-11).

2 *Chronicles 6:12-42; 1 John 5; Habakkuk 1; Luke 20*

∾

SOLOMON'S PRAYER OF DEDICATION (**2 Chron. 6:12-42**) is one of the great moments of Old Testament history and theology. Many of its features deserve prolonged reflection. Here we pick up on a few strands.

(1) Both the beginning and the end of the prayer fasten on God as a covenant-keeping God, the original promise keeper. In particular (and understandably), Solomon is interested in God's promise to David to the effect that his line would continue, his dynasty would be preserved (6:14-17). Similarly the final doxology: "O LORD God, do not reject your anointed one. Remember the great love promised to David your servant" (6:42).

(2) Although the temple was doubtless a magnificent structure, and although Solomon might understandably feel some sort of justifiable pride in its completion, his grasp of the greatness of God is sufficiently robust that he himself articulates, in memorable terms, that no temple can possibly "contain" the God who outstrips the highest heavens (6:18). There is no trace of tribal domestication of God.

(3) The principal burden of what Solomon asks may be summarized quite simply. In the future, when either individual Israelites sin or the entire nation sinks into one sin or another, if they then turn away from their sin and pray toward the temple, Solomon asks that God himself will hear from heaven, and forgive their sin (6:21-39). There are four remarkable elements to these petitions.

First, there is an astonishingly realistic assessment of the propensity of the people to sin, even to sin so badly that they may one day be banished from the land. A lesser man would have been tempted on such an occasion to introduce a lot of sentimental, Pollyanna-like twaddle about undying allegiance and the like. But not Solomon. He is a wise man, and he knows that sinners sin.

Second, however central the temple is to be as a focus for the prayers of the people (not least when they sin), God will hear their prayers not from the temple but from heaven, his dwelling place. Once again, God is not being reduced to the status of the tribal deities worshiped by the surrounding pagans. The phrasing of this repeated request for forgiveness makes the role of God the crucial thing—the God who fills the heavens, not the temple.

Third, insofar as the temple is critical, it is seen as the center of religion and worship *that deals with the forgiveness of sin* and thus restores sinners to God. The heart of the temple is not the choirs and the ceremonies, but the forgiveness of sin. In this day of ill-defined spirituality, it is vital that we remember this point.

Fourth, Solomon's vision extends far enough to include foreigners (6:32-33)—a missionary thrust.

∾

2 Chronicles 7; 2 John; Habakkuk 2; Luke 21

∿

WHEN SOLOMON FINISHED PRAYING, there was more than silence and hushed reverence. Fire descended from heaven to consume the burnt offerings, and "the glory of the LORD filled the temple" (**2 Chron. 7:1**). God himself approved both the temple and Solomon's prayer of dedication. The thousands of Israelites who were present certainly saw things that way (7:3) and sang again, "He is good; his love endures forever" (7:3). The festival of celebration described in the following verses (7:4-10) is peerless.

There is more. Just as the Lord had personally appeared to Abraham, Isaac, and Jacob—and to Solomon's own father David!—so now he appears, by whatever means, to Solomon. Note:

(1) "I have heard your prayer and have chosen this place for myself *as a temple for sacrifices*" (7:12; cf. 7:16 and the meditation for November 26, emphasis added). God himself sees the sacrificial system as the heart of the temple. He then summarizes afresh his willingness to respond to his people when they stray and then pray; for this temple, in line with God's gracious self-disclosure, institutionalizes the various offerings for sin that are the means by which guilty sinners can be reconciled to God by the sacrifices that he himself has both prescribed and provided.

(2) Much of the rest of God's words to Solomon run on one of two lines. *First,* in words of reassurance, God says his eyes will indeed always be open to his temple, and he will hear the prayers of those who repent. *Second,* this appearance to Solomon is also a warning, even a threat. God tells Solomon that if the nation (the "you" in verse 19; "but if *you* turn away" is plural) succumbs to rebellion and idolatry, the time will come when God will descend on them in judgment, drive his people from the Promised Land, and so decimate Jerusalem and this temple that people will be appalled; they will hear as the only sufficient explanation that God himself brought all this disaster on them because of their sin (7:19-22). From God's perspective, the people receive fair warning; from the chronicler's perspective, he is preparing the way for the tragic conclusion to his book; from the canonical perspective, Christian readers are reminded that all systems and structures, even those that point to Christ, were bound to fail in this broken world until the appearance of the One to whom they pointed.

(3) The promise of 7:14 is often quoted as a universal key to revival. But one should note the linked themes of covenant people, land, and temple—all contextually specific, in this form, to the old covenant. But there is a legitimate extension, grounded in the reality that righteousness exalts a nation, but sin is a reproach to any people. God calls on all peoples to repent.

∿

2 Chronicles 8; 3 John; Habakkuk 3; Luke 22

∿

THE SITUATION BEHIND **3 John** seems to be something like the following. The writer, the "elder" (1:1), presumably the apostle John, has written to a particular church in his purview, apparently asking that church if it would do what it could to help out some "brothers" (1:5) who have been sent out on evangelistic ministry. Unfortunately, that church had been hijacked by one Diotrephes, who, in the apostle's view, was much more interested in being "first," i.e., in self-promotion and autocratic control, than he was in the advance of the Gospel (1:9). With such values controlling him, Diotrephes was quite prepared to spurn the apostle's approach.

From a distance, there was little the apostle could do. Nevertheless, when he does show up, he will call attention to what Diotrephes is doing, exposing him to the church (1:10). Apparently John is confident that he has the authority and credibility to carry the day. Meanwhile, the apostle sidesteps the normal channels of authority and writes his dear friend Gaius (1:1), who appears to belong to the same church but is of a very different spirit to that of Diotrephes.

After some preliminary words (1:2-4), John enthusiastically praises Gaius for the way he has opened up his home to these traveling "brothers" (1:5). Indeed, some of them have brought back reports of Gaius's excellent hospitality (1:6). Gaius will do well to continue this excellent ministry, sending them out "in a manner worthy of God" (1:6)—an astonishing standard we should emulate today when we commission and support missionaries who are truly faithful. In short, stouthearted generosity among Christians, exemplified by Gaius, is bound to be mission-minded; bullheaded lust for power, exemplified by Diotrephes, is far more likely to become narrow and myopic in vision.

Observe the piercing clarity of the opening remarks (1:2-3). *First,* John prays that Gaius's health will prosper as his soul prospers. Note which of the two is the standard of the other! *Second,* the apostle remarks on what has given him great joy—namely, the report of Gaius's faithfulness to the truth, his walk in the truth. *Third,* John generalizes this last point: "I have no greater joy than to hear that my children are walking in the truth" (1:4). In a world where many Christians derive their deepest joy from advancement, ease, promotions, financial security, good health, popularity, and a host of other things, it is delightful, not to say challenging, to hear an apostle testify that nothing stirs his joy more than to hear that his "children" are walking in line with the Gospel. That tells us all we need to know of his heart—and of where we should find our pleasures too.

∿

2 Chronicles 9; Jude; Zephaniah 1; Luke 23

∽

"DEAR FRIENDS, ALTHOUGH I WAS VERY EAGER to write to you about the salvation we share, I felt I had to write and urge you to contend for the faith that was once for all entrusted to the saints. For certain men whose condemnation was written about long ago have secretly slipped in among you. They are godless men" (**Jude 3-4**). Observe:

(1) Sometimes it is right to contend for the faith. That is not always the way forward, of course: more often the primary emphasis must be on proclamation, articulating, and rearticulating the whole counsel of God. Sometimes a gentle answer or earnest entreaty will prove the wiser course. But here, Jude urges his readers to *contend* for the faith.

(2) That for which we must contend is the faith that was once for all entrusted to the saints. The place where the faith is being attacked in such cases is bound up with some stance that describes itself as "progressive," "contemporary," or "avant-garde"—but which is inevitably prepared to sacrifice something that "was once for all entrusted to the saints." Of course, sometimes the latter is nothing more than an appeal to unwarranted tradition, but that is not what is going on in this case. Here the "progressivists" are sacrificing something that has been essential to the Gospel from the very beginning.

(3) In some cases, contending for the faith (which is not to be confused with being contentious about the faith) is the most urgent thing to do. That is why Jude can openly admit he had hoped to write something else, but felt compelled to apply himself to this more urgent task. However discomfiting, when essential truth is being denied, and the denial is being believed by rising numbers, strategic wisdom foregoes other ministry for a while and focuses on the immediate pressing danger.

(4) The need for the firmest contention usually arises when the heretical voices arise *in the church*. When those who oppose the truth are outside the church, then although some Christians must respond to their various arguments (perhaps for evangelistic purposes), there is no urgency about contending for the faith once entrusted to the saints. Once such people manage to slip inside the church, however, so that many naive Christians accept their teaching without perceiving it to be pernicious, firm contention is inevitable. Such people must not only be refuted, but disciplined—and the latter cannot be accomplished without the former.

(5) The peculiar godlessness Jude confutes in this case is some perverse reading of the Gospel that transmutes it into "a license for immorality" (v. 4). Any reading of the Gospel that promotes immorality or denies the efficacy of Jesus' salvation must be wrong and dismissed as godless.

∽

2 Chronicles 10; Revelation 1; Zephaniah 2; Luke 24

∾

BEFORE THE OPENING VISION OF **Revelation 1**, which pictures the exalted Jesus in apocalyptic symbols that are reminiscent of the imagery of the Ancient of Days in Daniel 7 (Rev. 1:12-16), John provides us with a brief encomium: "To him who loves us and has freed us from our sins by his blood, and has made us to be a kingdom and priests to serve his God and Father—to him be glory and power for ever and ever! Amen!" (1:5-6).

(1) For all the startling and even terrifying pictures of God and of the Lamb in this book, we start out with a declaration of Jesus' love, his peculiar love for the people of God: *"To him who loved us . . . be glory and power for ever and ever!"* There is nothing that inspires our gratitude and awe more than the love shown us by the eternal Son of God on the cross. I believe it was T. T. Shields who penned the lines: "Was ever a heart so hardened, / And can such ingratitude be, / That one for whom Jesus suffered / Should say, 'It is nothing to me'?"

(2) Jesus Christ "has freed us from our sins by his blood." Some older versions offer instead "has washed us from our sins by his blood." The difference in the Greek is only one letter; the NIV is almost certainly right. By his blood, i.e., by his sacrificial and atoning death, Jesus expiated our sins and thereby freed us from their curse. Not only so, but all the benefits we receive—the gift of the Holy Spirit, the promises of God's enduring protection, eternal life, the consummating resurrection—have been secured by Jesus' death, and all of them combine to free us from our sins—their guilt, their power, their results.

(3) Christ "has made us to be a kingdom and priests to serve his God and Father." There is a sense in which we are *in* the kingdom—the sphere of his saving rule. There is another sense in which Christ now rules over all in unconditional sovereignty (Matt. 28:18; 1 Cor. 15:25), and in that sense everyone and everything is in his kingdom. But insofar as Christians are the peculiar locus of the redeemed community and the foretaste of the universe-transforming redemption still to come, we ourselves can be thought of as his kingdom. Moreover, he has made us priests. Christians do not have priests other than Jesus their great high priest: there is but one mediator between God and human beings (1 Tim. 2:5). But in another sense, we *are* priests: all Christians mediate between God and this broken, sinful world. We mediate God to fellow sinners by faithfully proclaiming and living out the Gospel, and bear their needs in our intercessory prayers before our heavenly Father. Jesus Christ has made us a kingdom and priests to serve his God and Father.

∾

2 Chronicles 11—12; Revelation 2; Zephaniah 3; John 1

～

THE CHRONICLER PROVIDES SOME fascinating insights into the reign of Rehoboam, the first king of Judah after the end of the united monarchy (**2 Chron. 11—12**). We note two of them.

(1) Predictably, many of the Levites who lived in the north drifted south (11:11-17). Their entire life centered on the temple, and this was the connection that Jeroboam, king over the northern ten tribes, wanted to break. Not only therefore did he establish his own idol gods, but he sacked all the Levites. The effect, at least initially, was to strengthen the hand of Rehoboam (11:17). Sometimes the principle of "unintended consequences" is quietly used by God's providence to bring blessings out of what at first appears to be unmitigated disaster. The most stellar example of this, of course, is the cross.

(2) Rehoboam proves to be a mediocre king whose total effect is bad. Certain early elements in Rehoboam's reign were good. He chose the right son, Abijah, to be his "chief prince" (11:22), preparing him for the throne. Learning from the stupidity of the initial decision that had cost him the unified kingdom (10:8; cf. 1 Kings 12:8), Rehoboam worked hard at maintaining contact with the people, dispersing his many sons around the districts and fortified cities of Judah. Sadly, once he had become comfortable, once his kingdom was more or less secure, he drifted away from the Law of the Lord, and so did his people (12:1). God responded by unleashing Shishak, king of Egypt, against this small nation. The prophet Shemaiah thundered, "This is what the LORD says, 'You have abandoned me; therefore, I now abandon you to Shishak'" (12:5).

King Rehoboam and the leaders of Israel humble themselves (12:6, 12). The result is that God does not permit the Egyptians to destroy Judah. Nevertheless, God says that his people will "become subject to [Shishak], so that they may learn the difference between serving me and serving the kings of other lands" (12:8). This development reminds us of God's reaction when the people of Israel entered the Promised Land and promptly compromised their faithfulness. The result was that instead of the clean sweep they might have had, they were embroiled in squalid skirmishes for generations.

There is a kind of evil that is not very bad and not very good, not too terribly rebellious yet not hungry for righteousness, a stance that drifts toward idolatry and hastily retreats at the threat of judgment. What it lacks is David's heart, the heart of a man who, despite failures, sets himself to pursue God with passion and delight. The final verdict on Rehoboam's reign explains the problem: "He did evil because he had not set his heart on seeking the LORD" (12:14).

～

2 Chronicles 13; Revelation 3; Haggai 1; John 2

∾

THE SEVEN CHURCHES OF Asia Minor (roughly the western third of modern Turkey) differ quite a bit from one another (Rev. 2—3). In most instances they reflect something of the cities in which they are located, either by mirroring their faults or by withstanding their oppression. Two of the seven churches, at Smyrna and Philadelphia, are small and under attack, and they receive no criticism. The other five are in various degrees of jeopardy.

The church that receives the least encouragement and the most condemnation is the church at Laodicea (**Rev. 3:14-22**), a church that reflects its surroundings far too closely. Laodicea was a banking center. Here travelers to the East changed their money, as did Cicero, the famous Roman orator, when he traveled beyond the borders of the Empire toward the East. The money business made the city wealthy. It was also known as an ophthalmic center. Eye infections were not uncommon, and at Laodicea doctors had developed a poultice that many found effective. The sheep in this area produced a particularly tough, black wool—the "jeans" material of the ancient world. The only real drawback to the town was its water system. Nearby Colossae had the only fresh spring water in the Lycus Valley; nearby Hierapolis boasted hot springs, renowned as a place for "taking the cure." Laodicea had to bring in its water through stone pipes from miles away, and this water was foul. It left thick calcium carbonate deposits in the pipes, and was infamous in the ancient world for its disgusting taste.

John picks up on these points. The church thinks it is rich, but does not realize it is spiritually bankrupt. It believes it can "see," i.e., that it is discerning, when in fact it is blind. It holds that it is well dressed, entirely presentable, whereas God perceives it is naked. This church has become smug and proud in all the ways the city is smug and proud. The exalted Jesus urges that this church "buy" the "gold" that only he can give, the eye salve only he can provide, and clothes, white clothes (signaling purity) only he can give them (3:18). For in his experience, in their current state they are to him like Laodicea's water: neither cool and refreshing (like the water at Colossae), nor hot and medicinal (like the water at Hierapolis), but frankly nauseating. They are neither cool and useful, nor hot and useful; they are merely disgusting and make him retch.

Many a church in the West finds itself in a similar position. Hear the Word of the Lord: "Those whom I love I rebuke and discipline. So be earnest, and repent. Here I am! I stand at the door and knock. If anyone hears my voice and opens the door, I will come in and eat with him, and he with me" (3:19-20).

∾

2 Chronicles 14—15; Revelation 4; Haggai 2; John 3

⌒

THE REIGN OF KING ASA of Judah is instructive on several fronts, and will occupy our attention both today (**2 Chron. 14—15**) and tomorrow.

Asa's long reign began with ten years of peace (14:1), "for the LORD gave him rest" (14:6). During this time Asa "commanded Judah to seek the LORD, the God of their fathers, and to obey his laws and commands" (14:4). The people sought the Lord, "and built and prospered" (14:7). At the end of ten years, Asa faced the devastating power of the Cushite forces (from the upper Nile). Asa could not possibly have forgotten how his grandfather Rehoboam was subjugated by Shishak of Egypt (2 Chron. 12). Asa's own conduct is exemplary, a foretaste of how his descendant Hezekiah would handle himself centuries later when he faced the Babylonians: he called on the Lord, frankly acknowledging his utter powerlessness against such forces. "Help us, O LORD our God, for we rely on you, and in your name we have come against this vast army. O LORD, you are our God; do not let man prevail against you" (14:11). By whatever means (the text does not specify), the Lord answers, and Asa's relatively tiny army crushes the Cushite host.

Enter Azariah son of Oded, a prophet with a message of encouragement for Asa and for all Judah and Benjamin (15:1-2). Reflecting on the terrible years of anarchy under the closing years of the judges and the opening years of the monarchy, when travel and trade were dangerous and when the Levites were not sufficiently disciplined and organized to teach the people, Azariah encourages king and people alike to seek the Lord, for "he will be found by you, but if you forsake him, he will forsake you" (15:2). Such a message strengthens Asa's resolve. He proceeds against the remaining idolatry in the land and pours resources into the maintenance of the temple. This is the covenant community, and under Asa it begins to act like one. "They sought God eagerly, and he was found by them. So the LORD gave them rest on every side" (15:15) for a further quarter century, to the thirty-fifth year of Asa's reign (15:19). The "high places" were not removed (15:17)—a residue of competition with the temple—but for the most part Asa was a straight arrow.

We should not be embarrassed by the blessing of God on integrity and righteousness. Righteousness exalts a nation: it lifts it up and strengthens its hand. This is not merely a sociological inference: it is the way God has structured things, the way he providentially rules. Inversely, corruption attracts the wrath of God, and sooner or later will bring a nation down.

⌒

2 Chronicles 16; Revelation 5; Zechariah 1; John 4

∾

BEGINNING WELL DOES NOT mean ending well. Judas Iscariot began as an apostle; Demas began as an apostolic helper. We know how they ended up. Asa began as a reforming king zealous for God, a man who displayed formidable faith and courage when the Cushites attacked (review yesterday's meditation)—but how he ends up in **2 Chronicles 16** is frankly disquieting.

The crisis was precipitated when Baasha, king of Israel, attacked some of Judah's outlying towns and cities. Instead of displaying the same kind of resolute faith he had shown twenty-five years earlier, when he had to face the more formidable Cushites, Asa opts for a costly political expedient. He strips both the temple and his own palace of wealth, and sends it to Ben-Hadad, ruler of the rising regional power of Aram, centered in Damascus. Asa wants Ben-Hadad to attack Israel from the north, thereby forcing Baasha to withdraw his troops from the southern assault and defend himself in the north. The ploy worked.

This was also linking Judah with Aram in dangerous ways. More importantly, the prophet Hanani puts his finger on the worst element in this strategy: Asa is depending on politics and money, and not on the Lord God. "Were not the Cushites and Libyans a mighty army with great numbers of chariots and horsemen? Yet when you relied on the LORD, he delivered them into your hand. For the eyes of the LORD range throughout the earth to strengthen those whose hearts are fully committed to him. You have done a foolish thing, and from now on you will be at war" (16:8-9).

Even then the situation might have been retrieved: God so regularly listens to the truly repentant. But Asa merely becomes angry, so enraged that he throws Hanani the prophet into prison. His dictatorial urges multiply, and Asa begins to brutalize the people (16:10). Four years later he contracts a wretched disease, but instead of asking for the Lord's help (let alone his forgiveness), he entrenches himself in bitterness and seeks help only from the physicians. Two years of disease later, he dies.

What about all those years of godly reform? We are not in the position, of course, to offer a final accounting: that belongs to God alone. But people can be on the side of goodness or reform for all kinds of reasons other than love of God; phenomenologically, people can have a heart for God for a long time (15:17) but wilt before demonstrating final perseverance. In a disciplined person, it may take a while before the truth comes out. But when it does, the test, as always, is fundamental: Am I number one, or is God?

∾

2 Chronicles 17; Revelation 6; Zechariah 2; John 5

CHAPTERS 4 AND 5 OF REVELATION, on which we have not reflected, constitute a major vision that prepares us for much of the rest of the book—including **Revelation 6**. Chapter 4 is to chapter 5 what a setting is to a drama. Revelation 4 depicts, in apocalyptic symbols, the throne room of Almighty God. The emphasis is on God's awesomeness, his holiness, his transcendent and spectacular glory. Even the highest orders of angels veil their faces as they bow in worship and extol God for his holiness. In Revelation 5, the drama begins. In the right hand of God rests a scroll, which turns out to contain all his purposes for redemption and judgment. The scroll is sealed with seven seals. In the symbolism of this book, opening the seals means bringing about all of God's purposes for redemption and judgment. If the book remains unopened, God's purposes will remain unfulfilled. A powerful angel launches a challenge to the entire universe: Is anyone worthy to approach this awesome and frankly terrifying God, take the scroll, and open the seals—in other words, to serve as God's agent to bring his purposes to pass? No one is found who is worthy, and in despair, John weeps. Then one of the elders tells him to stop crying. The Lion of the tribe of Judah has prevailed. John looks up through his tears, and sees—a Lamb. This is not an animal additional to the Lion. True to the mixed nature of apocalyptic metaphors, the Lion *is* the Lamb— and he emerges from the center of the throne. From then on in the book of Revelation, praise is offered to him who sits on the throne, *and to the Lamb.*

Revelation 6 finds the Lamb opening the seals. In due course, the seventh seal introduces seven trumpets (Rev. 8), which in turn are followed by the seven bowls of God's wrath (Rev. 16). Thus the entire drama of the book of Revelation is introduced by the vision of Revelation 4—5.

So far as Revelation 6 is concerned, I shall focus on only two points. (1) The martyrs who are "under the altar" cry out in a loud voice, "How long, Sovereign Lord, holy and true, until you judge the inhabitants of the earth and avenge our blood?" (6:9-10). It is a great comfort to know that justice will be done, and will be seen to be done; it is an even greater comfort to know that God is more forbearing than Christians. (2) But when that judgment does come, there is no escaping it, no reprieve. All who have rebelled against their Maker and never been reconciled to him, whether they are slaves or among the powerful and the mighty, cry out to the mountains and the rocks to hide them "from the face of him who sits on the throne and from the wrath of the Lamb" (6:16). But who can hide from the throne of God?

2 Chronicles 18; Revelation 7; Zechariah 3; John 6

∾

THERE ARE MANY DISPUTED POINTS of interpretation over **Revelation 7.** For instance, who are the 144,000 (7:4)? Are they the same people as the great multitude that no one could count (7:9), in much the same way that in chapter 5 the Lion is the Lamb? What or when is the "great tribulation" (7:14)? Is it a brief period of time? If so, when—in A.D. 70, or toward the end of the age? Or is it a way of referring to the entire period between Jesus' first and second comings?

But here I shall restrict my attention to three elements in John's description of the "great multitude that no one could count."

First, they spring "from every nation, tribe, people and language" (7:9). There is not a whiff of racism here. Moreover, this theme keeps recurring in the book. For instance, already in Revelation 5:9, the elders sing a new song to the Lamb: "You are worthy to take the scroll and to open its seals, because you were slain, and with your blood you purchased men for God *from every tribe and language and people and nation.*" The ultimate community of God is transnational, transtribal, transracial, translinguistic. In that sense, Los Angeles is a better anticipation of heaven than Tulsa, Oklahoma. Let the church, strengthened by the grace of God, live out now, as largely as possible, what she will one day be.

Second, everything significant about these people turns on the work of God effected through the Lamb—in short, it turns on the Gospel of God. So they stand "before the throne and in front of the Lamb" (7:9); they cry "in a loud voice: 'Salvation belongs to our God, who sits on the throne, and to the Lamb'" (7:10). While the angels worship God (7:11-12), John is told that these people "have washed their robes and made them white in the blood of the Lamb" (7:14). In short, whatever else is found in Revelation, this book overflows with the Gospel.

Third, the ultimate prospect for the great multitude is not located in this life. They "are before the throne of God and serve him day and night in his temple" (7:15). Nothing bad will ever again befall them (7:16). "For the Lamb at the center of the throne will be their shepherd; he will lead them to springs of living water. And God will wipe away every tear from their eyes" (7:17). The book of Revelation fans the flames of courage and faithfulness in this life, even in the teeth of the most virulent opposition, by holding out the most glorious prospects for the life to come.

∾

2 Chronicles 19—20; Revelation 8; Zechariah 4; John 7

∾

EARLIER WE WITNESSED A KING who began well and ended poorly (Asa; see December 13-14); still earlier, we witnessed a halfhearted reformer (Rehoboam; see December 11). Now we come across another, King Jehoshaphat, who does not degenerate, nor does he slide along in a gray zone between good and evil, but rather proves to be very good in some areas and not very discerning and even stupid in others—all his life (**2 Chron. 19—20**).

The two previous chapters (2 Chron. 17—18) can be divided into two parts. Chapter 17 depicts the strengths of Jehoshaphat—the man who diligently seeks the Lord and fortifies the entire southern kingdom. By contrast, chapter 18 depicts foolish Jehoshaphat, enmeshed in a needless and compromised alliance with wicked King Ahab of Israel, almost losing his life in a fight that wasn't his. Now in the chapters before us, the prophet Jehu, son of the prophet Hanani who had been imprisoned by Asa in his old age, confronts Jehoshaphat: "Should you help the wicked and love those who hate the LORD? Because of this, the wrath of the LORD is upon you. There is, however, some good in you, for you have rid the land of the Asherah poles and have set your heart on seeking God" (19:2-3).

Then the pattern repeats itself. Jehoshaphat works diligently to rid the judiciary of corruption (19:4-11). When he faces another military crisis, this time the nations of Moab and Ammon allied against him, he turns to God for help. The culmination of his prayer is intensely moving: "O our God, will you not judge them? For we have no power to face this vast army that is attacking us. We do not know what to do, but our eyes are upon you" (20:12). In his mercy, God sends his Spirit upon Jahaziel son of Zechariah, who carries a prophetic word to strengthen and encourage Jehoshaphat and the people of Judah and Jerusalem (20:15ff). The victory they win is extravagant, and the Lord graciously imposes "the fear of God" upon the surrounding kingdoms, thereby giving Jehoshaphat and Judah rest.

So what does Jehoshaphat do? He makes another stupid and unnecessary alliance, this time with Ahaziah, the new king of Israel, and is soundly rebuked by another prophetic word (20:35-37). Doesn't the man ever learn?

Today we would probably label such deeply disturbing repetitions "character flaws." They can occur in people whose lives, on so many levels, are entirely praiseworthy. At one level it is entirely right to thank God for the good these people do. But would it not have been far better if Jehoshaphat had learned from his first mistakes?

Would it be impertinent to ask if you and I learn from ours?

∾

2 Chronicles 21; Revelation 9; Zechariah 5; John 8

∽

WHATEVER THE REFERENTS BEHIND the horrific images of **Revelation 9**, the visions of mayhem and slaughter are clear enough. In war and plague, countless millions of human beings are slaughtered, one-third of humankind, some in great agony. Today I wish to focus on the closing verses of the chapter, setting this sweeping destruction in a certain framework.

(1) At one level, this destruction is the work of hell—more precisely, of "the angel of the Abyss, whose name in Hebrew is Abaddon, and in Greek, Apollyon" (9:11), the Destroyer. There is no doubt this is also Satan, the Devil himself (cf. 12:7-9; 20:10). For all his efforts to entice human beings away from the God who made them and whose image they bear, Satan's long-term goals for human beings are *never* benign. He may give temporary power or advantage to those who sell themselves to do evil, or to those who enter a Faustian pact with him, but his ultimate goal is the destruction of all human beings, or as many of them as he can harm, as ruthlessly, as painfully, as possible.

(2) For all that Satan himself is behind this destruction, in the larger narrative of the book, God himself has brought about this destruction as part of his righteous judgment. Satan is evil and powerful, but he is not all-powerful. Even at his most virulent he cannot escape God's control—and God is able to use even Satan's evil to bring about his purposes of righteous judgment on those who persist in their rebellion against God.

(3) So perverse are human beings that even the most devastating judgment frequently fails to get their attention or to drive them toward repentance. "The rest of mankind that were not killed by these plagues still did not repent of the work of their hands; they did not stop worshiping demons, and idols of gold, silver, bronze, stone and wood—idols that cannot see or hear or walk. Nor did they repent of their murders, their magic arts, their sexual immorality or their thefts" (9:20-21).

Few statements are more discouraging. What is God to do? When he maintains order and stable times, his image-bearers drift away from him, indifferent to his blessings. When instead God responds in judgment, his image-bearers charge that God is unfair, or assign these things to blind circumstance, or exclusively to the Devil, or to alien deities who need placating. Apart from the intervention of the convicting work of the Spirit, few reflect deeply on how these disasters are calling to us in prophetic terms.

What disasters has the race of God's image-bearers faced in the twentieth century? What is their message? How have most people responded?

∽

2 Chronicles 22—23; Revelation 10; Zechariah 6; John 9

∾

MANY IMAGES IN THE BOOK OF Revelation are drawn from the Old Testament. The antecedent to the scroll that John eats (**Rev. 10:8-11**) is a similar image in Jeremiah 15:16; Ezekiel 2:8—3:3.

Each of the three passages develops the notion of eating God's words a little differently. Jeremiah contrasts himself with his persecutors and tormentors, with "the company of revelers" (Jer. 15:17) with whom he never made common cause. How could he? He sat alone because the hand of God was upon him. He perceived the sin in the land and the judgment that were threatening, and he was filled with indignation. What was it that gave him this stance? "When your words came, I ate them; they were my joy and my heart's delight, for I bear your name, O LORD God Almighty" (Jer. 15:16).

In his vision Ezekiel is shown a scroll written on both sides with "words of lament and mourning and woe" (Ezek. 2:10). God tells him to open his mouth and eat the scroll, and then go and speak to the house of Israel (Ezek. 3:1). "So I ate it, and it tasted as sweet as honey in my mouth" (Ezek. 3:3). The context makes clear the meaning. Even though the message Ezekiel conveyed was full of judgment and lament, even though he explained the sins of Jerusalem to the exilic community and predicted the catastrophic fall of city and temple alike, Ezekiel was to be so aligned with God's perspective that he found God's words sweet. However hard the message, God's words of judgment, if they really are God's words, Ezekiel will find sweeter than all of the words of the received opinion of self-justifying sinners.

In his vision, John the seer is instructed to take a scroll and eat it. He is told that it will taste as sweet as honey, but that it will turn sour in his stomach (Rev. 10:9-10). The content is again judgment: John "must prophesy again about many peoples, nations, languages and kings" (10:11). But here the symbolism works out a little differently. It is still important for this scroll to taste sweet in John's mouth, i.e., for him so to align himself with God and his truth that he finds God's ways and words to be sweet. But now an extra layer is added: however important and right it is to side with God's perspective, however vital it is to say "Amen!" to God's good and necessary judgment, nevertheless judgment is still judgment. There cannot finally be pleasure at the prospect of the wrath of God, as utterly righteous as that wrath is, for the sin that has called it forth is utterly tragic both in its own reality and in the consequences it elicits.

∾

2 Chronicles 24; Revelation 11; Zechariah 7; John 10

∿

THROUGHOUT THE BOOK OF Revelation there are occasional visions of the end or of the throne room of God that anticipate the last two chapters. In other words, the line of development in Revelation is not always linear. The anticipation of victory, glory, and the perspective of the Almighty are sometimes placed in the context of the darkest scenes of judgment: e.g., Revelation 14:1-5, in the context of chapters 12—14.

When the seventh trumpet sounds (**Rev. 11:15-19**), the veil is rolled back a little to permit a glimpse of just such a scene—not in this case of the new heaven and the new earth, but of the reign of God over these scenes of terrible judgment. I may draw attention to two elements.

First, the notion of the kingdom of God is a dynamic one and changes its precise significance in various contexts. Here loud voices in heaven proclaim: "The kingdom of the world has become the kingdom of our Lord and of his Christ, and he will reign for ever and ever" (11:15). This suggests that there was a time before which this divine "kingdom" over this lost world had *not* begun. So what is in view is certainly not the universal kingdom of God's providential rule. Nor is this the onset of Jesus' reign, as inaugurated by his resurrection and exaltation. True, at that point all authority became his in heaven and earth (Matt. 28:18). Nevertheless, that reign is so exercised that it is still contested. What the following verses suggest is that God now so takes his great power as to destroy those who have destroyed his people. "The time has come for judging the dead, and for rewarding your servants the prophets and your saints and those who reverence your name, both small and great—and for destroying those who destroy the earth" (11:18). What this announces is the imminence of the final exercise of authority that shatters all residual opposition and judges all with perfect justice.

Second, we have already seen that mixed metaphors are characteristic of apocalyptic literature. Here in 11:19, God's temple in heaven is opened, and *within* the temple the ark of the covenant is seen, accompanied by an awesome storm. Terrible storms accompanying God's great acts of self-disclosure spring from what took place at Sinai; something similar is found in the vision of 4:5. The point of temple, ark, and storm in this verse is that God himself is present and reigning. By contrast, in the vision of chapters 21—22, there is no need for a temple in heaven, *for the Lord God Almighty and the Lamb are the temple* (21:22). Only pedants will perceive a contradiction.

∿

2 Chronicles 25; Revelation 12; Zechariah 8; John 11

～

THE VISION OF REVELATION 12 provides the ultimate cause of the ongoing tribulations of the people of God. That cause is nothing less than the rage of Satan.

The woman in this chapter is not Mary, but a figure representing the people of God. From her springs Jesus, the son "who will rule all the nations with an iron scepter" (12:5). Yet she is not simply Israel, for after Jesus ascends to God, the woman is left behind with "the rest of her offspring—those who obey God's commandments and hold to the testimony of Jesus" (12:17). The woman, then, represents the collective people of God, whether of the old covenant or of the new.

Satan in this chapter not only fails in his vicious attempt to destroy Jesus (12:4-5), but he is defeated by Michael and thrown out of heaven (12:7-9). He is hurled to the earth (12:9). Raging against this restriction (12:13), raging as well "because he knows that his time is short" (12:12) before his utter destruction, he is filled with fury against the woman and her offspring. Much of the rest of the chapter describes his attack on the woman and her children—on us Christians!—in symbol-laden language drawn from the Old Testament.

Among his attacks are accusations designed both to destroy our confidence and to engage God's wrath against people as sinful as we are: Satan is "the accuser of [the] brothers" (12:10). But in one crucial verse (12:11), John tells us how these believers overcome the devil.

(1) "They overcame him by the blood of the Lamb." The preposition translated as *by* in the NIV should be rendered "on the ground of." When all his accusations are brought before us—so many of them entirely justified, if we gauge things only by the quality of our faithfulness—Satan is silenced when we insist that our acceptance before God is grounded not in ourselves but in the death of Jesus Christ. "Who is he that condemns?" Paul exultantly asks. "Christ Jesus, who died—more than that, who was raised to life—is at the right hand of God and is also interceding for us" (Rom. 8:34). We neither have nor need another ground for our acquittal.

(2) "They overcame him by . . . the word of their testimony." This does not mean that they frequently gave their testimonies. It means, rather, that they constantly bore testimony to Jesus Christ; in short, they constantly proclaimed the Gospel. That is what spells Satan's defeat. Keep silent, and Satan wins.

(3) "They did not love their lives so much as to shrink from death." You cannot defeat an opponent who is not only willing to die, but for whom death means winning (Phil. 1:21).

～

2 Chronicles 26; Revelation 13; Zechariah 9; John 12

∾

IT TURNS OUT THAT SATAN HAS two unholy beasts to assist him, one that comes out of the sea (**Rev. 13:1-10**), and the other out of the earth (13:11-18). Together they constitute an unholy triumvirate that in some ways apes the Trinity.

Admittedly, many of the apocalyptic symbols in this chapter have been interpreted in mutually exclusive ways by different schools of thought. It is entirely beyond these brief meditations to defend a particular structure. In my view, however, these beasts represent recurring historical manifestations of evil—in the one case, evil in its guise as outright opposition against the people of God, and in the other, evil in its guise as religious deception. (It is not for nothing that the beast out of the earth is described later in this book as "the false prophet": e.g., 19:20.) Satan deploys not only agents who overtly and viciously attack believers, but also agents whose mission it is to seduce and deceive, if it is possible, the very elect.

Observe one of the extraordinary elements in the description of the first beast. He has received a fatal wound, but the wound has been healed. This sounds incongruous: surely if the wound has been healed, it was not fatal, and if it was fatal then obviously it could not be healed. But this symbolism is meant to describe the *repeated* historical manifestations of this monster. He emerges in a Nero, in the Roman Emperor, in Innocent III, in a Hitler. In every case, the monster is cut down. Many people think that evil in its worst form has finally been destroyed. The thousand-year Reich lasts a decade and a half: surely this was the war to end all wars. Then the genocide starts again—in the Eastern block, in China, in Cambodia, in Rwanda. The beast receives a fatal wound, but always the beast comes back to life.

Note some of the symbols used to describe the false prophet. He looks like a lamb, but he speaks like a dragon (13:11): this probably does not mean that he roars like a dragon and scares everyone off, but that he appears innocent, even though his speech is the speech of the dragon—the "great dragon" of 12:9, none other than Satan himself. This "lamb" turns out to be Satan's mouthpiece. He performs miraculous signs and thereby deceives the inhabitants of the earth (13:14). There is no suggestion that the signs are mere tricks; miraculous power does not necessarily attest divine power. Ultimately he uses the authority he derives from the first beast to constitute an exclusive identity for his own followers, excluding all others with severe economic sanctions (13:16-17). Even little historical knowledge can remember manifestations of such deceitful coercion.

∾

2 Chronicles 27—28; Revelation 14; Zechariah 10; John 13

∼

IN REVELATION 13, we discovered that all those under the authority of the unholy triumvirate have a mark on their foreheads. This means that they can participate in the world order of the dragon and his beasts and be spared the wrath of Satan. Here in **Revelation 14**, we learn that God's people also have something on their foreheads—the name of the Lamb and of the Father (14:1). These people stand on Mount Zion with the Lamb and are spared all the wrath of the Lamb. By contrast, those with the mark of the beast must now face the wrath of the Lamb, drinking "of the wine of God's fury, which has been poured full strength into the cup of his wrath" (14:10-11).

The imagery comes from quite a different vision, from Ezekiel 9, where Ezekiel sees God instructing a man dressed in linen to put a mark on the foreheads of all the people in Jerusalem who grieve over its sin. When the angelic executioners go through the city, bent on destruction and slaughter, they spare all those who have God's mark on their foreheads. That imagery has now been adapted in two quite different ways in Revelation. Now *everyone* has a mark on the forehead. Either you have the mark of the beast, and you are spared the wrath of the beast but must face God's fury; or you have the mark of the Lamb, which means you are spared God's fury but you must face the sanctions of the beast.

So whose wrath would you rather face? You will face one or the other. Would you rather face the wrath of Satan, or the wrath of God?

The Lord Jesus taught us that the person to fear is the One who can cast both body and soul into hell (Matt. 10:28). Few passages are more terrifying about that prospect than Revelation 14. We are bluntly told that "the smoke of their torment rises for ever and ever. There is no rest day or night for those who worship the beast and his image, or for anyone who receives the mark of his name" (14:11). Few passages are more explicit about the eternal longevity of this punishment. The final graphic portrait (14:19-20) is unimaginably horrific. In the ancient world, large stone vats with holes punched in the bottom were filled with grapes, and servant girls jumped in and tramped down the grapes, squeezing out the juice that ran out through the holes and was gathered for use in winemaking. But now in the wake of the final harvest, one must assume it is people who are thrown into this vat, for what flows out from "the great winepress of God's wrath" (14:19) is blood, flowing outward for 180 miles.

So, whose wrath would *you* rather face?

∼

2 Chronicles 29; Revelation 15; Zechariah 11; John 14

∽

WITH THE EXCEPTION OF only a few verses, most of the material in 2 Chronicles 29—31 has no parallel in 2 Kings. What these chapters provide is a detailed account of how King Hezekiah went about reinstituting temple worship that was in line with the Law of God delivered through Moses, and then called the covenant people together not only from Judah but even some from Israel to celebrate the Passover in a way that had not been done for some time.

Here we may focus on **2 Chronicles 29**. Paganism had taken such a hold on the people that temple service had fallen into disuse. The temple had become a repository for junk; even the doors needed fixing. Still only twenty-five years old, King Hezekiah, in the first month of his reign (29:3), opened the doors and repaired them. He found some priests and Levites and instructed them to consecrate themselves according to the rites established in the Law, and then to set about cleaning, repairing, and reconsecrating the temple. Moreover, Hezekiah recognized that the past failures in this respect had invited the wrath of God (29:6). He was not so foolish as to think the failures were merely a matter of ritual: he saw the larger picture, but perceived, rightly, that the utter neglect of the ritual demonstrated that the hearts of priests, Levites, people, and king alike were entirely alienated from God. His open intention was to reverse this pattern and inaugurate a covenant with the Lord (29:10).

The rest of the chapter details what was done. More priests and Levites came on board. The musical instruments secured by David were restored to use. Even small deviations from the Law are recorded, such as the permission to allow the Levites to help with the skinning of the animals for the sacrifices, owing to the fact that at this point too few priests were consecrated (29:32-34).

"So the service of the temple of the LORD was reestablished. Hezekiah and all the people rejoiced at what God had brought about for his people, because it was done so quickly" (29:35-36).

So it is when genuine revival comes in considerable proportion. Inevitably, God raises up a leader whose prophetic insistence proves irresistible, first to a few, and then to a great crowd. And in the best instances it is not long before men and women look back and marvel at how fast the face of things was massively transformed. They conclude, rightly, that the only explanation is that God himself has done it—that is, that the transformation is not finally attributable to reforming zeal or organizing skill, but to a God who has changed people's hearts.

∽

2 Chronicles 30; Revelation 16; Zechariah 12:1—13:1; John 15

∾

THE SEVEN BOWLS OF GOD'S WRATH (**Rev. 16**), containing the seven last plagues (see also Rev. 15), are poured out on the earth. Doubtless much of the language is symbol-laden; some of it is transparent, some of it more difficult to understand. Here I wish to focus on one clause that is repeated. When the fourth angel poured out his bowl, the people "cursed the name of God, who had control over these plagues, *but they refused to repent and glorify him*" (16:9, italics added). Similarly after the fifth bowl: people "gnawed their tongues in agony and cursed the God of heaven because of their pains and their sores, *but they refused to repent of what they had done*" (16:11, italics added).

We must reflect on these somber passages.

(1) They occur immediately after the semi-poetical lines of the previous verses: "You are just in these judgments, you who are and who were, the Holy One, because you have so judged; for they have shed the blood of your saints and prophets, and have given them blood to drink as they deserve. . . . Yes, Lord God Almighty, true and just are your judgments" (16:5-7). We have come upon this theme before. If God ignores the persistent attacks on his covenant people, if he pretends that the massive evils that have been perpetrated in the world never happened, he himself is diminished: he is at best amoral, perhaps immoral.

(2) In some ways, the terrible words of 16:9, 11 explain something of hell itself. Hell is not filled with people who have learned their lesson. It is filled with people who still refuse to repent. Like those who suffer from these plagues, they suffer and curse God because of their suffering, but they refuse to repent of what they have done. That is what hell is like: an ongoing cycle of sin, rebellion, judgment, sin, rebellion, judgment, world without end.

(3) These passages of horrible judgment must be seen in the framework of the entire book of Revelation. Already Revelation 5 has drawn attention to the Lion/Lamb whose triumphant suffering has rescued men and women from every tribe and language and people and nation. Revelation ends with an invitation: the Spirit and the Bride (another word for the church, the people of God) still cry "Come!" (22:17). "And let him who hears say, 'Come!' Whoever is thirsty, let him come; and whoever wishes, let him take the free gift of the water of life" (22:17).

It is written: "Let him who does wrong continue to do wrong; let him who is vile continue to be vile; let him who does right continue to do right; and let him who is holy continue to be holy" (22:11).

∾

2 Chronicles 31; Revelation 17; Zechariah 13:2-9; John 16

∾

THE VISION OF THE PROSTITUTE OF **Revelation 17** is replete with colorful language that has confounded many an interpreter. Yet the main lines are reasonably clear, and even the more disputed points are not completely obscure. Here we may reflect on three matters:

(1) Her basic identification to any reader in the first century would not have been in doubt. Reference to the seven hills on which the woman sits (17:9), plus the explicit statement that the woman "is the great city that rules over the kings of the earth" (17:18), would identify her with Rome.

(2) Formally, she is identified in slightly obscure terms: "Mystery: Babylon the Great, the Mother of Prostitutes and of the Abominations of the Earth" (17:5). Historical Babylon was by this point a ruin of a place, a relatively small and certainly enfeebled center without significant influence. But Babylon had stood in Old Testament times for all that was pagan, powerful, self-promoting, and vile. Babylon was the city that had sent Judah and Jerusalem into exile (however much the people of God had earned the judgment). Now the ancient city's name is transferred to Rome, the new geopolitical center. The word *prostitutes* is not in the first instance referring to ordinary human prostitutes, but to spiritual prostitution (once again drawn from the Old Testament). "The mother of all X" is a Semitic way of saying something like "the archetype of all X." And at the time, Rome was certainly, in this sense, the mother of all spiritual prostitution, the fount of the abominations of the earth. The title was merited not only because of her paganism, political corruption, endless violence and perversion, extraordinary wealth and wretched poverty, but also because this was the center where a human being, the current Caesar, was addressed on minted coins as "Our Lord and God," and from which emanated the political will that was increasingly directed against the people of God.

(3) The seven heads of this prostitute, we are told, point in two directions. On the one hand, they point to the seven hills of Rome. They also point to seven kings, five of whom have fallen, "one is, the other has not yet come" (17:10). It is extremely difficult to align this list with the known Caesars of the first century. Various connections have been drawn; I am uncertain which one is right. But the beast on which the woman is riding, certainly identified with the beast out of the sea from chapter 13, this beast that receives a fatal wound and then is healed, "is an eighth king" (17:11). This suggests to many (rightly, I think) a manifestation of evil *beyond* the Roman Empire.

∾

2 Chronicles 32; Revelation 18; Zechariah 14; John 17

∾

IF REVELATION 17 EXPOSES THE abominations of "Babylon," **Revelation 18** announces her imminent destruction. Much of the language is drawn from Old Testament passages that predict the destruction of historic Babylon or some other pagan city characterized by corruption, violence, and idolatry.

Read the chapter again, slowly and reflectively. It is worth remembering that although Rome faced several major reverses during the ensuing three hundred years, it was not until the time of Augustine that the city was thoroughly sacked by the barbarians to the north. So much of the description of this chapter came to quite brutal and literal fulfillment. But by that time, Christianity had itself become the state religion, and many Christians therefore found the sacking difficult to accept, let alone explain.

It was Augustine who wrote a book that set the sacking of Rome in a theological context that helped Christians make sense of it all. His volume *The City of God* traces out two cities, the city of God and the city of man. (See the meditation for January 9.) These categories for him become the controlling typology not only for his rapid scan of biblical history, but for his analysis of good and evil within history. The work is masterful and deserves close reading even today.

Above all, Augustine warns us against associating the church and the Gospel too closely with the cities and kingdoms of this world, cities that are all temporal and temporary and slated for destruction, hopelessly compromised. By contrast, Christians should identify themselves with the new Jerusalem, the city of the great King, the Jerusalem that is above, whose builder and maker is God.

Getting these matters right is never easy or simple. "Come out of her, my people, so that you will not share in her sins, so that you will not receive any of her plagues" (18:4). In the context of the book of Revelation, this is a compelling exhortation not to align with any of "Babylon's" corroding riches and perverted values. One must "come out" and "leave" this doomed city which stands under the judgment of Almighty God. But these words have been used to justify second- and third-degree separation, as if that is what the Apocalypse were teaching. If some enjoy Babylon so much they end up being destroyed with her, others expect to build their own centers entirely removed from Babylon's corroding influence, without perceiving that until Jesus returns the people of God must constantly be tugged in different directions by the city of God and by the city of God's rebellious image-bearers. Our ultimate hope is in God himself, who not only introduces the new Jerusalem (Rev. 21—22), but who brings down this "mother of prostitutes" in his own sovereign judgment.

∾

2 Chronicles 33; Revelation 19; Malachi 1; John 18

∾

REVELATION 19 IS DIVIDED into two parts. In the *first* part, John hears the roar of a great crowd in heaven shouting out various lines of unrestrained praise, joined by various others in antiphonal unity. The first stanza of adoration (19:1-3) praises God because he has condemned the great prostitute (see the reflections for December 26-27), thus demonstrating the truth and justice of his judgments (19:2). This stanza elicits a chorus: "Hallelujah! The smoke from her goes up for ever and ever" (19:3), and the elders around the throne join in adoring approbation (19:4). A voice from the throne exhorts all God's servants to join in praise—"you who fear him, both small and great" (19:5)—and again John hears a vast multitude in the thunderous acclamation of worship. Now the focus is less on God's justice in condemning the prostitute, and more on the sheer glory of the reign of "our Lord God Almighty" and on the imminent "wedding of the Lamb" (19:6-8).

The *second* part of the chapter depicts Jesus in highly symbolic categories. Once again it is important to remind ourselves how apocalyptic can mix its metaphors. He who from chapter 5 on is referred to most commonly as the Lamb (a designation that is still very common in chapters 21—22) is now presented as a warrior riding a white horse. This warrior is called "Faithful and True" (19:11); his name is "the Word of God" (19:13; compare John 1:1, 14), and his title is "King of kings and Lord of lords" (19:16). He leads the armies of heaven in the final assault on the two beasts (i.e., on the beast and the false prophet) and on all who bear their mark. His weapon is a sharp sword that comes out of his mouth: he needs only speak to win. It is he who "treads the winepress of the fury of the wrath of God Almighty" (19:15), which returns us to the terrifying image of 14:19-20.

In one sense, Revelation 19 does not advance the plotline of the book of Revelation. It does not try to do so. We have already been told that God destroys the great prostitute, that those who bear the mark of the beast must face the wrath of God, and so forth. What it adds—and this is vital—is the entirely salutary reminder that God is in absolute control, that he is to be praised for his just judgments on all that is evil, and that the agent who destroys all opposition in the end is none other than Jesus Christ. Moreover, all of this is conveyed not only in the spectacular language of apocalyptic, but with the exulting tongue of enthusiastic praise. Implicitly we readers are invited to join in, even if at this stage we do so by faith and not by sight.

∾

2 Chronicles 34; Revelation 20; Malachi 2; John 19

∽

IN THE MEDITATION FOR November 9, I briefly reflected on the reforming zeal of Josiah, who led the last attempt at large-scale reformation in Judah (2 Kings 22). About three-quarters of a century had passed since the death of Hezekiah, but much of this was presided over by Manasseh, whose reign of more than half a century was almost entirely devoted to pagan evil. Now we return to the same event, this time recorded in **2 Chronicles 34**. Here we may pick up some additional and complementary lessons.

(1) The rediscovery of the book of the Law (probably Deuteronomy) in the rubbish of the temple discloses to Josiah how dangerous is Judah's position: the wrath of God hangs over her head. Josiah tears his clothes, repents, and orders reform. Moreover, he instructs his attendants to inquire of the prophetess Huldah (34:22) as to how imminent these dangers are. God's response is that disaster and judgment on Jerusalem are now inevitable—"all the curses written in the book that has been read in the presence of the king of Judah" (34:24). The pattern of deliberate and repeated covenantal breach has become so sustained and horrific that judgment must come. However, the Lord adds, "Because your heart was responsive and you humbled yourself before God when you heard what he spoke against this place and its people, and because you humbled yourself before me and tore your robes and wept in my presence, I have heard you" (34:27)—and Josiah is assured that the impending disaster will not occur during his lifetime.

There are two obvious lessons here. *First,* we are afforded a glimpse of what God expects from us if we live in a time of cataclysmic declension: not philosophizing, but self-humbling, transparent repentance, tears, contrition. *Second,* as so often in the Bible, precisely because God is so slow to anger and so forbearing, he is more eager to suspend and delay the judgment that is the necessary correlative of his holiness than we are to beg him for mercy.

(2) The picture of the king himself calling together the elders of Judah and solemnly reading to them the Scripture (34:29-31) is enormously moving. There is nothing that our generation needs more than to hear the Word of God—and this at a time of biblical illiteracy rising at an astonishing rate. Moreover, it needs to hear Christian leaders personally submitting to Scripture, personally reading and teaching Scripture—not in veiled ways that merely *assume* some sort of heritage of Christian teaching while actually focusing on just about anything else, but in ways that are reverent, exemplary, comprehensive, insistent, persistent. Nothing, nothing at all, is more urgent.

∽

2 Chronicles 35; Revelation 21; Malachi 3; John 20

∾

AT LAST WE REACH THE CLIMAX of redemption (**Rev. 21**). In his final vision, John sees "a new heaven and a new earth" (21:1). Some notes:

(1) The absence of any sea (21:1) does not establish the hydrological principles of the new heaven and new earth. The sea, as we have noted before, is symbolic for chaos, the old order, death. And so the sea is gone.

(2) John also sees "the Holy City, the New Jerusalem, coming down out of heaven from God" (21:2). We are not to place this New Jerusalem *within* the new heaven and the new earth. They are two quite separate images of the final reality, two ways of depicting the one truth—not unlike the Lion and the Lamb in Revelation 5, where although there are two animals there is only one Jesus to whom these two animals refer. One way of thinking about the consummated glory is to conceive of it as a new universe, a new heaven and earth; another way of thinking about it is as the New Jerusalem—with many entailments to this latter image.

(3) Yet a third way of thinking of the consummation is to focus on the marriage supper of the Lamb (21:2, 9; cf. 19:9)—and here the bride is the New Jerusalem. The metaphors have become wonderfully mixed. But all can see that the consummation will involve perfect intimacy between the Lord Jesus and the people he has redeemed.

(4) Doubtless the perfections of the New Jerusalem are so far outside our experience that it is difficult to imagine them. But one way of getting at them is by negation: we are to understand what ugly things connected with sin and decay will *not* be present: there will be "no more death or mourning or crying or pain, for the old order of things has passed away" (21:4).

(5) The city is an inherently social reality. The consummation is not a place of lone-ranger spirituality. Nor are all cities bad, like "Babylon," the mother of prostitutes (chapter 17; see meditation for December 26). This city, the New Jerusalem, is described in many symbol-laden ways to depict its wonder and glory—too many to unpack here. But note that it is built as a perfect cube. This no more reflects its architecture than the lack of sea betrays the ultimate hydrological arrangements. The cube is symbolic: there is only one cube in the Old Testament, and that is the Most Holy Place of the temple, where only the priest could enter once a year, bearing blood for his own sins and for the sins of the people. Now the entire city is the Most Holy Place: in the consummation all of God's people are perennially in the unshielded splendor of his glorious presence.

∾

2 Chronicles 36; Revelation 22; Malachi 4; John 21

∾

BOTH OF OUR PRIMARY READINGS for this last day of the year convey hope.

The first, **2 Chronicles 36**, depicts the final destruction of Jerusalem. The Babylonians raze the city and the leading citizenry are transported seven or eight hundred miles from home. But the closing verses admit a whisper of hope. Babylon does not have the last word. Decades later the Persian empire takes over and becomes the regional superpower, and Cyrus the king authorizes the return of the exiles to Jerusalem and the construction of a new temple. Historically, of course, the Persians established this policy for all the peoples that the Babylonians had transported: they were all permitted to return home. But the chronicler rightly sees the application of this policy to Israel as supreme evidence of the hand of God, and a new stage in the history of redemption that would bring about the fulfillment of all God's promises.

The hope depicted in the second reading, **Revelation 22**, is of a superior order. The opening verses complete the vision of Revelation 21. The blessedness of the consummation turns on such matters as these: the water of life flows freely from the throne of God and of the Lamb; all the results of the curse are expunged; God's people will constantly see his face, i.e., they will forever be in his presence; there are no more cycles of night and day—again, the point is moral, not astronomical, i.e., there will be no more cycles of good and evil, of light and darkness, for all will live in the light of God.

Granted the sheer goodness and glory of this sustained and symbol-laden vision of the consummation and the triumph of redemption, the rest of the chapter is largely devoted to assuring the reader of the utter reliability of this vision, and therefore of the absolute importance of being among those "who wash their robes, that they may have the right to the tree of life and may go through the gates into the city" (22:14). Here, then, is the ultimate hope, such that if one turns away this time, there is no more hope. There is only a fearful anticipation of final wrath. We are not there yet, the author says, but the climax is not far away, and when it comes, it will be too late.

The resurrected and exalted Jesus, the one who is the Root and Offspring of David and the bright Morning Star (22:16), solemnly declares, "Behold, I am coming soon! My reward is with me, and I will give to everyone according to what he has done. I am the Alpha and the Omega, the First and the Last, the Beginning and the End" (22:12-13).

∾